AMBUSH AT VELLA GULF

AMBUSH AT VELLA GULF

THE DESTROYER BATTLE THAT CHANGED THE COURSE OF WORLD WAR II IN THE PACIFIC

REX A. KNIGHT

STACKPOLE
BOOKS
Essex, Connecticut
Blue Ridge Summit, Pennsylvania

STACKPOLE
BOOKS

An imprint of The Globe Pequot Publishing Group, Inc.
64 South Main Street
Essex, CT 06426
www.globepequot.com

British Library Cataloguing in Publication Information available

Library of Congress Cataloging-in-Publication Data available

ISBN 978-0-8117-7848-0 (cloth)
ISBN 978-0-8117-7849-7 (electronic)

Contents

Preface vii

Chapter 1: Commanders: Leadership in the Making 1
Chapter 2: Pearl Harbor: Reality Strikes Home 26
Chapter 3: Guadalcanal: Gateway to Hell 50
Chapter 4: The Tokyo Express: "Hellova Nuisance" 77
Chapter 5: Tulagi: The Gathering 98
Chapter 6: The Mission: Facing the Challenges 122
Chapter 7: All Ahead: Into Destiny's Darkness 146
Chapter 8: Execute: The Moment of Truth 167
Chapter 9: Commence Fire: Finishing the Deed 188
Chapter 10: Scenes of Victory: God This Is Awful 208
Chapter 11: Well Done: Summation of Victory 228
Chapter 12: Final Notes: Debates, Controversies, and Conclusions 246

Notes 267
Bibliography 289

Preface

In the spring of 2002, I made a promise to a group of heroic Pacific war veterans. The promise was to tell their story as completely as possible, and have it published for the world to read. I already had a good grasp of what I intended to do. The research was already being gathered and organized. I was confident that I had what it took to write the story, with the greatest amount of detail, and do so in a way that would have publishers racing to make offers. Boy, was I wrong.

The book was to capture the full story of the battle at Vella Gulf, in the Solomon Islands, on the night of August 6-7, 1943. This battle was small but precise, perfect in fact, and lasted only forty-five minutes. There was not a single enemy-inflicted American casualty, and no American ship received any damage. So, how does one write an entire full-length book about such a small, lopsided battle, and make it exciting to read? My solution was to personalize the engagement by using a number of biographical inserts, as the personalities (on both sides) were, in my opinion, key to understanding the full development of this important engagement. Where these men came from, what influenced their lives, and how they arrived at this crucial point in history was as much of the story as was the engagement itself. The historical course leading up to this engagement is a most fascinating read, to say the least. And sure, it was just a forty-five-minute engagement, but it changed the course of the Pacific war. So, how was there any problem with a book?

The research phase went very well, as too did the writing—initially. I truly enjoyed delving through all of the old documents in search for more details to this amazing story. Moreso, I was excited by all the fine people I met, especially the veterans with whom I became friends; I was honored by their many contributions to my effort. The interviews and conversations were given with a true respect and appreciation for what I was endeavoring to accomplish. They believed in me, and they shared stories and thoughts liberally, stories that even their own families were not privy to hear. I was blessed, and I knew it. But the journey was to be far more trying and lengthier—so frustratingly so—than I ever imagined.

I was not completely new at being a published author, but publishing had made many dramatic changes since my earlier successes. Many of the smaller houses and imprints with which I was familiar had since been consumed by bigger publishers, eliminating most of these small-market options. Development of the internet had drastically changed how books were sold, as online sales quickly cut into the market share of the brick-and-mortar stores, and especially so for the smaller "mom and pop" shops. With such changes, it was now far more difficult to approach the traditional publishers. It was a real struggle to even get a proposal submitted.

As time progressed, I became more and more concerned that my promise could not be kept. Time became my enemy. My veteran friends and confidants began to lose battles with age. Progress became a slow crawl. My confidence fell, to a point where I even shelved the work for a period of time. The development of the manuscript was not coming together as I knew was needed. I nearly gave up entirely—but that promise still lingered.

More of my veteran friends passed on, leaving me feeling that I had failed them. I sent portions of the completed manuscript to those who still lived, allowing them at least some opportunity to know my efforts were real. They relished the read, and their comments remained encouraging. Even so, I was no closer to having the work published.

In 2004, I decided to send out the proposal with sample chapters to some literary agents. I was hoping for some interest—or, at a minimum, some helpful comments. I got both. There *was* serious interest—but in nearly every response it was pointed out that the development of the story still needed work. By the comments, I at least knew that I was on the right track. So, I continued to refine the story, and I continued to approach the agents, some a second and third time. The comments became more promising. "This is a very good revision." "I can see a book now . . ." "You've made significant improvements . . . it seems tighter and more focused." Even so, there was still a concern that it was not an easy sell. Despite the importance of the story, and the writing being good, I had no widespread notoriety as an author and, without this element, the work was just not strong enough on its own. Time continued to pass, my veteran friends continued to succumb to time, and my frustration and fear of failure grew more. Even so, I pressed on.

There were many distractions. My real job—that of a regional development planner—consumed much of my writing time. And caring for aging and ailing parents consumed what was left. It was life, and I was blessed by my roles. By now, however, more than two decades had passed. The veterans to whom I had made my promise were all gone. My own veteran father, as well as my mother, also passed. I had since retired. The thought returned that I needed to fulfill that long-ago promise. The story remained alive and the research remained relevant, given as a gift to me by the very men who had lived it. I alone possessed it. My obligation had not ended with the deaths of those veterans. Every piece of research came back out, as did the manuscript. It had been a while since I had read it through. The writing was fine. It really only needed a few tweaks here and there, just some minor refinements to be ready. I set to the task, determined as never before to fulfill my promise. The timing was finally right. I sent the proposal and sample chapters out to a publishing house specializing in such historical material, said a little prayer . . . and this time . . . success!

Now, please allow me to digress just a bit. My journey to this point has been a long but thrilling affair. My love for history began at the young age of ten. This passion was continually nurtured by numerous individuals—actually far more individuals than I could ever list. I had many mentors, and I feel honored to have been so blessed. But this specific project was directly inspired by some very key individuals, whom I need to acknowledge and give credit.

I already mentioned my parents. However, I should point out that my father, a World War II Navy veteran of the Pacific war and a destroyer sailor, was a key reason this story developed. He had served on the destroyer USS *Lang* from May 1944 through to the end of August 1945, and he had served under the leadership of Frederick Moosbrugger, while part of the deadly picket defensive network established north of Okinawa, during that campaign. He was proud of his service, his ship, and the men he had served with. For his sixtieth birthday, I decided to organize a reunion for the *Lang*, on his behalf. I had no idea of the gift it would be to me. These former sailors had not been together since the war ended. It was quite the challenge, but I succeeded at finding a rather large number of these veterans. Eighteen of the men came together for their first reunion, a most emotional gathering, in the summer of 1985, welcomed by a personal letter of congratulations from then President Ronald Reagan. From this point on, the reunions continued on a yearly basis, with a growing roster. It was an amazing opportunity to learn. And it was through these gatherings that I first met and communicated at length with some of the Vella Gulf veterans listed in this story: Kenny Arthur, John Ballantine, Dan Gray, Charles "Chuck" Lee, Pemberton Southard, Charles Stirrup, and Leonard "Woodie" Wood. All of these men openly shared their experiences for my research.

Later in 1985, I began working on a complete history of the USS *Lang*. I took this effort very seriously, knowing I had a veteran market and that they would be my toughest critics. This work took a number of years to complete. I self-published the work in 1998, entitled *Riding on Luck: The Saga of the USS*

Lang (DD-399). The book sold quite well, as all of the *Lang* veterans and their extended family members bought one or more copies and a good many small-market bookstores eagerly purchased copies for their shelves.

It was also in 1998 that I first met and started a friendship with Capt. C. Raymond "Cal" Calhoun, author of *Tin Can Sailor* (Naval Institute Press, 1993) and a veteran of the destroyer USS *Sterett*. Cal would become an invaluable aid and encouragement throughout my future efforts.

It was during my research and writing period of *Riding on Luck* that I took another additional step, reaching out to C. Brian Kelly, editor of *World War II* magazine (Empire Press), for perhaps a try at a feature article. I needed to establish myself as an author. My first offering was a story on the Battle of Vella Gulf. It was accepted and published in the March 1990 edition, entitled "Clean Sweep by Destroyers." Throughout the next decade, I wrote a number of other articles for *World War II*. C. Brian Kelly's acceptance of my style of historical storytelling was truly a confidence builder for my future efforts. It even presented me with the opportunity for an invitation to the commissioning ceremony of the USS *Vella Gulf* (CG-72) at Norfolk, Virginia, on September 18, 1993. There I was awarded an introduction to the new ship's captain, Capt. Constantine L. Xefteris, presenting him with a special gift photo of the USS *Lang* (DD-399) and a copy of my "Clean Sweep by Destroyers," in a mint *World War II* edition. More importantly, it was here where I first met a number of other Vella Gulf veterans.

The year 1999 opened even more doors. That year I began approaching some smaller book imprints/traditional publishers to see if any interest was out there for a more serious publishing effort of *Riding on Luck*. There was. Kathy Marshbank (Acquisitions) of PSI Research/Hellgate Press was interested. A contract was soon agreed to, and we quickly began working together on a full-size paperback version of the book. The new version of *Riding on Luck* was published in 2001, having a wonderful foreword written by my now good friend, Cal Calhoun. It was now time for the next step.

Ever since writing "Clean Sweep by Destroyers" for *World War II*, I knew that this was the story. Cal had a chapter in his book about this important battle, I had a chapter in mine, and numerous other books over the years captured the story in one way or another. Even so, no book had ever been devoted to the complete story. Study of the battle was part of the curriculum for U.S. Naval Academy cadets, but—despite over fifty years having passed—there remained no truly devoted detailed account out there anywhere. It was an important story that needed to be told.

Due to my earlier efforts, I already had a considerable amount of research gathered for the story, but most of my interviews centered around the USS *Lang* veterans. There was so much that I knew I was missing. So, in 1998—even before *Riding on Luck* was first released—I made a concerted effort to contact the veterans of the other ships involved. Not many of these veterans had computers or email, so I started out with a letter and questionnaire to send out by snail mail. The response was phenomenal. Nearly every veteran who I approached promptly responded. Not only did they provide answers to my questions, but many sent additional materials that far exceeded my expectations. Information and details about the Vella Gulf action were rolling in, filling my mailbox to capacity with dozens of letters and packages. Then came the phone calls, and additional discussions over the landline. I was so thrilled.

Despite this apparent quick start, during the next decade piecing together the story became a slog. The progress was disappointingly slow. I needed help. And, it was not till 2007 that two events occurred to meet that need. Finally, I could once again feel a renewed sense of optimism beginning to build.

One of the agents who I had earlier contacted was James D. Hornfischer. Jim was not only a literary agent, but he was also a very successful naval historian and author. He was one of a number of agents who took interest in what I was trying to accomplish. In 2007, Jim gave me a number of ideas and suggestions for reaching my ultimate goal. A problem that I was having was with my effort at combining a historical narrative with a number of biographical narratives. I understood the difficulties with the development; such does not easily allow for smooth transitions. I was covering a lot of history as well, from Pearl Harbor to Vella Gulf. However, I felt all of this background and the personalities were so very important to the overall story. It was not just a narrative about an important naval engagement of the Pacific war, it was a story of how the right men came together at the right time for perfectly pulling off what appeared to be a nearly impossible feat. To understand the victory, one needed to fully understand the men involved (on both sides), where they came from, what defined them, and what motivated them. Jim understood this, and he didn't discourage my effort. In fact, he liked how I had "broadened the coverage," but with a caveat that I needed to work harder at making "the various component parts come together . . . successfully." I really believe Jim was seriously considering representing my manuscript—but for one critical aspect—he was working on his own book on the Guadalcanal campaign, of which my chapters 3 and 4 also covered. His comment was, "I would be competing with myself were I to take on your book." It was a letdown to be sure, but I understood. I actually felt good about his seeing my work as competition. Remarkably, a couple days later I received an unexpected phone call. It was Jim. He was worried that his remarks might have caused me some discouragement, and he wanted to assure me that he felt that I was on the right track and not to feel otherwise. We had a great conversation, and I felt very reinspired afterward. I so appreciated this man's kind insights. Unfortunately, Jim was lost on June 1, 2021, a victim of cancer at the young age of fifty-five.

Another important introduction also occurred in 2007. It was around the fall of this year that I received a call from naval historian Dave McComb. Dave was the founder of the Destroyer History Foundation, and he worked closely with the Tin Can Sailors Association. He had three books to his credit, and he oversaw his own website, destroyerhistory.org. Dave had gotten wind of my Vella Gulf history effort, and he called me with some information that he thought would be helpful. The discussion was good, and I had gained another supporter of my project. Dave would later contact me regarding the upcoming commissioning ceremony for the USS *Sterett* (DDG 107), a new Arleigh Burke Class destroyer. The event took place at Baltimore, Maryland, on August 9, 2008. A number of the Vella Gulf veterans were to be there, and so was my friend, Capt. Cal Calhoun, who was to be a guest speaker. The skipper for this new ship, Comm. Brian P. Echerle, like myself, was from southern Indiana. His father and my father were friends and had worked together for many years at the Naval Weapons Support Center at Crane, Indiana. Both men were World War II destroyer veterans and former gunner's mates. There was no problem getting an invitation for myself and my family.

Again, the commissioning ceremony allowed me some more face-time with a number of the Vella Gulf veterans. It was the first time that Dave McComb and I met in person. What a wonderful and opportune time this was. I had made a list of additional questions to ask, and the Vella Gulf vets were eager to respond. I really didn't have to do much, other than just listen and take notes. When a group of "Old Salts" get together, the stories abound.

Dave McComb's support at this critical time was invaluable. He was so looking forward to what I was to pull together. Unfortunately, we lost Dave too soon, too. He lost his fight with cancer on July 4, 2014, at the age of sixty-five.

Still, obstacles persisted. It would take yet another decade of work and struggles, but on October 15, 2025, I finally reached the pinnacle of my lengthy journey. That long-sought publishing agreement was signed. In the fall of 2026, *Ambush at Vella Gulf* was in print and a reality. Thank you to Dave Reisch (Stackpole Books) for recognizing the importance of this story and seeing the worth of my efforts. The great assistance that he—and the excellent staff at Stackpole Books—gave for making this work a success is so greatly appreciated. Thank you for helping me honor my promise and for formally honoring all the veterans who played such an important role at Vella Gulf on August 6-7, 1943.

I already mentioned the *Lang* veterans who so kindly shared their recollections and responded to my many questions. In addition, were the following veterans: From *Dunlap*—E. Ralph Barber, Clyde A. Conner, John W. Huber, Albert R. Olsen, Loyd Peters, William Rivera, Max Schaffer, and Robert J. Wallick; representing Frederick Moosbrugger—sons Edward and Dave Moosbrugger (each who willingly shared about their great father, both through written correspondence and phone conversations); from *Craven*—Richard L. Allison, William L. Caylor Jr., Henry D. Davison, Wilber O. Fultz, Patrick J. Gaither, Jack B. Gilmore, William P. Hayden, John A. Hall, Gene Hansen, Carl W. Lanz, William A. Lazarz, Anthony P. Lucia, James D. Oliver, John J. Poitevin, George J. Pritchette, and Ferdinand S. Yannotti; from *Maury*—Russell S. Crenshaw, James W. Fisher, and John T. Olcott; from *Stack*—Harold E. Shear; and from *Sterett*—C. Raymond "Cal" Calhoun (Cal passed away at the age of 101 on August 29, 2015). All of these men were important contributors to this work. My appreciation for them cannot be expressed enough.

I would also be remiss to leave out the support of my immediate family. My loving parents always had my back. And my lovely wife, Linda, provided her unwavering support as well. She often did not understand the depth of great importance which I placed on this project, but she never ceased at giving me her full attention when talking about it. There is no end to my love and appreciation for her. My children, too, often found me isolated at times, at study or typing on a word processor (boy, isn't that a bit dated) or computer. It is sometimes difficult to explain the passion of a historian to teenagers (or even adults, for that matter), but my children received this as pretty normal in our household. Thank you, Shane and Shauna.

Finally, but most importantly, I thank God for giving me this wonderful opportunity. What talents I have, I give full credit to His award and direction. He placed in my path of life all the right people for me to become the person I am today. I have been so blessed. While this is a book about the terrible outcomes of warfare, I pray that in some way it shares the importance of fellowship, forgiveness, and fortitude to live a good life. The "Greatest Generation" was not happenstance. They were—I truly believe—of Divine providence designed with purpose. I am truly grateful to have known such great human beings.

I will conclude with a final thought: In nothing are we ever truly alone. We share life with a wealth of humanity. How we recognize and utilize this wonderful treasure is up to each individual. Again, the list of great people who have influenced my life is very lengthy, and it continues to grow daily. I would have had little success without them. As a historian, I am entrusted with properly capturing stories of people. I merely put words to paper. Others lived the experience. And still others shared their wisdom for knowing how best to extend this important story on to yet others. Thank you all!

Chapter One

Commanders

Leadership in the Making

World War II in the South-Central Pacific had become a contest of wills, a question of which combatant could take the most punches without crying "uncle!" In the twelve months following the August 1942 American invasion of Guadalcanal, the Solomon Islands had transitioned from an unknown and trivialized piece of South Pacific real estate to a war zone of immense notoriety and a coveted ground to be purchased with seemingly unending amounts of human sacrifice. And this fight looked to continue with little pause and no decrease to the violence.

On the one side, the U.S. Pacific Fleet commander-in-chief, Adm. Chester W. Nimitz, was determined to press forward one offensive strike after another, intent at keeping his Japanese opponents off balance and on the defensive. These efforts soon developed into the ultimate goal of initiating a speedy advance, isolating some of the more foreboding Japanese bastions—like the two massive naval bases of Rabaul (on the island of New Britain, Papua, New Guinea) and Kavieng (on the island of New Ireland, Papua, New Guinea)—and bypassing these for more strategic targets while pressing across the Pacific toward Japan proper to victory (a strategy to become known as "island hopping" or "leapfrogging"). But to attain this fast track he first had to ensure that supplies to these bypassed islands were completely cut off, or otherwise risk continued harassment and detriment to his future offensive flank—a prospect he dared not need to contend with. At the moment, however, the Solomon Islands archipelago was his Achilles' heel. If he could not achieve a concise termination to Japanese resupply in the Solomons, how could he be expected to achieve it elsewhere?

The Japanese, on the other hand, were just as equally determined to make this isolation effort impossible or of such a cost that the Americans would eventually see the losses as too great to continue, forcing a negotiated settlement. By this time, most Japanese leaders understood that an outright defeat of American forces was impossible, but they equally believed that Americans, on the whole, had no stomach for continually throwing their sons into the "meatgrinder" that was currently the South Pacific. They envisioned that the exaggerated losses in the battles for the Solomons would bring the wrath of American mothers and wives down on the leadership in Washington and force these leaders to consider a diplomatic resolution. Here, they felt, was America's weakness. For this, the Japanese leadership was willing to press forward its own military at great sacrifice. It certainly appeared a worthwhile strategy, as this was indeed a great concern for the American leadership—but for one critical error the Japanese had already made. This strategy for the Japanese was mostly lost the moment their first bomb struck the surface of Oahu on the morning of December 7, 1941.

Regardless of a year and a half having already passed since that fateful day, America's outrage over Pearl Harbor still remained powerfully strong. The wound was too fresh for solely the ointment of diplomacy. America was out for vengeance, and negotiating a settlement was currently not a consideration—though American leadership knew with certainty this was not to remain an infinite sentiment, especially if successes at defeating the Japanese did not move faster (the capture of Guadalcanal had taken the better part of a half-year to conclude). The slow crawl across the South-Central Pacific needed to increase to more of a spirited sprint—or at the very least a fast jog.

For the many American sailors who currently prowled the deadly waters of the Solomons, these prospects came with a fearful unease. They were the ones seemingly at the tip of the spear, having embattled Marine and soldier associates screaming for the Navy to get its part of the job done and quickly. Certainly, the situation of the current conflict was far from determined, and it cast a long and unrelenting deathly shadow that few could escape. This arena of warfare remained intense and provided little avenue for error. Every patrol was high risk. Throughout this hostile realm, constant dangers lurked and death impatiently awaited its opportunity to pounce. Numerous men and ships had already perished here. Even with a good plan in hand, survival was measured by disparaging percentages. Few sailors expected to venture into these sinister waters and return completely unscathed.

Indeed, there was a serious flaw with the American battle strategy. While American airpower—for the most part—ruled the day, providing a growing measure of security for Americans at sea and on the ground, the night—where a typically dense darkness often proved itself to be impenetrable to the eye and most horrifying to the imagination—belonged solely to the Imperial Japanese

Navy. It ruled these darkened hours with unnerving determination and skill, even despite lacking the American technological advantage of radar. This should not have been.

Numerous efforts were pursued at ending this ongoing bond between the darkness and the Japanese, but with mostly devastating results. Indeed, the Japanese continued to run supplies to their beleaguered garrisons with near impunity, and these successes were making the battles for each piece of sand and rock intensely protracted. To this point the Japanese strategy was working.

The so-called "Tokyo Express" of fast destroyers was the most effective and menacing of the Japanese resupply efforts. They ran only in the wee hours of the night, avoiding American airpower and submarines, and were delivering thousands of reinforcements and tons of supplies on a regular basis. And when the Express was confronted, it typically dished out more punishment than it got. This had to end, and the frustrations of the American commanders were noticeably reaching a breaking point. They desperately searched for some positive understanding of how to dethrone this Japanese rule of the darkness so usurped by the Express. Surely there had to be an answer. Surely there was some aspiring talent among the fleet that could stop this seemingly unending nuisance. And there was—but it had heretofore been overlooked and misused.

Indeed, the fleet had its answer all along, but its accepted doctrine of the day determined capital ships—battleships and aircraft carriers—should lead the offense, leaving other options to be errantly dismissed. With these capital ships in short supply and critical to preserve, cruisers quickly inherited the primary naval role of offense in the Solomons campaign. But this too proved problematic, and by mid-1943 cruisers were also in short supply. Finally (and more out of desperate need than actual change of heart), the leadership turned their gaze a different direction, and an unsung group of veteran American destroyers were unleashed and given their chance. For months destroyer commanders had been begging for this charge, and so when offered this opportunity to finally display their full mettle, there was no hesitation. They quickly set to the task, sailed into the night without delay, and pulled off one of the most perfectly fought naval actions of the entire war. And just how this victory and these victors came to be is a most magnificent story.

* * *

At the age of eighteen, neither Arleigh Burke nor Frederick Moosbrugger knew of the great plans being reserved for their futures. Both young men were standing at a great pinnacle in their lives, though without true understanding of the course that either would soon pursue. They had no premonitions of how their individual—or collective—decisions and efforts might one day affect the overall course of a future war, even to afford a path to assured victory. Such contemplations—though perhaps warranted of such forward thinkers—were at this time completely absent their youthful minds. Truthfully, they could not have known; what lay ahead was well over the horizon. For the moment, only the present held their most immediate concern.

For Burke and Moosbrugger—and a number of other young men as well—June 26, 1919, was far too significant to be awarded anything other than a most profound sense of pride. This was their first day at the U.S. Naval Academy, pursuant to each their own individual dream of becoming an officer in the U.S. Navy. Annapolis, with its elite halls and trusted instructors, welcomed them only after their meeting the lofty markers long established at keeping the household of a quality membership. This historic campus now greeted them with inspiration and purpose. Great men—Dewey, Fletcher, and so many others—had studied here. John Paul Jones was entombed here. These grounds, adorned with such an abundance of temple-like limestone structures, were so beautiful and compelling. They strolled along the red brick walkways and between the park-like courtyards with a great sense of awe, exploring every facet of the estate destined the next four years to be their home. This was surely the beginning of some of the most important days of their lives. Here they would be classmates and acquaintances, two persevering souls standing collectively among several other outstanding midshipmen set to graduate in 1923. They had but one common purpose, to become specialists in both the lessons of seamanship and the art of leadership. Momentarily, nothing else mattered. This was their time to shine, and most assuredly they would approach this joint venture with mutual ambition—but they would do so displaying little else of like comparison.

Outside of their professed determinations at becoming naval officers, Arleigh Burke and Frederick Moosbrugger exhibited almost no discernable similarities. Their backgrounds, physiques, demeanors, first impressions, as well as nearly every other distinction about them were different. It just did not seem possible that both men could harbor the same mettle or ever share in similar honors. But fate was to see otherwise. Twenty years later, on another common ground, these two gentlemen officers would meet yet again. Though their encounter would be fleeting, hardly more than a passing exchange, it would prove to be a pivotal instant in history and a milestone for both of their aspiring careers. These two exceptional though very dissimilar personas, groomed—as were so many other young men of their time—by a myriad of worldly and personal events, would one day set their combined talents to a unique challenge. Indeed, far in advance of their individual knowledge, it seemed almost predetermined that Burke and Moosbrugger were to be key components in one of the most remarkable victories ever recorded by the U.S. Navy.

The blond-haired, blue-eyed Arleigh Burke, a third-generation Swedish American, was born in 1901 on his parent's farm near Boulder, in landlocked Colorado. Arleigh obviously lived a long way from the ocean and was just as equally distant from the life of a sailor. Such an environment would surely reveal in him no youthful promise for his future skill as a naval officer, let alone that of a naval hero. Nor would he display any early aspirations for such direction to his life. Moreover, the rural family farm in the early 1900s offered few opportunities at expanding one's choice of careers, of which seamanship remained far outside the spectrum. But none of these mattered. This young man would one day chart his course, set his sights on success, and find at sail a triumph far beyond anything he could have earlier dreamed possible.

Indeed, there seemed little doubt that Arleigh Burke was destined to be a leader. He was a powerful presence, projecting confidence and inspiring loyalty, who no one could dismiss. A big man with big ideas, Arleigh had an unyielding passion for pursuing his future. Once focused on an objective, he was nearly impossible to stop. But, despite being so self-driven, Burke also maintained a great sense of modesty. He seemingly never forgot who he was or from where he had come. His advancements, when they came, were always proudly received—though in humble recognition that they were never his alone.

Surely life had blessed Arleigh with many positive influences. Foremost among these was his determination to succeed, and this should be rightly credited to his well-rounded upbringing. The nurturing received by Arleigh while growing up was assuredly responsible for his determination and direction, eventually leading him to achieve his goals. Everything he was destined to become appeared in some way attached to the experiences of his youth. His amiable disposition, his strong resolve, his undying devotion, these traits and others were all attributes passed on to him by parents who demonstrated these very same characteristics—virtues championed with every lesson they taught.

Success, as the Burkes understood it, was dependent on the performance of the whole, which in their terms was the family. A farm family of the time was reliant on all its members pitching in and playing a critical role for its ultimate survival. Such dependence certainly made for no easy life. The operation of an early twentieth century family farm was never to be given over to passive efforts, as it was a hard and dirty vocation, routinely requiring many hours of heavy labor that regularly began early in the morning and often lasted far into the night. Like so many others of their time, the Burke children were taught early on the important lessons of responsibility.[1] Chore assignments were non-negotiable and given with high expectations that these would be completed as given and in a timely fashion. Moreover, development of strong work ethics became an unquestionable demand. Arleigh, the oldest of six children, surely found his responsibilities were even greater, as he was often given charge over his siblings during work and play—adding to his development a strong sense of supervision. For these reasons and more, the family farm proved to be a fine institute in character building and just as equally a powerful educator in the lessons of life. By itself, however, the family farm could offer little else in the way of real opportunity.

A formal education was the only true avenue toward advancement. Clearly, Arleigh's parents, Oscar and Clara, understood the importance that school was to have with their children's futures, as they both placed a high priority on such educational development—Arleigh's mother was an elementary school teacher and obviously this attributed greatly to such determination.[2] Certainly Clara's tutoring influences were used to good advantage at assisting her children with their progressions in scholarship, but even this had limited reach. Having this in mind, and nearing the end of his high school years, Arleigh began giving careful consideration to the direction of his own future. Though he truly appreciated the family farm and all it provided, and had great respect for his father's work, he saw for himself no future in the farming trade. His parents understood.[3] They also wanted a better life for their son and wished for him some opportunity at an institution of higher learning. But the cash-strapped Burkes found the cost of postsecondary education one step beyond their means. With such revelation, the potential for Arleigh's future advancement appeared to be dismal—though perhaps not entirely.

As the choices were so very limited, finding an economical route to a career was sure to be a difficult task. There was, however, one promising alternative to young Burke's educational dilemma; he could request and possibly receive an appointment to a military academy. This option intrigued both Arleigh and his parents. But this too presented a critical obstacle. The Burkes needed political connections and had none. Fortunately, an influential neighbor did have the proper connections, and on Arleigh's behalf, he introduced the family to their district congressman, Charles Timberlake.[4] With this introduction, a hopeful journey appeared set to begin.

Arleigh's initial meeting with the honorable Timberlake was assuredly an exceptional opportunity, and he approached it with extraordinary energy and determination. He made a resounding appeal to the congressman for an appointment to West Point, hopeful of acceptance into this famed U.S. Army officer training school. Certainly, young Burke's high grades and notable recommendations were well received but, as the congressman explained, there were no West Point appointments remaining open.[5] He was sorry, but he could be of little help. Obviously, this was not the news the family had hoped to hear. It was a terrible disappointment, and again Arleigh's prospects appeared rather bleak.

Noting Arleigh's discouragement, a high school teacher intervened and approached her favorite student to persuade him not to give up just yet, suggesting that perhaps he could ask the congressman for an appointment to the U.S. Navy's officer candidate school, at Annapolis. Arleigh had never given the Navy a thought, nor had his parents, for he had never even been outside the state of Colorado, let alone near the ocean or aboard a ship. But, why not ask? So, he did. Unfortunately, the response was nearly a repeat of before. The congressman could only apologize. Again, he had no appointments remaining open for Annapolis.[6]

Regrettably, it appeared that Arleigh's every option had been exhausted. The young Burke was devastated. Even then, however, not all was lost. Just prior to Arleigh's graduation, the congressman announced to his local constituents that his two appointments to Annapolis for the year had withdrawn.[7] The door was suddenly reopened for two new candidates to enter, and the timing could not have been better.

Arleigh was exuberant. This was the opportunity he had been praying for. To be fair, the congressman opened the appointments to all capable young men, ages sixteen to twenty-two, within his district.[8] Such openness did not matter to Arleigh; his big chance had come and he was fully determined to win its offering. He knew the competition would be stiff, so he doubled his study efforts during the final weeks of his senior year. Still, nothing was to come easy for the young Burke. A severe influenza outbreak caused the temporary closing of his school—a setback to be sure. Aware of his circumstances and confident in his abilities, three of his teachers came to his aid and began private tutoring to ensure that he did not fall behind. It was also during this time that Arleigh learned of an examination prep course that was to be offered at a school near Columbia College in Columbia, Missouri. His teachers recommended that he apply.[9]

Arleigh was determined to find a way into the school, but he was short of the required funds. Aggressively attacking the problem, he quickly found some additional paying work and, as a result, was able to gather enough money for the train fare and tuition, even to be left with a few dollars in reserve.[10] Having now overcome the greater financial obstacle, the young Burke appeared to be on the road to success. However, there was still the issue of how to sustain his living once he was at the school, especially considering that his remaining cash was sure to fall well short of such expenses. Regardless of this one uncertainty, Arleigh was far from dissuaded. He packed his bags, bid his farewells, and headed east, confident he could manage.

After arriving at the school, Arleigh began an immediate search for a place to stay and was soon successful. He bartered a deal for a room at a local boarding house, trading his labor as part-time kitchen help and janitor for the greater cost of the rent.[11] Arleigh's small bankroll would now suffice, providing him a meager allowance for meals and leaving him to concentrate his mental energies solely toward his schooling, which he would do quite ably and with substantial reward.

Three months later, in early April 1919, Arleigh returned to his Colorado home, somewhat confident but as yet unconvinced that he was fully prepared to pass the highly competitive exam. The test site would be in nearby Boulder, where he arrived on horseback a day early—trying to avoid late travel in a developing blizzard-like snowstorm.[12] To save money he spent the wintry night in a local stable, where he slept with difficulty, nervously anticipating the following day and the repercussions it was assured to deliver toward his future. By sunrise Arleigh was up and wide awake, anxious to face this important day and resolute in his determination to meet its challenge.

Burke promptly arrived at the test site—joined there by the many other hopeful candidates—and found immediate encouragement with the exam. The test was so very similar, even near identical to the simulations he had studied at the Columbia prep school. He had overcome many inconveniences and difficulties to take the course, and it now appeared to have been worth all of his efforts. He completed the test in record time, handed it in, and headed home for an anticipated long and excruciating wait for the outcome.[13]

Though his future remained in limbo, Arleigh had for the first time in a long while just cause to display some real sense of relief and confidence. He was certain he had responded well to the exam's many challenges, and for this reason he felt secure in that a good portion of his weighted educational burden had finally been lifted from his broadening shoulders. Still, had his effort been enough?

Young Burke was obviously very anxious. His heart seemed to pound a continuous beat of nervous anticipation. Minutes passed into hours and hours into days, as the clock seemed to slow to an intolerable crawl. Though Arleigh tried hard not to continually dwell on the matter, he found it nearly impossible—patience was never one of his strong suits.

At the Burke family farm, Arleigh went about his work as usual. Chores became his only escape from the slow elapse of time. Obviously, he tried not to get his hopes up too high, but it was a difficult effort. His desire for the appointment was so strong that he could hardly think of anything other.

Finally, the moment arrived. The letter was placed in his hands. It seemed a lifetime had passed. He now held the document bearing the news of his future, but—even in spite of the many long days of anticipation—he hesitated to open it, fearful of the rejection that might be contained inside. The answer he had so impatiently waited for was within his grasp, but his desire to know had for an instant abandoned him. Nevertheless, he braved a peek. His eyes widened as his grasp of the letter tightened, and a shout of jubilation suddenly burst forth from across his lips. He quickly turned to his observing parents to give each a huge hug, and then off he ran to the homes of his three high school teachers with the news, thanking each one for their timely help.[14] He had won the right to one of the two open appointments. Arleigh Burke was going to Annapolis.

But Arleigh was not alone. Half a continent away, in Philadelphia, Pennsylvania, another young man was just learning of his own similar success.

Frederick Moosbrugger was a reclusive spirit, whose full measure of talent proved impossible to judge and to fully appreciate at face value. To many first-time observers he appeared as an enigma, quiet and genteel, providing few hints to his true underlying character. His slim frame and passive persona did not appear as a combination equal to one who might be destined for a great role in leadership or that could easily pass the tough rigors of Annapolis, but the youthful Moosbrugger was far more of a force than his appearance displayed. He was every bit as determined to succeed as any who were to walk the great halls of the academy grounds—including his soon-to-be classmate, Arleigh Burke.

A humble young man with humble beginnings, Frederick Moosbrugger had been born to immigrant parents in Philadelphia on October 9, 1900. His father, Jacob, was a native of Germany, as was his mother, Rosine (Matilda Maier). Jacob and Rosine were married in 1892 and quickly moved to establish their new home in the ethnic community of East Falls, a suburb of Philadelphia that had built up around a group of local textile mills. Times here were initially quite good and life appeared to be very promising.[15]

Frederick's father, a cabinet maker prior to his move from Germany, made his new livelihood as manager of a saloon, at a new establishment that was part of the local Hohenadel Brewery. Here Jacob built an honored reputation, becoming well known as a man of fairness, watchful for the best interest of all his customers—he often sent weekly paycheck–bearing men home to their wives, ensuring their family income was at least marginally protected before serving them drinks. This type of thoughtfulness and concern reflected well on his personality and won him considerable respect. As a result, the saloon quickly became a flourishing business, while Jacob's influence within the community grew to considerable importance (even today the family name remains memorialized in the neighborhood, listed as donors of one of the fine stained-glass windows of the old historic Trinity Lutheran Church, on the corner of Queen Lane and Germantown Avenue).[16]

The Moosbrugger home was originally established in a small house that sat on Queen Lane, just a couple blocks from the saloon where Jacob worked and a short distance from the Lutheran church where the family worshipped. East Falls, with its steeply sloped streets and quaint German inspirations, offered the Moosbruggers a good life, just as Jacob provided the family with a nice income and Rosine filled the time-honored role of homemaker and mother. The family prospered, just as it also increased in number, adding three daughters (Louise, Sophie, and Mathilde) and one son (Frederick), leading the Moosbrugger patriarch to build a new, more accommodating home, which he conveniently located next door to the first.[17]

Freddie—as he was known to family and friends—the youngest of the Moosbrugger children, was merely the typical boy, full of energy and a bit on the mischievous side.[18] He appeared nothing out of the ordinary. Once in his teens, however, his demeanor grew more reserved and direct. The inherent traits of his father, those of an independent thinker and careful observer, became predominant with his evolving personality. Freddie was growing into manhood. Late at night, while lying in bed and listening to the huff and chug of some lonely sounding locomotive passing on the nearby railway, he carefully considered his future and the path his life should take. He hoped to one day breach beyond his urban confines, to do something meaningful and exciting with his life—and indeed he would.

In the meantime, education became the driving force behind Freddie's young life. Learning was his passion. He attended Philadelphia's public schools and graduated from Northeast High School in 1918, having maintained his still reserved though bright persona.[19] Even so, and regardless of his initial successes, Freddie faced some very uncommon—as well as common—youthful dilemmas.

The Great War in Europe had thrust a new and unkind spotlight on the nation's many peoples of German descent, harshly framing them with unfounded suspicions and criticisms of disloyalty. In addition, an increasingly popular movement toward prohibition of alcohol sales used this growing antipathy to focus attention on the many German breweries, accusing them of profiteering and wasting the national supplies of grains at the expense of American soldiers who were sure to soon be involved in the war "over there." It was perhaps these very stresses that led to the unfortunate and premature death of Jacob in 1916.

Having to deal with the grievous loss of his father and while nearing his senior year of high school, Freddie now had to be concerned with his own future. His options, however, appeared limited. Postsecondary education was hardly a choice as this was sure to be an impossible financial strain for his now widowed mother. He could not afford such a venture on his own. The only alternative, if he wanted to pursue further education, was to apply for an appointment to a military academy. This too would surely be no easy route, especially considering the anti-German sentiments brought on by the recent war, but this became his resolve nevertheless.

Much like Burke, Freddie's first choice was West Point, and, like Burke, he was unable to receive an appointment.[20] So he turned to the U.S. Naval Academy. Despite the burden of its cost, Freddie's mother found the means to send her son to preparatory school, where he aptly applied his skills at study for the upcoming exams. His scores were more than sufficient; shortly thereafter he won a coveted congressional appointment.[21] With it came one of the most important moments of his future. Like Arleigh Burke, Freddie was finally on his way to becoming a naval officer.

Annapolis would indeed—as it had and would for so many other notables—prove itself the catalyst for the launching of the future careers of Arleigh Burke and Frederick Moosbrugger. The academy, with its great lessons in leadership, loyalty, and winning spirit, was truly their common ground. Here their characters were not altered but enhanced, emboldened, and challenged never to falter. Both men proved themselves to be remarkable students. Once having graduated, however, the paths of these two fine young officers quickly separated. Their pursuit of careers proceeded without one having any thought of the other. Though they would share some very similar experiences, their paths would not directly cross again—until destiny was ready for their timely reunion, twenty years later.

For Arleigh Burke, graduation day—June 8, 1923—began with dual significance. This was not only his first day as a naval officer but was also his wedding day, as he had pledged to marry Washington debutante Roberta "Bobbie" Gorsuch, a petite brunette whom he had met during his first year at the academy and with whom his affections were instantly anchored.[22] Certainly Navy life and marriage are never an easy combination, especially considering sea duties and the inherent long separations in tandem with regular moves from one assignment to another. But Arleigh and Bobbie were of similar spirit and embraced challenge as much as they did one another. Both were determined to make their partnership succeed.

Moves came quickly for the Burkes. Arleigh was given his first assignment aboard the battleship *Arizona*, and was destined to remain a part of the big battleship's roster for the next five years. He and his new bride immediately headed west by train to Seattle, Washington, where *Arizona* waited in port. The experience was demanding for both husband and wife, as there was much to learn, but they adapted well. Bobbie established her new home with base housing at Bremerton, while Arleigh eagerly moved into his new quarters aboard ship.[23]

Burke loved being a part of *Arizona*'s roster. Early into this tour—though clearly a wet-behind-the-ears ensign—Arleigh's strong devotion to duty and keen ability at leadership quickly gave cause for him to be challenged at deciding on a specialty. The choice was simple; he picked gunnery and torpedoes, the two things he felt were most important to know on a warship.[24] His talent in this arena soon awarded him a job in the *Arizona*'s plotting room, at one of the ship's most important duties, that of controlling the vessel's massive 14-inch guns. Without a doubt, nothing about these monstrous weapons or the machines controlling them was to escape Arleigh's careful study. He learned every aspect of their function, right down to each complex calculation. His superiors were greatly impressed, for each day his skills shone brighter and his confidence grew stronger—as did his promise for an outstanding career.

By mid-May 1929, Arleigh's superb performances won him acceptance into the Navy's Postgraduate School. He and Bobbie returned to Annapolis. By this date a lieutenant junior grade (jg)—a promotion received in the summer of 1926—Burke arrived back on the academy grounds with tremendous enthusiasm, and even more so after he was chosen to be among a select few to participate in a new ordnance program.[25]

The yearlong course was intense, but Arleigh successfully met its challenge and immediately advanced on to graduate school. Offered the option of several fine institutions, he chose to attend the University of Michigan—and again he and Bobbie were on the move. Another year of classes followed. Then, on June 22, 1931, with his schooling complete, Lt. (jg) Arleigh Burke was presented a master of science degree in the field of engineering.[26]

The Navy took quick notice of his valuable new education, and Arleigh was next assigned to the Bureau of Ordnance. He and Bobbie moved back to Washington, DC, where, at the request of her widowed mother, they took up residence in Bobbie's childhood home.[27] The arrangement—especially considering the financial strains created by the Great Depression—worked out well, especially for Bobbie, as Arleigh was often away, traveling to one munitions factory and then to another.

These were hard times, both at home and abroad, from which even the military had no immunity. During his many travels Arleigh saw and experienced—surely with considerable alarm—just how the U.S. Navy was being plagued by this new money crunch.

The economic hardships were indeed far reaching, even creating immense financial difficulties for most government agencies. Severe reductions in appropriations were forcing drastic cuts throughout the Army and Navy, which for both branches meant less money for equipment, wages, and critical training. The Navy, in particular, was hit hard due to tandem blows of a weakening purse in combination with newly signed international naval treaties, creating a whole list of shipbuilding restrictions and threatening to derail much of the new construction that could be afforded.[28] Certainly this all came at a most inopportune time, as rumblings in Europe and the Far East were once more signaling the very real possibility of another new war on the world's horizon—a war that America was by no means prepared for.

By June of 1932, Arleigh, now a full lieutenant, was again reassigned, this time to the cruiser *Chester*. Again, the Burkes moved, making the long journey back to the West Coast, to San Pedro, California. This assignment, however, was short lived, lasting only nine months.[29]

Arleigh was then ordered to report to the fleet auxiliary ship *Antares*, where he was to become a member of the Base Force Ordnance-Camera Party.[30] Home base for this assignment remained the same—which was fortunate for Bobbie—even as Lieutenant Burke's location was constantly changed. Such was to be a grueling schedule, bouncing the lieutenant around from ship to ship, as he was charged with photographing various aspects of gunnery throughout a growing number of fleet exercises. All the while, however, Arleigh was gaining a greater knowledge about gunnery and gunnery tactics, becoming more and more the expert.

Since completing his rather lengthy tour with *Arizona*, Arleigh had so far managed no more than two years at any one location. The trend continued with his assignment to Base Force, when in April of 1934 the command was ordered to the East Coast for observations with the ships of the Atlantic Fleet. Arleigh made the transit by sea, via the Panama Canal, while Bobbie made the trip cross-country, and the two reunited in New York. Shortly after, Lieutenant Burke applied for a transfer back to the Bureau of Ordnance, and within the year he and Bobbie were back in Washington, DC. But, as the Burkes' two-year trend continued, by May 1937 Arleigh and Bobbie were again moving their nest, this time to Quincy, Massachusetts.[31]

At Quincy's Bethlehem Shipbuilding Corporation, a brand-new ship awaited Burke's arrival. Arleigh had received the assignment as the vessel's new executive officer, second only in the progression of command to the ship's captain. The ship, destroyer *Craven*, was the third ship built of the Gridley class, a newly engineered design uniquely separate from the so-called "tin cans" of old. Sleek, compact, powerful, and fast are all adjectives that gave fabulous descriptions of this new warship. Arleigh found himself in complete awe of its sculpture. Two boilers joined to a single stack (ship's funnel) supplied steam to two powerful turbines, already proven to produce speeds in excess of 39 knots. Even more noticeable to Arleigh was this ship's firepower; despite a compact 1,500-ton package, this destroyer mounted four 5-inch guns and sixteen 21-inch torpedo tubes. Such a combination of speed and weaponry was sure to make its mark in naval presence. Suddenly, whereas he had always before thought his service preference was to remain with the battleships, the lieutenant had reason to rethink his partiality. The destroyer was quickly winning his heart—and this love affair was only just beginning.

Arleigh was to serve aboard *Craven* for the next two years, during which time he gained a promotion to lieutenant commander. At the conclusion of this tour, he was finally offered the opportunity for which he had been longing, his own command. On the morning of June 5, 1939, he arrived on the deck of *Mugford*—a sister ship to *Craven*—and dominantly stepped into his next important role, that of commanding officer.[32]

It was on this occasion that Arleigh first met and made acquaintance with Gelzer Loyall Sims, the thirty-five-year-old lieutenant who had been chosen as *Mugford*'s new executive officer. A native of Orangeburg, South Carolina, Sims was a man of small stature, standing nearly a foot shy of Arleigh's large 6-foot-plus frame. Even so, it was immediately evident that the lieutenant's size was no indicator of his ability. Sims could be quite a force, being a highly intelligent man, seriously spoken and quick with accurate evaluations.

Burke found his second in command a very interesting character, as his responses were relaxed and exact, and his speech was given to the drawl typical of his Southern roots. During their initial meeting the lieutenant told Arleigh an unusual story, one about a town bum hired to shine the brass barrel of an artillery piece decorating the local courthouse lawn. He went on to explain that the man did fabulous work, as the gun was always immaculate and bright. One day, however, the man suddenly declared that he was tired of polishing someone else's property, and he quit. When he was asked what he planned on doing, he responded, "I'm goin' in business for myself."[33] As the story went, the man had purchased his own artillery piece, and he intended on finishing out his career with its maintenance only. In the midst of this homespun yarn Sims suddenly declared, "I figure you're the kind of man who's got to have his *own* cannon!"[34] The characterization was a bit unorthodox, but it was true of Burke; he was indeed a man who demanded control of his own destiny—and "cannons" just happened to be his expertise. On *Mugford* this characterization was to become even more apt.

Indeed, *Mugford* and Arleigh Burke were to prove to be the perfect match. Their record would be hard to surpass. As captain, Arleigh stood as proud as any who had held the post, and for good reason. *Mugford* was noted as one of the tautest ships in the U.S. Navy and was home to a crew that was second to none. In an early exercise, Arleigh's team won the Navy's coveted fleet gunnery trophy, scoring an unprecedented thirty-six hits out of thirty-six shots fired.[35] This exhibition set a high standard, but each successive challenge saw *Mugford* set the bar even higher. There seemed to be no limits to the success of this duo.

Indeed, Arleigh's first command was exemplary and of it he was very proud, but he was not arrogant. He was first to note that *Mugford*'s every success was due entirely to the talented team that served under him. Even so, no one doubted that his leadership was that one element responsible for having built this team.[36]

Known as a tough commander, Arleigh's toughness was not in the orders he spouted but in the examples he set. He demanded perfection—as he expected no less from himself—and was intolerant of mistakes, yet he needed to scold only with a momentary sear of the eye or a mere word of caution. He demanded speed, of both ship and crew, but not at the expense of oversight. He demanded complete control, though not by usual expectation of his rank, but by a respect that he would work hard to earn. Respect, Arleigh taught, was an honor best given if it was to be received. Officers and sailors alike found him eager to reward them with praise, never failing to acknowledge their good efforts. He demanded the best of himself and those around him—and he almost always got it because his officers and men always wanted to make their captain proud. At some point, Arleigh knew, such devotion to duty would bring far greater rewards than mere respect and expertise at seamanship: It would bring survival.

Frederick Moosbrugger, on the other hand—while his initial avenue into the ranks was a bit similar—experienced a mostly dissimilar path to his leadership role than did Burke. While still at the academy, just as was true of his earliest school days, academics remained foremost among Freddie's pursuits. No doubt his abilities to perform well in the classroom were noted. Still, these intellectual talents did not truly divulge the fullness of his character. There proved to be far more to this quiet young man than just books.

When encouraged to participate in sports, Freddie elected to join the academy baseball and boxing teams; and it was this competition that quickly spurred a passion in him never before seen, hinting for a first time to his otherwise hidden aggressiveness. Indeed, though ever the quiet and genteel person, Freddie was fast maturing into a tough, well-rounded midshipman, bright and full of promise—and he quickly gained notice.

Interestingly enough, a classmate once wrote, "Freddie has the most consistent luck of anyone," noting his amazing ability to escape trouble.[37] Apparently, Moosbrugger's mischievous, daring side was somewhat resurrected during his academy years, sometimes causing him to catch the "fat" of his superiors.[38] But it appeared he used his unassuming character to his own advantage, as he so consistently avoided retribution that his ease at escaping wrath became widely expected.

As a newly commissioned ensign in the U.S. Navy, much like Burke, Moosbrugger began his first assignment aboard a battleship. His first sea duty was aboard the *Nevada*, and the experience for him was both impressive and memorable.[39]

His new home, a massive dreadnought vessel, having an armored steel structure that extended over 580 feet in length and displaced over 27,000 tons of weight, exhibited a formidable presence.[40] Ten large 14-inch and twenty-one medium 5-inch guns bristled about her armored frame, ensuring a respect from any would-be adversaries. Above the ship's decks and dwarfing its great superstructure, two cage-style masts towered high into the sky, housing crow's-nests that at their highest pinnacle offered—at an age before radar—early visual detection of any distant vessel or land. It was the age of the battleship, and no ship of the time projected more power or authority. Being a part of *Nevada*'s complement was certainly a proud period of service for Moosbrugger—but it was a service yet in its infancy.

Indeed, so much was to impact Moosbrugger's career. The next four years brought several new and exciting experiences for Freddie, expanding his knowledge of seamanship while raising his awareness of the world's instability.

In June of 1925, *Nevada* departed on a "Goodwill Cruise" to Australia and New Zealand.[41] This trip was twofold in purpose: (1) to assure America's allies in the Pacific of friendship and an ability to assist in their defense, and (2) to demonstrate to the Japanese a need for their caution with any plans at future aggressiveness and/or unwelcome expansion along the Pacific Rim. (Though war between the two nations remained far beyond the horizon, there were expectations that it would eventually happen.)

Shortly after the "Goodwill Cruise," Moosbrugger transferred to the destroyer *Truxtun*, whereupon he received his first experience with one of the Navy's feisty tin cans.[42] *Truxtun*, a four-stack destroyer of the Clemson class, was assigned to the Asiatic Fleet and based out of Manila, Philippines. Between September 1926 and October 1927, this destroyer spent much of its time in China, patrolling up and down the Yangtze River in the effort to protect American interests and American civilians from the widespread rebellion consuming this land and its people.[43]

1926, however, was also to be a troubling time for Moosbrugger. Freddie's mother, whom he loved dearly, died that year, leaving him to suffer through another period of grieving.[44] Despite this, he went about his duties, competently meeting their requirements while remaining his usual reserved self—so much so that some in his company were not even aware of his pain. In truth, Freddie rarely shared his inner feelings with anyone, even family, especially when he was hurting—and he *was* hurting. On the outside he cautiously displayed a character of self-control and self-determination, something he had learned as a youth to help him overcome a perception by others that he was physically weak. It was this hidden character that so often caused others, especially his enemies, to misjudge him.

Many years later Frederick's middle son, Edward, would share a family story about his father that confirmed this misconception of weakness. Edward wrote: "There was a rather large youth who lived in Freddie's neighborhood in Philadelphia who loved to pick fights and generally make life miserable for other youths. This particular day, Freddie, who [had been] away at the Naval Academy, was on leave and was walking home after coming up from Annapolis. As he passed by, this bully made some very insulting remarks about Freddie and how he looked in his uniform. Freddie ignored him at first, but when the bully added taunts and threats to his insults [,] it couldn't be ignored any more. Freddie, not tall [or] heavily built, invited the bully to 'have it out!' under a nearby railroad bridge, which the bully was apparently very happy to hear. What the bully didn't know was that Freddie was on the boxing team at the Naval Academy. The thrashing Freddie gave him became a permanent part of the neighborhood lore."[45]

All personal dilemmas aside, Freddie most assuredly was conscious of the chaos brewing around him. His experience in China was most disconcerting and proved to be only a hint of what was to come. The China he witnessed was in the midst of transition, passing from feudal rule to a republican style of government, resulting in much infighting. The evolution was painfully slow, bloody, and stiffly resisted by many of the nation's powerful warlords. In addition, there were many outside influences at work in China, fanning the flames of revolution: The United States and Britain usurped the opportunity to use political prowess and financial reward at supporting a movement toward westernization; Stalin's Russia offered military training and supplies in its bid to support a movement toward socialistic communism; and Japan saw the upheaval as further opportunity for expansion. (During the First World War, Japan had seized the German holdings of Shandong Province, and then at the war's conclusion brokered a deal with Beijing to retain their claim over Shandong and assert protectorate control over eastern Inner Mongolia and southern Manchuria—the latter to become the Japanese puppet state of Manchukuo.[46]) *Truxtun*'s many river patrols gave Moosbrugger a firsthand glimpse into the severity of this Far East turmoil and to the true brutalities of war. Though he surely did not comprehend this at the time, he was witnessing the spark that was set to erupt into a wall of uncontrollable flames, certain to consume the Far East and Pacific in massive world conflict—a conflict he was destined to play an important role in extinguishing.

By May of 1927, Moosbrugger had completed his tour in China and was ordered back to the mainland United States, given an assignment with the 13th Naval District Headquarters at Seattle, Washington. This assignment was, however, quite brief, as in less than three months Freddie was back at sea, this time finding a new assignment aboard the fleet oiler *Brazos*.[47]

Service aboard the oiler lasted for the next twenty-two months, most of it at sea, sailing with the fleet on various occasions from the West Coast to Hawaii, to Samoa, and to Australia.[48] Obviously, this experience lacked much of the glamour and excitement of those aboard the warships, but it was still a very valuable education. Freddie was now a lieutenant (jg), and his knowledge and abilities at leadership were increasing rapidly.

From battleship to destroyer to support vessel, Moosbrugger proved himself a very capable and promising young officer. Each new assignment brought with it a great many new challenges. Each was set upon a new environment, requiring Freddie many adjustments to his routines and responsibilities. Having adapted to these quite well, in June of 1929 he was given his next test, an assignment with the U.S. Navy's adolescent submarine service.

Following a period of instruction, which he completed in December, Freddie arrived at New London, Connecticut, to board his new home, the submarine

S-6.[49] It was not what he expected. His newest assignment was rather lackluster. The boat was ten years old—small, confining, and uncomfortable—and nearing the end of its service. *S-6* had once served in the Far East as a part of the Asiatic Fleet, and was among the first American submarines to make the complete journey from the West Coast to the Philippines on its own. For three years she had patrolled coastal China, providing protection for American interests. Since then, however, newer submarines, having far greater range and capabilities, had replaced her class. *S-6* was now awaiting its retirement, serving only as a coastal patrol boat, having duties limited to the eastern seaboard and ranging no farther than the Panama Canal.[50] Still, despite such bland duty, Moosbrugger found his service aboard *S-6* to be a worthwhile experience, adding to his résumé of knowledge a valuable understanding of subsurface warfare, torpedo technology, and tactics. His service aboard *S-6* lasted through the next fifteen months, till the boat's decommissioning on April 10, 1931.

Moosbrugger's next assignment landed him back ashore at Annapolis, where he was to spend the next three years of his service as an instructor at the academy.[51] The shore duty suited Freddie quite well. He was by this time a husband, having married his Philadelphian sweetheart, Dorothy E. Britt, on January 29, 1931.[52] Family life came quickly—a first son, Fred, was born on January 20 of the following year—and Freddie lost no precious moments at enjoying its rich rewards.

By June of 1934 Freddie's stint at the academy had come to an end. He said his farewells to family and friends and headed back to sea, aboard one of the Navy's newest cruisers, *Houston.*[53] This proved to be a very opportune assignment, as he arrived aboard just in time to participate in an honored presidential cruise.

On July 1, President Franklin D. Roosevelt was welcomed to the decks of the cruiser for the beginning of a 12,000-mile adventure. Departing Annapolis with considerable pomp and circumstance, *Houston* sailed south into the Caribbean, through the Panama Canal, ranging far out into the vast Pacific, on to Hawaii, to then return to the West Coast, ending its journey at Portland, Oregon.[54] The experience was quite wonderful, as the president, a former secretary of the navy, applauded the officers and crew for an outstanding venture—a moment that would prove to be only a taste of times to come.

Houston was destined to spend the next year and a half sailing the Pacific. Based out of San Diego, California, her assignments during this time included a cruise to Hawaii (hosting the assistant secretary of the navy, Henry Roosevelt), a cruise to Alaska, and an additional presidential cruise that would conclude on the East Coast, at Charleston, South Carolina. Afterward the cruiser returned to its base, and on July 28, 1937—just one day before Moosbrugger's scheduled departure for reassignment—she participated in the great celebration to mark the grand opening of San Francisco's Golden Gate Bridge. As a result, Freddie closed out his service with *Houston* just as it had begun, in salute to a remarkable moment in history.[55]

Moosbrugger then returned to Annapolis, where he was to spend the next two years instructing on what had now become his expertise, gunnery tactics.[56] Having now returned to a stable stateside assignment, Freddie was once more able to resume his role as husband and father, enjoying some long overdue quality time with his darling love, Dot (Freddie's pet name for Dorothy), and his two young sons (a second son, Edward, had been born November 26, 1936).

These were good times for the Moosbruggers. Even despite the lingering effects of the Great Depression, the nation's economy was slowly improving and the country was at peace, which was of obvious benefit to all those in the employ of the nation's military. Freddie felt well advised to take full advantage of this rare offering—he rightly suspected it would not be long standing. He was well aware that the tranquility being experienced here at home was far from a true reflection of the unsettled disposition being felt by the rest of the world. Europe was a tinderbox set to ignite, while China and Japan were already aflame with open warfare that threatened to spill over into other regions of the Far East. Every effort at diplomacy had up to this point failed, and miserably so. The arrival of each new day announced even greater uncertainty as the rumblings of war grew more and more pronounced. Freddie watched the situation with keen interest. He had witnessed firsthand and clearly understood the world's volatile state, and suspected, quite correctly, that it would be only a matter of time until even more chaos would rear its ugly head and beckon him back to duty at sea.

Certainly, the U.S. Navy was not standing idle. By early 1939, the Navy was hastily pressing forward in preparation for the likelihood of a new massive conflict, and especially so in the Pacific where the offensive threat created by the powerful Imperial Fleet of the Japanese navy was most worrisome. More and more new ships were being built and the demand for experienced officers was ever increasing. By June, as expected, Freddie was headed back to the West Coast, having in his hand the orders for his next new assignment, returning him to a fleet battleship.

Moosbrugger, now a full lieutenant, had been awarded a new responsibility, that of gunnery officer aboard the *Tennessee*.[57] He arrived on the deck of the battleship without any illusions about the nature of his new job; the assignment was to be a critical juncture in his development as a naval officer and an ongoing test of his evolving skills, both in providing mastery over the vessel's powerful weapons as well as delivering competent leadership to the teams in charge of their operation. Certainly, if war did ensue as it was expected, Freddie knew *Tennessee*'s twelve 14-inch guns were sure to be an important asset to the Navy and likely play heavily in the outcome of any major naval surface engagements. There could be no room for inefficiency. When the time should come, he intended to be ready.

Time, however, was not a luxury for anyone, and especially not for the U.S. Navy. On September 1, 1939, the perils of world instability were suddenly given over to full realization. As threatened, European discord finally exploded into full-fledged disorder. After nearly a decade of charismatic prodding, Adolf Hitler—with tyrannical rants that had long been open with his intent at European domination—unleashed Nazi Germany's powerful fighting forces on its immediate neighbors, beginning with an invasion of Poland. The action forced the only plausible response; two days later England and France declared war against the rogue dictator and his countrymen. As a result, chaos spread quickly, in Europe but also in Europe's many extended colonies, with the strategic shipping lanes lying between them becoming instant battlefields.

The turmoil even extended its reach to the distant Pacific Rim, giving rise to legitimate fears that an unruly Japan would likely take full advantage of the situation to further expand its own dominating influences in the region, which it would surely do if not quickly checked. For this reason, the U.S. Navy was put on immediate notice to be ready, and its leadership quickly advanced preparations for its next series of fleet war games, entitled Fleet Problem XXI.[58] This exercise was to be held in the Pacific in early spring 1940, just west of the territory of Hawaii. Nearly every available U.S. Navy vessel was ordered to this Polynesian assembly. Burke and the mighty *Mugford* were among the participants, arriving in the waters off the Hawaiian Islands in early April. Moosbrugger, aboard *Tennessee*, was also present.

The gathering was massive, as warship after warship filled the tight confinement of Pearl Harbor, Oahu, forcing yet others to drop anchor at the less inhibitive Lahaina Roads, Maui. It certainly appeared—as diplomacy had become fully dysfunctional and with conflict spreading across the globe as a windswept wildfire—that some of America's leadership were hopeful that this bold display of military power and prowess might be enough to deter any enemy aggression against America and its interests. It would not.

No doubt there were some astute players within the government and military who did indeed understand the full gravity of this growing war and the massive threats it posed, wanting of greater direct participation at bringing it to an early end. But these were too few. Preparation for any overt involvement in an unpopular war posed a great many risks, and especially so within the realm of American politics. Due to the overbearing influences of a powerful isolationist movement, led by hero aviator Charles Lindbergh, most politicians chose to take the "safe" approach to the escalating warfare rather than set their own personal careers at jeopardy, regardless of any future cost to the nation.

President Roosevelt was not immune, as he too was mostly deterred at becoming directly involved in the volatile European affair. His "Short of War Policy" did allow for a fair amount of aid to those countries (mainly England, Russia, and China) resisting the encroaching Axis (Germany, Italy, and Japan), even dared some covert meddling, but little more.

Rather than risk direct intervention in the widening conflict, America would instead wager that its allies could hold fast on their own and, if not, then rely on a moat of two massive oceans for its own front-line defense, with the U.S. Navy widely expected to protect these waters and coastal territories along their edge. This meant that if both the eastern and southern coasts of the United States were to be properly protected, the Navy would have to police the entirety of the Caribbean plus an extension of the coastal Atlantic outward by some 300 miles. If these were not daunting enough tasks, especially in the face of other warring world-class navies, there remained the need to protect the western coastline, where the Pacific created a far greater challenge. Indeed, American territories in the Pacific extended all the way to Alaska and the Aleutians far to the north, to Samoa deep in the south, and to the Philippines in the distant west. This was a lot of water to police and was to prove quite a tax to the Navy at its current levels. Even so, this challenge, in particular, was not without one very positive benefit, as it did allow President Roosevelt the flexibility at posturing for a very strong military presence in the Pacific—which was one opportunity he was sure not to let slip by.

Determined at boosting war preparations wherever possible, the president had in April 1940 ordered his Pacific Fleet to be permanently headquartered in Hawaii—a decision that at the time was very unpopular with many of his military commanders but one that the president deemed necessary.[59] In addition, Roosevelt demanded that the Navy's newest fleet problem, Fleet Problem XXI, should be exercised as far west as possible yet not so far west as to cause an international incident—forbidding the fleet to cross west of the International Date Line.[60] Obviously the president's foremost intent was to use his fleet's move and conjoining naval exercise as a way of sending a stern warning to the

Japanese, for the purpose of conveying that the United States would not stand idle to any of their aggressive antics—to which the Japanese were receptive, but clearly unimpeded. Additionally, Roosevelt also hoped the exercise might convey to every officer and sailor of his own Navy, if they were any bit unclear, who their enemy would likely be, cautioning them to be ready for whatever might come—to which they too were receptive, though with apparent arrogance and oversight with respect to their enemy's true capabilities.

As for Fleet Problem XXI, it was to proceed in a somewhat normal application of protocols, setting in opposition U.S. warships in simulated combat, with one side posing as an aggressor fleet, this time predetermined to be ships of the Imperial Japanese Navy. This enemy aggression would be presumed as closing to attack the Hawaiians—an ironic and premonitory situation that few truly believed likely. Regardless of its plausibility with most strategists, this exercise was set to test the fleet's preparedness against just such a major seaborne attack.[61]

Neither Burke nor Moosbrugger appeared surprised by the scenario, as both officers clearly expected some type of conflict with Japan—even if they did not fully understand the events that were forthcoming. Obviously, being that he had witnessed some of the Far East turmoil in person, Moosbrugger appeared to have a good comprehension of the Japanese bent on expansion as well as a clear understanding of the risks associated with the interventions. Burke, whose extensive time within the Bureau of Ordnance had provided him with some unique insight, understood how the U.S. Navy, so previously underfunded and ill equipped, remained well behind at matching the massive building programs previously launched by the Japanese. Even so, surely no one knew just how emboldened the Japanese truly felt or how far they were really willing to go at reaching their lofty goals of Far East domination.

It seemed justifiable that the Navy should feel optimistic about flexing its muscle in overt warning, just in case someone (the Japanese in particular) doubted its resolve. What most analytical prophets failed to grasp, however, was just how the Japanese were to receive this message. Their perception of the American moves was not so much deterrence as direct threat, and they began immediate preparations for quick elimination of this new obstacle—and on such a grand scale as to nearly mimic the imaginary scenario of the problem. This was every bit unexpected.

Such a potential hazard should not have been so surprising. But, even despite numerous foretelling events, there remained overconfidence prevalent throughout the U.S. Navy—of which neither Burke nor Moosbrugger was immune. Not only did the Navy presume its own skills at naval surface warfare as dominant, but it seemingly also displayed a pure disregard for the true strength and ability of the Imperial Japanese Navy, and the disastrous results were only too soon to be revealed.

Even the Fleet Problem, as it had been intended but not completely as planned, exposed some of these very weaknesses. Set to be conducted in two separate phases, a variance of training exercises and concluding combat scenarios were employed, all to be held in the open sea during daylight hours. All elements of the problem were to be heavily scrutinized by a myriad of official observers, whereby they were to score the outcome and make note of any successes and failures.[62]

The first phase of the problem, as it was judged, was well handled and quickly scored as a victory for the U.S. ships. However, the second phase inadvertently extended into the late evening hours and concluded in a night engagement wherein, with all its complexity, the exercise turned into a fiasco that was a certain premonition to a good many future combat debacles. Within the darkness, ships lost track of one another and nearly collided, while communications became confused and corrective maneuvering became frustrated, ultimately causing the formations to disintegrate and offensive/defensive posturing to fail.[63]

Most of these failures were duly noted, but—outside the recommendation for faster integration of radar on all ships—few concrete solutions or serious corrections were set in motion. Even the lower echelon commanders, such as Burke and the other destroyer commanders, despite the assured vital importance of their future roles, were given no clear understanding to the pretext behind the predetermined maneuvers and were later left only to guess at its concise conclusions.[64] Secrecy of the failures became paramount—as Japanese ears were sure to be listening—overriding any mass sharing of exposed weaknesses or for expediency at overt improvement of the overall performance. Nevertheless, it was quite clear to *all* observers, regardless of rank, that the Navy's nighttime tactics were seriously flawed and in need of major review—future combat was to prove it so, and to the detriment of many young lives.

Indeed, events long set in motion were quickly establishing the destiny of many. A perception of weakness and unwillingness to fight was emboldening America's enemies, and the result was to set the nation on course for exactly what it had hoped to avoid. In addition, an unfounded arrogance, this of ignorant presumptions and beliefs in the ineptness of the nation's enemies—especially of the Japanese—was to prove devastatingly wrong and the root of a good many gross miscalculations and bloody failures in the future. Unfortunately, these were lessons not easily learned, with many duplicated repercussions, each being exceedingly more painful and unnecessarily deadly. Future combat leaders, whose destinies set them at the tip of the spear, at the forefront in the conflict, were often forced to improvise when meeting these inherent challenges. Many were to fall well short. Fortunately, the right men with the right decisions did appear, and at just the right time.

Arleigh Burke and Frederick Moosbrugger—combined with the tough veterans their commands would ultimately inherit—were to be among the elite. For both men, their entire lives had been built upon a vast array of inescapable challenges, each one requiring from them some strong responsive planning and fast reflexive thinking to overcome. Life had taught them well. Transference of such earned talent at the successful meeting of any additional dilemmas seemed only second nature to these two. But the extreme test had yet to arrive. The ultimate challenge remained just beyond the horizon and—like so many others in their company—neither man was quite as ready for this future as he initially thought.

Chapter Two

Pearl Harbor

Reality Strikes Home

The Pearl Harbor attack of December 7, 1941, caught all of America napping. An unsuspecting society, long resting on overstated security, was abruptly awakened to two new horrible realities—a personal war and a stinging defeat. The immediate question that followed was not easily answered, not at first. A declaration of war was assured—but just how would the nation, on the whole, truly respond?

American life, as it had been, instantly changed, and drastically so. The nation was wholly unprepared for such transformation. Even despite the extent of the European conflict, the protracted instability of the Far East, and the raw aggressiveness previously displayed by Japan, few people (military or civilian) expected such a direct assault on this U.S. territory—let alone one with such savage and successful results. For a population once so contented with and so compelled at remaining isolated from the worldly chaos, the shock of such a bruising blow proved itself a very painful awakening indeed. The warned-of "unavoidable" war—so long knocking at America's doorpost—was now very real and had in its impatience suddenly burst through the threshold to grab the country directly by the throat, threatening a severe harm and instilling a newfound fear unlike anything before experienced.

For those individuals so unwittingly caught in its initial onslaught, the true seriousness of this deadly affair needed only to be evidenced by the woeful masses of gathered dead, the pitiful throngs of grievously wounded, and the smoldering numbers of wrecked planes and ships that had been left behind on Oahu.[1] Others of the nation were not nearly so privy to this reality. Their early news of the event came by way of compelling commentaries on radio, by typeset "Extra" editions quickly printed by ticker-tape newspapers, or by the proverbial word of mouth. Most of these initial reports remained impersonal as well as inconclusive, even to the point of significant error. As more facts were disclosed, as names were given to the numbers of casualties, and as grieving families from across the country were witnessed mourning the losses of their sons, the consciousness of the nation came bounding from its self-induced hibernation.

The nation had been "suddenly and deliberately attacked" by an "unprovoked" enemy.[2] America was now at war. Internal squabbling no longer seemed relevant, and even in the realm of American politics a rare truce emerged, projecting a strongly unified front. It did not matter that almost no one comprehended the full magnitude of what was beginning or understood the ultimate cost; the nation was now determined to rise to the challenge.

Young men lined the streets in front of recruiting offices, eager to sign up for a conflict they did not fully understand, while those already in the services went on a full war footing, preparing for immediate action that was neither to be immediate nor fully prepared for. This was how it was to begin, an affair full of uncertainty and replete with unknown risk, of which no one—from the highest of leadership to the most common of everyday folk—knew how it might conclude. The fate of the nation, indeed the entire world, rested in the need for America to unite with one common purpose—just as she would, and at great sacrifice too. A nation's treasured youth were soon sent into harm's way, and at great peril to both life and limb.

Lt. (jg) Henry D. Davison was one among many who was desperately trying to make some sense of what had just befallen the nation. The twenty-five-year-old native of McGehee, Arkansas, was a highly opinionated young man, very smart and very proud of who he was—proud of being an American, proud of his Southern roots, proud of the U.S. Navy, proud of his ship, and so very proud of his being a product of Annapolis.

A 1940 graduate of the academy, Davison would write, "I am a naval officer, one of the 'trade school' boys the government spent time and money training."[3] He was by the very precepts of his training a professional, and he did not take his profession lightly. Glamour was not a part of his trade. "[Such] related forms of eyewash [do not] exist in real life," he noted.[4] He had been trained "in terms of cold facts" and was thoroughly convinced that the quality of his training would be more than sufficient for any conflict that might arise.[5] He knew of the threats, but the Japanese did not concern him, not really. He—as did most Americans—believed the U.S. military was far and away a better fighting force than anything the short-sighted Nipponese, miniatures in both body and intellect, could possibly muster. If the Japanese tried to attack, they would surely catch a thrashing that would quickly whip them into submission. How wrong he was, and how shocked he was to experience the reality.

On the morning of the attack, Davison was standing his assigned post, at station as officer-of-the-deck aboard his ship, the USS *Arizona*.[6] The day began much as any day within the Polynesian realm, beautifully calm and quiet. Due east of the lieutenant the sun revealed itself brightly, announcing the birth of a lovely azure sky, its domain interrupted by only a few sculptured variances of large white cumulus clouds. The morning breeze, as usual, was warm and fresh. This was, after all, "paradise," and one expected little other. Furthermore, it was Sunday, and activity at the base was nearly nonexistent. No one had any suspicion of imminent danger. Nothing appeared out of the way. Most men were sleeping late in their berths, oblivious to the world. A few fortunate souls were ashore, taking advantage of welcomed weekend passes, resting up from a night out on the town or up early for a wandering stroll along one of the island's magnificent beaches. Others, like Davison, stood their stations aboard their respective ships, unconcerned for their own welfare and less than astute in their watch. Nothing alluded to any need for extra caution. No alerts had been issued. A large concentration of planes, arranged in classic "V"-shaped formations, was noticed racing into the arena, engines roaring deeply as their silhouettes glistened brightly in the light—which was unusual for a Sunday, but not entirely out of character. The alarms remained quiet, so no one suspected anything foul. Then the Vs broke up into pairs, and the engine tones rose to a tenor as the incoming crafts dove swiftly toward the surface of the harbor. Still no alarms sounded. The concern remained mute. Suddenly the entire harbor shook as with one massive explosion, as thunderous booms and crackling pops simultaneously echoed from all directions. In an instant Lieutenant Davison found himself enveloped within a hostile shower of bombs and bullets. The speed of the action was tremendous, like that of a mighty rushing whirlwind spinning on a wicked course that no one could stop. There was nowhere to be shielded from its hideous destruction, no place of true safety to escape the angry torrent. Finally, warning sirens began their belated wails and clattering bells rang their repeated call to arms, only, it seemed, to add to the ongoing confusion and growing chaos.

Regardless of the peril, sailors responded with all able haste, rallying forth in desperate defense of their ships—but such was not nearly soon enough for *Arizona*. The vision that followed was horrific, burned so deeply into the subconscious as to never be forgotten. Davison's mind would repeat the scene over and over, recreated in agonizingly slow motion, eternally capturing the ungodly roar and the rise of the hellish ball of flame that shot upward by hundreds of feet into the morning sky. His memory would be forever haunted by the screams of those unfortunate sailors whose bodies he watched thrash in torment, tortured by a final few seconds of excruciating pain before being consumed in the super-heated fire. He had never before witnessed such dreadful carnage or felt so completely helpless at aiding those in need. Within the lapse of only a few short minutes his ship—what had once been a magnificent brute of a proud battleship—was turned into a burning, twisted wreck of nearly unrecognizable structure.[7]

Arizona's now hideous form quickly settled deep into the harbor's mud, taking with it hundreds of officers and crew to their eternal rests.[8] But Davison survived—one of only a very few souls who avoided the flames to escape into the harbor for rescue. Later, when finally wrested from the water, oil soaked, bleeding, and exhausted, the lieutenant emerged a changed man.[9] No longer was he the naïve gentleman officer as before, but rather the wounded veteran of enemy aggression, steeped with anger and determined at revenge. Obviously, it went without question that the Japanese had won this early bout, but there would surely be hell to pay for their wanton aggression—and certainly Henry D. Davison stood as ready as anyone to settle the score.

Across the channel at the submarine base, Torpedoman 2nd Class Wilber Fultz stood affixed in the openness of the nicely groomed yard that fronted his barracks, observing the developing attack with a dire concern.[10] A stalwart young man whose appearance of maturity was well in advance of his true age (of just eighteen), Wilber had been jarred awake by the first of the explosions and sent recoiling from his bunk to race half-dressed outside in curious pursuit of the source of the ongoing clamor. His initial observations revealed unfamiliar warplanes circling wildly all around, men running from one place to some other place seemingly without any sense of direction, and billowing black smoke rushing high into the sky at every angle of his search—all while horrendous booms continuously shook the ground beneath him. He could not readily explain the chaos, but he knew it was the beginning of something very bad. Indeed, the world he had come to love was exploding all around him, and it angered him that such was happening again.

Born and raised on a rural homestead farm near Fort Benton, Montana, Wilber Fultz's world had exploded once before. In 1928, at the age of five, Wilber had experienced the harshness of the breakup of his family. His mother and father divorced after suffering several years of extended financial hardship and uncertainty. The worst of the event came the day his mother packed up his two sisters and left for Texas, tearfully leaving him and his two brothers to remain behind at the homestead with his father—neither parent could afford to raise all the children on their own and so separation of the siblings seemed their only recourse. Many years would pass before he would see his mother and sisters again.[11]

Wilber's father, Coy, a weathered man, hardworking and intent, loved his sons and gave every effort at providing for them the best he could. The task proved to be extremely difficult. Life for the Fultzes would be subsistent at best. The Great Depression only added to their woes. Facing potential loss of the farm, Wilber was forced to leave school right after the eighth grade so that he might add his physical labor helping his father maintain the crops. Later, when his younger brother needed surgery, Wilber took it upon himself to find additional work, hiring on as a cowboy at a local ranch to raise the necessary funds to meet the added medical expense. Not a single day of Wilber's young life had passed without his being severely burdened and tested, and the experience had taken its toll on him.[12]

In 1940, when Wilber turned seventeen, he determined enough was enough. Life surely owed him something better. He and his older brother had often discussed it; if there were to be any opportunities for them, they likely lay in the military. Joining the service seemed the only practical way for the two to make a life for themselves outside the impoverished lifestyle they had come to know. The future prospects of war did not weigh into their common decision. They wanted to see things, do things, and travel as far away as possible from their hard life in Montana. Their choice for such a life-changing experience was the U.S. Navy and, with their father's blessing, they enlisted.[13]

Certainly the transition from Montana farmhand/cowboy to ocean-borne sailor was to be quite an adjustment for Wilber, but he took to his new role in life with considerable enthusiasm. After all, considering his previous experiences, how tough could it really be? Following boot camp—a meager amount of difficulty compared to what he was used to—Wilber was assigned to his first ship, the Pearl Harbor–based destroyer, *Craven*, which he would note as one of the "so called 1500 ton ships."[14] With this assignment, the moment he had been striving to meet had finally arrived. His life as a true sailor had begun. But the experience it was about to bring was to prove well beyond the scope of any of his imaginations.

By early November 1941, Wilber had acclimated to his new profession quite well, even aspired to a new expertise, acquiring the rate of torpedoman. For this reason, he had been temporarily transferred to the confines of Pearl Harbor's submarine base—sent here for the purpose of taking a required training course at the base torpedo school. And here he remained on the morning of December 7, to be eyewitness to the entirety of the vicious Japanese assault.[15]

His station provided a rather advantageous panorama. The barracks' yard offered a disturbing view of the destruction, embellished by multiple, seemingly endless eruptions of pyrotechnics in the forefront of a black colonnade of telescoping smoke plumes. The surety of disaster was undeniable, and Wilber could not believe his misfortune. How was it that he could so profoundly escape the harsh deprivations and cursed uncertainties of one world only so soon to be caught by the same of another? It just wasn't fair. As in his youth, here he stood, again the helpless bystander, watching in disbelief as his world once more went spiraling out of control. His heart sank—faster it seemed than even the most battered ship in the harbor—at this realization of loss. But despite the very real wounds to his emotions, his physical well-being was never once jeopardized—the Japanese bombers for some unfounded reason bypassed the submarine base, leaving its facilities scarred by only a light splattering of stray bullets. Nevertheless, it was certain that there would be no escaping the future consequences of this attack—for the Navy was now at war and the conflict was sure to require great sacrifice from all of its members.

No doubt, Wilber was bitterly ready to do his part, begging for revenge, though a quick study of the aftermath was more than sufficient at acknowledging that such would not happen soon. For the moment the only offense available to this young sailor was the spouting of a few angry innuendoes. "Jap sons of bitches," he uttered with disdain.[16]

Some distance to the west, Wilber's ship, *Craven*, sailed confidently toward the Hawaiian Islands, and did so without any obvious concern. Her officers and crew remained oblivious to the ongoing attack on Pearl. As a part of Task Force 8—the *Enterprise*-led contingent sent to deliver fighter planes to the isolated outpost of Wake Island—this small haze gray destroyer now served what was becoming its common role, that of escort for the larger, capital ships.

On this day, *Craven* shared a part of the carrier's defensive screen, primarily tasked with what appeared to most as a futile search for some unlikely menace of an unfriendly submarine.[17] The charge was pursued without any great concern. There were no premonitions of any pending danger. *Craven*'s crew worked their stations and did their duties as usual. Their greater focus remained on returning to port, where they presumed a resumption of fine liberties awaited them. Everyone was anxious for the journey to conclude, exasperated by an arrival that was already well behind schedule (originally slated to be returned to Pearl by December 6, an encounter with bad weather—the same weather that was responsible for hiding the advancing Japanese carrier fleet to the north—and an associated engineering problem with one of the other screening destroyers, *Dunlap*, had together delayed the force by nearly twenty-four hours). Had things gone as originally planned, these sailors knew they would have already been in port, ashore at either Pearl City or Honolulu, recouping from a previous night of bar-hopping or otherwise enjoying some other escape from the confinement of their ships. They had no clue of the action ongoing less than 150 miles to their east; news of the attack had yet to be received by any of the task force. The fact that this inadvertent delay had saved the carrier, its screening cruisers (Cruiser Division 5—*Northampton*, *Salt Lake City*, and *Chester*) and destroyers (Destroyer Squadron 6—*Craven*, *Maury*, *Fanning*, *Dunlap*, *Gridley*, *Benham*, *Balch*, *Ellet*, and *McCall*) from being caught squarely center of the deadly Japanese assault was not yet known.

Earlier that morning, at around 6:18 a.m., a flight of eighteen scouting torpedo bombers had launched from the carrier, sent aloft on a routine precautionary dawn patrol—having no suspicion of any potential trouble. As ordered, the flight was to search in advance of the ships by the remaining distance to port and, providing nothing out of the ordinary was sighted, proceed on to Pearl to land at Ford Island. This the pilots would indeed do. The timing, however, could hardly have been any worse. These planes arrived over the base just as the attack was developing, caught right in the middle of its initial melee and forced to take quick evasive action.[18] (The awkward Dauntless SBDs were no match for the highly maneuverable Zero fighters and their skilled pilots; but even so, most of the Americans did manage to land their planes intact—three of the SBDs did fall victim to the enemy, two came up missing, while one other was inadvertently shot down when Fort Weaver gunners mistook the plane as an attacking Japanese.[19]) An overheard radio dispatch, a final plea for help from one of these less fortunate pilots, was the first warning to the *Enterprise* force.[20] The call of the panicky voice obviously caused quite a frenzy of questions, while the searing Admiral Kimmel dispatch, "*Air Raid, Pearl Harbor—This is not a drill*," that followed (received at just shortly after 8:00 a.m.), confirmed the worst possible explanation.

This warning came as a complete shock, sending a ripple of apprehension throughout every ship. Klaxons instantly rang out their deafening tones, joined in their alert by speakers blaring excitedly, "*Man your battle-stations . . . Man your battle-stations!*"

This call to general quarters sent everyone scurrying. Sailors hurriedly raced to their respective posts, passing each other through the tight corridors while searching the eyes of every man they met, curious for some answers to their new dilemma. But no answers were readily available. Only one thing seemed certain: This call to arms was no high-ranking pretend scenario meant to challenge everyone's skill; this alert, they understood, was real. This was serious, and how so very disquieting this was, having been caught so completely off guard.

Aboard the escorting destroyer *McCall*, the anxieties were equally high, but the officers and crew managed to react to their uncertainties with a discipline expected of a finely drilled team. General quarters stations were quickly occupied. Guns were manned, lookouts were posted, water-tight hatches were dogged down, and damage control parties were strategically placed. Posts promptly reported, "Manned and ready!"

Then, as if to defy even the shrill song of whistling stays and the deep vocals of churning screws, the moment yielded itself to a deafening stillness. All conversation became noticeably subdued. Anxious eyes directed their focus heavenward, diligently searching the sky above, expecting something though without any certainties as to what.

From a lofty perch, and at critical observation from his pilothouse vantage, *McCall*'s skipper studied the current situation carefully. He cautiously watched for the unexpected, ready to act or react in whatever manner deemed necessary to defend his ship and the rest of the accompanying task force. Frederick Moosbrugger currently held the seat of command aboard the destroyer, and he did so with complete confidence (having been promoted to lieutenant commander while still aboard the *Tennessee*, Freddie had been awarded command of the *McCall* on April 28, 1941).[21] His leadership had now reached a milestone and was perhaps facing its ultimate test, that of real combat. He therefore stood steadfast, staring straightway through the opened pilothouse port-lights, focused yet without displaying any premature alarm. Indeed, Freddie's common demeanor had changed very little. Even in this time of extreme uncertainty, he still projected the same illusive and reserved spirit exhibited in his past—coolly prepared, if and when needed, to order his ship and crew into some type of deadly action.

Moosbrugger had no doubts about his ship and crew; he thoroughly believed they could fight and fight well. *McCall*, a Benham class destroyer (often referred to as the McCall class due to the lower-numbered *Benham* being delayed in its construction and *McCall* actually being completed first), was another of the single-stack vessels similar to the Gridleys that had so captivated Arleigh Burke. This ship was fast, well armed, and carried all the latest electronics, including radar, providing it the extraordinary capabilities of locating enemy planes at great distances and of even seeing in the dark. More importantly, she was manned by a fine crew, an excellent group of officers and men in whom Freddie had great confidence. This trust was verified just a couple months later, captured in a letter he wrote to his sister, Louise. In it he confided that if she should "happen to see a ship with 400 painted on its bow in any of the news reels . . . you'll know it is the 'Merry Mac' in there doing its stuff."[22]

But as confident as he was, Freddie could not completely escape all of the mounting anxieties. He was indeed experiencing some profound unease, even to the point of distraction—not so much for his current situation but rather for the welfare of his family. Not long after taking command of *McCall*, Freddie had moved Dorothy and his (now) three sons (the youngest, Dave, was born September 10, 1940) to Hawaii, so he and they could be close. He had rented a quaint home located within a small community in Manoa Valley, on Oahu and not far from Honolulu, and here he had settled Dot and the boys.[23] It now appeared that this choice had been a good bit unwise. News from the island was at this point sketchy. Details as to how widespread the Japanese attack had been or if there were any civilian casualties remained unclear. Obviously, this gave Freddie good reason to worry—even as he carefully refrained from displaying the emotion to the men of his command. In time he knew he would have his answers. Until then, he would lead his ship.

Nearby, on board the destroyer *Dunlap*, twenty-seven-year-old Waukegan, Illinois, native, Lt. (jg) Albert R. Olsen, had his own set of concerns. He was the gunnery officer aboard the destroyer and was busy enough just assuring that his guns were at the ready. Like every other man in his company, the shock of his hearing of the attack had yet to diminish, just as his questions about the disaster grew. Everyone was wondering what was happening at Pearl. But Olsen also pondered how very close the task force was to having been a part of this destruction. Had they maintained their schedule, all of the nearby ships would have been in the Hawaiian port, experiencing the attack firsthand. In fact, his ship was probably most responsible for delaying the task force and at keeping *Enterprise* beyond the crosshairs of Japanese bombers. However, this satisfaction, this new understanding that their earlier propulsion issue (an overheated propeller shaft) had by its end result been a good thing, was not at all reassuring to him. The lieutenant knew enough about engineering to understand the down side. Despite severe weather being at the root of its cause, the engineering failure could not be dismissed as some timely happenstance. It was a serious matter. Any recurrence in the future must be avoided. Twenty-four hours was way too much time to lose in an important transit, even in spite of all of the ships of the task force having been slowed by the associated inclement conditions. Mobility, speed, and maneuverability were all critical to a warship, to its mission and its survivability, and even more so now that there was a real war with which to contend. That this delay had on this occasion been a good thing was, as Albert knew, of no matter to the lessons of seamanship—the next time could result in disaster; the next time could be deadly.

Albert Olsen, a well-rounded young man who almost always displayed a pleasant smile, was well versed in seamanship and clearly understood its importance to success at sea. He came from a family rich in naval tradition. Prior to his move to New York in 1880, Albert's father, Hjalmar, a Norwegian-born immigrant, had served six years as a merchant seaman (beginning as a cabin boy at the young age of fourteen). After coming to America, and while yet unable to find suitable work, Hjalmar elected to sign on for a stint with the U.S. Navy. Here he found a home. He would serve through two wars (the Spanish-American War and World War I), eventually to progress through the ranks to become an officer, to then retire as a lieutenant. This impressive journey was but the beginning of a multi-generational family tradition, which the senior Olsen first passed on to his six sons, of whom Annapolis proudly graduated five (one son, Lawrence, tragically lost his life in a dormitory fire at Alabama's Marion Institute while enrolled in a preparatory course, or the graduation count would have been all six). Certainly few families could boast such a grand accomplishment, and the Olsen legacy was only just beginning.[24]

Albert, the youngest of the Olsen brothers, graduated from the academy in 1938, initiating his service in the Navy aboard the cruiser *Quincy*. He proudly noted in simple statement of fact that, "My naval career began."[25] One year later he moved to the *Dunlap* (one of only two ships built of the Fanning class), still had his home on this feisty tin can on December 7, and was afterward willingly acceptant to extend this association for however long it might be needed.

Now that Olsen and *Dunlap* were locked into this deadly new war and forced into an uncertain future, there seemed to be no escaping the obvious concerns. This conflict, Albert knew, would surely be a naval war, likely to span the entirety of the Pacific Ocean, and with perilous venture. The casualties the Navy had taken this day were only the beginning. Many more sailors, Marines, and airmen were assured of having a similar end before this fight would have any lasting conclusion. Thankfully, none of the Olsen boys were at Pearl at the time of the attack, but the certainty that the escalating and lengthy consequences would at some point place each one in harm's way was in no way encouraging. Albert had already lost one brother, and he certainly wished to lose no others.

He was far from alone with such concern. A similar thought—since they had no knowledge of his absence from the base—was equally shared of him by all in his family and perhaps by none more so than his aging, eighty-one-year-old veteran father, who knew all too well the dangers of war and the sea.

Similar concerns for a son's safety were equally shared by the parents of Lt. (jg) Russell Sydnor Crenshaw Jr., who was currently stationed aboard the destroyer *Maury*, also in escort of the *Enterprise*. The news of the surprise attack being broadcast over the radio at their Richmond, Virginia, home was received by the Crenshaw family with extreme alarm. Their son was stationed at Pearl. They had no clue of his absence, and rightly had reason to feel anxious.

Though a young officer, the twenty-one-year-old Crenshaw certainly stood his station astutely and with confidence, just as though he was the veteran. He knew the Navy well. His father, Russell Sr., was a retired captain who had graduated from the Naval Academy in 1907 (the academy class first to dedicate the U.S. Navy anthem, "Anchors Aweigh"), who later served in the First World War and had several important assignments with the battle fleet as well as with the Navy Department. That the son of such a proud naval officer might follow in his father's footsteps seemed never in doubt. Russell Jr. would not disappoint.

Crenshaw entered the academy in 1937, having received an at-large appointment, making him eligible for graduation in June 1941.[26] But as the potential for war increased—heightened by escalating conflicts in both Europe and the Atlantic while in conjunction with the ongoing saber rattling coming from regions of the Pacific—the amplified calls for active-duty naval officers forced the graduation of Crenshaw's class to be moved up by five months, to February 7. Assignments soon followed, and as the destroyer fleet was the one group most seriously understaffed, it was imperative that these positions be filled first, and quickly. As a result, Crenshaw promptly found his new home to be aboard the destroyer *Maury*, another of the Gridleys. Now, just ten months later, he clearly understood the reason for the rush.

Though perhaps expecting some type of conflict to erupt—just like Moosbrugger, Olsen, and the others around him—Crenshaw was shocked by the news coming out of Pearl. And he was equally desperate for some answers. He knew nothing of the loss of *Arizona* or of the turmoil currently being experienced by his good friend and academy classmate, Henry Davison, just as he knew nothing of any other details of the attack.[27] All he readily understood was that the base from which he had recently departed was under assault, his nation was at war, and he sailed with the one fleet left with any immediate power at retaliation. Indeed, the *Enterprise* group—even shy eighteen of its torpedo bombers—

remained a very formidable force (Vice Adm. Chuichi Nagumo, commanding the powerful Japanese carrier fleet responsible for the Pearl Harbor attack, was overtly aware that this threat was somewhere nearby). The expectation that combat might occur at any moment was obvious. An enemy fleet sailed somewhere close by, and Crenshaw had no illusions that if one side located the other that a battle would be assured.

For the service men and women at or near Pearl Harbor, the immediate threats at hand were seemingly directed wholly at them. But there was no doubt that this massive Japanese air attack—as it was now understood—was only the beginning of something far larger. This was a new war, and it would by no means be confined only to Pearl or even to those ships solely stationed in the Pacific. This was an attack on all of America, and this reality spread quickly.

Some 5,000 miles to the east and in port at Norfolk, Virginia, another Crenshaw classmate and good friend, Lt. (jg) Pemberton Southard, was just himself getting word of a Japanese attack on Pearl. Pem—as he was known to all of his many friends—learned of the news just shortly after 2:00 p.m. (East Coast time) but was not immediately convinced of its accuracy. His ship, the destroyer *Lang*, had back in May been a part of the Pacific Fleet stationed at Pearl. The lieutenant knew the base well, and he found it a bit hard to believe that such a powerful facility could have been so easily caught unaware. Furthermore, at the time of this initial report, *Lang* was being assisted by yard tugs to its assigned berth, and everything seemed as usual, without hint of any concerns.[28] This caused him to doubt the attack even more—though not for long. Moments later Norfolk erupted into a frenzied state of activity. Confirmation of the attack had been received. It was true.

With the snap of a finger, the base instantly converted from peacetime to a wartime operation. Emergency calls were sent out, ordering sailors who were on leave to return to their ships immediately. Alerts were sounded and security abruptly tightened. Contact with the outside world ended. Crews were confined to their ships, and all wondered with uncertainty of what to expect next.[29] Because this was the East Coast, any real threat of Japanese ships being anywhere nearby appeared quite minimal, but obviously no chances were being taken, as every possible outside threat was received with all due seriousness.

Of greatest concern to the base was the possibility of sabotage. For this reason, shore patrols were quickly beefed up and ships within the port were soon posting around-the-clock watches, all to be vigilant for anything out of the ordinary. Southard was *Lang*'s first lieutenant and assistant gunnery officer, making him responsible for a good portion of the destroyer's security. This job was to be his primary focus, and he oversaw this duty with every expediency and the professionalism it required—but, as with so many others around him, his mind was not always loyal to only those tasks at hand.

Such a sudden upheaval to life gave every individual due cause for instant pondering of the future. So much about tomorrow was now in question, and there was no clear understanding of what to expect next. For Pem, there was the obvious concern for duty; yet he could not escape the poignant thoughts of his girl, Jane Duvall, the pretty "Southern belle" from Charleston with whom he was passionately devoted. What now would happen with them?

Pemberton had first met Jane back in July, at the Charleston Officers' Club, where having braved a dance with her he instantly lost his heart to her endearing enchantments.[30] Since then, the two had missed no opportunity for being at each other's side. Pem had even braved a moment to ask Jane to marry him, to which she had responded in the affirmative. He expected that they would be together forever. Now, in an instant, everything had changed. Pem knew *Lang* could be called to sea at any moment, urgently directed into an unruly conflict with no promise of return—at least any time soon. He might not see Jane again for a very long time. He felt a desperate need to have another brief moment with her, just to reassure her that he would be okay and to affirm his love for her—but this, too, was surely not to happen, not readily anyway. For the time being, he clearly understood where his loyalties must stand—to his ship and to the needs of the nation—and to these he was committed with the professionalism of a naval officer, just as he had been taught. He suspected that Jane would understand. But she might not understand him leaving without first setting a date for the wedding. Under such restrictive circumstances, however, how was such a simple task to be met? Pem stressed over the matter for days, but it would get him not one step closer to a solution. Finally, he was forced to conclude that it would surely work out in the end—just as it always had for him.

Lieutenant Southard knew a little about having last-minute situations work to his favor—he did indeed have *some* previous experience. Pemberton had been born on a blustery sub-zero (-20 degrees Fahrenheit) night, on February 4, 1918, to parents Col. Frank E. and Edith (Pemberton) Southard, at their home in Augusta, Maine. This arctic evening was far from the most ideal time for Pem's life to begin. Even less opportune, however, Edith developed some complications with her labor. When called upon to help, the local doctor initially refused his aid, unwilling "to take his horse out in the cold." Pem's birth was suddenly at terrible risk, and the dilemma appeared to have no immediate solution. Perhaps it was Pemberton's father, a rather influential lawyer, who convinced the doctor to reconsider. Or maybe the doctor's conscience just pestered him to a change of heart. However it was determined, the physician did arrive on time and Pemberton—as well as the horse—survived quite well.[31] Thus the youngest Southard passed his first great trial of life.

Trials, however, were not to conclude at Pemberton's birth. Being placed to the test seemed an everyday part of his journey toward adulthood. The Southard family was affluent, but this did not always transfer to a life of ease, at least not for Pem. He had advantages unavailable to some, but so too did he have some rather uncommon pressures.

As a youth, Pemberton's most elusive ability and greatest ongoing burden was that of keeping up with the standards set by his older brother, Frank Jr., who was an academic prodigy (started the first grade at age four, graduated high school at age fifteen, college at age nineteen, and Harvard Law School at age twenty-two). Pem could never match such towering intellect, even despite his own keen accomplishments (skipped sixth grade and was a member of the National Honor Society). Altogether opposite his genius brother, whose focus was solely on academics, Pem preferred excelling at sports, including baseball, football, and hockey. Above all, he loved the water, swimming, and boating. From 1928 through 1935 he spent his summers at Lake Cobbossee, near Augusta, entering outboard and sailing races, competing in challenge after challenge. In 1930 he won his first outboard race, the Summer Regatta. "I guess my Navy career began then," he fondly noted later. So—though not following in either his father or brother's footsteps—by his junior year at Coney High School, Pemberton had definitely decided the direction he intended for his future. He was set on going to the U.S. Naval Academy to become a naval officer.[32]

It was not the Ivy League, obviously, but Frank Sr. gave full support to his youngest son's aspirations. In the fall of 1935, arrangements were made for Pem to attend Bullis Prep School in Silver Springs, Missouri, where he was to prepare for the academy exams.[33] This was to be an exciting time for Pem, as he had never before been farther west than Washington, DC, where one of his uncles lived. So, this trip was to be quite special and full of promise.

Indeed, Bullis proved to be very much to the youngest Southard's liking, and he studied long and hard at taking advantage of its education. When Pem returned home the following spring he felt fully prepared to compete for the important appointment. As might be expected, Pem passed the exam rather easily—but only as a fourth alternate. His appointment was not assured.

Fortunately for Pem, the principal appointee and the three alternates before him were each to falter, either with the entrance or physical exams. The door was immediately open to the next alternate. Pem took his turn—but he would also fail the physical exam (a congenital hernia was found which would require surgery to correct). The physical issue was soon medically corrected, but this was not in time for entrance to the academy by enrollment in 1936. Pem's first real opportunity at starting his career had been missed. So instead, he enrolled in the University of Maine, taking up studies to match academy curriculums while still being hopeful of pursuing his academy dream.[34]

Even as he studied at the university, Pem continued to take additional congressional competitive exams, endeavoring to improve his alternate status. He was only able to rise to third—and even with his father's strong influences Pem could not get the sought-after appointment. Summer of 1937 was quickly coming to a close and further chances at success were looking pretty bleak (at this time one could not be more than twenty years of age to enter). Time was running out. Finally, on August 1, with nearly every option exhausted, Pem received the call he had so diligently sought. He was told to report to the academy on the 7th for entrance and, after packing in great haste, off he took to his future.[35]

The years that followed passed by with amazing speed, and at their conclusion—just as was the case with his new classmate and friend, Russell Crenshaw—Southard found his tenure at Annapolis shortened. He too would graduate from the academy five months early and be expeditiously sent on to his first assignment. His orders directed him to the decks of the destroyer *Lang*, which he finally caught up with at Mare Island Navy Yard, Vallejo, California, on March 1, 1941.

Arriving at the pier where *Lang* stood, Pem headed up the ship's gangway, and was immediately met by Lt. (jg) Jack Murdock, officer-of-the-deck. Pem first saluted the ship's ensign (national flag) and then repeated the honor to the confronting lieutenant, announcing afterward, "Ensign Southard reporting for duty, sir." But the response he received was particularly surprising. "Am I glad to see you," the lieutenant fired back. "You're the new First Lieutenant of the *Lang* and as soon as you unpack your bags, I'll stand relieved." Pem stood in shock. "I became a department head and division officer in less than five minutes of reporting aboard," he would later write.[36] Thus began his career aboard the destroyer. Now, less than a year into this service, he was bracing for what would assuredly be the greatest trial of his life, deadly combat at sea.

Also at Norfolk and not far from Pem's station, naval reservist and hospital apprentice 1st class Ralph Barber was at his usual duty, working the ward of the Norfolk Naval Hospital. His background and reason for being in the Navy were in stark contrast to that of Southard's—even as they were to share shocking similarities in their future. Nevertheless, when the announcement about Pearl was first received, he reacted to the news with much of the same stunned disbelief as the lieutenant. But it was indeed true.

Confirmation of the attack spread quickly throughout the facility, instantly drawing small crowds around the few strategically placed radios brought out for gathering the latest information. None of the news being heard was good. Reports directly from the distant Pacific base were sparse and incomplete. It was unclear what was happening. "The attack is ongoing," stated the broadcasters.[37] Enemy planes flying over the islands were said to be seen throughout the day and enemy ships were rumored to have been spotted offshore. Invasion of the islands was expected at any moment. Other reports told of American merchant ships being torpedoed at sea and of enemy warships even being sighted off the coast of California. Casualty figures remained unknown, but the hospital at Pearl was said to be receiving large numbers of wounded. Certainly, of all he had heard so far, the report of the casualties was the one thing that Ralph related to, as he had been learning how to suture wounds and care for the injured. Even so, the patients he had been used to seeing were mostly victims of mishaps. He had never before seen a war wound—though this was sure to change, and soon.

Ralph Barber never intended to be caught in the middle of a war, and even if such a fate was to catch him, he especially did not expect it so soon. Joining the Navy had been more of a knee-jerk reaction rather than a carefully developed plan. He only happened to be at Norfolk at this time due to a bit of a twist to his original assignment and most definitely a distant path from his youthful intent. But this was just how things seemed to work out for Barber.

Ralph was from Birmingham, Alabama, born to Irving and Annie Barber on July 7, 1922. His family was of a normal size for the time, having seven children, of whom he was the third. Ralph would later describe his family's situation as "rich in children but poor in finances."[38] The Great Depression made life almost unbearable, yet the Barber family managed, even if at a meager minimum.

Able to remain in school—though having little appreciation for the privilege—Ralph graduated from Ensley High School in January of 1941. Throughout his high school years Ralph had found consistent employment at a local pharmacy, making a decent ten-cent hourly wage.[39] Here he also made a valuable new acquaintance.

Bob Steele, another employee of the pharmacy, whose job was that of managing the establishment's fine soda fountain, became another of Ralph's many teenage friends. The two hit it off well but, like most high school friendships, they separated after graduation and had little expectation of seeing each other ever again.

Bob went off to college and Ralph found employment with TCI (Tennessee Coal and Iron & Railroad Company) making exceptional pay for the time, receiving sixty cents an hour working in the company's machine shop. This was the summer of 1941. By this time the ongoing conflict in Europe was threatening America's involvement, and this was forcing a new military draft for young men twenty years old and older into the Army. With the possibility of war growing, Ralph knew his days were numbered. The older men where he worked, many being veterans of the First World War, took great pleasure at telling the young Barber stories of the dreaded trenches. These stories and subsequent kidding finally prompted Ralph not to wait any longer with his decision. Wanting nothing to do with the Army, he quit his job and enlisted in the Naval Reserve, hopeful of a safer and more satisfying service. A few days after making this fateful decision, Ralph entered the Naval Office housed in the Federal Building in Birmingham, and there to his surprise he found his old buddy, Bob Steele, now working as a recruiter.[40]

Ralph approached his old friend and quickly explained his plans. Bob listened carefully and then told Barber that he would take good care of him. He recruited Ralph as a hospital apprentice 1st class, awarding him a pay of $36 a month rather than the customary apprentice seaman rate of $21.[41] Everything appeared to be going young Barber's way. Despite his having no training at caring for the sick, he was assured that there would be no problems; other men for various reasons had also received the rate, and they had no training either. Later, however, when he and the others arrived at Pensacola for duty at the Naval Air Station Mainside Hospital, their lack of training quickly became very evident. The Navy intended to have nothing to do with such shortcuts.

Bob's fine efforts failed. Adjustments were quickly made to the situation, sending Ralph and nearly twenty others over to Norfolk to catch up on their bypassed training, placing them directly into boot camp. Obviously, this was not so good, but Ralph managed.

After the dreaded boot camp, Ralph was then sent on to the base hospital where he was to complete his training for the rate of pharmacist's mate. Again, he settled in and made the best of his situation, finding satisfaction with both his schooling and location. But now that the country was involved in this new war, he once again saw his future placed in jeopardy. Just nothing seemed to be going his way. A decision that was supposed to have provided him with a soft duty, at station in Pensacola and close to his Alabama home, was now to award him intensified training, in wartime conditions, and with promise of quick deployment to some hot zone in the far-off Pacific. Planned for or not, here he was just the same—and even more unfortunate, this would not be the last time such a well-intentioned decision on his part would lead him somewhere he did not expect.

Indeed, the consequences of this new war were to have a grievous effect for many young men. Even back at the Naval Academy—where news of the devastating Japanese attack reverberated through the halls with the same shocking notice as being experienced throughout the rest of the services—wartime adjustment began in speedy earnest. Plans were quickly set to fast-track the Class of 1942 to an early graduation (on December 19th) and have them placed aboard ships as soon as possible, ready for active duty. Two of these midshipmen, Joseph D. Jeffrey and Harold E. Shear, much like Crenshaw and Southard, were to be given assignments with the destroyer fleet. Neither of these young men had a clear grasp of what was awaiting them, as both were surely venturing into an abyss of uncertainty. Nevertheless, both men stepped up to the challenge and, without regard to life or limb, prepared to perform their duties to the best of their abilities.

Joseph Jeffrey, a handsome young man, having a well-defined face with dark piercing eyes, radiated complete confidence. Originally from Boulder, Colorado—giving him something in common with Arleigh Burke (which meant very little to him at this early moment in the war)—Joe was athletic and outdoorsy. Others referred to him as a light-hearted individual, being noted in his academy yearbook as one who "will join in anything that gives promise of a laugh."[42] Obviously, however, Joe knew there was nothing funny about this new war, and his future experiences were to give him even less reason to think otherwise.

Harold Shear's personality could also be defined as one with great confidence. An equally handsome fellow, featuring a head crowned with well-groomed wavy locks and a torso boasting a pair of very broad shoulders, he stood with poise and determination. Originally from Shelter Island, New York, this young man had grown up with the sea very much a part of his young life. Shear was a sailor through and through. He loved to sail and did it well. His classmates quickly bestowed upon him the nickname of "Admiral," which was to prove quite prophetic.[43] But, much like Jeffrey, Shear also knew his next experience at sea was to be a far different venture than those of his recreational past.

Indeed, the rush of war instantly sent Jeffrey and Shear barreling toward some new future, grossly uncertain, and with neither young man hardly given even the time for proper farewells. Barely had the ink dried on their commissions when they were both sent chasing after their initial assignments. Jeffrey was ordered to report to the destroyer *Sterett*, while Shear was directed to the *Stack* (both ships being of the Benham class). The rush seemed a bit premature as, due to their ships' deployments, neither man was able to meet up with his assignment till mid to late January. Once they were aboard, however, there was again little time for adjustments, as both ships were scheduled for immediate return to the sea, demanding fast adaptation by both officers. Even hereafter, the pace would rarely slow.

Such changes were sure to happen just as quickly for others as well. This was certainly true for Vining A. Sherman. His decision to join the Naval Reserve had been made without premonition to any attack but proved timely nonetheless—as the attack on Pearl came just as he was concluding his third of six months' worth of officers' training. He now knew that he was assured a very lengthy experience in the Navy. Despite his education in naval leadership skills being at best basic, in no way equal to that of the academy grads, his service was sure to be of equal demand—just as his call to duty was equally pressed with all due haste.

The twenty-five-year-old Sherman was a New Englander from Plympton, Massachusetts. Tall, slender built, and resonating with determination and focus, Vining gave an appearance of one in command of his own destiny. He had graduated from Dartmouth College in 1938, and was intellectually sharp and artistically gifted—ready, it seemed, to take on the world and do so without falter.[44] As it was, however, his future was far less determined.

Vining had but two true interests in life: painting and seamanship. To "obtain local color" for his artistic expressions, he disregarded all offerings through his formal education and took a job "as a commercial fisherman," working out of the Florida Keys—truly a favorite haunt of many artistic adventurers.[45] He hired on as a mate for a savvy veteran fisherman by the name of Paul Demerrit. The adventures that followed were an impressive time for Sherman, offering many life experiences unavailable to him in the classroom, and none for which he was ever to regret. Still, and despite this contentment, the constant talk of war had captured his attention and—suspicious of the implications—encouraged him to temporarily set aside both his fishing career and artistic ventures for a stint in the Naval Reserve. He hoped this move might avoid him being drafted into some branch of service outside his interests. Immediately afterward, he went to San Diego for training, where he began his schooling in leadership, and where he remained when he learned of the attack on Pearl.

This new reality of war caught Vining just as unexpectedly as the next person. Like all other young men of the time, his future fell into instant disarray. Only his ongoing training was assured (unlike the Academy Class of '42, the current class of reservists were not to be rushed through an abbreviated training) as reserve training was abbreviated enough as it was. Sherman was to complete his schedule as originally established. Only one thing was certain to follow: After completion of his next three months, he would surely experience all the seamanship and adventure he wanted—and more.

Also at San Diego was Fire Controlman Loyd Peters, who was just finishing up his fourth month of service training at the base. Having just concluded his classes for the year, Loyd was on the morning of December 7 preparing the final touches to a rather lengthy letter to his folks, telling them to expect him home for the holidays. He had hardly dotted the period ending his last sentence when he was informed of the news about the attack. "All leaves and liberty [were] cancelled," he later recalled.[46] There would be no holiday—not for a very long time.

Born in Garnett, Kansas, on December 29, 1921, Loyd Peters (a twin whose brother also served in the Navy) was a jolly young man who always seemed to meet his personal dilemmas in stride. This was not the first time his plans had been disrupted.

Loyd and his family had lived an "unsettled" life. His parents were hard workers, enterprising with their efforts and having ideals for a most promising life. After considerable investment, Loyd's father had just established a fine farm implement and feed business when the stock market crashed in 1929, causing the business to fail. The Peters family went bankrupt and lost their home. They became migrants, moving from one rented home to another, working farms wherever work was available.[47] The constant moving was tough but, in hindsight, it became preparation for a future that Loyd had no way of knowing was coming. Later, in the South Pacific, he found his new family and home, these being his shipmates and ship, equally unsettled. For Loyd, this new war was proving to be just another of life's many unexpected detours.

For Arleigh Burke, news of a Japanese attack was perhaps not altogether as surprising. He had long been convinced that war between the United States and Japan was inevitable, but the disaster at Pearl was not at all as he envisioned this war to begin. He was shocked by the tremendous loss, and even more so upon learning the fate of the *Arizona*—a first ship holds a special place in a sailor's heart, endearing and undying, at competition with a mother's comfort and a girl's first kiss. Arleigh's blood boiled with a demand for revenge, and he pledged to get himself into this fight. The war could not be permitted to pass without him. He owed it to the *Arizona* and his former fellow shipmates that the Japanese would not sustain victory from their cowardly attack. But Arleigh's every initial attempt at being allowed this pursuit was to fail.

Arleigh had parted ways with his celebrated command of *Mugford* back in July, had since returned to Washington, DC, and was currently assigned once more to the Bureau of Ordnance. His new job was that of ordnance inspector at the Washington Navy Yard—more commonly known as the "Naval Gun Factory"—where the work of inspecting the guns and ammunition was well within Arleigh's expertise.[48] At the time of his transfer, he had looked forward to this new challenge, and he had so far responded to it with the type of energy and perfection displayed with his every previous occupation. But this new move had not gone without some emotional uncertainty.

Leaving his beloved *Mugford* had not been an easy event for Arleigh, nor was it popular for the men of the ship. Just prior to his leaving, he had called his officers and crew together. He stood before them and proudly praised, "I couldn't wish for a better ship's company. I have been particularly well pleased by two things, two indispensable attributes for a man-of-war: your loyalty to your ship and your hard work. I have seen many ships, but I've never seen one that could excel the *Mugford* in these two characteristics. I have the utmost faith in you."[49] It was a mutual admiration; because, as the officers and crew knew, and as one junior officer was to state, as good as they were, Arleigh "was the catalyst that welded the team and made it click."[50]

Still, Arleigh's overall considerations were far broader than solely for career, as this new relocation would also allow him some long-desired quality time with his other love, his dear Bobbie, and for this prospect he was quite thrilled. Nevertheless, these were unsettled times. Even then the world was at the brink of total chaos, with both the European war and the Japanese conflict with China at the height of jeopardy. Little true stability existed. It was almost assured that it would be only a matter of time till the United States would also be drawn into the fray, and being the true warrior that he was, Arleigh wanted in when it happened—and certainly Bobbie knew he would go.

So, when notice of the attack on Pearl was given, this was all the invitation that Arleigh needed; he immediately applied for transfer back to a duty at sea. Unfortunately, and even despite a desperate need for his talent, his course to combat was not to be so readily navigated. Many months were to pass and many battles were to conclude before this gifted officer would find his route to success.

Indeed, December 7, 1941, had awakened the entire nation to a whole new era of uncertainty. No one was sure of what to expect next. By December 8, the complete reality of the disaster at Pearl Harbor was finally being more clearly understood. News reports were by this time becoming more detailed, and the truest sense of loss was finally beginning to hit home. With firm expression and determined tone, an angry President Roosevelt addressed the nation, asking Congress to formally declare that "a state of war" existed between the United States and Japan.[51] His pronouncement was assurance that the path to peace no longer relied on further isolation but rather on a dark, perilous venture that was sure to be one of the costliest in the history of humankind.

The grimness of this broadcast noted the seriousness of the mission. Far out in the Central Pacific, sailors and airmen of the *Enterprise* group were listening carefully, attentive to the president's words, but his speech had far less impact than the landscape before them.

Task Force 8 finally completed its late return to Pearl on the morning of December 8. As they slowly sailed into the harbor for a first true view of the chaos, the sight was stunningly surreal. Entering into this once perceived secure shelter, the returning warships moved cautiously forward, while all along their railings an unbroken line of sailors stared solemnly in disbelief at the terrible devastation that spanned their vision. Thick black smoke still hovered all around the base, while the anchorage displayed a ring of shattered shipping. The surface of the water was coated with a dark, rainbow-accented slime that smelled of a putrid mixture of fuel oil and sulfur. Rescue efforts were still ongoing, and a sense of chaos and disorder permeated every scope of the eye. Truly this was a moment unlike any these men had ever before experienced, and the shock was inscribed heavily on every face.

Like others, Frederick Moosbrugger stood still, silently observing from *McCall*'s bridge and was equally awestruck by the sights of such massive destruction. Among the first victims Freddie would see was his old ship *Nevada*, displaying itself heavily damaged and grounded in the mud at Hospital Point.[52] Further in, while passing battleship row at Ford Island, he spied the horribly disfigured and sunken remains of *Arizona*. Nearby was his beloved *Tennessee*, having her structure tightly pinned between the concrete moorings by the wrecked hulk of *West Virginia*, with her exposed superstructure and 14-inch batteries—the very guns that were once his responsibility—blackened by the previous explosions and fires. But, for more obvious reasons, Moosbrugger's greater concern remained for the fate of his family, and especially so now that he had seen the true extent of the attack.

Freddie wanted ashore. A short time later he would take his liberty—and, to his greater relief, he would finally learn that Dot and the boys were unharmed.

The commander's oldest son had, in fact, witnessed some of the Japanese planes, as during the previous day's attack little Fred—while on his way to church with his mother—had seen a portion of the Japanese second wave when it flew overhead. Edward and Dave, on the other hand, who had remained home that morning in the care of a maid, knew little of the events around them nor were they of the age to have much true understanding of the repercussions.[53] At no time, however, was any of the family in any direct danger. Nevertheless, life for the Moosbruggers—as with everyone else on the islands—was to dramatically change.

Since Hawaii was no longer deemed a safe area, Freddie made immediate preparations for getting his family off the islands and back to the States. He needed Dot and the boys out of harm's way, and the sooner the better. The commander booked the next available civilian sea transport from Honolulu for their passage. Even so, the departure was not to happen readily.

Civilian transports were few, and of these military personnel were given obvious priority. Evacuees outnumbered the means of evacuation, and delays were commonplace. Additionally, as defensive patrols outside the islands became standard duty for the remaining warships, Freddie was rarely in port to aid with his family's endeavor. Success of their evacuation was not noted by Moosbrugger until March, when in a letter to his sister he stated, "The times I was able to see the 'flock' were few and [this] length of time short but I happened to be in when they left."[54] With their bags packed and their quaint little home vacated, Dot and the boys were finally boarded on the liner SS *Lurline* and headed east to safety.[55] Freddie was now free to concentrate solely on the business at hand, this new war in the Pacific and the overall victory so hoped for by all Americans.

Moosbrugger was ready—even eager—to go to work, but the job before him remained terribly uncertain. There was little in the way of good news to be heard. The commander was, however, quite pleased to learn that, despite his initial observations, his old ships had survived the attacks quite well (protected from the torpedoes by neighboring *West Virginia* and fortunately missed by most aerial bombs, *Tennessee* was soon to be sailing back to the West Coast for repairs and refitting; while *Nevada*, too, was expected to be fully repaired in only a few months' time) and that all of the fleet aircraft carriers were still intact. This was indeed promising.

Even so, the Pearl Harbor debacle was a tremendous setback and great embarrassment for the U.S. Navy. In one swift blow the Japanese had successfully placed America's most prominent Pacific-borne defense, its powerful battleship fleet, temporarily out of action. A battleship navy was now without its main weapon. Adding salt to this wound, the destruction had been caused by carrier aircraft alone and without the aid of any other warships' weaponry.[56] There was no defeatism among the ranks, however, and this was an obvious encouragement. Moosbrugger's own confidence appeared unaffected. In a February 11, 1942, letter to his sister, Louise, he boasted, "You can rest assured that the Navy is in there fighting and you will be hearing more and more of their exploits"—just as everyone soon would.[57]

Chapter Three

Guadalcanal

Gateway to Hell

Less than ten weeks after the Pearl Harbor attack, Frederick Moosbrugger passionately predicted that the "Japs are going to start taking punishment on an increasingly progressive scale because we are beginning to roll."[1] This bold statement was made in early February 1942, just after the commander had returned from supporting a successful carrier-based air raid against the Japanese-held Marshall Islands. Obviously, this recent mission had provided him with some good reason for his overt sense of encouragement. Still, such optimism, especially for this early juncture of the war, was truly a stretch of reality—for at this point in time taking the fight to the Japanese was proving to be no easy task.

The news coming from the Pacific was at best dismal. The Japanese juggernaut remained in full control of its offensive thrust and with every bit the same—if not more—shock of any German blitzkrieg. There were indeed some early skillful attempts at throwing some stinging jabs back at the Japanese, as with this mission against the Marshalls, as well as with the later raids on Wake and Tokyo, sporting minor successes. But these were mostly propaganda strikes, providing a boost to sagging morale, and had little lasting consequence to the overall direction of the conflict. The Coral Sea battle in May concluded as a draw. Only at Midway—where during an early June melee U.S. carrier-based airpower fortunately outplayed their counterparts—were the Japanese to be tremendously hurt and with any lasting effect (the IJN lost four of its main aircraft carriers and many valuable pilots and support crews). Even this, however, was sure to be of little use if the window of opportunity it provided was not quickly entered and a true American offensive in the Pacific was not expedited and with some positive import. Remaining on the defensive was at this point no longer an option, and time was no longer a luxury. So, with a boldness completely unexpected by the Japanese, the U.S. Navy quickly made its daring choice and, with full approval from the War Department, the decision was made that the Solomon Islands should be its first great step toward Tokyo.

The Solomons, however, would prove to be a very hard lesson. The contest here turned far tougher than any of the earlier predisposed expectations. Lt. Henry D. Davison spoke of this campaign in his usual unabashed manner: "If you can find anything romantic in the daily grind the South Pacific offered, brother, you've got more imagination than I have. Monotonous, uninspiring patrolling, a heat that slammed at you by day and clung like a wet blanket at night; and through it all the nerve-wracking strain of constantly keeping alert to gain the few precious seconds of warning when the ever-present possibilities became realities—uncharted reefs, torpedoes, Bettys [Mitsubishi G4M1/G4M3 Navy Type I attack bombers] that sneaked in, minefields, shore batteries. In my book that comes under the heading of work—and plenty of it."[2]

"Work" it was too; a deadly work, beginning in the very early hours of August 7, 1942. On this predawn morning nineteen American transports (just barely scraped together in time for the event) off-loaded 11,000 Marines of the 1st Marine Division (the only U.S. combat unit adequately trained for amphibious warfare then available to the Pacific) to ride destiny's path to the shore of Guadalcanal (an island of no initial notoriety and with a terrain almost completely unknown to its new assailants). Given an operational nickname of "Shoestring" by the sailors and Marines supporting it, Operation Watchtower was the first true American ground offensive of the Pacific war. Less than four weeks of planning had gone into its preparation. Success depended far more on the element of surprise than on overwhelming force. Some professional nay-sayers had argued that this effort was premature, an unwarranted gamble, too soon after the disaster at Pearl Harbor to go on an all-out offensive. This was exactly what others hoped the Japanese were also to think. It was a risk, for sure; but it was a risk considered by Watchtower's planners worth the taking.

With the commitment made, the necessary ships were amassed, the invading troops were readied, and the hastily pieced together plan was quickly executed. The first American amphibious operation of the Pacific war was begun. To everyone's amazement the landings were carried out with what seemed an almost effortless exercise. Hardly could any campaign have had a smoother start; by the end of the first day's actions the contingent of U.S. Marines had established a solid foothold on Guadalcanal's north shore—and the startled Japanese opposition (consisting mostly of construction troops) was sent fleeing for deep cover within the island's rugged interior. Such ease of success was by no means expected. It was eerie—surreal even. Surprise had been so complete that the enemy had barely even fired a shot in their own defense. But this early taste of victory was indeed a false security; the Japanese were stunned only, and far from defeated. The fierceness of the many battles to follow, along with the extreme costs to be incurred by both sides, proved just how consequential this initial action—and the Solomons themselves—was to be to the future of the war. And so, the bloodletting began.

The days and weeks to follow brought many uncertainties, many disasters, and many losses of life. Neither side was fully prepared for the experience. Old mindsets, old rules, and old technologies were quickly abandoned, while newer, more creative, and more effective ways were demanded in the effort to successfully meet this new and ever-changing environment of warfare. Many leaders—on both sides—were to rise to the challenge, permanently etching their names in the pages of military history; while many lesser-known men were to have their exploits frozen in these same historical annals, sacrificing life, limb, and youth for a cause they likely did not fully comprehend. For here, well within the visages of Guadalcanal's mountainous heights, where awaited tall grassy highlands and thick jungle river valleys, common men would establish the course to an uncommon conflict. Here, both sides knew, the very conclusion of the entire war might well be echoed. Here, sailors, Marines, and soldiers would fight with every ounce of their resolve, pursuant to the victory, hopeful of the fatal act that should seal the fate of their adversary. And here, at this unexpected arena of sand, rotting jungle, and treacherous sounds, individuals, mostly stripped of all family and comforts of home, struggled to survive one more day—hopeful at avoiding a lonely death in a faraway land they knew little about.

This was to be the war in the Pacific, an uncommonly horrific charge, infinitely different from the great land campaigns fought on the soil of massive continents. Throughout this vast ocean expanse, the Japanese had established a multitude of small island fortresses—many far more powerful and combat ready than Guadalcanal—all strategically located and each awaiting the opportunity to suck the life-flowing blood from any force that dared to face their wrath. The ground campaigns to secure these fortified atolls were sure to be fiercely fought. Marines and soldiers were certain to spearhead any such operation, but it was just as certain that the safe delivery and constant support of these troops were the keys to any achievable victory. From the outset, both the United States and Japan clearly understood this critical objective. Both nations had invested a great abundance of their wealth in amassing great fleets of powerful warships. It was therefore assured that—as disclosed by Japan's initial strike at Pearl Harbor—victory was to hinge on the success or failure of the two opposing navies. And perhaps no greater example of this was to be given than that of the campaign to win the Solomons, wherefore both sides were to commit their navies at a terrible cost. "The Solomons were a navy problem," wrote historian Edwin Hoyt.[3]

The Solomon Islands were indeed "a navy problem," and a massive one at that. In short order it became clear that this arena was to be the premier testing ground as well as the torchbearer for the future course of this new war. Such was grossly unexpected. Neither side initially held these remote islands at such a vital importance, especially to each of their own overall strategies. For the Japanese, the Solomons were but a secondary extension of their eastward advance, support areas rather than massive bases. For the Americans, they were a mere offensive start, a perceived weak link in the Japanese chain of outlying defenses that could serve as a jumping-off point for what was their true target, the Japanese bastion of Rabaul, on New Britain. These islands, however, soon proved themselves to be a far different reality. The Solomons quickly developed into a fiercely contested battleground, on land, sea, and in the air. The investment soon became too great for either side to concede. Even more consequential, these islands became the proving ground for a new type of warfare. Here, within this bloody arena, new ideas, new tactics, new weapons, and new leaders were all to emerge, each to gravely affect the future course of the entire war. The lessons to be learned here were brutal. Mistakes here were unforgiving. The islands themselves took no side, equally spreading their harsh inhospitalities to either of the combatants without any sense of bias. If there truly is any such place that is a good place for battle, a good place to die, the Solomons were not.

But many *were* to die here, and mercilessly so. Even as Marines and soldiers gave their all in the desperate struggle to secure these isolated spots of rock and sand, it was assured that victory could not rest in the pure control of these islands but rather in the control of the sea and air that surrounded them. This was the "problem" for the navies. Without the Imperial Japanese Navy, the expanse of Nipponese island fortresses could not long survive. Without the U.S. Navy, the new American offensive could not move. The Japanese had struck the first blow at Pearl Harbor. The United States had retaliated at Midway. Still, the Japanese held the greater edge at sea. At Guadalcanal the two navies fought to a standstill, with neither side initially able to gain a decisive victory. American naval airpower ruled the day and Japanese gunnery and torpedoes ruled the night—while the deadly realm they split promised its loyalty to no one, or even hinted of ever doing so.

This was the very war that Arleigh Burke—and so many other warriors like him—aspired to be a part of. Arleigh had expected this conflict with Japan, and he had many ideas on how it should be fought. Surely this was his intended destiny. Even so, Burke was missing from the venue. Due in part to his unequaled expertise with naval ordnance—more so to a stubborn superior—Arleigh remained stranded stateside, anchored to a desk in Washington, DC, and absent the first full year of the war. Despite one transfer request after another, this renowned destroyer commander found himself a derelict at the Naval Gun Factory, unable to obtain a release from his oversight duties or to even be heard above his most immediate boss. His only headway came in the manner of a promotion, to commander, which he would have gladly traded for a resumption of his old command of *Mugford*—and still the conflict in the Pacific proceeded without him.[4]

It appeared as complete insanity to Arleigh that a naval officer with his proven talents and abilities could not get into this fight; but no amount of formal complaining got him one step closer to his desired duty. The Solomons campaign was especially suited to Burke's aggressive style; but the commander—one of the Navy's finest gunnery experts—could only watch this ongoing "navy war" from a distance, fighting the fight as some armchair tactician, without means of direct intervention of his own carefully crafted ideas. Such was so grossly unsatisfactory to such a specialized and determined officer. Obviously, as these days passed on and the war progressed further—or at least continued on—without him, Arleigh's frustrations were to grow ever more pronounced. He was willing to do whatever it might take for a command in the South Pacific, right arm and all—but to no avail. Finally, the war itself provided the true means for his calling.

Far off in the embattled South Pacific a new need developed. The fight, for the Solomons in particular, was not going as hoped. To the chagrin of America's highest leadership, the front-line surface fleet on which they were depending was not performing nearly as well as expected. At Guadalcanal, the Navy repeatedly failed to make good on promises to subdue the enemy, unable—it seemed—to utilize its own strengths and to exploit Japanese weaknesses at gaining the upper hand. Victories at sea were few, and these few positive results usually had more to do with luck than leadership. There was a lack of aggressiveness among the fleet commanders, and this would not do.

Vice Adm. Robert Lee Ghormley, who had initial command of the South Pacific Force, was a good and well-respected leader, but the Solomons quickly gained a reputation for destroying the careers of mere "good" leaders. Ghormley's fate was sealed on the second night of the Guadalcanal offensive, when in the early morning hours of August 9—at just past midnight—a fleet of his patrolling warships was sucker punched just off Savo Island. Having quickly responded to the American landings, Adm. Gunichi Mikawa, the shrewd commander of the Japanese Eighth Fleet at Rabaul, had skillfully sortied his own ships to Guadalcanal to successfully dispatch one Australian (*Canberra*) and three American cruisers (*Astoria*, *Quincy*, and *Vincennes*) to the depths of Davy Jones's Locker, and without loss to his own force. The "good" admiral never overcame the defeat or the great respect he instantly gained for Japanese prowess and power. Ghormley's future advances were marked by an obvious tentativeness and caution that could not long suffice in the Solomons. By October a new leader, Vice Adm. William F. "Bull" Halsey, replaced him.[5]

Halsey, a man known to be pointedly direct, had a style of leadership as acute as the intent of his nickname. He had but one rule: *Attack*. Even so, this admiral—alone—did not possess nearly enough aggressiveness to see his fleet to the greater victory. He needed other aggressive commanders for this to happen. Soon, lower ranks were being reorganized, as Halsey promoted and introduced stronger-willed leaders to the theater—names like Kinkaid, Wilkinson, Ainsworth, and Merrill. Above all he desperately needed more fighting destroyers, and to command these ships he needed spirited leaders with proven records. Arleigh Burke was surely one such promising candidate and—with strings soon pulled on his behalf—the personal war he had long waged for his own transfer was finally ended. Arleigh headed to the South Pacific and into the midst of the fight, just as he desired.[6]

A turning point was nearing, but the newly promised "aggressiveness" that Halsey so vehemently preached remained to be witnessed by many of the frontline combatants. Lt. Henry Davison was certainly not satisfied. The frustrated Pearl Harbor vet had since found a new home aboard the destroyer *Craven*, thrust into the Solomons campaign in early November, and was obviously still experiencing some bitter disillusionment with the overall experience. His ship's numerous regional operations, all deemed high-priority missions, were nearly always charged with the escort of transports to the embattled island of Guadalcanal. He referred to this work as a "danger and monotony."[7] This was not the type of fighting he had imagined, not at all the type of role he had expected for his fighting destroyer. After all, he still had a bone to pick with the Japanese. He wanted nothing less than the freedom for his ship to engage the enemy, with the offensive independence as it was intended.

Davison—just as others of his kind—perceived the destroyer as a hunter, a trained killer stalking the sea for the enemy, not a babysitter of "friendlies," *being* the hunted. He loathed the tediously monotonous escort missions. He did not doubt the importance of the task, providing protection for the slower, lightly armed transports, but this was primarily a defensive duty, high on risk and low on opportunity. If just on some occasion his ship could be allowed a part of a real offensive operation, given a chance to flex its muscle and do what it had been designed for, perhaps then he could feel better about this less intriguing work. But such was not to happen—not readily anyway.

The lieutenant's aggravation was not his alone. Disillusionment with how destroyers were being utilized in the Solomons appeared universal among all their officers and crews. It was regularly discussed in the wardrooms, in the galleys, in the berths, and every other corner where men were to gather. The question was almost always the same: "When are they going to cut us loose?"[8]

This query seemed never to receive a positive response. Even *when* included in an offensive effort the destroyer commanders were kept tightly secured to a short leash, unable to set their ships toward the performance of their greater potential. The U.S. Navy, in the Solomons at least—beyond the excellent use of its air force—and even with Halsey at its lead, was predisposed at determining that—while within the confinement of waters set between these islands—cruisers were to be its main weapon against Japanese surface incursions. After all, battleships (excluding *North Carolina*—which after Pearl Harbor was quickly transferred to the Pacific from the Atlantic but at assignment with the carrier fleets only—and the late 1942 transfers of *South Dakota* and *Washington*) were unavailable, and cruisers were the next biggest guns. Most in the upper echelons of naval leadership seemed thoroughly convinced that the key to victory remained in the success of its close-order gunnery, even at night (with tactics already proven flawed and despite radar not being fully introduced or readily accepted by many commanders). Therefore destroyers, with their torpedoes and smaller-caliber guns (even despite many already having radar), were placed in close support of the cruisers and were subsequently given few opportunities to strike first and with any impunity.

The Japanese, on the other hand, realized a far different determination of naval engagement, and especially so when forced within the confinement of restricted space, as with the Solomons. Nighttime action was their forte. Even without radar technology (and regardless of such technology being available to them and even despite a less-capable variant than used by the United States and Great Britain being introduced on some of their naval warships), Japanese sailors were excellent at spotting enemy ships within the darkness and even at exceedingly great distances. The Japanese had the highest quality optics, sporting superior magnification capabilities, and their crews were well versed in how to use these and in what to look for when at search. The Japanese had also perfected the torpedo (a reality that the U.S. Navy would not fully learn till after the war ended) as well as its use (having incorporated the weapon on both their cruisers—an advantage unknown to U.S. cruisers—and destroyers, with both incorporating reloadable torpedo batteries). Therefore, for the Imperial Navy, gunnery—at which they also excelled—became a secondary instrument of engagement, while destroyers—with their deadly torpedoes and great speed—were a primary tool when initializing any attack against opposing ships. Unfortunately, the U.S. Navy learned this lesson slowly and harshly, and the results were nearly damning.

For Lt. Albert Olsen this savage reality was to strike all too early. His ship, *Dunlap*, first arrived at Noumea on December 5, 1942, and had yet to experience the terrible struggle that was this campaign for the Solomons. Nevertheless, his welcome to the region could hardly have been more devastating.

The weeks prior to this stop had not been a pleasant time for Olsen. He had recently been notified of the death of his aged father, and obviously this news came as a tremendous blow. Terribly heartbroken, Albert was even further aggrieved knowing that neither he nor any of his active-duty brothers could be home for the comfort of his mourning mother and sister. At Noumea, however, he did find some occasion for what he hoped would be a generous lift to his own sagging spirit. Albert's older brother, Earl, was serving as the chief engineering officer aboard the cruiser *Pensacola*, and it just so happened that this vessel was in port at Noumea for repairs. To see his brother, especially at this time of recent family loss, would surely be a boost to the morale of both men. Albert immediately requested permission to give the ship a visit—and permission was granted.[9]

Albert departed *Dunlap* having high expectations, displaying energy to his step that had of late otherwise been missing. But the closer he got to his destination the more clearly he could see that not all was as he supposed. The *Pensacola*, as she stood at dockside, could be seen listing a bit to port and she appeared very much in a bad way. The cruiser, he soon learned, had just recently returned from a battle with the Tokyo Express, which had taken place off of Tassafaronga, Guadalcanal, on the night of November 30—a fight that had not gone well for the Americans. She had been hit by a Japanese torpedo and was sporting a huge, gaping hole at the waterline portside of amidships. Much of her structure was heavily damaged and scorched from the intense fires that had followed, and the lieutenant knew that these were surely to have produced some very severe casualties. Far from dissuaded in his mission, Albert arrived at the cruiser's gangway still mostly blinded by his eagerness at seeing his brother. He quickly requested "permission to come aboard."[10] Given his permission, the lieutenant boldly marched forward, but was almost immediately taken aback by the harsh welcome of grim reality that greeted him, for there was no welcome to be had here at all. The battle had obviously taken a terrible toll on the crew, as those who were nearby gave him a quiet and hollowed-eyed stare, making him acutely aware of the distress that was so duly present. Still, he remained hopeful. He reached the officer-of-the-deck and, after a brief introduction, he inquired of the officer if he or someone else might be able to direct him to his brother. The query met instant silence. There was an agonizingly long pause, and then he heard the dreadful words: "Your brother is dead."[11] Albert received the news with obvious shock. His stomach began to knot up, his face paled, and his legs weakened. How could this be—first his father and now his brother? There was no making any sense of such misfortune. It was explained to him that during the battle Earl had been caught in a flooded engine compartment, where he had directed the successful evacuation of many others and was trying to carry a fellow officer to safety when he became trapped. There he was to succumb to the intensity of the fast-moving fires.[12] Earl had died a hero; but such was of little immediate comfort to Albert. Psychologically exhausted, the bereaved lieutenant quietly returned to his ship torn between grief and anger, and completely unsure of how to deal with either emotion. One thing, however, was most certain for Albert Olsen; this fight with the Japanese had suddenly become very personal.

This fight had also become very personal for young Ens. Joseph Jeffrey. In Jeffrey's case, however, he *had* met the enemy, in combat, and it had been a fearsome experience—one he hoped never to repeat again.

Joe had first boarded his new assignment, the destroyer *Sterett*, only a month after his early graduation from the academy and, though highly trained, he had almost no true experience at sea. He had hoped for at least a little time for adapting to his new environs, especially before being handed some major leadership post. Imagine his surprise when in the very first moments of his arrival he was notified that he was the relief for the ship's assistant gunnery officer (to replace Ens. Hillard Marver, who had received an unfortunate and debilitating injury while in port at Norfolk and who remained hospitalized and unable to report back to the ship). Obviously, this new responsibility would be quite demanding of a young ensign (as he was at the time)—especially considering an imminent departure to the war-torn Pacific—instantly requiring Joe to make speedy study of his ship's weapons systems as well as quickly familiarize himself with the director crews that ran them. He hurriedly set to work and, despite his perceived inexperience, seemed to acclimate to the new duty quite well. Jeffrey's immediate boss, Lt. (jg) Charles R. Calhoun, found his new assistant to be a very capable officer.

Calhoun wrote, "I was especially impressed with [Jeffrey's] knowledge and intelligence . . . [as he] repeatedly demonstrated his dependability and competence."[13]

Jeffrey did indeed learn his duties quickly, but his lessons were ongoing, and none would prove more sobering for this young officer than the terrifying test he encountered on Friday, November 13, 1942. On this date Jeffrey—as well as the rest of *Sterett*'s crew—would personally experience the true horrors of naval warfare, a fast and furious type of close-order battle that the Solomons were most known for. The contest would nearly cost him his life.

During the predawn hours of that early November morning, *Sterett* sailed as part of Task Group 67.4, a cruiser/destroyer group that was providing support for transports taking men and supplies to Guadalcanal. As fate would have it, at this very same moment Japanese forces were also on their way to the island, having a like-minded purpose and supporting it with battleships, cruisers, and destroyers. A confrontation was assured; and within the deep darkness of Savo Sound the two groups collided and proceeded to duel in what was to become the longest and most heated sea battle of the entire campaign.

That night Ensign Jeffrey sat alongside his boss Lieutenant Calhoun high atop their perch at *Sterett*'s gun director, just as his general quarters duty required. All was quiet, yet he remained ever watchful. Jeffrey had powerful optics at his employ and could search in almost every direction—but he could see almost nothing. Despite his near perfect point of observation, his desperate view remained blocked by an infinite curtain of intense blackness—a characteristic of the Solomons that Jeffrey had already learned to be a common dilemma. Suddenly and without warning the destroyer made a sharp turn and he heard a fearful roar echo from his aft, quickly followed by an audible din of repeated explosions reporting in the distance. He instantly twisted around in time to see the horrifying flares of a burning ship illuminated within the darkness. Then, as if this were some great signal, the entire region immediately erupted into a frenzied dance of light. Bright yellow flashes of gunfire, blurring red streaks from arching tracers, deep orange glows from burning oil, showering silver sparks of exploding ordnance, and phosphorus green splashes from near-miss explosive shells seemed to envelop his ship from every direction. The spectacle was one of mass confusion, instantly sending one's every emotion into a furor of spasms. But Jeffrey gathered himself expertly and alertly gave every effort at tracking the targets provided him by radar, even to keep up with the fast transitioning of the ongoing fight. Then from his headphones he heard a dire warning. The outline of a sinister pagoda was seen approaching through the intense darkness. Jeffrey spotted the target and watched as its menacing silhouette grew in its fast approach. Suddenly the only sound prominent to his hearing was that of his own heart heavily thumping to an exaggerated beat. He was experiencing real fear as never before.[14]

The monstrous shadow was that of a Japanese battleship—the *Hiei*. Jeffrey knew *Sterett* was hopelessly outgunned but, regardless of the odds, she would respond rapidly to the challenge. The destroyer fired a spread of four torpedoes and her 5-inch batteries took careful aim at the behemoth's towering pagoda-like superstructure. Fortunately, *Hiei* was far too busy with other targets to give *Sterett* her fullest attention, even as her gunnery still took a serious toll on the destroyer. Another accompanying destroyer (*Laffey*) took a direct hit, sending her quickly into the depths of the unforgiving sound. An escorting Japanese destroyer (*Yudachi*) entered the fray, though she too was soon silenced by some other opposing gunfire. The American cruiser *Atlanta* was hit several times and left a burning wreck. *Hiei* was also set ablaze. *Sterett* had by this time already taken two to three hits, starting a fire in one of her aft gun turrets, when another round slammed heavily into the destroyer amidships. More fires broke out, but her excellent damage control teams quickly extinguished each blaze. Finally, incapable of adding more to the fight, *Sterett*'s astute skipper (Comm. Jesse Coward) decided it was time to get his ship out of harm's way, and the destroyer made good her escape.[15]

The captain's wise decision was timely. The destroyer had survived, but barely and at a steep cost. Twenty-eight men of the destroyer's veteran crew were killed, and an even greater number were wounded. Jeffrey was among the casualties, having received wounds to his back and head from steel splinters of a close hit.[16] The ensign's wounds were not life threatening, but the scars they left behind would run far deeper than the depth of his skin. Though Jeffrey had indeed survived his first face-to-face encounter with the Japanese navy, he did so narrowly and with residuals—for the fear he experienced on this dark night was never to be forgotten and the clarity of recollections was never to fade, even despite the spread of time.

As it were, this great battle—an intensely fought naval/air action that lasted close to three full days—would at its conclusion prove to be a strategic victory for the U.S. Navy and a decisive win in the struggle for Guadalcanal. The American transports, so key to the operation's success, were kept safe and able to deliver their precious cargo as planned. Additionally, two Japanese battleships (including *Hiei*), a heavy cruiser, two destroyers, and all eleven of the transports they were to protect, were sunk (one ship that did survive was the destroyer *Amatsukaze*, commanded by Comm. Tameichi Hara, an officer who was destined to be heard from again). Just the same, it was a bittersweet victory. Seven American destroyers (five on the first night of action) and the cruisers *Atlanta* and *Juneau* were lost (among the dead aboard *Atlanta* was Rear Adm. Norman Scott, while on the *Juneau* almost 700 of her crew lost their lives, including the five Sullivan brothers—only ten sailors survived). Jeffrey would later write, "In November 1942 the waters between Savo and Guadalcanal marked the gateway to hell. . . ."[17] And still the battle for the Solomons raged on.

Indeed, the great naval engagements so far waged at winning these islands were of a most terrible consequence. They were deadly, unrelenting, and destined to be among the last close-order naval engagements in modern history. Neither side had so far given up a bout without first delivering—or receiving—all the punishment possible. Few ships were to escape without bearing the scars of battle and/or loss of life. Many were not to survive at all.

Rarely did a night go by that the flames of a burning ship did not brighten the darkened Solomons seascape. Far too many times patches of burning oil and flotsam were all that remained at marking the tragic death of a ship and its crew. In some cases, heroic ships were witnessed to slip below the ocean's surface with their guns still firing, while within their bowels trapped sailors spent their last few moments of life screaming for help, as flames sucked all the remaining oxygen from their air and/or water consumed their last bit of space. During these great gun battles, direct hits sent jagged bits of shrapnel and mangled chunks of steel slicing through the air, indiscriminately ripping apart the flesh and bones of any man unfortunate enough to be in their path. Flash fires instantly burned the clothes off sailors, searing their flesh with second- and third-degree burns, leaving them in a horrifying state of agony. Additional flames, fed by exploding munitions and unspent fuel, raced from one end of the ship to the other, creating a floating funeral pyre. To escape these terrifying and deadly fires, sailors often leapt from their ships to the perceived safety of the sea—only to plunge into an ocean full of flaming oil.

For those who survived the loss of a ship, the trials were only just begun. Escape from a sinking vessel was only a first step toward survival. Sailors had to swim frantically, as hurriedly away from their sinking ship as possible, or risk being pulled under by the great suction created at its final dive. Failure meant almost certain death. Success, on the other hand, only assured the sailor a treacherous wait for rescue, forcing him—often singly or in small groups—to spend many long hours in the water, hoping to be found, while suffering with wounds and fighting off sharks. And, as one sailor once stated with a bit of dry humor, "the sharks were not particular"; it didn't matter if the meal being served was American, Australian, or Japanese.[18]

Even when on the side of victory—as when sailors witnessed distant opposing ships burning and slipping silently into the eternal depths—the Solomons gave due cause for emotional restraint. Without question victorious crews were well within their right to cheer the hellish demise of their enemy, especially when having a direct hand in the outcome, but such cheering was rarely awarded a lengthy stay, usually dulled instead to a quiet thankfulness, better the enemy had suffered the sad fate rather than themselves. Everyone seemed to know that, with the winning of a single battle, the fight was far from over. Guadalcanal had promptly proven that this war was not to be short lived or easily won. Sailors were quick to understand that a victory today only left them in the contest to fight another horrifying battle tomorrow. There were no assurances of peace, of a safe return to home, or even of a single day's survival. All were in question.

Putting this in a more simplified perspective, Russell Crenshaw would later relate the Solomons to "an athletic field with a goal at each end and lots of obstacles in the middle."[19] It was a contest, too, seemingly without specific rules, referees, and/or time limits—though it did abound with many promising players.

Whether regular or reserve, officer or enlisted, this campaign almost daily exposed the mettle of all who participated. The Solomons had become a classroom of tough lessons for an ever-growing number of students. Here no grades were given. There were no curves. The tests given in the Solomons were of harsh reality; they were tests of survival. A wrong decision in the heat of battle usually meant death—while even a right decision was no guarantee of safety. It took a special breed of men with a special toughness to lead others through this "gateway to hell," to face the tests of uncertainty that lay beyond its threshold, and do so with some sense of confidence that they could bring everyone back alive.

Among these tough players was Oregon-born Rodger W. Simpson, an outspoken forty-four-year-old destroyer commander with a bent toward the flamboyant. During his academy years—while among the graduating class of 1921—Rodger Simpson's classmates quickly learned of his notoriously "ready smile," and just as aptly learned to receive it with all due suspicion, as "Simp" had a "fury" of a temperament when faced with competition. Whether on the football field or in the classroom, Simpson sought the "limelight," and he gave every effort to stand out, even if the attention might fall upon negative terms. He was known to have a "good nature," but his peers were prudent not to be fooled by such display; "he had the appellation of snake thrust upon him by earning it," a classmate once cautiously noted.[20]

During the First World War the demand for naval officers placed Midshipman Simpson in advanced training aboard the battleship *Ohio*, providing him his first working experience at sea and precursor to his future role in leadership. But, even as this old dreadnought proved to be an impressive learning center, Simpson was to find no endearments here. Between the wars he went on to serve mostly on the decks of destroyers, having assignments with six different of the fleet's mighty tin cans, and it was within the confines of these feisty little warships that he found his home. Simpson would later serve as a member of the staff of the commander of Destroyer Squadron 14. Afterward, he attended postgraduate school at Annapolis and Yale University, from which he emerged with a major in communications engineering, taking his new skill with him back to the destroyer fleet.[21] With such combination of skill, experience, and natural aggressiveness, there was no question that Simpson possessed every one of the leadership qualities sought by Halsey for the Solomons—and still there was more to this commander's story.

By March 1941, Simpson—at this time a lieutenant commander—had assumed the leadership of the destroyer *Mahan* (namesake of her own class and first built of the single-stack destroyers), a ship long on assignment in the Pacific and regularly a fixture at Pearl Harbor.[22] His arrival had come at a precarious time, as the threat of war loomed more and more acute with each passing day. But along with this threat (as numerous repeated alerts continuously proved premature and false) there also evolved a lethal lethargy and passiveness. Even as the population at Pearl Harbor grew steadily, crowding its limited facilities to capacity, few individuals truly understood the factors behind the gathering storm. Simpson was a skilled officer for sure, but he was a warrior in title only, and was no more convinced of the approaching peril than any other of his peers, even as the crosshairs of destiny were quickly drawing down to bear where he stood. When the Japanese attack did come, Simpson was missing, as fortunate *Mahan* was absent from the harbor, on patrol far to the south and well out of immediate danger. More than surprised, however, Simpson was angry; for this former pigskin "Hustler" had missed the initial kickoff to a critical contest, and he wanted in the game—and most assuredly he would not be kept out of the contest long.

Surely Simpson's display of aggressive spirit was well warranted. But, outside the defense of the Hawaiians, these early months of the conflict afforded *Mahan* no opportunities for pursuit of the enemy. Simpson's destroyer was restricted mostly to inter-island patrols. But, when in August the invasion of Guadalcanal began and the Navy's attention suddenly shifted from a mode of defense to offense, *Mahan* was among the campaign's earliest beneficiaries. By October, Simpson had his ship on the move, directing the destroyer into the heat of the South Pacific action—and he would waste no time at displaying his great skill and courage for challenging the enemy.

Sent specifically to join in with the Solomons campaign, *Mahan* departed Pearl on October 16; but once well out to sea, Simpson received a new set of orders directing him to divert his ship—along with the destroyer *Lamson*—for a raid south of the Gilbert Islands, where a group of enemy gunboats were known to be operating. This, Simpson knew, was an exceptional opportunity, and the commander was very happy to oblige the undertaking. The two ships made their detour and arrived near their targets on October 22, successfully escaping all enemy observation. Then, so as to not chance losing their advantage, *Mahan* and *Lamson* aggressively raced forward, daring a daylight gunnery action rarely nerved at this juncture of the war. The surprised enemy reacted poorly, and two of the Japanese gunboats were quickly dispatched to their watery graves (though only one, the 3,300-ton converted minelayer *Hakkaisan Maru*, is actually confirmed as sunk on this date).[23] Subsequently, the two destroyers made their successful escape and, despite numerous ensuing aerial attacks, did so without any casualties. As a result of this "extraordinary heroism," Simpson was awarded the Navy Cross. The citation read in part, "Boldly engaging an enemy patrol line in a daring daylight raid, [Simpson] . . . launched determined aggressive attacks in which two Japanese vessels were sunk. . . . Despite terrific aerial opposition, he brought his ship and crew through this successful engagement without loss or damage. . . ."[24]

This bold aggressiveness was to continue too. On October 27, while sailing as part of Task Force 61 just north of the Santa Cruz Islands, Simpson's destroyer again came under heavy aerial assault. Neither side was to give an inch. Fighting back with a ferocious hail of defensive gunfire, *Mahan*'s crew successfully splashed four of their determined attackers.[25] As a result, Simpson and his destroyer quickly gained a reputation as one of the toughest combinations in the South Pacific.

Still, even such an emboldened duo as Simpson and *Mahan* could not avoid all the troubles that the Solomons insisted on delivering. On October 30, while making emergency maneuvers in avoidance of a contact with an enemy submarine, *Mahan* accidentally collided with the battleship *South Dakota*, buckling the destroyer's nose and causing a brief fire in the ship's forward section. The damage was not terminal, but it was serious enough to require his destroyer to return to

Pearl for repairs.[26] Simpson was forced to leave the fight, though his absence would certainly not be for long.

Simpson, like Burke, had proven that he was made for this type of warfare, and, like Burke, he appeared very much predestined to be a part of it. In some ways, both commanders displayed similar natures, especially in tune with the art of aggressiveness. Their very appearances reflected confidence, strength, and resilience. They were loud, outspoken, and demanding. If opportunity did not readily come their way, they raced toward it, encouraged it, and even dared it. They both seemed more than groomed for the challenge that this war brought; they were born for it. The term *warrior* defined them as much as they defined the term. They were a breed apart, but not alone. Others were evolving, such as Moosbrugger. Though perhaps far more subdued with their talents, these too were to prove just as capable—just as they would prove equally important to the overall victory.

Lt. Russell Crenshaw had heard of Simpson—as *Maury* was a part of the same destroyer screen as *Mahan* during the Santa Cruz action—though he did not appear overly impressed. That Simpson could be counted as a hero was at this point in time of no immediate consequence to the lieutenant. As *Maury*'s new gunnery officer, Crenshaw was far more impressed with his own ship's role, especially as the many stresses being usurped by the Solomons were proving exceptionally brutal. Indeed, *Maury* had been serving as escort for the carriers since Midway, and had arrived at Guadalcanal with the invasion force as "plane guard" for the carrier *Enterprise*, and participated in the Battle of the Eastern Solomons, August 24-25, where *Enterprise* received heavy damage. Throughout this time *Maury* had been in the thick of it all, but her skipper, Lt. Comm. Gelzer Sims—the same that had been Burke's executive officer while he was in command of the *Mugford*—had so far managed to keep all within his command safe. This was the type of leadership that impressed Crenshaw. To have remained in the middle of this contest and escaped its deadly hand was no easy trick and was a worthy tribute to the talent and determination of all who were aboard the destroyer. So, when tasked with escorting the wounded *Enterprise* back to Pearl for repairs, *Maury*'s complement was well within their right to welcome the reprieve.

Maury's absence was brief, lasting only till mid-October. With *Enterprise* having her repairs completed, both she and her escorting destroyer were immediately dispatched for return to the Solomons—just in time to join in the action off Santa Cruz—whereupon the *Enterprise* was damaged once more. *Maury*'s return was just as though it had never been absent. For this reason alone, Crenshaw had no time for pondering the conquests of some other destroyer captain—or any future whereby they together might join in advancing the course of the war. His thoughts for the moment were reserved solely for his own duties and little else.

Much like Crenshaw, Lt. Pemberton Southard was another preoccupied officer, far too concerned with his own obligations to ponder the successes of others. Like Crenshaw, Southard—at least during these concluding months of 1942—had no great impressions of Simpson or Burke. In fact, he knew even less of these commanders than did Crenshaw and understood nothing of their demeanors as leaders or of their skills in combat—even though he was destined to learn. Southard's ship, *Lang*—another of the tough veterans of the Solomons campaign—would soon serve a few days under Burke's command and was destined to become the flagship for Simpson, during his leadership of Destroyer Division 15: a pairing that was to have its significant union in the Eastern and Central Solomons throughout much of 1943 and a marriage that was destined to be as turbulent as it was to be historic. This, however, remained several months away; and, for Pem, such a future marriage was far less consequential than the one this campaign had already interrupted.

In the meantime, just as with so many other servicemembers of his time, Pemberton's most earnest efforts were focused on day-to-day survival, and were without forethought of any destiny that might be waiting. He worked just as he had been trained, with devotion to duty. Even so, his most personal thoughts remained very much human. His truest desires were to be elsewhere. He was obviously loyal to the defense of freedom and country, but the harsh realities of this war were giving him new reason for concern. The frustrations of dealing with all of the many inconveniences of this conflict were extremely trying for everyone, and Lieutenant Southard was not at all immune. The war in the Pacific had taken on a life of its own, as did its timeline, which was promising to be quite lengthy. Moreover, this South Pacific struggle—and especially the Solomons—drew much early disaffection, as this theater quickly proved itself to be an extremely perilous venture, being every bit as much "work" as had been so acutely described by Henry Davison's earlier discourse. In Pemberton's case, however, there was an additional issue; this campaign was also responsible for keeping from him the only other affection having equal or greater status to that of his beloved Navy—this being his betrothed, Jane.

Pem's journey to the Pacific began when *Lang* was ordered to join in the assembly for the Guadalcanal invasion, sailing two months ahead of the invasion date as escort for the carrier *Wasp*—a duty that had been the destroyer's since late March (first assigned to the carrier for a joint British/American mission to resupply desperately needed fighter planes to Malta in the Mediterranean). These latest orders—into the far-off regions of the South Pacific, where President Roosevelt had initially determined the commitment should be secondary as opposed to the war in Europe—had caught *Lang*'s complement of officers and crew completely by surprise. There had been no expectations for such a transfer, and certainly the timing could have hardly been worse for Pemberton. The lieutenant had plans to be married in September (even despite their wartime separations, Jane and Pemberton had finally managed to use correspondence and phone calls to set a date for their commitments). He had foreseen no good reason why he should not be available. After all, everyone seemed to agree that any full-scale offensive operations in Europe were likely more than a year away and equally so in the Pacific. Even should he be temporarily absent, away for some escort duty or at sea on patrol, all the necessary arrangements could still be made—the church scheduled, the wedding dress made, family and guests invited, etc., etc. As long as he remained stationed somewhere along the East Coast—as he expected—then he should have little trouble receiving the necessary liberty for such an important occasion. Shipping out to England for the Malta mission surely did bring a temporary shudder of doubts to his cause, but the *Wasp* and *Lang* were safely returned to Norfolk by the end of May and everything looked to be back on due course. But then, on June 7, *Wasp* and *Lang* were once again handed orders, sending the tandem back out to sea.

The destination was not readily disclosed, but the scuttlebutt had it that they were heading to the Pacific. This news was truly upsetting to all aboard, especially after having just so recently returned home from their rather lengthy—and successfully completed—mission to distant European waters. It had been everyone's hope that their stateside stay would be at least long enough for being rewarded some well-earned liberty—but such was not to be. To Southard's dismay, instead of being provided an opportunity for a long overdue visit with Jane, his stay at Norfolk was only an abbreviation to a far lengthier journey. Within hours he was back at sea and sailing right on past Charleston Harbor—where his fiancée waited without initial knowledge of his departure. *Lang* continued on south and beyond, through the Panama Canal and farther into the Pacific, stopping only briefly in San Diego before proceeding on to the hazard-ridden Solomons invasion. (At San Diego, Pemberton called Jane to let her know of his departure, but he could not disclose his new location. Such did not matter, as Jane already knew. She worked in a Navy office in Charleston and had inadvertently seen a transfer order with the names of ships, seeing *Lang* noted among the list.[27]) The future was pretty obvious. Pemberton knew no return by

September should be expected. The wedding he was so looking forward to would have to be postponed.

For the better part of a year the Solomons campaign would occupy much of *Lang*'s itinerary, and it would be September before the destroyer would have even a modest break in this new action. On September 4, *Lang* was finally relieved from her lengthy escort of *Wasp*, replaced by the newly arrived destroyer *O'Brian*. *Lang* proceeded on to Noumea, New Caledonia, for a brief but greatly needed rest for her crew—despite being less than a month into the campaign, the stresses of the Solomons were so extremely taxing that any departure from this unruly and brutal region, even if only for a few days, was a welcomed occasion. This exodus, however, proved especially fortunate for *Lang* and her crew, for on September 20 the *Wasp* was sunk and the *O'Brian* was heavily damaged by dual strikes from a single marauding Japanese submarine. So, after having served a full half-year of constant duty with *Wasp*, only sixteen days had separated *Lang* from apparent disaster.

Despite this apparent good fortune, any feeling of reprieve for *Lang* was truly short lived. The destroyer went back to work quickly, this time escorting highly vulnerable fleet oilers back and forth between Australia and Noumea. Though these escorts proved to be quite unremarkable, they were quickly followed up by one of the truest bits of wartime irony. Quite unexpectedly, *Lang* was ordered to escort the patched-up though still hurting *O'Brian* back to Pearl for more permanent repairs.

Sailing on October 10, *Lang* along with the oiler *Cimarron* helped to nurse the terribly ailing *O'Brian* along its way. Each nautical mile saw the *O'Brian* deteriorate even more. Every effort was made to keep the ship afloat, but on October 19, just off Samoa, the vessel began to break up, expediting the immediate removal of her abbreviated crew. Southard watched, as did many observers, helplessly gazing on as the structure of this unlucky ship suddenly split and bid its final farewell. Collapsing into a V before surrendering to the depths, *O'Brian* disappeared with a concluding strangled gurgle of escaping air. The destroyer that had stood in *Lang*'s stead was gone, and the Solomons had accounted for yet another of its many victims. The vision was so very haunting, and disturbingly so, as the lieutenant could hardly help but ponder how easily this could have been *Lang*'s destiny he watched. It was a powerful reminder of just how vulnerable and uncertain life could be in this war. Even so, Pem and his ship survived—and so too did his promise to return to Jane—so far at least.

With similar respect, Ralph Barber, the disconcerted pharmacist's mate from Alabama, had his own dubious list of frustrations and concerns with the

South Pacific. In the early part of April 1942—just as Pemberton and *Lang* were beginning their first trek to Malta—Ralph began his first move, transferring from Norfolk to Brooklyn's Flushing Avenue Barracks. Here he and other medical personnel were to train as part of a newly organized Mobile Operating Base, MOB-5. As usual, Barber was not especially thrilled with his prospects—knowing full well that his workload was sure to intensify and that he was just one additional step closer to some further deployment. Despite this reality, the change of scenery did at least produce for Ralph one bit of undeniable good fortune.

One day while on liberty, Ralph took the opportunity to visit downtown Brooklyn, and there, while walking the people-crowded streets, his attention was suddenly affixed on a single individual. He could hardly believe his eyes; the petite brunette whom he had just seen walk by had a very familiar face. Could it really be? It was! The pretty young lady he spied in passing was his old high school sweetheart, Virginia Adair. Ralph quickly ran to catch up to her, calling out her name. Virginia instantly turned to him and was caught with equal surprise. She had just recently moved to Manhattan and had by no means any expectations of running into anyone she knew, let alone someone for whom she had affection. The romance was almost instantly rekindled and just as quickly aspired to becoming quite serious. The two saw each other nightly, and on April 19, Ralph proposed. Virginia accepted and "I placed the $50.00 engagement ring on her finger," Ralph proudly noted.[28] But, as in the case of Pemberton and Jane, wartime uncertainty would just as assuredly interrupt Ralph and Virginia's plans for marriage.

MOB-5's training was unexpectedly accelerated and the unit was made active in the briefest amount of time. By June 1, the medical teams were all aboard a troop train and ready for transport to the Navy's destroyer base at National City, near San Diego, California, where they would prepare for even further deployment. There would surely be no opportunity for a proper wedding. Almost as instantly as it had begun, Ralph and Virginia's relationship was forced to go long-distance—and their marriage too was placed on indefinite hold.

Like Pemberton, Ralph was destined for a rendezvous with the Solomons. At National City, MOB-5 waited, but for only eight weeks before once again being ordered to move. No one seemed privy to their next destination, causing many unfounded rumors. Word had it that they were going to Hawaii. No, they were going to Panama. No, they were really going to Australia. And so, the conjecture continued, adding further to the uncertainty and without any credible resolution to its mystery. In the end, all that Ralph and the others could learn officially was that they were going somewhere and soon.

This "soon" came at the end of the first week of August, when Ralph and the rest of MOB-5 were crowded aboard the passenger ship SS *President Monroe*—an old passenger liner turned troop transport—and were sent sailing off toward some still undisclosed destination. About this voyage Ralph would later recall, "The days were very long."[29] Despite their transport's former glory, there remained no conveniences aboard the ship. The former liner had been mostly stripped of its luxuries and Ralph duly noted his frustrations with the inherent discomforts. The "enlisted men received two meals a day [scrambled eggs in the morning and stew in the evening], and it was impossible to get anything [extra] to eat at the Ship's Service."[30] The journey itself—as the ship sailed a course south by southwest, across the equator and beyond the International Date Line—became more and more of a discomfort with each accumulated mile. The heat became sweltering, and there were very few opportunities for refreshment. "Only salt-water showers were allowed to the enlisted men," Ralph complained.[31] It quickly became apparent that this sailor had little fondness for the sea and ships.

The dissatisfaction with this journey was far from Ralph's alone. Nearly everyone aboard the crowded vessel was ready for this voyage to end. Despite the sea being mostly calm, the combination of heat and pitch still caused a great many cases of seasickness, and many areas of the vessel reeked of vomit. The one good thing, at least, was that MOB-5 members were finally notified of their destination. Once well out to sea, their objective was finally disclosed; they were headed for Noumea, New Caledonia, a key staging area for the recently initiated American campaign in the Solomons. There, at a spot near Anse Vata Beach, MOB-5 would erect its hospital. Ralph would later refer to this site as "the most beautiful location on the island."[32] Truly his experiences here were to prove very much to his liking, even as the ugly results of warfare were always evident—many horribly wounded patients were received at the hospital and almost all were from the ongoing conflict in the Solomons. Still, here he remained safe from harm, even as the scarred and dying were always around him. He wrote Virginia often, confidently reassuring her that he would be okay. He was far from the front and never expected to face any true risk to his own life—until, that is, another of his spontaneous decisions would once more send him in a direction he did not thoroughly plan out.

Indeed, plans in this war—as Barber had found but had yet to fully grasp—were rarely to turn out for anyone as first hoped. This was certainly true for one very youthful and bright-eyed gunner by the name of Charles "Chuck" Lee. Chuck had in late September just shipped over from San Francisco to Pearl. Arriving at the docks on *Lang*'s first day back in port—just after the destroyer had completed its long trek from Noumea, less unfortunate *O'Brian*—the eighteen-year-old Lee clamored up the gangway with a plucky spirit to his step, orders in hand and surely expectant of a cordial welcome. His arrival, however, proved not so endearing. This ship, Lee knew, was a veteran warrior that had just returned from the Solomons; still its testy demeanor caught this young gunner completely unexpected. Chuck immediately sensed a dire wariness from the crew. The faces he met were of young men, but men who exhibited a spirit far more mature than their true years. Even in the midst of their humor these men appeared dry and displayed a curt seriousness, overly experienced and nearly monotone. They were a no-nonsense crowd, who looked to offer little in the way of compassion to new arrivals, as exemplified by his initial greeting, which came by way of a tough-looking boatswain's mate by the name of A. B. Clifford. "Put your gear in the deckhand's area and start to chip paint," the boatswain growled loudly.[33] Chuck was immediately taken aback. He was instantly reminded of his younger civilian teenage days when he had worked at the shipyards in Staten Island, where he had spent many grueling hours chipping paint. He despised the task. He had no new desire to restart the trade. This was surely a mistake, he thought. He was a gunner's mate, not a seaman. He shouldn't be expected to do such labor. Obviously, the boatswain misunderstood. So, Chuck tried to enlighten the older sailor by pointing to the badge he wore on his sleeve. But there *was* no mistake; the boatswain didn't seem to care who or what Chuck was. "Get to work," he said with a scowl. "See the Yeoman after you finish."[34] Perhaps it was Chuck who had made the mistake, having so recently chosen to volunteer for such duty and with little thought to the consequences. He knew better than to argue, however, and so he did the work as instructed—though afterward he did indeed march directly to the yeoman's office.

At the ship's office Chuck was met by Charlie Stirrup, a sharp-appearing fellow who displayed a pleasant smile. Frustrated and angry, the young gunner quickly went into sharp detail at explaining to Stirrup who and what he was, and of his initial treatment. The yeoman seemed to understand and forwarded him on to Lieutenant Southard, who greeted Chuck with his characteristic patient stare. There the gunner repeated his story, to which Southard appeared quite attentive. Knowing just how to handle the situation, Pemberton sent Chuck on to see *Lang*'s chief gunner's mate, Leonard "Woodie" Wood. Wood, a soft-spoken man, a laid-back "Hoosier" who hailed from Vincennes, Indiana, and who had been aboard the destroyer since its commissioning, was no novice with such dealings. Pemberton expected, and rightly so, that Woodie's wisdom and experience could surely handle this upset gunner.

Chief Wood patiently listened to Lee as he repeated his complaint for yet a third time and, after doing so, found good reason to be impressed by this sailor's spunk and determination. The recent "welcome" aboard *Lang* had indeed struck a foul note with this gunner—as Chuck had been profoundly "shocked" by his initial treatment—and he had no intention of letting the episode pass without his concerns being heard. Chuck wanted his rightful place among the gunner's gang, and he let the amiable chief know that he felt that he was due some type of reassurance.

Though certainly seen as impressive, Chuck's drive was by no means unusual for his character. Lee had learned early on to be proactive when facing challenges, which was an attribute that served him well throughout all of his life.

Raised in the rural mountain region of West Rutland, Vermont, Chuck had certainly experienced one of nature's most alluring landscapes—but this environment could also be quite harsh and extremely challenging. Winters here could be very difficult, and summers were usually spent preparing, as cutting wood, gardening, and canning took precedence over most family leisure. Chuck, his three sisters, and two brothers were always busy helping out. Still, these were happy times, "thanks to a great set of parents."[35] Chuck's mother, Mildred, was a homemaker, and she did a wonderful job at overseeing the everyday needs of the family. Chuck's father, Victor, an immigrant from Sicily and veteran of the First World War, had originally worked as a crane operator for the Vermont Marble Company in West Rutland, and made a good living. But during the Depression this source of income was lost, leaving the family in a desperate strait. Nevertheless, Victor did not give up, and later he acquired a job with the WPA (Works Progress Administration) involved with public works as part of President Roosevelt's "New Deal." Still, life for the Lee family remained very difficult. Chuck would note, "It was very hard times but we managed to survive."[36]

As a matter of convenience, Chuck started school with an older sister at an age of "four-years and three-months," causing him even further challenge—though he maintained better than average grades throughout his educational years. At the age of fifteen and while still in high school, Lee joined the Vermont National Guard, as a member of the 43rd Division, 172nd Infantry, Company A. "The armory was in Rutland," he explained, "which was [only] a short

4 miles away [from my home and the] pay was $1.50 a drill."[37] In November 1940, his guard unit was fully activated and preparations were made for it to be deployed to the Philippines—but Chuck was only sixteen and was disappointedly discharged (left behind to later ponder "if any of my pals wound up in the infamous 'Bataan Death March'").[38] This same month Chuck's parents moved to Brooklyn, where his father finally found some good-paying employment at the Navy Yard. Chuck also found a new job, with a federally sponsored program at Staten Island wherein he worked at chipping paint from old Navy ships being prepared for part of President Roosevelt's Lend-Lease program—though this work soon found disfavor with him. In late November 1941, he acquired another new job as a stock clerk at a brush factory in downtown New York. He was just getting settled in when the unsettling news about Pearl Harbor was first heard.

As with most young men of the time, revelations of the attack quickly inspired in Chuck a new sense of direction. "Everyone . . . was ready to go to war," Lee wrote.[39] So was he. But Chuck was only seventeen, and to join would require the signature of his parents. It took some time and some rather powerful persuading before finally getting his wish. "I enlisted in the Navy on February 10, 1942."[40] Then off he went to Newport, Rhode Island, for boot camp.

At the Newport training facility all of the inductees were quickly encouraged to choose a vocation. Chuck initially thought he might like a position as a yeoman, where his skills at typing, shorthand, and bookkeeping might serve him well. But his drill instructor, evidently recognizing his greater talents, convinced him otherwise. So, after an aptitude test placed Chuck in the top 10 percent of his class, offering him an abundance of options, he chose to become a gunner. "I chose gunnery as I wanted to handle a gun in battle," he wrote later. "[It was] not a hero wish, but I thought that was what I wanted to do."[41]

Chuck was then sent on to the Great Lakes Naval Training Center in Chicago, where he entered gunnery school. After completing this training, he was then transferred to Treasure Island, San Francisco, where he arrived in late August. But just prior to his leaving the Great Lakes, Chuck made a last-minute commitment, as he signed up for aerial gunnery school. He had done this due almost solely to the pay incentives. "Aerial gunners were given an extra 50% for flight pay. This sounded great to me."[42] But soon after making this decision, something unexpected happened that gave this young gunner reason to have second thoughts.

One pleasant Saturday afternoon Chuck and some friends went downtown to a local USO-sponsored dance. It was here that he first met seventeen-year-old

Patricia Skinner, a pretty San Francisco native with whom Chuck immediately became infatuated. He asked her for a dance, and she agreed. This girl was instantly the love of his life; she was the one, of this he had no doubts. He soon had her convinced to accompany him on a series of dates. But when one evening Chuck asked Patricia to go steady, to be *his* girl alone, she politely refused. She certainly had a strong affection for this young man, but the reality of this new war, the promise of long separations, and their short romance made her reluctant for any long-term commitment, especially to a fellow she had only recently met. Moreover, Chuck was now preparing to train as a belly gunner on a "TBF" (Grumman TBF-1 Avenger) torpedo plane, arguably one of the most dangerous jobs in the Navy. The expected survival rate for such men was quite low. Such odds could not be a comfortable beginning for any aspiring romance.

Chuck returned to his base thoroughly frustrated, disappointed with the choices that both he and Patricia had made. Adding further to this discontent, he had been weeks waiting for his transfer to come through for aerial gunnery school in Hawaii. Chuck was losing his patience. He was anxious to get involved in the fighting, especially after learning of the new South Pacific offensive at Guadalcanal. On the way back to his barracks he just happened to stop by a bulletin board, and here he saw a notice seeking fifty volunteers for destroyer duty in Hawaii. It was time for another quick commitment. Without much regard for details, he walked straight over to the yeoman's desk and signed up. It was 10:00 p.m. and the troop ship he was to leave on was scheduled to depart at midnight. He quickly grabbed his gear and left. Even his closest friends would not know of his departure.

Now that he was aboard the *Lang*, heated and a bit unnerved from his recent episode with the boatswain's mate, Chuck began to question his latest choice. Chief Gunner Wood had been careful to give Chuck his fullest attention, displaying an honest interest and compassion to every concern he raised. Understanding the need to be supportive, Woodie quickly assured Chuck that he was indeed a member of the gunners' gang, and that he would be treated as such in all future matters. Obviously, this was exactly what the young gunner's mate was hoping to hear. Chuck had not only found a reasoned man in Chief Leonard Wood, but a friend and a leader with whom he could place his whole trust.

Chuck was never to forget this first meeting with his new immediate boss, nor was he ever to ignore the many lessons that this wise man was to demonstrate in the future. Woodie was to teach lessons of survival, and in the South Pacific nothing was more vital. "Leonard Wood . . . was an excellent teacher," Chuck noted with passion. "This great man took care of [the gunner's gang] . . .

and instilled much confidence in us to do the job well, especially when under fire in battle situations. We were fortunate to have him as our leader . . . We won because of men like him."[43]

But winning the war was at this point, quite obviously, a long way off. Loyd Peters, who had originally joined the Navy in search of steady work—believing such service in the Navy "sounded romantic"—found far more of it than he ever wanted, or would ever again refer to as "romantic."[44] Immediately after the attack on Pearl Harbor, Peters was sent to Goat Island, San Francisco, to await further transfer. On December 31, while waiting for his next move, he volunteered to assist with aid for wounded servicemen and civilian evacuees who had just arrived from Pearl Harbor aboard the liner *Lurline* (the same ship that would in March carry Moosbrugger's family back to safety). It was an eye-opening experience, instantly divulging the grim reality of this new war. Three days later he boarded the *Pyro*, an ammunition ship, to head the opposite direction for his own part in the conflict.

At Pearl, Loyd would await his next assignment and on February 10 (the very same day that Chuck Lee was signing his enlistment papers) he finally stepped aboard the ship that would prove to be his home for the duration of the war, the destroyer *Dunlap*. Fortunately, for much of the remaining year, Peters remained near the Hawaiians. But on December 2, 1942, his turn finally came to join the fight in the South Pacific. On this date, *Dunlap* arrived at Noumea (Ralph Barber's island of residency) to begin its part in the struggle against the Japanese—and what a struggle it would prove to be.

Even in Moosbrugger's optimism—as initially shown back in February—there was surely by this point in time a bit less energy. Freddie, like many other naval commanders in the Pacific, was finally learning firsthand the harsh realities of this new war. In his case, however, he would have likely even welcomed a bit of the heat of the Solomons, as his own fight—though with the same determined enemy and in the same mass of ocean—was at the complete opposite end of nature's extremes. After nearly eight months of duty in and around the Hawaiian Islands, by the end of July 1942, Moosbrugger—who having just received his silver oak leaves in promotion to commander—was now leading his new command, Destroyer Division 11, into the paralyzing cold and extreme hardships of the campaign to win the Aleutians. Here, far to the north, the warring with the elements was to take an even greater toll than was the fight with the Japanese. Weather in the Aleutians was highly predictable; it was almost always bad. A terribly frigid, rough sea made patrolling for the enemy by ship a most difficult task. Visibility was often very poor, as fog hindered almost every operation. Collision with another vessel was as much of a threat as was an enemy torpedo or bomb. And there was little national focus on this region, leading the greater efforts of the commanders to go almost unnoticed, awarding them with little recognition for their successes. So, despite the many frustrations it held for others, to Moosbrugger the South Pacific looked to be an improvement—and he would indeed set his course there, and soon.

Chapter Four

The Tokyo Express

"Hellova Nuisance"

The frustrations of the Solomons were not solely American. The campaign proved to be just as trying for the Japanese, and with even greater liability. The challenges were fully unanticipated, as Japanese commanders had never really considered the need for throwing back enemy invaders at this location. Guadalcanal was thought to be barely noticed. With its only airfield still under construction, it was manned mostly with construction troops and without any serious defenses. But it did have strategic value. Now, it was in danger of being overwhelmed, making a hasty reinforcement of the island essential if the American aggression was to be defeated. Vice Adm. Gunichi Mikawa, Eighth Fleet commander at Rabaul and victor of the First Battle of Savo Sound, knew he had little time to waste. Vast numbers of combat troops and supplies would be needed on the island quickly, if the attackers were to be stopped. He needed a plan.

Mikawa knew that the slower, more vulnerable marus (civilian-type cargo ships) commonly used for naval transport would stand little chance at success, especially with American carrier-based airpower operating around the islands. He needed something better, something better suited to the task, and so he quickly devised an alternative for just this type of reinforcement; he would use fast cruisers and destroyers.

The admiral also understood that in order for his plan to work he needed a courageous and skilled commander at its lead. He had no trouble making his choice; he confidently chose the only officer he knew who might take this admittedly high-risk and hastily planned initiative to a higher plateau of success. Mikawa's selection proved quite brilliant. Rear Adm. Raizo Tanaka was given the tap.

A handsome officer with a superb history, Tanaka's speedy rise through the ranks could not help but bring attention to his talents. Born on April 27, 1892, this leader's more youthful and inexperienced days were—by the time of the Guadalcanal campaign—long behind him. His service in the Imperial Navy began early in 1913, as a midshipman, training at sea on various cruisers and destroyers. By December 1914 he had earned his sub-lieutenant rank (equivalent of a U.S. Navy ensign). Two years later he was again promoted, to lieutenant (junior grade), and immediately transferred for an assignment at the Imperial Navy's torpedo and gunnery schools. He then returned to sea duty and by December of 1919 had reached the rank of full lieutenant.

After being reassigned to torpedo school for a short period of advanced training, Tanaka again returned to sea duty, serving as chief torpedo officer aboard three different destroyer assignments. In the interim, his expertise in the use of torpedoes had reached a peak of proficiency, and by the end of 1925 he was once more reassigned to the torpedo school, but this time as an instructor. On November 21, 1930, Tanaka was given his first command, the *Tachikaze*, an older 1,200-ton destroyer of the *Minekaze* class. Ten days later he was promoted to commander. Then on November 14, 1931, he was given command of one of the Imperial Navy's newly constructed Fubuki class destroyers, *Ushio*. From here Tanaka's career soared.

Having reached the rank of captain in 1935, Tanaka returned to shore duty and entered into the Imperial Navy's War College at Yokosuka. By January 1937 he was commanding the 2nd Destroyer Squadron, and by the end of this same year he was in command of the cruiser *Jintsu*. From November 1939 through to April 1941 he had command of the battleship *Kongo*. By the time of the Japanese attack on Pearl Harbor, Tanaka held the rank of rear admiral and was in command of the destroyers supporting the highly successful landings in the Philippines and Dutch East Indies. His destroyers would also participate in the Japanese victory at Java Sea on February 27, 1942. But it was at Guadalcanal that Tanaka was to make a name for himself. Here his bold actions would gain him the greatest respect of his adversaries, who hated his every success yet referred to his abilities by such adjectives as "superb," "greatest," and "perfect." Unfortunately for Tanaka, his own superiors were not to share for him the same respect as did his adversaries. Guadalcanal and the electrifying destroyer force he nurtured were to engrave his name deeply into the pages of history, but it would also end his career—not in death, but in a disgrace not of his own doing.

Tanaka had never expected the highly critical and expeditious task that was handed him. He later noted, "It came as a surprise to me in mid-August 1942, to learn that, as Commander Destroyer Squadron 2, I had been chosen to assume command of a force to bring troops and supplies to Guadalcanal. The impact of this new responsibility may be appreciated when I say in all candor that neither I nor any of my staff had the slightest knowledge or experience in the Solomon Islands. Of Guadalcanal itself we knew no more than its location on a chart. We had much to learn, in little time, of the plan and scope of the operations to be carried out."[1] Even so, his persevering was to pay off greatly, and with amazing effect; while introducing ingenious new tactics and perfecting the execution of existing ones, his forces provided a most critical roadblock to the American offensive in the Solomons. And had the Japanese not wasted his efforts with ridiculously suicidal offensives in the land campaign, Tanaka might well have won for them the battle—perhaps even the war.

Lieutenant Sherman would write of Tanaka's efforts, "The Japs started raiding our outfits in the Solomon[s], in the early days, with a fast-traveling unit of cruisers and destroyers. We got to know this bunch as 'The Tokyo Express.' It was a 'hellova' nuisance. They used it well. They'd slip down through the darkness and the rain squalls, lash out at our beachheads, shoot at anything that floated, and then disappear into the north and the night."[2]

At its critical infancy—from August 18 through 31—Tanaka held the helm of responsibility for this reinforcement/bombardment effort and did so with unbreakable resolve. The birth of the "Tokyo Express" and its charge toward success was his to deliver—even despite his own low expectations of the prospects. "With no regard for my opinion," he would later write, "this order called for the most difficult operation in war—landing in the face of the enemy—to be carried out by mixed units which had no opportunity for rehearsal or even preliminary study. It must be clear to anyone with knowledge of military operations that such an undertaking could never succeed."[3] Still, he accepted his orders in stride and nearly pulled off the unprecedented victory.

With no time to waste, Tanaka spent many long, tension-filled hours trying to organize his forces for the difficult task ahead. It was a trying and tiring venture. "I realized," he noted, "that much had happened during my few short weeks in this command. I had lost many ships and men in difficult battle situations, one of my subordinate commanders had proven inadequate to his assignment, and there had been [a] delay in one reinforcement operation because of my conflict with the stubborn Army commander." Furthermore, he stated, "I was so exhausted—mentally and physically—that I could hardly keep going."[4] But his efforts were not without effect. On the last day of August, his forces completed the midnight landing of another 1,000 troops on the shores of Guadalcanal, and in avoidance of all opposition. Tanaka proudly noted, "This was the third time that a complete Army unit had been landed successfully from destroyers."[5] The total amounted to nearly 3,500 fresh troops delivered to Guadalcanal in less than five days, and to the detriment of the American Marines facing them.

As Sherman so ably indicated, the Tokyo Express was quickly proving itself an outright threat to the American campaign on Guadalcanal—and it needed to be stopped. The menace was quickly placing the American operation in severe jeopardy. Every successful delivery of enemy troops and supplies only guaranteed the fight to drag on, and impatience with this dilemma was increasing by the day. The U.S. Navy made several attempts at shutting down Tanaka's tenacious force, but his slippery Express consistently made good on their deliveries, to then escape to their home base with hardly a scratch—oftentimes leaving behind a wounded and dispirited adversary, scratching his head at what had just happened. And the Express just kept on coming!

Even despite his lack of knowledge of the new theater handed him, Tanaka adjusted to the challenge well. His quick, impromptu training of his crews, on the "how to" of fighting their destroyers while encumbered with an overburdening cargo of troops and supplies, was minimal but efficient enough to meet the requirement. He wisely emphasized to his subordinates the need to use the darkness of night to their own advantage, confident that his destroyers and their crews were far better versed than their American counterparts in nighttime tactics. He was right; his ships were fast and the quality of their torpedoes far exceeded any of their opposition, and he was to use both to great gain.

Indeed, the complexity of his mission was great, but Tanaka did not have the luxury of creating a complex plan, nor did he give such an effort. His plan was to be as simple as he could make it; his ships were to use the shortest routes possible, time their transit to have optimal darkness for avoiding the highest risk of air attack, race to the drop-off point for troops and supplies, search for and attack any targets of opportunity, and then race back home to safety. It was a bold endeavor, requiring officers to have nerves of steel. And, whenever one of Tanaka's commanders failed to show such mettle, "he was transferred shortly to the homeland."[6]

For Tanaka, however, this assignment proved to be the most stressful that he had so far experienced. The admiral was soon nearing total exhaustion. Mikawa knew his commander was being taxed well beyond his limits and, after three grueling weeks of near nonstop challenges, he ordered Tanaka and his squadron back to Truk for needed rest and replenishment. Tanaka later noted, "My first reaction to this unexpected transfer order was a feeling of indignation because I had spared no effort to fill this assignment successfully. On second thought, however . . . it was only proper that I be given relief from the strain of this command."[7] He was "gratified" too by the knowledge of who had been chosen to replace him. Rear Adm. Shintaro Hashimoto (an old academy friend to Tanaka) was to assume command of the Express, and Tanaka was sure that his old friend would continue to facilitate the organization in the direction that he had established.

Finally, Tanaka was free to turn his attention to other affairs, primarily toward rebuilding his beloved 2nd Destroyer Squadron—even despite the Express never being far from his thoughts. For the next two months his ships were to remain based at Truk, serving as part of Vice Adm. Nobutake Kondo's 2nd Fleet.

In the meantime, the effort to reinforce Guadalcanal remained a priority mission for the Imperial Navy, as this was critical at stopping the American offensive. Traditional means of re-supply and reinforcement were also utilized, employing conventional transports supported by escorting warships, but—just as Mikawa had already surmised—these missions mostly ended with heavy losses and failure. The Express, therefore, remained at the forefront of operational success. As a result, high stress continued to take an extreme toll on both destroyer commanders and their crews.

Initially, Mikawa rotated his precious destroyer divisions in and out of the theater solely to reduce this stress and to keep morale high. However, as time progressed, the eventual strains of increasingly greater losses soon forced the admiral to recall units at shorter intervals and keep them in action for more extended periods. For this reason, morale became more and more difficult to maintain. Even so, the Express warriors proved themselves to be a resilient group of sailors, all being very proud of the reputation they had built. Their skill and daring were paramount partners with a gifted leadership that allowed the reinforcement to continue. But the availability of experienced destroyer commanders and crews was often wanting. It was, therefore, of no surprise to Tanaka when in early November he was once again hearing from Mikawa and being ordered to return to the deadly Solomons.

To the credit of the Express, some 20,000+ Imperial troops were now fighting on Guadalcanal, but they were on perilous ground. Food and medicines were in short supply, and American airpower grew stronger almost daily. Even the bravest efforts of the Express were at this point near suicidal. Mikawa needed help, and he hoped to find it in Tanaka.

The enterprising Tanaka was not to disappoint his superior. "None of the usual methods [of supply] had been successful," Tanaka wrote, "and our losses in destroyers were proving prohibitive . . . daring expedients were called for to provide them. The first novel method of supply to be tried was what was called the drum method. Large metal cans or drums were sterilized and then filled with medical supplies or basic foodstuffs such as cereals, leaving enough air space to insure buoyancy. Loaded on destroyers, these drums were linked together with strong rope during the passage to Guadalcanal. On arrival all drums were pushed overboard simultaneously while the destroyer continued on its way. A power boat would pick up the buoyed end of the rope and bring it to the beach where troops would haul it and the drums ashore. By this means unloading time was cut to a minimum, and destroyers returned to base with practically no delay.

"Transport was also attempted by submarines which would be loaded with supplies brought to the landing point, and cruise there submerged during the day to avoid air attacks. Surfacing near the friendly base at night, the supplies would be carried ashore by motor boats.

"Yet both of these were makeshift measures and, even when successful, resulted in the provision of only a few tons—enough for a day or two—of supplies."[8]

The short of it was, Tanaka's greatest efforts were too little too late. The supply chain was too long and the resources were simply not up to the challenge and, as a result, Japanese forces were to suffer greatly. Tanaka knew the campaign could not last much longer. Still, under orders, he pressed forward with his supply efforts. With sacrifice and blood, he bought for his superiors the time they required to save face, to find excuse for failure and point blame. And so, the struggle on Guadalcanal continued to extend—to the disillusionment of all combatants in the field.

On Guadalcanal, whether or not the campaign was a lost cause for the Japanese made little difference, as death and misery was still ongoing for those still fighting there. By the closing days of November 1942, the battle had lasted nearly four full months, and no end appeared to be in sight. Thousands of Japanese had been killed on the island, but they just kept coming. Blame for this pointed directly to the Tokyo Express—and the U.S. Navy's inability at stopping it. Halsey was under increasing pressure to find an answer. His superiors, from Washington, DC, on down, were demanding that the enemy reinforcement of Guadalcanal be ended. There was a growing impatience and nervousness with the length of the campaign. The matter was, however, far more complex than these leaders—including Halsey—fully understood. To stop the Express required the

American fleet to have complete control of the waters around Guadalcanal, both day and night. Considering the growing strength of Halsey's available airpower, daytime control was already well in hand. It was at night—when airpower had limited effectiveness—where the problems continued to persist. Despite the possession of radar, a superior technology in night warfare, Halsey's ships were consistently outfought in one night engagement after the other. He couldn't make sense of it; there were no apparent justifications for the poor results. How was it that the Japanese ships, having no radar and often inferior in numbers, were able to keep control of the night? The answer was not readily available, and was soon to seem farther away than ever.

Tanaka's first attempt at dropping off the buoyed supply drums he had devised took place off Tassafaronga on the night of November 30. This, he hoped, would prove successful at helping to alleviate some of the sufferings of the soldiers in the field. It would prove to be an explosive event, for sure—and though rarely alluded to, was likely another inadvertent rotation to the wheel that would soon give full advantage at sea to the U.S. Navy. For Tassafaronga was to be *the* greatest—yet equally *the* worst—moment of Tanaka's inspiring naval career. And, sadly, it was a moment from which he would never rebound, either with his career or his emotion.

After the war Tanaka wrote briefly of the event and described its intent. "Of eight destroyers that were to take part," he noted, "six were to be loaded with 200 to 240 drums. To accomplish this, reserve torpedoes were removed from these six ships, leaving each with only eight torpedoes—one for each tube—cutting their fighting effectiveness in half. No drums were loaded onboard flagship *Naganami* (or) destroyer leader *Takanami*, which carried the commander of Desdiv 31.

"Preparations were completed on November 29 and I led the ships from Shortland that night. In an attempt to conceal our intentions from the enemy we sailed eastward during the next morning. Nevertheless, we were shadowed constantly by his alert search planes. Around noon we increased speed to 24 knots and shaped a southward course to Guadalcanal . . . we continued toward designated unloading points off Tassafaronga and Segilau."[9]

Tanaka's attempts to keep his movements hidden and objectives secret nearly worked. The "search plane" he noted never spotted his formation and, therefore, reported nothing of his approach. A sharp Australian coast watcher did, however, report that eight destroyers were missing from Shortland's harbor, and this was enough to alert Halsey to the Express run. In addition, considerable boat and barge traffic had been reported around the Tassafaronga area of western Guadalcanal, and this was enough to lead Halsey to suspicion that this would be the enemy drop-off point. As a result, the stage was set for a showdown with "Tenacious Tanaka" and his mighty Tokyo Express, with Halsey hoping to end this reign of "nuisance" once and for all.

On the morning of November 30 an American task force of five cruisers and four destroyers were quickly dispatched for the assignment. These ships appeared more than adequate to fulfill the mission, but Halsey ordered two additional destroyers to join up with the force as added insurance. The Express had proven itself a tough contender in the past, deadly in combat, unpredictable and evasive, and the South Pacific commander did not want to fail at this next opportunity.

Unfortunately, whereas most of these task force ships and crews were experienced in the Guadalcanal Theater, their commanding officer, Rear Adm. Carleton Wright, was not. He had just arrived two days before, replacing the more knowledgeable and gifted Rear Adm. Thomas Kinkaid. As a result, Wright had little time to plan and even less time to acclimate himself to the region. Despite these shortcomings, Wright, who wisely adopted a plan left behind by Kinkaid, proceeded to intercept the enemy force as instructed.

Tanaka's ships had no radar and, though he did have a radio report of an enemy cruiser force in the area, he had no idea of the peril awaiting him.[10] Nearing Tassafaronga, the Express commander slowed his ships to 12 knots, preparing to launch the buoyed supply barrels at their designated pickup points. Everything appeared to be going as planned when the commander of the lead destroyer, *Takanami*, suddenly broke radio silence to report "*enemy ships*!" Tanaka had already begun the process of unloading the barrels but immediately ordered "*battle stations*" and increased his ships' speed in anticipation of battle.[11] However, before he could resume battle formation, flares lit up the night sky exposing Tanaka's destroyers. *Takanami*, since she was closest to the enemy formation, was immediately assailed by a swarm of incoming high-explosive shells, left crippled and burning furiously, though still able to fight. The gunfire, in turn, exposed the American column to Tanaka, and he quickly set to commencing headlong attacks, allowing his destroyers the independence to pursue the enemy ships at their own discretion.

Wright had made a tremendous error. Early in the action, his van [lead] destroyers had captured Tanaka's force on their radar, set themselves up for the perfect angle of attack, and immediately requested permission to fire their torpedoes. But Wright refused their request, refused to allow his destroyer muscle to flex at the most critical moment—and this would cost him the battle. Surprise was his, but Wright's decision to wait—though only four minutes—allowed Tanaka just enough time to be warned and to turn toward his attackers.

In the ensuing minutes Wright's cruisers took a pounding. Captured in the beams of Tanaka's powerful searchlights, the American cruisers were to draw no quarter from the irate Express. Like angry hornets shaken from their nest, the Japanese destroyers came straight for those who would dare to disturb their efforts. The night-fighting skill of Tanaka's battle-hardened crews was to shine its brightest this night. Torpedoes and shells persistently found their mark, and Wright's ships were quickly placed on their heels. The American destroyers were forced—by Wright's own cruiser gunfire—to move out of the way, leaving the cruisers completely open to torpedo attack. Wright's own flagship, *Minneapolis*, was first in the cruiser line to receive Tanaka's wrath, solidly punched by two well-aimed torpedoes, left slowed and blazing. *New Orleans* was next, struck by a torpedo that set off explosions in two forward magazines, the powerful blast ripping away the whole forward section of the ship from gun mount #2 all the way to the bull nose, though she managed to stay afloat and in motion. *Pensacola* (Earl Olsen's ship) tried to maneuver an escape but, in avoidance of a collision with the two crippled cruisers before her, steered directly into the path of yet another well-placed torpedo, crippling her as well. *Northampton* was then struck by two torpedoes, leaving a massive hole in the cruiser's port side and setting her oil-soaked afterdecks alight in what appeared as one massive flame, eventually sending her to the sound's bottom. Of Wright's cruisers, only the *Honolulu* was to escape without damage.

Caught completely by surprise, the engagement should have been Tanaka's end. His outgunned destroyers, encumbered with supplies and out of defensive formation, should have been easy prey. But Tanaka was able to turn the table, and his fast and aggressive actions led to an unprecedented victory that left the Americans stunned and once again searching for answers. Tanaka had lost but one ship, *Takanami*, yet he was far from jubilant. In an interview given several years after the war, Tanaka gave a brief response to questions about this battle. With tearful expression he noted, "We were able to defeat Admiral Wright's ships in this action only because of *Takanami*. She absorbed all the punishment of the enemy in the opening moments of battle, and she shielded the rest of us. Yet we left the scene without doing anything for her or her valiant crew."[12]

Tanaka also left the scene without delivering to Guadalcanal the precious cargo of supplies he carried, and this infuriated his superiors. Regardless of his resounding victory against a superior enemy force, he had failed his mission. "I accept the principal criticism leveled by fellow officers," he added. "It was an error on my part not to deliver the supplies according to schedule. I should have returned to do so . . . Had I but known that only one cruiser and four destroyers remained in fighting trim!"[13]

In his heart, Tanaka knew his failure mattered little to the outcome of the Guadalcanal campaign. It had long been lost, way before Tassafaronga. He even boldly recommended to his superiors that Guadalcanal be abandoned and the troops there to be evacuated. To put it politely, the recommendation was not well received. For those proud elites of the Imperial Navy, this was the last straw. To have a flag officer, one of their own, make such a severe recommendation could not be tolerated—even if it were right—and it was.

"A simple statement of the facts," Tanaka later wrote, "makes it clear that the Japanese attempt to reinforce Guadalcanal ended in failure. The causes of this failure, however, are probably as diverse as the people who may offer them. From my position as commander of the Reinforcement Force[,] I submit that our efforts were unsuccessful because of the following factors: command complications, [inferior] force composition, inconsistent operation plans, communication failures, [lack of] Army-Navy coordination, and underestimation of the enemy."[14]

Someone had to take the fall, however, and—due in part to his outspoken criticism—the decision was made that Tanaka was to become the scapegoat. His failures at getting the required number of troops and supplies to Guadalcanal—despite his amazing successes—were to be blamed for this first major loss of Japanese territory in the Pacific war. The time he had purchased for his superiors to save face was bought at his own expense. Although he had proven to be a brilliant commander, his success mattered little to his superiors. He was to be denied any meaningful role in the future of the war. Such was no doubt a very grievous mistake on the part of the Japanese command, as his talent and ability would have likely been to their advantage in future operations.

In the interim, though feeling disgraced and betrayed, Tanaka continued to fulfill his obligations, making additional Express runs to Guadalcanal, delivering several more tons of supplies in the days following Tassafaronga. December 27, however, he received his new orders, sending him off to an obscure staff job in Singapore; and two days later he turned over his command to Rear Adm. Tomiji Koyanagi, a former chief of staff to the Second Fleet. Still, even despite his imminent departure, he was to play one more key role in the conclusion of the Guadalcanal campaign.

Regardless of their initial objections, the Imperial Naval leadership finally gave approval for the evacuation of Guadalcanal, and Tanaka was asked to plan the operation, which he did. He would not, however, be allowed to lead the effort, as this was given over to his successor, Koyanagi. Just the same, due greatly to Tanaka's skillful planning—and in part to the defeat at Tassafaronga still being fresh on the minds of Halsey and others of the U.S. Navy—the "miracle" evacuation of Guadalcanal met complete success. In three night-runs (February 1, 4, and 7), fast destroyers of the Tokyo Express assisted by numerous submarines were able to extract to safety well over 11,000 troops from the war-torn and inhospitable island, known simply as "The Canal." Diseased, wounded, and starved, the haggard soldiers were eager to leave. Indeed, their relief was long overdue.

Halsey did not learn of the Japanese escape for several days, and the news, when learned, was received with serious concern. The admiral still faced a great dilemma. Guadalcanal was won and Tanaka was gone, but the Tokyo Express still remained a contentious obstacle. The evacuation success served to emphasize the matter and was just one more embarrassment that Halsey had to explain. And the potential of the next fight on the next island having the same lengthy results was almost assured if something could not be done to stop the continual "nuisance" of the Express. He just could not afford another Guadalcanal. There had to be an answer.

The obvious next step toward Halsey's initially planned objective of Rabaul was through the New Georgia and Vella Lavella regions of the Solomons chain, and the Japanese knew this and were already preparing for the likelihood of this new campaign. They had another powerful presence at Munda, New Georgia, and operations to strengthen this area were quickly set into play.

Even before the fighting on Guadalcanal had concluded, elements of the Tokyo Express were already being directed to assist with shoring up the defenses at Munda. During the month of December 1942, no less than eight Express runs of troops and supplies were made directly to the shores of New Georgia Island, as preparations for this assured next fight were given considerable attention. Still, throughout this time, reinforcement of Guadalcanal remained the top priority and, despite its admitted uselessness toward any type of victory, Tanaka continued to pursue his missions as ordered.

By early February 1943, however, the focus was forced to change. As Tanaka was now absent from the theater and the final evacuation of Guadalcanal was complete, the status of the Express was questioned. A short three-week sabbatical was ordered. Koyanagi was to use this time to rest, replenish, and reorganize his ships and crews, while he was to study how best to continue the next series of assured reinforcement operations. Obviously, the feasibility of such an effort was not his to determine, yet his direction would surely affect the outcome.

As suspected, the reprieve did not last long. Regardless of the strain it placed on the remaining destroyer forces, by the first week of March the Express was once again back to its old activities. Hoping to make any additional advance by the Americans as costly an effort as possible, the Japanese hierarchy was determined to throw before their adversary as much men and materiel as possible—even though they stood no tactical chance at winning. There did, however, still remain an open window for the award of some type of negotiated settlement; and if the Americans could be kept off balance and hampered from gaining a speedy advance, such opportunity could still be won. The war was at this point a war of attrition and wills, as to who was willing to suffer the most pain. Japanese leadership continued to believe the Americans were weak in resolve and that continued heavy losses would drive them to a table of truce. This remained their only true hope toward victory.

The Express was obviously in the forefront of keeping this hope alive, this by attempting to keep the attention of the Pacific war centered in the Solomons and far from the shores of the homeland. But the new challenges being faced by the Express were increasingly more difficult. American airpower controlled the Eastern Solomons' skies. This wide-reaching air arm made any daylight efforts by the Express an impossible venture. Additionally, despite Japanese efforts to shut down their networks, the coast watchers continued their reporting and, in conjunction with air reconnaissance, allowed almost no opportunity for the Express to move without notice. Despite this, Koyanagi still maintained the structure of the Express force, and determined, as had Tanaka, that success—if any were possible—could only be attained by using these fast destroyers and capitalizing on what these teams did best, night missions. But, during this next campaign, instead of taking troops and supplies directly to their objective (New Georgia Island) as Tanaka had done at Guadalcanal, Koyanagi chose instead to deliver his Express cargoes to a neighboring island and from there ferry the troops and supplies the rest of the way by boat. Kolombangara became the chosen medium. From here it was but a short distance across open water to Munda, and the Japanese could use armed barges to complete the transport of men and goods, allowing his destroyers shorter and safer routes. It proved to be a wise decision, and gave new life to the Express and its "nuisance."

By using armed "Daihatsu" barges to complete the final stages of the Express deliveries, Koyanagi was able to provide some added insurance to the survivability of his precious destroyers. The various routes available to his Express conveniently allowed his ships the luxury of hugging close to the coastlines of the nearby islands, an important aid at masking them from enemy radar. This increased the dangers of striking uncharted reefs, but the destroyer commanders were willing to take such risks in lieu of the alternatives. Kolombangara, too, offered several convenient drop-off points whereby the commanders were allowed some variances of approach while possibly avoiding enemy contact altogether. But, if contact was made, Japanese commanders also had confidence that they remained the superior force in nighttime combat, that after dark in a head-to-head bout with American cruisers and destroyers they could and would prevail. Their night engagement training was better, their optics for seeing at night were the best, their torpedoes were beyond the scope of anything their adversaries could field, and their gunfire had consistently proven more accurate and deadlier than any of the opponents they had so far faced—all of this despite a lack of radar.

Use of the Daihatsu barges, in addition to allowing the Express even greater flexibility and advantage, would also prove to be a highly effective mode of troop reinforcement. These barges, some armed with their own torpedoes and mounting as many as three 25-millimeter machine guns, could also fight quite effectively on their own, and give a potent sting to any would-be attackers.

First and foremost, however, these barges had to be found to be stopped. The Daihatsu had its greatest advantage at night as, while traveling close to shore, they were almost invisible, either to the naked eye or to radar. Even on the open sea, if spaced correctly, they were difficult to detect. In addition, their shallow draft, even when fully loaded, made them immune to torpedoes, while only the most accurate gunfire could stop them.

The most feared nighttime menace to either the Express destroyers or their Daihatsu cohorts was thought to be the pesky American torpedo boats that consistently prowled close along the islands and around the narrow passages, and for these they were constantly vigilant. American planes, though extremely deadly during daylight hours, were only a secondary threat at night, while cruisers—with their continued poor performances—rated a distant third, and destroyers—due to the way the Americans had deployed them in every previous combat situation—were likely to be of minimal issue. The fact remained, at this point in time, that Japanese naval commanders still had very little respect for the fighting capabilities of the opposing surface fleet—and such was to be a critical error.

Newly assigned to the Tokyo Express, Capt. Tameichi Hara had a devout wariness of and a fervent distrust for the disregard his superiors placed in American ability. He stood tall and rigid at his place on the bridge of his flagship, *Shigure*, as his gaze was frozen forward, oblivious to any others around him while in study of his new assignment. He was no novice to the dangers presented by this war. He had served under Tanaka during the landings on the Philippines and during the action at Java Sea. He had even served in the Solomons already, having participated in some of the deadly naval engagements fought for Guadalcanal (surviving the deadly November 13–15, 1942, battle). He, therefore, found his surroundings to be very familiar. Rabaul's Simpson Harbor had changed little in appearance since his last visit here; it was still a busy hub of activity and remained a haven for many of the Imperial Navy's powerful warships. There was, however, one marked difference. It was not so much noticed in the landscape, but it was seen in the eyes of every other officer and sailor he met. Morale here was lower than he had ever before experienced. That the war was not going well was obvious, but the truth of it was far worse than he expected. It was just as he had feared; the stubborn pride of a closed-minded leadership was directing the fleet to certain disaster—and Hara was not looking forward to the experience.

Tameichi Hara, the son of a poor farm family, had a very humble beginning, in some ways very similar to that of Arleigh Burke. He was born on October 16, 1900, just one year and three days before Arleigh. He was part of a large family, having two brothers and two sisters, of whom he was the youngest. Work on the farm was shared by everyone in his family, and the hours were long and tiring. Learning respect for the family and for the strong work ethics demanded by the farm was an essential part of growing up, and was to affect the strong character of Tameichi's future. But, much like Arleigh, he had little desire for pursuing the farming trade.

Tameichi's home was on the outskirts of Takamatsu City, situated on Shikoku Island and facing the Inland Sea. Here he was offered a wonderful view of a land rich with great seaside history and tradition. This land held special meaning to his family, as their ancestry was once part of the region's upper class, wealthy and extremely influential. The Haras were of the lineage of the once powerful samurai, the centuries-old warrior sect considered the elite among fighting men and the most loyal guardians to the warlords of old. The land had, however, greatly changed since those long-ago days. A more moderate and modern Japan had since stripped the regional warlords and samurai of their power and wealth, favoring instead a centralized form of government with far more worldly acceptance. Still, a distinct pride at having had such an esteemed heritage remained widely present among those families who once held such position—and they dreamed of the day when they would once again hold such honor.

Moichiro Hara, Tameichi's grandfather and patriarch of the Hara clan, was one of the dreamers. He was the last of the family to hold the title of samurai, and he still lived during the first few years of Tameichi's youth. This old warrior was to be a powerful influence on the boy, as the elder Hara reveled at telling his favorite grandson the many stories of his days as defender of the emperor. He often recounted the days when he bravely struck his sword in combat while charging on horseback into some opposing throng. His stories captivated young Tameichi, and he would never forget the spark of excitement each recollection created in the old man's eyes. His grandfather beamed at the telling of each tale, as each recounting seemed to restore in him a long-lost hope that such pride might again one day find its place with the family, perhaps with Tameichi himself.

Sadly, Moichiro passed away in 1907—just prior to Tameichi entering grammar school—but not before passing on his dream. While on his deathbed, the elder Hara called his youngest grandson to his side. Tameichi later wrote of the event: "He called my name and asked that I come close. As I was just six, my parents brought me to his side and put my hands in one of his. The other hand clutched his treasured samurai sword, which he finally placed in my tiny hands. He coughed and struggled to say, 'Tamei, this is yours. Now listen carefully to your grandpa's last words . . . Tameichi Hara! You are the son of samurai and you will remember that. *A samurai lives in such a way that he is always prepared to die.* Don't misinterpret that teaching. Never seek an easy death, for that would be against the true spirit of Bushido. I have told you many times about fine samurai who suffered great hardships to achieve their missions. Try to do likewise . . .' Though I was too young to understand all he said, the dying man's expression of great affection for me was clear and unforgettable."[15]

Instilled with his grandfather's pride, Tameichi entered school with a mission. He proved himself to be an exceptional pupil, graduating from grammar school at the head of his class and the first of his family ever to be an honor student. Despite such effort, the next step to furthering his education remained in doubt. None of his brothers or sisters had ever gone on to middle school, as the family could not afford the extra expense. Tameichi, however, presented his family with a bit of a dilemma, as they could not readily justify a waste of their son's promise to mere farm work. Still, how would it be possible to overcome such a financial burden? The solution was offered by Tameichi's older brothers; they would help pay for his education, if their father would agree. He did.

In Japan, middle school accepted only a select few. Applicants were given entrance exams and from these only a small percentage was selected to go on. Remarkably, Tameichi managed to be chosen, and for the next five years he maintained a high position within his class, ranking 10th out of 150 boys.

Clearly Tameichi was smart enough to advance on to college, which provided him with ample opportunities for a positive future. Considerable thought was to be given to his career. Finances, however, remained for him the one most critical obstacle. If he chose a government assisted education at a "normal school," the only career option open to him was that of teaching. But, if he chose a military school, a whole range of exciting careers awaited him. Since he was "the son of samurai," the choice seemed only too clear.

As his grandfather had been a cavalry soldier, Tameichi first considered the Army as his career choice. On second thought, however, the area of his home was rich with naval tradition, as many important naval battles had been fought in the Inland Sea just off Takamatsu. Hara noted, "My desire for a navy career was no doubt inspired by the naval heritage of my native province."[16] He suspected his grandfather would understand.

But getting into the naval academy at Eta Jima was a most difficult proposition. The entrance exam was notoriously tough to pass. For added security, Tameichi decided to take both the Army and Navy entrance exams, just in case. The decision required twice the study as well as travel to two different locations, yet he felt it to be the right thing to do. The Army exam was given close to his home and he felt very comfortable with his performance. The Navy exam, however, required him to travel to Hiroshima, on the island of Honshu, and the distance and unfamiliarity of location caused him considerable anxiety. This was his first time being away from home, on his own, and he found the experience a bit unsettling. He returned to his family very uncertain as to how he had fared with the tough exam. He needed not worry, however, as he passed both exams quite handily.

Choosing the Navy, Tameichi entered the Eta Jima Naval Academy to become a part of the graduating class of 1921, formally known as Naval Academy Class 46. The rigors of the academy were extremely difficult, even brutal, but Tameichi survived to graduate 40th out of a class of 150 cadets. It was a very proud moment. Still, being the perfectionist that he was, Hara later stated, "I knew . . . I could have done better."[17]

In the immediate months and years that followed, Tameichi grew in both knowledge and experience. While still a cadet he participated in a training tour that allowed him to visit many of the world's major ports, including San Diego and New York. He trained on cruisers and destroyers, and gained special instruction in naval torpedo and gunnery tactics. He watched with curiosity as the Imperial Navy adjusted to—and often circumvented or outright cheated—the post–World War I restraints imposed on its fleet by the despised Naval Limitation Treaties. He participated in and saw firsthand the turmoil ongoing in China and was seemingly confused by the world's negative reactions to Japanese interventions. That a broader war was on the horizon was almost certain, yet Hara gave world events little of his attention. He was still young, and his mental focus remained more on his immediate personal agendas and internal naval training rather than on the state of world affairs.

Tameichi's life seemed filled with continuous and delightful moments of change, and these were to consume his energies. By the summer of 1927 he reached the rank of lieutenant. In the spring of 1929 he married Chizu Asayama, the daughter of a wealthy businessman; and one year later she bore him his first child, a daughter. Also, at this time he met and became friends with then-Captain Chuichi Nagumo—the same who as an admiral would later lead the attack on Pearl Harbor—from whom Hara found a great deal of encouragement at seeking higher pursuits within the naval hierarchy. Despite such encouragement, Tameichi could not find the determination required at reaching staff rank; his mind was more obsessed with other, more personal agendas. Principally, after having spent considerable time as a torpedo officer aboard the destroyer *Akikaze*, Hara was thoroughly convinced that Japanese naval torpedo doctrine was outdated and in desperate need of revision. He was confident that he could improve the faulty doctrine and he spent the next two years secretly assembling a new set of rules based on his own complicated set of calculations.

To prove his new theory, Tameichi secretly began using his new doctrine during fleet exercises and quickly gained a reputation at being the highest scoring torpedo officer of the whole fleet. Once having gained such a title, he finally felt the timing was right to release his new manual to the Imperial Navy for critique. Surprisingly, Hara's theory was energetically accepted and his manual—though having some revisions and adaptations—was made the official new torpedo doctrine. Tameichi later wrote, "I still take more pride in my achievement of correcting Japanese torpedo doctrine than in any other activity of my naval career."[18]

In the Solomons campaign, Hara's torpedo doctrine was used with destructive effect. During the November 1942 naval battle of Guadalcanal, while serving as commander of the destroyer *Amatsukaze*, Tameichi witnessed firsthand and executed action that displayed the great gravity with which the Imperial Navy's superior torpedo tactics played in this new struggle. During this action, however, his destroyer received some very pronounced wounds of its own, requiring several months of convalescence for his ship and crew. In the interim, Hara again found favor for promotion; in February he was given command of

Destroyer Division 27 and in May he was awarded the rank of captain. His new division was supposed to consist of four destroyers, but he found his command down to three, and two of these were on loan to other divisions with higher priority missions.

Hara arrived at Rabaul aboard his flagship, the older and terribly weathered destroyer, *Shigure*—and without the rest of his division in tow—in the closing weeks of July 1943. The situation was not good.

So much had happened since Hara's previous days in this region. Every report Hara received disturbed him more. The number of ships and men lost to recent actions was staggering, yet the direction of the Navy's leadership seemed determined to continue down the same old paths. He was confused and bewildered by a leadership that seemed so unable—or unwilling—to adjust to the reality that their enemy was strong, even superior, and growing stronger by the day. During his previous visit to the homeland, he marveled at how—even while facing correlated economic strains—everyone seemed so detached from the war while seemingly being totally complacent to the losses received by the combined military in the South Pacific. There was such a disconnect from the truth, even among the upper echelon of the military command, as the misguided propaganda campaigns were successfully misleading everyone. Even at Saipan, the military nerve center in the Central Pacific, he found complacency, as during his northern passage of the island a flight of patrolling planes completely ignored his advance and failed even to seek recognition of his ship. Hara noted, "Such . . . laxity . . . was unwarranted and unforgivable while Japanese were being bled white in the Solomons."[19]

Despite his misgivings, Hara was grateful for the opportunity to have had time to visit his home in Japan. The rest he received was welcomed and the time spent with his wife, Chizu, and his two little girls, Yoko and Keiko, was a joy. Still, the desire to return with his ship to the Solomons and the fight they had left behind remained paramount on his mind. It was an impassioned feeling, the drive of a true warrior, a samurai, wherein the powerful lure of combat begged his participation. However, now that he was back, he found plenty of reasons to give such a desire second thought.

The situation was far worse than he had ever anticipated. The gifted Tanaka—under whom Hara had previously served and greatly respected—had long since been relieved of his command of the Express and tragically demoted to a desk job in Singapore, which Hara believed was a great mistake. In another demoralizing blow, the Navy's March attempt to reinforce Lae, on New Guinea, had ended in doleful disaster, with fourteen of sixteen ships sunk and thousands of men lost during a massive enemy air assault. To add to this downward spiral of events, on April 14, Admiral Yamamoto—the Imperial Navy's elite commander-in-chief and planner of the Pearl Harbor attack—and several officers of his staff were killed in an aerial ambush during a planned visit to Bougainville. This obviously left a terrible void in leadership within the fleet. Then, on June 30, just as had been anticipated, the next offensive, the American invasion of New Georgia, began in earnest. To this point the American advance was continuing and nothing was having any real success at slowing it—nothing that is except the reconstituted efforts of the Tokyo Express. Hara noted with pride, while hinting an underlying sense of regret, "the destroyers of the celebrated 'Tokyo Express' were the real work horses of the South Pacific."[20]

No doubt the awkward use of destroyers in the Express effort was looked upon by the fleet commanders as a necessary sacrifice, but the high price could only have value if the American advance could be forced to stall—and this was a tall order to fill, especially at this late stage of the Solomons campaign. Hara was not confident of its success.

As another newcomer to the Express, the genteel Capt. Kaju Sugiura also was not blind to the sacrifice ongoing in the Solomons. He would have likely agreed with Hara's evaluation of the situation; yet he would do so only in private as—Tanaka's experience had taught most regional commanders—open criticisms of high command decisions were damaging to one's career. Sugiura, who had aspirations of reaching flag rank, did not intend to challenge his orders, regardless of any concerns he might have. He would obey and execute.

As commander of Destroyer Division 4, Sugiura was another of a small group of highly skilled destroyer commanders just recently pressed into service in the Solomons. The forty-seven-year-old captain was among the best destroyer officers produced by the Imperial Navy, and his abilities were expected to keep the Express at the top of its game. There was no doubt that Sugiura had noteworthy credentials. He was a graduate of the prestigious Naval College. He was an expert in the arts of gunnery and torpedo tactics, and had even spent several years of his prewar career instructing these and other classes at Yokosuka. He had on two different occasions commanded destroyers, *Tade* and *Uzuki*, and subsequently commanded Destroyer Divisions 5 and 17 prior to taking command of Division 4. But, regardless of such an illustrious background, Sugiura had very little experience in the Solomons and even less under true combat conditions.

Hara initially held great respect for Sugiura and referred to him as a "friend" and a "highly regarded" officer, but he soon doubted the commander's competency at leadership in a theater where the threats posed by the opposing surface fleet were increasing daily.[21] Like Tanaka, Hara saw in many of his fellow officers a lack of respect for the enemy and his ability to learn from his mistakes, and he was often very vocal about his concerns. "We could not count on the enemy for such stupidity," he wrote.[22] Sugiura, on the other hand, allowed his combat inexperience and personal ambitions to intervene and dictate that he not take any bold stance on the side of prudence. He would not challenge the slightest detail of his orders, regardless of any concerns that might arise, which Hara understood only too well.

Despite their obvious differences, both Hara and Sugiura were destined to join in the next round of reinforcement missions. At Rabaul, Hara had hoped to be joined by the rest of his division so that he might have some control over his own destiny, but such did not happen; his other two destroyers still remained on loan to other units. As a result, he and his flagship, *Shigure*, were the odd players out.

The situation was similar for Sugiura. Though he did have a one-ship advantage over Hara by commanding the destroyers *Hagikaze* and *Arashi*, he too was operating with less than full division strength. Both divisions were therefore forced to supplement where needed, and where needed was with a mixed command of troop-laden destroyers bound for the Eastern Solomons. Hara expressed his doubts quite loudly when he wrote that he "hoped luck would be with us."[23] Within a week's time he would have his answer.

By August 1, 1943, the Express had made well over one hundred reinforcement and bombardment sorties into the deadly region of the Solomons. Regardless of the fact that the American advance had in no way been stopped, it had certainly been slowed—and this continued to provide the Japanese with unfeigned hope.

Truly the cost had been devastatingly high. But, despite heavy losses, when boldly confronted by its adversaries the Express consistently gave more punishment than it took—and this added to its courage. In reality, the "Tokyo Express" was far more than Sherman's colorful "hellova nuisance," it was a proven obstacle that remained for the Americans a steadfast threat to the entire South Pacific offensive. The very fact that the Express continued to operate, often with impunity, was an extreme embarrassment to Halsey and the U.S. Navy. Well over half of the Marine and Army casualties in the Solomons, as well as a large number of naval casualties, could be attributed to the reinforcement and bombardment successes of the Express. For as long as it had such potential it would not voluntarily retreat.

The Express had established itself as the Imperial Navy's samurai fleet, fearless and determined, and was willing to suffer many hardships at meeting its objectives. It would not surrender. To stop it would require far more than a good bruising—this had been done already—it would require a sound defeat. When charged with a mission, only death could stop the samurai. Halsey had tried, on several occasions, to do just that, to end the life of the Express, but with disappointing and often devastating results. He desperately needed someone or some group to close out the contest, to boldly take the fight directly to the Express, someone or some group who could be just as fearless as their opponent and climb into the Solomons ring to score a knockout. He was about to get just that.

Chapter Five

Tulagi

The Gathering

If indeed Halsey was to find a match for the meddlesome Tokyo Express, he was most likely to find it at Tulagi. A small sliver of an island and, by any description, less than appealing, Tulagi was hardly more than a slender tropical tuft of green surrounded by water. It was terribly dwarfed by its most immediate neighbor, Florida Island, and even more so by its other neighbor, Guadalcanal. Its significance to the campaign appeared, at first glance, a good bit meager. But Tulagi was the natural guardian of the region's most protected anchorage, the deep-water haven of Purvis Bay, currently the lair to a large number of the fleet's destroyers and boasting a conclave of the region's most tested veterans. It was here, well forward and in the midst of this cruel campaign, where these roving Solomons sailors were to find a rare safe refuge, a modest but sufficient shelter providing them security, provisions, and rest. The real estate was highly treasured. For it was from Tulagi that nearly every destroyer-related mission was to have its start—and hopefully at Tulagi every mission would conclude.

To Lieutenants Albert Olsen and Vining Sherman—since their ship, *Dunlap*, had only first entered Purvis Bay on the morning of July 30—Tulagi was far less than impressive. The island they viewed seemed void of any obvious appeal and, despite the busy activity ongoing all around, displayed itself as uninviting. Still, both gentlemen were intrigued just enough to feel beckoned to go ashore and investigate what if anything this place had to offer.

In the afternoon, not long after their ship was securely moored, the two officers obliged their desires and disembarked on a joint passage to visit dry land. Surely this otherwise unremarkable spot of rock and jungle could produce something for their enjoyment, or so they hoped. At the very least, they would stroll along the island's narrow sandy shoreline for a bit of relaxation or venture into its dense interior in pursuit of its hidden natural treasures. But, once ashore, the two appeared quite content to progress no farther than the local watering hole, the Tulagi Club, a mere shack of a structure that was home to the officers' canteen.

Here at this rudimentary tavern, they quietly paused, each briefly satisfied by this facility's offering of refreshment, a liquid cleansing of both mind and soul that seemingly met their most immediate need. They had hoped to find some escape from the daily pressures of duty and stresses of war, and here they had found it—even if only temporarily.

These two officers, however, soon had their fill of the Tulagi Club, grabbed a couple of beers to go, and proceeded on with their predetermined investigations. Just as they had initially surmised, their venture quickly divulged that the island offered little in the way of true excitement. This place was no vacation spot. It was busy, hot, and cluttered.

Along their meandering path Olsen and Sherman observed several sailors and Marines, as well as a large number of native workers (stevedores), tasked with nonstop motion, their prominent purpose that of loading and unloading large quantities of equipment and supplies. This was critical work, needed for keeping the nearby destroyer operations ongoing. A torpedo and ammunition storage area was located nearby, and many workers were here busily removing such deadly stores from the belly of an LST (Landing Ship Tank) and transporting this stock to its proper shore locations. Other workers were loading the same types of cargo onto yard boats, to be distributed to the warships anchored in the nearby harbor. Progressing yet farther they passed by "Calvertville," a shanty town that was headquarters to Motor Torpedo Boat (MTB) Flotilla One and home to its leader, Comm. Allen P. Calvert. Though most of the flotilla had by this date moved on to a forward base on Rendova, a couple of the plucky PTs remained dockside for their viewing.

Off to the north and east, gazing past Tulagi's small harbor and farther still across the turquoise blue of Purvis Bay—where their ship *Dunlap* and a few other destroyers were presently at anchor—the two officers could clearly see the large mountainous island of Florida. This island was covered in rich green foliage and crowned by a pale white cloud of heavy mist. To the south, they could see only as far as Tulagi's high ground. Nevertheless, they both knew that in this direction, no more than 15 miles distant, lay the infamous island of Guadalcanal, the embattled ground that had taken six long months to conquer. In between lay Savo Sound, more ominously known as "Iron Bottom Bay," the eternal resting place for an alarming number of warships and their crews—and the spot where eight months earlier Olsen's brother had met his tragic fate.

Olsen suddenly stopped his stride, paused at the narrows of the sandy beach, and looked determinedly toward the top of a nearby palm. Then, with careful aim, he drew back his throwing arm and tossed his empty beer bottle skyward. With the accuracy of a major leaguer's pitch, the bottle streaked a line to knock loose a nice-sized coconut, sending it tumbling to the sandy ground below. "Lieutenant Olsen . . . and I were after coconuts with which to make a cocktail cup," Sherman later noted with a bit of jest.[1] But, for Olsen, this was no joke. The reasoning for the proposed drinking vessel was unspoken but the sentiment behind it was well known; Olsen begged for even a small part in a great victory against the Japanese, someday, any day when he might hoist his new cup in a toast for avenging his brother's death. Sherman picked up the fallen trophy and handed it to his friend, understanding his pain while nodding his agreement—the victory would surely come.

Triumph in the Solomons, however, had so far remained an elusive commodity. Even so, there was finally reason for having some confidence that it would one day be reached. For, despite the fight being frustratingly slow, there had been progress to report: The battles for Guadalcanal were now concluded, the Russells had been occupied, Rendova had been captured, and a whole new operation was ongoing. "The New Georgia campaign was in full swing," Lieutenant Davison noted. "Harmon had cleaned up Rendova, landed at Onavisa [*sic*] Inlet and Rice Anchorage, thrown up effective roadblocks and was closing in on Munda airstrip."[2] The march toward Tokyo was at long last moving forward—even if at a feeble pace.

Davison—whose dire realisms often cautioned otherwise—had acquired a renewed sense of optimism for the future, and for good reason. The New Georgia campaign brought with it some interesting new challenges and, with these, a promise of some real change in naval aggressiveness. First and foremost, there were new leaders in town; Adm. Theodore Wilkinson was now the new task force commander, and with him came a new task group commander, Arleigh Burke. The lieutenant had heard many positive things about both officers and was anxious to learn of their plans for the future. In addition, Davison had earned a promotion and, with it, a new position of authority. "I was Exec [Executive Officer—the very same command position, on the very same ship, held by Arleigh Burke less than five years earlier] of one of a group of six 1500s, three *Gridleys* out of my squadron and three *Benhams* out of the other outfit, that had been thrown together as a high-speed striking group in an effort to clean up on the barge traffic." Davison then added with rare approval, "We were based at 'Nervous Purvis,' just adjacent to Tulagi. . . ."[3]

Tulagi, as experienced by Olsen and Sherman and as noted by Davison, had an important role to play in this campaign—a role that already carried a good amount of history. Before the war, as the Solomons were originally under the protection of the British Empire, Tulagi was the regional capital of an insignificant and virtually unknown colonial occupation. For the most part, the surrounding islands were a wilderness, mostly void of inhabitants, except for a few indigenous tribes of Melanesians, who had long settled here, and an occasional copra plantation or missionary outpost. Even as late as 1939 the only notable settlement of the islands was that of Tulagi, though it was hardly anything to speak of. The settlement itself was small, having a single road that passed between a dual line of rudimentary structures, made up of some "Chinese shops and a small hotel, a wireless station and neat bungalows on the hill for the British officials."[4] The local church was built of palm wood and thatch. Life here was difficult, to say the least. No one who braved the isolation was to remain long—and, of these, most were to return to their native homelands bearing the lifelong effects of malaria.

It was also in 1939—with the world on the verge of all-out war—that a small defense force was established on the island. This force consisted mainly of a squadron of Catalina PBY "flying boats" of the Royal Australian Air Force, a reconnaissance group, and was supported by a small contingent of less than 200 police, most of whom were local natives. In the event that war did erupt, the Australians were given the broad task of defending Great Britain's numerous South Pacific interests, which included the Solomons—and, considering the nature of world events at the time, war did indeed appear inevitable. But Australia's military was more meager than massive, having greater concern for the defense of Australia itself rather than the many regions of inhospitality that surrounded it. A few minor bases, as at Tulagi, were initially established, but the extent of their worth was doubted. Even as the Pacific war exploded into reality, no one expected this region of the Eastern Solomons to become such a vital center of attention.

The surprise attack on Pearl Harbor changed most former perspectives, as every previous dynamic of the entire Pacific region was immediately placed at risk. With the U.S. Pacific Fleet severely wounded and temporarily incapacitated, the Japanese war machine was free to move across the Pacific at a mind-boggling pace. Within the first three months of this new Pacific war the Japanese made unparalleled gains, capturing Guam, Hong Kong, Wake, Singapore, Borneo, Java, New Guinea, Timor, and the Celebes. Soon after, they would add Burma and the Philippines. In addition to the great blow dealt the U.S. Fleet at Pearl, the Japanese just as ably disabled Britain's Royal Navy, quickly dispatching to the "Deep Six" (ocean's bottom) its two regional battleships, *Prince of Wales* and *Repulse*. The Japanese appeared unstoppable. Obviously, such offensive capabilities had been greatly underestimated by the Allies—a defensive mistake for which they were to pay dearly.

Having quickly gained one of their most primary objectives, the key capture of the oil-rich Dutch East Indies, the Japanese understood that assured defense of this new strategic holding would eventually require the defeat of Australia. Additionally, the Japanese also understood—acknowledging that the Pearl Harbor strike was only a temporary reprieve from the U.S. Pacific Fleet—time was not on their side. To aid in the isolation of the Australian homeland and to gain a true defensive edge in the South Pacific, the Imperial Japanese Navy quickly established two new powerful bases in the Bismarcks, one at Rabaul on New Britain and the other at Kavieng on New Ireland. They planned next to overrun New Caledonia, Fiji, and Samoa, this in the effort to cut all communication between Australia and the United States. The isolation was nearly complete—only three nasty little thorns remained capable of disrupting Japanese plans: (1) a spiteful fleet of American aircraft carriers under the command of Rear Adm. Frank J. Fletcher, (2) a strong Allied naval and air holdout at Port Moresby, Papua, New Guinea, and (3) the long-range reconnaissance capability of tiny Tulagi.

To eliminate these threats the Japanese set out with a three-pronged operation they christened "Operation 'MO'," a daring naval assault that intended to capture both Tulagi and Port Moresby while simultaneously drawing the American carrier fleet into a final, decisive battle. To accomplish their broad goal, the Japanese set sail with five task groups: an invasion group and a support group for Tulagi, an invasion group and a support group for Port Moresby, and a carrier strike group to round out the ticket. The operation was to begin on May 1, 1942.

Unfortunately for the Japanese, their plan was no secret. Due partly to Japanese operational arrogance, partly to an ingenious array of strategically located Australian Coastwatchers, and partly to an initial breakthrough by American intelligence at deciphering portions of the Imperial Japanese Navy's code, the commander of the Pacific Fleet, Adm. Chester W. Nimitz, was aware of Japanese intentions. He knew of their plans as early as mid-April; but stopping such new aggression was a whole other matter. With much of his main battle fleet sunk or severely damaged at Pearl Harbor, Nimitz had very few options available for a response. Frank Fletcher's carriers *Lexington* and *Yorktown* (less *Hornet* and *Enterprise*, not yet returned from their famous Doolittle Raid on Tokyo) and their supporting cast of cruisers and destroyers were all the fighting ships that were immediately available. Nimitz could perhaps count on some additional support from land-based fighters and bombers stationed within range, but their aid would likely be minimal at best. Nevertheless, the order was given.

The primary objective for the Allies was to hold Port Moresby. If the freshly arrived Gen. Douglas MacArthur—new commander of the Southwest Pacific recently transferred from the Philippines—was to have any chance at starting an offensive push in New Guinea, he must be able to retain control of this strategic base. The Australians, on the other hand, could find no worthwhile reason to fight for Tulagi. The outpost was of no serious consequence—or so they thought—and the small garrison stationed there had no chance at defending itself against a powerful Japanese landing force. In addition, the Americans would not, could not waste valuable time, ships, and materiel at aiding in the defense of such a perceived out-of-the-way and unimportant sector of the Pacific. So, on May 1, the Australian command ordered the island evacuated, conceding the ground along with all of the Solomons to the Japanese without a fight.

To this point, the Japanese plan appeared to be working. Tulagi was easily captured and the American carriers were coming out for battle. But this was as far as the Imperial plan progressed. Fletcher's planes quickly sortied for a surprise raid on the Japanese forces at their newly won Tulagi base, sinking three minelayers and one destroyer. Soon after, land-based bombers located portions of the Japanese navy's Port Moresby group, and their directions guided Fletcher's planes on another successful sortie, sinking the light carrier *Shoho*. The battle was, however, only just beginning. In response, Japanese planes located and lashed out at the American ships, sinking the fleet oiler *Neosho*, destroyer *Sims*, and the fleet carrier *Lexington*. A "crisscross" naval air battle ensued. During the melee that followed, the Japanese carrier *Shokaku* sustained heavy damage and was forced to make a premature departure from the operation. *Yorktown*, on the other hand, as with the rest of Fletcher's task force, survived the fight and escaped with only superficial wounds. Both sides were bloodied and neither could claim a knockout. This first major carrier battle in history ended with no clear-cut victor; yet it did force the Japanese to abort the rest of their operation, and this was no small matter.

Tactically, comparing the types of losses, the Coral Sea engagement was a victory for the Japanese—but strategically, by having thwarted the Japanese invasion of Port Moresby, the real victory was with the Americans. Just the same, the Allies had been forced to surrender more ground. Neither combatant fully realized just how important a role tiny Tulagi and its larger neighbor Guadalcanal would soon play in the future of the war. Nor did the Allies perceive the cost that would be exacted at taking these back. Had they known, perhaps they would not have been so eager to have given them away. Nevertheless, they would be retaken.

Tulagi was by early 1943 a fully secured possession of the U.S. Navy and was welcoming to its charter Arleigh Burke. The union had been a long time coming, and when the commander did finally arrive in the Solomons, in late January, he did so knowing that nearly all the major actions leading to the final capture of Guadalcanal were concluded. Even so, this new division commander was finally where he wanted to be, eager to play a role at seeing this war to a greater victory—as indeed he would. He hoisted his flag on the destroyer *Waller*, took his post on the bridge, and prepared to direct his ships off into mortal combat—completely unaware of the impact that his leadership was about to have toward winning this hard-fought campaign.

Despite his late arrival to the theater, Arleigh had long been working on a new set of destroyer tactics that he felt certain would show great success against the Japanese, and especially so in the Solomons. But to this commander's utter disappointment he quickly learned—as every other destroyer officer in the Solomons already knew—that destroyers had little or no opportunity to operate freely in the South Pacific and were more often than not refused any real chance at engaging the enemy one on one. Therefore, any true test of Burke's ideas was not to come readily, even regardless of his persistence at pitching them to his superiors.

Despite this limitation, Arleigh wasted little time at displaying his mettle; as on March 6, he tallied his first score, successfully blasting a Japanese destroyer, *Murasame*, while in support of the bombardment of Munda airfield, on New Georgia Island. This initial success brought considerable attention to Burke's presence and to his ideas, but far more importantly it taught the commander a very valuable lesson for the future.

During this action Arleigh had very nearly made a fatal mistake. He had failed to accept the validity of the information being forwarded to him by his talented veteran crew, and he waited—waited almost too long—for a visual confirmation of the enemy ships that were reported. As a result, he nearly lost the tactical advantage of surprise. It was this very same type of mistake that had cost Admiral Wright so dearly at Tassafaronga. This hesitation was against every lesson that Arleigh had ever taught; he had failed to respect his veteran crew and he had failed to act boldly. Burke was humbled in a way he did not expect, and he promised he would never fail in this manner again—and he would not.

More determined than ever, Commander Burke aggressively pitched his ideas for a new destroyer doctrine, and did so to anyone within earshot. For the most part he was ignored. But he did find a friendly ear with his new boss, Rear Adm. A. Stanton "Tip" Merrill.

Merrill, who was thirteen years Arleigh's senior and had a far more reserved character, found himself greatly impressed by his junior commander's persistence. The admiral liked Arleigh, thought highly of his talent, and enjoyed listening to his bold new ideas. He often encouraged Arleigh not to give up on his proposals—even requested that he submit them in writing—though he cautioned whether the theater was quite ready for such initiatives. Still, this positive attention was indeed inspiring to Arleigh, to say the least.

By June, Arleigh was again on the move, reassigned to the command of Destroyer Division 44. The commander transferred his flag to the destroyer *Conway* and immediately set to establishing his leadership. To his delight, he learned that his new assignment was soon to encompass far more than command of a destroyer division, but also that of a destroyer task group, designated as Task Group 31.2. In addition to his own division, he was to command any otherwise unattached destroyers for the elite purpose of independent missions against the Japanese throughout the Central Solomons and along the infamous Slot (the common track used by the Tokyo Express between New Britain and Guadalcanal). Arleigh was elated. This was the very opportunity he had been waiting for.

Arleigh's new boss was Rear Adm. Theodore S. "Ping" Wilkinson, a man with a fatherly appearance, strong and caring. He certainly was an inspirational figure, having a colorful history and a Medal of Honor as evidence of a courageous past. Just as Merrill had, Wilkinson quickly took a liking to his younger commander. They had a great deal in common, especially that they had both had important assignments with the Bureau of Ordnance. He truly expected great things from Burke, if not sooner than later.

During one of his many encounters with the admiral, Arleigh confided his destroyer doctrine. Wilkinson was intrigued, and was even willing to allow Burke some future lead, but other missions would first have to receive the commander's attention.

For the next full month Arleigh's ships continued their role as support, though on a more independent basis and with considerable latitude toward mobility. Beginning on July 22, two important missions were to occupy much of the commander's time. The first was an escort and bombardment mission at Enogai, New Georgia. It was during this operation that Arleigh fell against equipment on the bridge and cracked two of his ribs.[5] Not to be deterred, Burke hid his injury and accepted a second mission—a highly critical and extremely precise bombardment—at Munda, also on New Georgia. Throughout a period of over seventy-two hours the commander had little opportunity to rest. Still, Arleigh did not disappoint those who depended on him. His gunnery proved outstanding, and his mission was met with complete success.

For a reward, upon his return to Tulagi orders awaited Arleigh sending him and his division back to Noumea for some well-deserved rest and recreation. These orders were well intentioned, but, despite their positive intent, they did not set well at all with the commander. He was not about to deny his ships and crews their earned break from the action, but *he*—especially considering all that he had gone through to get here—he was not ready to leave, not just yet, not before getting his shot at the Tokyo Express. He immediately requested a meeting with Wilkinson. The admiral agreed. There were still other unattached destroyers in the area. "Let me have them," Arleigh begged.[6]

Wilkinson pondered the request. The activities of the Express were indeed increasing. And General Harmon, the commander in charge of the operations on New Georgia, was screaming for the Navy's help at stopping its deliveries. "Okay," Wilkinson conceded, "but only till I can find you a replacement. Then you go get your rest. Understood?"[7] Arleigh agreed.

Burke departed the headquarters a happy man. He had won his reprieve, though he knew time was not long on his side. He quickly returned to *Conway* and gave his ships their leave. Without much ado, he said his farewells and moved his flag to another destroyer, *Maury*, happy to once more be working with his old friend, Gelzer Sims. He would also retain his command of TG 31.2, now consisting of DesDiv 15 (under the flag of the most aggressive Comm. Rodger W. Simpson aboard *Lang*) and three to four other unattached veteran destroyers now a part of DesDiv 12 (an ad hoc group, most being recent reassignments given to the leadership of Arleigh's old classmate Frederick Moosbrugger aboard *Dunlap*). It was this very type of team Arleigh could have only dreamed of, well trained and experienced and led by the best—the perfect combination.

Arleigh's opportunities at testing his new command came quickly. On two different nights, July 31 and August 1, *Maury* departed Purvis Bay, Tulagi, on missions into enemy territory.

On the first operation Burke led four of his newly assigned destroyers (*Maury, Gridley, Craven*, and *Dunlap*) as escorts for a fast transport group to take supplies to embattled Marines at Oniavisi Inlet, New Georgia Island. As was typical of his aggressiveness, he hoped the Japanese might give challenge so he could engage his ships in a headlong attack; but the enemy did not appear.

Just the same, he did not waste this chance to practice the types of maneuvering he was to expect from his destroyers, and he put them through the tough rigors.

The second mission was even more direct, a search and destroy mission, seeking out an expected Tokyo Express run through Kula Gulf. *Maury* again departed Tulagi, this time leading five others (*Gridley*, *Craven*, *Sterett*, *Stack*, and *Wilson*) of the commodore's new destroyer team. As with a plan he had only recently devised, he divided his ships into two supporting columns, and they began their search.

Throughout this night Burke spent much of his time in *Maury*'s cramped combat center, located directly behind the bridge in the captain's former emergency cabin, where he watched as the ship's new executive officer, Lt. Russell Crenshaw, skillfully led his talented CIC (Combat Information Center) team. The heat within this small confine, amplified by the warmth emitted by a myriad of electronics, was sweltering. Arleigh did not relent. He mopped the sweat from his forehead and diligently conferred with Crenshaw, keeping pace with each movement the team tracked while consuming each bit of information they extracted. Somewhere out in the darkness an enemy force was making its move, of this he felt certain. He was right, too; a four-destroyer Tokyo Express (including Sugiura's *Arashi* and *Hagikaze* as well as Hara's *Shigure*), loaded to the gunnels with troops and supplies and under the overall command of Capt. Katsamori Yamashiro, was indeed proceeding into Kula Gulf. Unfortunately for Arleigh, Yamashiro had entered through the back door, driving through Vella Gulf and Blackett Strait to deliver his goods. Despite an intensive effort, Commander Burke's ships failed at locating Yamashiro in the misty black; on this first try he wasn't even close. Yamashiro made a near perfect escape (his flagship, *Amagiri*, received damage when it accidentally sliced through Lt. John F. Kennedy's PT-109 on his return), leaving Arleigh to search for him on another hopeful day.

Despite this initial miss, the commodore's ships and crews returned to base with their morale high and their adrenaline pumping. They were ready to go again, and they would not hesitate to say so. Arleigh alone was responsible for these loyalties, and especially so from *Maury*'s complement. He made both the junior officer and the average seaman feel special around him. He cut no quarter at getting to know the men who worked for him. He would briefly converse with them, laugh with them, and offer a friendly disposition. And he did so with purpose. For he needed these men's abilities and he sought out their trust. If he was to have any success in the grueling Solomons theater, he needed more than officers and sailors who were willing to work for him; he needed a *team* that was willing to work *with* him, and with the same type of mettle and intensity that he himself displayed. He would lead by example, exhort by command, and congratulate by personal praise. And sailors would proudly follow wherever he dared to challenge.

On August 3, however, Arleigh's time did indeed finally run out. Admiral Wilkinson sent for his commander to meet him at his headquarters at Koli. Arleigh knew what this meant. Arriving on shore, alone and tired, he took his time with his approach to the admiral's command center. His exhaustion was evident in every step he took. Still, he considered trying one more argument on his own behalf, but then he thought better. It was no use; there could be no further delay in his relief. He saw the admiral standing outside his headquarters. And he saw a jeep with a driver waiting nearby. This he knew was to be his transport over to Henderson, the airfield from where he was destined to fly to Noumea. Deep down he hoped the admiral had changed his mind, as he hoped that he might be given just a little more time to continue his quest. He truly knew otherwise.

Wilkinson greeted Burke with both congratulations and concern. He admired Arleigh for his excellent efforts. He would like to keep him. But he could find no good excuse for risking any losses due to exhaustion. As good as Arleigh was, he was human and needed rest. The admiral understood the commander's disappointment. The timing was not the best, but it was necessary. Arleigh would not be gone long. Wilkinson knew this talented commander would be back, and soon. Besides, he was receiving a promotion, to captain, and being handed a new command, a squadron of brand new 2,100-ton Fletcher class destroyers—sure to be a powerful combination. And there was plenty of war left, plenty more opportunities to challenge the enemy. When he returned, he would be well rested, clear of mind, and ready to beat the pants off the Japanese. Until then, Arleigh's torch, his command of Task Group 31.2, would have to pass to someone else.

Back aboard *Maury*, the decks seemed a bit more vacant than with the usual departure of just one man. The ship was far quieter than it had been in a very long time. Her crew appeared reserved and much more distant than just a few hours before. Burke was gone and his departure had brought a real sense of loss.

Commander Sims and Lieutenant Crenshaw, in particular, returned to their duties feeling a special concern at having witnessed Arleigh leave. Long before Burke had arrived aboard *Maury*, Crenshaw had grown to admire the man. Sims spared no salt at telling stories of his former captain—some he even requested his officers not repeat . . . especially to the commodore. Overall, however, Sims's yarns correctly described Arleigh as a gifted leader, widely respected by those who knew him, and one with whom one's life could be entrusted to wise decisions during combat.

Both Sims and Crenshaw were in agreement; the theater could not long do with Burke's absence. "It was with genuine regret that the officers and men of the Striking Force saw him go," wrote Crenshaw. "He had been just what the force had needed."[8]

The commodore's presence had indeed been truly special to *Maury*'s officers and crew. His time aboard had only been for a few days, but it was enough to create a great sense of pride among all of the warriors of the striking force. The men that had served under him had found Burke's aggressiveness very appealing, as he was intent at forcing a duel with the enemy at every opportunity but intelligently so. No one had questioned his command, as everyone felt at ease with his leadership, confident that wherever this commander might lead, he would lead with purpose—and with success. They did not feel as sure with Burke's replacement.

To most South Pacific sailors, Frederick Moosbrugger remained a somewhat obscure individual, thin of face and slightly built; he displayed little resemblance to the tough destroyer commanders the Striking Force was accustomed to seeing. Freddie was an unassuming figure, exhibiting far less charisma than his predecessor. His name was far from the ordinary and a bit hard to pronounce. A good portion of the men had never even heard of him. He was neither brash nor boastful, and he projected no outward disposition toward aggressiveness. Indeed, he appeared to have more of the persona of a schoolteacher than that of wartime naval officer. "Freddie . . . was well known . . . as a pleasant, quiet gentleman," Crenshaw wrote. "He was certainly experienced and qualified, but we in *Maury* didn't expect him to be an Arleigh Burke." The lieutenant's sentiment was equally shared among most others of the force, as few could imagine the courage and ability this man was soon to display. "We had a lot to learn," Crenshaw concluded.[9]

Lt. Comm. Clifton Iverson, the broad-shouldered Texan who skippered the destroyer *Dunlap*, found no surprise in Moosbrugger's new appointment. He knew the commander quite well, as he had served with him for several months. The thirty-five-year-old native of Houston thought highly of his immediate boss: "He was a great shipmate and Commodore," Iverson wrote.[10] "Swifty Clifty," as Iverson was affectionately known to his crew, felt honored to call Moosbrugger his friend.

Even as Freddie first raised his flag on *Dunlap*, in late March 1943, then establishing his new command of Destroyer Division 12, he and Iverson quickly developed into quite a team—both on a personal and a professional level. Throughout their time together, on several different occasions, the two had—as commanders and confidants—often discussed the crucial role of the destroyer and destroyer tactics. Much like his old classmate, Burke, Moosbrugger held a steadfast belief that the destroyer was being improperly used in the Solomons, having a concern "about the way destroyers had been used in some of the earlier night actions where we had suffered heavy losses."[11] Iverson agreed. Foremost among their concerns was the aggressive use of torpedoes—or, more to the point, how they perceived the fleet's improper use of torpedoes and lack of aggressiveness. It was an area about which the commander had considerable expertise, and he had developed some sharp opinions about how a greater success could be better achieved.

Unlike Burke, however, Moosbrugger tended to be far more selective and reserved when sharing his thoughts. He was not known among the inner circles as a harsh critic, outspoken or otherwise. This passionate side of the commander was mostly hidden, and as such was a characteristic that Iverson had a bit of monopoly at witnessing, offering him some rare insight that others did not readily see. Therefore, unlike Crenshaw and others of the Task Group, who appeared to doubt Moosbrugger's warrior-like instincts, Iverson exhibited a firm confidence in Freddie's ability to aggressively lead. He applauded Wilkinson's choice, and he suspected (correctly) that the admiral had not made such a choice lightly. After all, Burke had left a large pair of shoes to fill, and the inherited challenges were sure to require a sure-footed leader if stumbles were to be avoided and successes met. There appeared no doubt in the admiral's decision; he displayed no need, as some fairytale prince, to search throughout his dominion for a proper fit to his empty set of slippers. He knew exactly to whom he should go. Wilkinson's selection of successor was made swiftly and without reservation, even before the toll of the midnight bells, and it was to prove a very wise choice indeed.

Nevertheless, such an abrupt change in command, especially while employed in the midst of a dangerous war zone, was always a reason for experienced veterans to display their concern. Some officers were the strict, hard, impersonal types, who could make life tough on the ordinary seaman. Others were more liberal, compassionate and interactive with their command, making them more tolerable. Either type, regardless of personality, was certain to bring change, if not in method, then in expectations. Rarely, therefore, did a friendship relationship ever evolve between an officer and his charge of enlisted men.

By regulation, intermingling of the two was not permitted, and especially so during wartime. Such was understood; good leadership often measured on the ability to make tough, quick decisions without regard to personal biases. But the atmosphere on destroyers, where there were such small numbers and closeness of living, often forced a relationship that was indeed far more personal than the norm. Officers, especially ship captains and unit commanders, had to manage differently when leading such a unique charge under such trying circumstances. As could be expected, destroyer sailors were a demanding lot and, more so than any other courtesies, they expected two things from their leaders: (1) fairness of treatment and (2) smart decisions when their lives were on the line. If a commander could meet these, regardless of his style of leadership, he was certain to find loyalty—and little had greater power toward overall success.

Moosbrugger, however, gave no initial hint to his style of leadership, as he appeared to change nothing. Instead, Purvis Bay awakened on the morning of August 4 in typical fashion. At 5:30 A.M., while the sun was yet hidden and the horizon hinted but just a trace of light, a clamorous tolling of bells instantly aroused a great commotion throughout each and every anchored vessel. The din of alarm persisted and, despite the expectation that this was only another routine precaution, sailors instinctively sprang to their feet and raced to their designated battle stations, each duly prepared for some type of impending defensive action. As usual, they grumbled at such necessity, cursing the enemy—whether he was present or not—for once again disturbing another moment of their quiet rest. They hated this unrelenting drill, morning after morning, day after day, forcing them to such a special attentiveness to detail. Still, this alarm could never be taken lightly; to do so, to fail with a swift response when the warning was true and the danger imminent was certain to invite disaster. More so than duty, survival demanded this constant preparedness, and especially so in the Solomons. The officers and men of Task Group 31.2 clearly understood this—so too did Moosbrugger. They were all veteran, front-line sailors, well trained and full of experience. They all understood the dangers. In this, their own terrible corner of the war, every moment brought great uncertainty, challenging their very existence.

For nearly every ship serving the South Pacific this ritualistic start to each and every morning, this mandatory call to arms, was the measure of assured preparedness. Such was indeed a necessary precaution, and even more so for the thin-skinned, unarmored destroyers, especially while being at anchor within a confining bay, like Purvis, where speed could not be used in their own defense.

The timing was critical. Sunrise and sunset were the two optimal times for enemy air attacks. The sun is low on the horizon, bright and glaring across the ocean's wrinkled surface, and is most blinding to the eyes of the weary gunners searching its direction. Since the earliest days of aerial warfare pilots had learned to use the sun to their own advantage, masking their offensive approach by flying directly out of the sphere's fiery brightness. The moment could be deadly and the outcome severe—for one side or the other it almost always was.

This morning the first hour passed and no threats materialized. Nevertheless, the sailors of the task group persisted with their caution. Their nervous eyes searched the entire breadth of the sky, alert to any movement that might forewarn them of attack. Another hour passed and still their surroundings remained void of any enemy challenge. Finally, the morning was deemed safe, and at 7:15 A.M. general quarters were secured. Now, for a brief while at least, these men could relax, perhaps make their way to the ship's galley for an offering of powdered eggs and hot black coffee and/or take a private moment to pen a letter to home. Officers also took advantage of this moment, gathering themselves within the wardrooms, welcomed by stewards and seated to a business-like breakfast, where they were likely to discuss the plans for the day. Elsewhere, at various other stations, a few key watches continued their vigilance, always the watches, never ending at their search for the unexpected. Still, the morning remained undisturbed; only the departure of *Dunlap* was duly noted. Such were the common, everyday events rarely given to change.

There had been change, however. For the men of Task Group 31.2, this day did indeed prove distinctly different from the day before. Commander Burke, the notable mentor of this group, was gone, on his way to distant Noumea for a needed rest. In his place of charge now stood Commander Moosbrugger, the new leader of whom so little was known. This untimely change, knowingly on the verge of assured action, was plenty reason enough for these men to feel added anxiety. Beyond their common questions of, "What's next?" or "What should we expect today?", they now had additional: "Who is this new commander?" "What kind of man is he?" "Is he a man of experience?" "Will he lead well and bring us back alive?"

With this war there were always a certain number of unknowns, and this was especially true within the hostile environs of the Solomons, and these men certainly needed no additional. Here they were always in the forefront of danger, and always under extreme pressure to be alert, to be fully prepared at executing the performance of their duties and do so within the excellence of their training. Soon they would be in action again. Their anxieties were justified. Still, regardless of who led them, they were sure to do what was asked of them. More importantly, they would fight, fight expertly, and fight to win, for this was their character and they knew nothing less.

This was the spirit that would work to Moosbrugger's advantage, and rightly so. For it should be duly noted that though every class of ship has its own distinctive character, from its very conception the destroyer has always been a breed apart from all others.

The destroyers of World War II were no exception; they had a special magnetism that few ships could boast. "The lure of the destroyer is something of the spirit," wrote war correspondent Foster Hailey. "The ship is a cottage compared to the mansion-like battleship or carrier, and you acquire for your own tin can an affection that is difficult to feel for a ship only half of which is familiar to you and many of whose ship's company you never get to know."[12]

Hailey's words echoed the sentiments of men like Arleigh Burke, Rodger Simpson, and Frederick Moosbrugger. They had all experienced this "lure" early into their careers, with each having acquired a deep personal attachment to these unique seaborne warriors. Many men have, in fact, found reason to claim affection for these small fighting ships, known as the "workhorses of the fleet." Why? Obviously, this fondness was not due to these vessels' extraordinary luxury. "Cramped quarters," Hailey went on to describe, "and the all-steel decks, now stripped of all linoleum, make them much more uncomfortable in hot weather than the bigger vessels; the bridge is open to all the winds that blow, the sun and the weather; watches are tighter and sleep in rough weather, even if you are strapped in your bunk, is almost impossible short of exhaustion."[13]

Most assuredly, the destroyers engaged in the South Pacific were never to be confused with yachts. They were of an extremely cramped configuration, void of all fineries. Still, despite their many obvious discomforts, destroyers projected a very powerful attraction, and especially so to the veteran sailor. For some this attraction was due to status, as the destroyer had a history as a proven fighter, capable of defeating an adversary of almost any size or form, making it a "David" among the "Goliaths." Sailors were impressed with such a claim to power, and were proud of such association. But, the greater attraction, more so than any other quality, was atmosphere. The officers and crew of a destroyer were not only a team, they were a family. "All the men of the destroyer know one another," Hailey added, "and there is a close association between officers and men. . . ."[14] And this, this "close association," this equivalent to a family atmosphere, became the destroyer's greatest of lures.

For most destroyer sailors their ship was as much their home as was that place from which they had originated; for a few, in fact, it was the only true home they had to this point ever known. For this reason alone, destroyermen were unfailing in their loyalties. They would fight for their ship, for her defense and her honor, anytime, anyplace, and against any foe. Sometimes they would even fight among themselves, as brothers so often do, and that was fine too; but outsiders beware, to challenge a destroyerman is to challenge all his mates. This closeness, this strength of brotherhood, made these destroyermen among the tautest associations in the military. Such a brotherhood when combined with the power of the destroyer produced a daunting force, a force of great reckoning, a force of near unstoppable determination. Indeed, it was this type of association that was the destroyer's true lure—and so powerful was this that its attachment was destined to extend far beyond any ship's lifetime.

Certainly, the reputation of these fine men-of-war is well known. The World War II destroyer was truly a powerful weapon, a hunter-killer welcomed by friends and feared by foes; yet, by itself, it was but a hollow vessel made only of strong steel. These destroyers were nothing without their heart and soul, and their heart and soul were the very men who sought their strengths and called them "home." These men were what gave these ships life. They were the energy within. Without them, the destroyer was a powerless fabrication, unable to function. With them, it was a fearsome beast, capable of considerable stealth and deadly force. It was they, these men on a restless pursuit, who, in fact, created through the destroyer's many successes the very lure that drew yet others.

Moosbrugger's inherited force, the destroyermen of Task Group 31.2, were among the best in the business; these men were true front-line warriors, most already tested in combat and all highly skilled at their art. Even so, they remained common men in an uncommon time, where life was given to a need to be determined and resilient. They were part of a unique generation, tempered by the experiences of their youth. Though they had a natural tendency to be independent—and even despite their varied backgrounds and degrees of learning—they proved to be tightly knit and uniform. Loyalty and devotion, those precepts long instilled as part of their upbringing, was what drove them forward, and did so with unyielding resolve. A tough lot to be sure, these men were never to faint from hard work or shrink in the face of desperate odds. By their often-dramatic demonstrations of courage, some observers were even tempted to refer to them as "insane" or "suicidal," though they most assuredly were neither; they had a strong desire to live, though if winning offered no alternatives they were indeed ready to make the ultimate sacrifice. They did require a bit of confidence toward success to be effective, but with just a pittance of this they were nearly unstoppable. There was no wonder that commanders, as Burke, Simpson, and Moosbrugger, coveted such a charge.

Moosbrugger inherited such spirited talents as Southard, Crenshaw, Davison, Olsen, Sherman, and Jeffrey, and so many others. The combined experience was monumental, and he knew how fortunate he was to be leading such a great band of warriors. Arleigh Burke had masterfully gathered the very best, and Freddie was now the grateful beneficiary of the gift.

Another among this gifted gathering was Joseph Jeffrey's former classmate, the "Admiral," Lt. Harold Shear. Serving aboard the destroyer *Stack*, Shear was truly another elite example of the type of membership afforded Moosbrugger's new charge. Neither Shear nor his ship was a novice at fighting this war. The experience had come early for both. Just shortly after Shear had reported aboard, on January 29, 1942, and while enroute to Reykjavik, Iceland, *Stack* was ordered to sweep a nearby area for a German U-boat. The enemy intruder was known to be responsible for the torpedoing of the U.S. Coast Guard cutter *Alexander Hamilton*, and *Stack* was given the mission to end its mischief once and for all.

Later that night the suspect submarine was sighted "close aboard" and the destroyer's alarms rang out, sending the crew rushing to their battle stations. This would be the ship's first offensive action of the war. What followed would prove to be a common scenario for destroyers and their crews.

Stack's speed increased and great phosphorus wakes rushed past her knifing bow as she raced to catch the unsuspecting enemy. It was a speedy attempt at surprise, but the destroyer's approach was spotted. The U-boat commander quickly ordered his crew to crash dive the vessel, hopeful of an escape from assured attack. Despite this effort, *Stack*'s soundman easily located the eluding sub on his sonar. Through the soundman's headset the repeat of pinging echoes reverberated, revealing the elusive sub to its would-be attackers. The pace of the echoes quickened, acknowledging that the destroyer was closing on its prey, and depth charges were ordered rolled off the ship's stern. A few seconds passed and a series of deep underwater explosions suddenly hammered the destroyer's deck plating, testifying to the power of the charges' forceful concussions. Far behind *Stack*'s stern and in line with her visible trail the sea's surface began to boil, and geysers of foaming water burst high into the air, confirming the violence of the deep-sea blasts. Two such attacks were made. Then, after a brief pause, two more followed. The sub was assured a good bruising, but the true results were initially proven negative (only after the war was it learned that the sub, *U-132*, had indeed suffered severe damage and was forced back to Germany for repairs).

Regardless of this outcome, *Stack* and Shear had their first introduction to open sea combat, and it was pure heart-pumping, adrenaline-rushing excitement. More importantly, this was an invaluable experience that in the future would equate to surviving the odds while facing additional life and death decisions in the field. This was war, real and unscripted—and in the Solomons, *Stack* and Shear were due to face far greater and with much more peril.

Lt. (jg) Dandridge M. Gray, another of Freddie's new charges who was *Lang*'s first lieutenant and damage control officer, had a prewar experience dissimilar to most other officers of Moosbrugger's gathering. Born in Bronxville, New York, Dan was a gangly young man. He was a happy fellow, with a pleasant attitude, and feeling very fortunate to have had a life that up to this point was somewhat at ease as compared to many others of his time. He had attended college at Amherst, where he had studied business and had expected to enter professional life soon after. But, like others of his time, the attack on Pearl Harbor was to change Gray's course in dramatic fashion. After his graduation in 1942, Dan immediately signed up for the Naval Reserve. Like Sherman, he enrolled in the Navy's midshipmen school and not long after was heading off to war. "It was amazing to me to see how the government could train so many so fast," Gray later noted. But he was not at all boastful. "They called us '90-day wonders,' but . . . we really were '90-day blunders.' We learned to become sailors [only] once we got aboard [our assignments]."[15]

Dan's assignment was the destroyer *Lang*, where as an ensign he finally caught up to her at Noumea in February 1943, right at the close of the Guadalcanal campaign. His new home was a good bit discouraging, as he found his welcome here not to be all that warm. *Lang*'s regular officers did not look upon the untested reserve with great favor. The same was true of the enlisted personnel, as they were nearly all veterans, wise with experience, while Gray was not. Even *Lang*'s commanding officer, Comm. John L. Wilfong, gave Gray a bit of a hard way to go. "He was quite intimidating, not particularly warm—perhaps a little gruff, and not very friendly to young '90-day blunders' like me," Dan stated of his captain.[16] In a rather brief amount of time, however, Gray proved himself to be a very capable officer, quickly gaining the respect of his superiors—including that of Wilfong—and even the approval of those over whom he was to command. When July arrived, he was by this time a lieutenant junior grade and newly awarded the responsibility of a deck division commander. He still had a lot to learn—and many hard lessons lay ahead—but he was more than meeting the expectations.

It would not be till November 12, 1942, that Wilber Fultz would again find his destroyer, *Craven*, destined toward the offensive effort, along the dangerous shores of Guadalcanal. The Solomons, Wilber knew, were deadly ground. He was well aware of the recent history of the struggle that had gone on here. The Japanese had proven themselves to be a far more lethal opponent than previously expected. The numbers of ships and sailors being lost for control of Guadalcanal alone were terribly staggering, giving every sailor in the region good reason for concern. For this was only one of many islands yet awaiting them, each far deadlier than the previous, making the end to this new war appear to keep slipping farther and farther beyond the horizon.

Wilber Fultz, however, remained convinced that his choice to join the Navy had been right. Three years earlier he had left his home in search of a life change, and he had indeed found it aboard *Craven*. By August 1943, this former cowboy from Montana held the rate of coxswain and was another of Moosbrugger's overall command. He was by now in every sense of the term a veteran, clothed with considerable confidence in himself, his ship, and his fellow shipmates. The Solomons remained a brutal arena, but he foresaw nothing in any of the upcoming operations that was beyond his previous experiences. "It was old stuff," he wrote. "We had been in that part of the islands since December of 1942, up and down under attack by torpedo planes and subs."[17] He expected little to change, even with Moosbrugger at the lead. Whatever was to come he would meet, and he expected he would survive.

For nineteen-year-old Charles "Chuck" Lee, the gutsy gunner's mate now serving aboard *Lang*, life among the cramped spaces of his destroyer was a far-cry from the secure liberties he had known growing up in the mountains of rural Vermont. Surviving in this war was sure to be a terrible struggle, by its very nature forbidding, yet this young man had found among his shipmates a unique strength and assurance. Here he was surrounded by a brotherhood that provided a great abundance of wisdom and welfare, and he had great respect for what it taught. "The age difference aboard the *Lang*," he noted, "worked to our best interests, as the older shipmates from other gangs would talk to us and we learned much from them. Some [of these men] were of pre-war status and had experience that none of us had, as of yet."[18] This positive wielding of an "old hand's" big-brother influence was always well received, and proved to be far more than an education. It was lifesaving!

Still, there was no doubt that Chuck missed his biological family, the father, mother, and siblings he had left behind in Brooklyn. He—as did most all his shipmates to their respective families—wished every day that he could be back with them. And he still could not escape having kind thoughts about that pretty young lady he had left behind back in Frisco—though he would not attempt to write Patricia, despite a sincere desire to do so, just in fairness to her wishes. Of foremost importance to him now, however, and especially so while in the deadly embrace of the South Pacific, was his new family, this brotherhood he found aboard *Lang*. Many a night he would rest his head in deep sleep, feeling secure and at ease, not by a warm word from home but by a confidence in the fine talents and abilities of those officers and men that surrounded him. He, in turn, felt just as determined at providing these men with the same type of confidence. There was always that common awareness that everyone must be at their best at all times. Survival, especially in the Solomons, depended upon it.

Pharmacist's Mate First Class Ralph Barber had for most of a year spent his time at relative ease on Noumea, expecting little to change. Ever since his initial sailing experience, Ralph seemed sure to avoid a revisit of such duty, and certainly he was never to consider an encounter aboard a destroyer. He knew very little about them. However, on August 4, 1943, here he was, standing on the deck of *Dunlap* and preparing for some unknown and sure to be deadly mission somewhere up the Solomons Slot.

Barber's reason for being here was once again a bit unorthodox. He had just recently enrolled in the Navy's V-12 program (another of the Reserve's training programs) and was on schedule for an early return to the States, destined for college and a chance at becoming a doctor. When told of his acceptance, he wrote Virginia to give her the good news; he would soon be home. Shortly after, however—and in what was surely a direct contradiction to his past attitudes toward sailing—he decided to sign up for duty aboard a ship. "I wanted a little sea duty," he explained, "before I returned to [the] USA. . . ."[19] He obviously thought the experience would look good on his record and, besides, he would soon be given his ticket home anyway, so it should be a short ride. His decision was spontaneous and given with little consideration to the obvious uncertainties that surrounded him, or to the common administrative snafus that often persisted in the military, and the results were to prove both unexpected and life changing.

These men represented only a handful of the many talents that were to serve under Frederick Moosbrugger. A multitude of fine sailors, from all aspects of life and not so dissimilar to that of Shear, Gray, Fultz, Lee, and/or Barber, made up this new command. And though some of these men may well have displayed some initial misgivings of Moosbrugger, he was never to express any doubts of them. He had had the honor of serving with many others like them of similar character and determination. His past commands had been full of such men. He appeared to trust their toughness and was duly confident in their many keen abilities, just as they were destined to perform with a remarkable adeptness to any and all challenges placed before them. For, no doubt, what they were destined to face together would indeed mold them into even a greater refinement of teamwork.

Truly there was no more dangerous arena for this group to serve than the Solomons. Still, for most of them, it was exactly where they wanted to be. Sure, they would prefer to be back home, securely and peacefully living life among their family and friends. But this war had not come by choice; home and life were now being threatened. There was a duty to defend the nation and to exact some revenge for the "unprovoked" attack against it. They thought of it in no other terms. Moosbrugger had no concerns as to the motivation of these men. He did not need to meet each individual nor read each record to know what to expect of them. They would do what was asked of them, and they would do it well.

As close-knit, highly observant and watchful as these veterans were, it was certain that nothing of worthwhile importance was to miss their attention. In fact, little of anything aboard a destroyer passed without notice. Therefore, the sailors of Task Group 31.2 were clearly abreast of *Dunlap*'s departure on the morning of August 4, as she made the short passage from Tulagi over to Guadalcanal.

Scuttlebutt quickly traveled throughout each ship's company that another new mission was surely forthcoming. They had seen this before: the call for the commander to proceed to headquarters, the impending meeting of officers, and the assured increase in each ship's preparation. This, as Fultz had duly noted, was "old stuff." Only the details remained to be explained—and this, these men knew, would come in due time.

Meanwhile, sailors pursued their routine tasks, practiced and confident. Such sharp responses to duties were a credit to the commanders who made certain that, beyond regular periods of required rest, their crews were never idle for long periods of time. Idleness could lead to low morale and lack of preparedness, neither of which was acceptable in this deadly theater. Shipboard duties and maintenance were always in demand, but so too were the need for reactionary skills.

Drills were a constant feature of life at sea in the war-torn Pacific, and especially so in the Solomons, where sudden enemy attack was always at high risk. The speed with which men could meet a challenge—whether it be in defense from attack, damage control, fire control, and/or medical aid—often made the difference between life and death. These tiring efforts were often bemoaned, but their necessity was clearly understood. These were the times, as Chuck Lee appreciatively noted, when questions could be asked of the older more experienced men and when their wisdoms could be safely gleaned and their critiques securely shared—whereas during the reality of combat it was often too late.

In truth, no commander of the time could afford to allow his crew unabridged latitude toward complete relaxation. The Pacific of 1942-43 had developed into the world's largest battlefield, where no region was fully secure and no corner appeared free of conflict, with the Solomons at its epicenter of turmoil. Here, of all places, alertness was a constant requirement. Here death was often the most violent of experiences, both brutal and horrifying. Unlike the Atlantic, Mediterranean, and/or Europe, here the very essence of civilization seemed so nonexistent. The Pacific could well be described as a wilderness, crude and cruel. It was a span of thousands of miles of endless sea, only sparsely covered by loose-knit island chains, many poorly charted, and many just like the Solomons, beautiful in their nature but bristling with inhospitality and treachery. Here was spied a wonderment of eye-catching splendor, enchanting and alluring, but it was often an illusion, hiding an elusive enemy, both natural and humankind. Here, where wide open spaces were everywhere, living required some form of confinement, always bound by the sea. Here everything good seemed so distant: the horizon, the next destination, true security, home, and family; all of the desirables were always somewhere just beyond reach. Here, where even war news was limited and letters from home were so very sparse, isolation was real. For here only bad things, like death and destruction, seemed quick with their handiwork. In such an arena, retaining the determination and will to continue on with this fight was of the most trying of challenges; yet the only alternative was to quit, and sailors, especially those who rode the destroyer—regardless of side—were to have nothing to do with this.

The tough reputation of the destroyerman was by this date well established, and he was to relinquish no part of it. He expected to be in the forefront of action, for this is what he had been trained for. The demand for his talents was never ending. "No Task Force Commander ever had enough destroyers," wrote Vice Adm. Walden Ainsworth, commander of all destroyers in the Pacific Fleet from July 1942 through January 1943. "Those . . . men . . . who joined the war to live and sweat, fight and die, in these small ships . . . held their heads high, with fierce pride. They became the soul and spirit of the Destroyer Navy. Of them we may all be very, very proud."[20]

The men of Task Group 31.2 were indeed proud. But they were also very frustrated, having knowledge that something was amiss. There were so few ready destroyers, and so great were the requests for their services, that they had yet to be offered any meaningful opportunity to operate strictly as weapons of offense. Nearly twenty full months into the war and destroyers still remained bridled with escort and support roles.

Simpson was nearly alone at having had any chance at leading destroyers on their own mission, and he had shown quite well how efficient and complete the destroyer could behave. Such was good enough for some high praise and commendation, but it did not help loosen the destroyer's bond to the larger ships.

Burke had been determined to change this, intent at convincing his superiors that such tight control over these powerful little vessels was a terrible mistake, that allowing the destroyer commander to operate with greater freedoms could dramatically change the dynamics of the enemy's approach and offense. When timing disappointedly interfered with Burke's greater efforts, Moosbrugger humbly took charge and was to wisely pursue in proxy with the fine plan that his predecessor had left behind.

Fine ships, fine men, fine officers, and a fine plan had finally come together for one of those rare great moments in history—all together waiting at the small island of Tulagi. And the outstanding results were only hours away.

Chapter Six

The Mission

Facing the Challenges

Commander Moosbrugger visited Koli Point for the first time on the morning of August 4, 1943, and he did so as the new commander of Task Group 31.2. His arrival was greeted by a spectacular sunrise, revealing itself as a golden crescent edge slowly peeking above an eastern horizon. The display seemed to mimic a distant mass of raging fire and served as another reminder of this region's volatile past as well as to ongoing traumas.

The demeanor of Guadalcanal had changed little; the island remained an intolerable old cuss, content at wreaking its many inhospitalities on all those individuals forced to live within its unruly interior. Hot and malaria ridden, this landscape was no more welcoming now than when the war first arrived at its shoreline. That so many young lives had perished for control of such harshness seemed such a waste. But, in truth, there *was* change to be found here, and promising change at that.

After many months of brutal warfare, Guadalcanal now stood in a relative state of peace and calm. Men were once again witnessed walking about boldly and with little or no fear. The vision seemed such a paradox to the scope of death that was this place only a few short months before. Even in Freddie's haste to reach his destination and despite a rush of thoughts playing upon his mind, the panorama of this morning could not help but impress upon him at least some positive optimism for the future.

Guadalcanal was in and of itself a testimonial to nature's fortitude. Here out of the midst of war had returned a peaceful setting, where stood quiet beaches cradled by the comfort of light breezes and an embrace of a guardian sea. Here constant rhythms and light slaps of incoming breakers were once again soothing and serene. Here outstretched palms of neighboring coconut trees stirred only ever so slightly, watched over by local fowl that swept gentle circumferences through a shared space of sky above, hinting of a paradise. And here tranquility had come back to rest, overpowering to even the scars of battle and waste of war. But in the midst of this grand exhibition a powerful statement was also being delivered; nature boldly pronounced she would never retreat in the face of an unwanted intrusion by mankind. One could direly afford, it seemed, to dismiss such strength. This bit of land—a hallowed ground, stained with blood and sacrifice and hard won from a determined human enemy at tremendous cost—refused to be owned or controlled. It reacted to each new day just as it had for thousands of years, as it so desired. Long after the armies would leave, it would remain. In time, even its scars would disappear. For Moosbrugger, the lesson was clear: Nature is her own force, and she has no accountability to man or concern for who might be victorious in his wars. She takes no side. Nature remains, therefore, that one uncertain element that could never be dismissed, regardless of the venue.

Moosbrugger did not need to be reminded of the lesson. Nature should be viewed as the beautiful mistress—a teaser ready to fool the unsuspecting. Freddie had already experienced her unfaithfulness. The Aleutians had tempered his awareness of nature's bad side. He knew the irony of her friendship was that she could not be trusted. When he would soon stand among others of his peers, making plans for whatever important operation was forthcoming, he knew too that nature would be present, spying on their every conversation. It would be wise to give her careful notice. If she decided not to be a willing accomplice in this new venture, then he must be prepared. He had no power over her, yet he could perhaps exploit her powers to his own benefit and purpose and to the detriment of his enemies. But nature was to prove only a fraction of Freddie's overall concerns.

As a byproduct of *Dunlap*'s early departure, Moosbrugger's men were now becoming ever more suspicious that something was being planned for their immediate future. Having a new leader—one whom they saw as untested in the local arena—and being faced with the likelihood of some new combat were in combination a prospect not well received. Regardless of such dubiousness, the morning hours at Purvis passed by in rather routine fashion. Six of the eight destroyers belonging to Task Group 31.2 stood secure at their moorings, and work details aboard each ship were given out as usual, with no sense of urgency. Outside of *Dunlap*, the only other vessel noticeably absent was *Craven*, which had departed earlier on a prearranged mission to aid with escort of some LSTs destined for New Georgia. The anchorage itself displayed only a minimal amount of activity, having only its customary traffic of small boats and barges, and the day would otherwise proceed without remark. But this appearance of normalcy did not necessarily reflect reality, for little was ever normal in this war, and these men knew it.

One thing that was normal, however, was the constant pace with which this struggle continued and the toll it persisted at accruing. The destroyers of Task Group 31.2 had all been at sea for several months, having much of their exposed structures beaten by the constant harshness of both wind and sea and their internal equipment taxed with overuse and abuse. This campaign had allowed these ships and crews almost no opportunities for real rest, and both men and machines were tired. In addition, the hectic schedules of this campaign were sure not to offer a respite any time soon. Regardless of such stresses, these sailors were to perform their duties with an amazing high rate of efficiency. They clearly understood what elements were important to their survival, and the greatest among these was keeping within a constant state of preparedness.

A warship had to be battle ready at all times. Beyond any ability of its crew to fight, a ship had to function as it was intended. The harshness of an unforgiving sea can quickly degrade any ship and its machinery, and keeping up with the maintenance is for any crew a daunting task. This was especially true for those sailors serving in the wartime South Pacific, where they usually had little to work with. Repairs, when needed—outside an occasional rendezvous with a tender (the floating machine shops that provided maintenance support to the fleet)—fell squarely on the shoulders of these sailors. They were either to find a fix for their problems or find themselves at a disadvantage that could prove most deadly. Fortunately, these were men who, being so well trained and expert with so many specialties, often performed miracles far outside the box of innovation and enterprise. Creativity became their forte and was among their most valuable assets.

But there were yet other challenges. In this fast-paced conflict, where unexpected change occurred often, the ability to conform readily to new directions, new protocols, and new aggressions was paramount toward success. From its outset, this new war placed doctrines in a constant state of revision and demanded ongoing adjustments in processes. The bar of standards was raised higher and higher with each new pursuit, persistently testing the limits of each and every crew. Thus, those who managed to meet hardship and change with the greater amount of resilience often proved the ones with the greater chance at avoiding catastrophic failure.

Chief among the tests of ingenuity was that of adaptation to new equipment, and this was especially true on the destroyer, where space was extremely limited and overcrowding was a constant issue. The Benhams and Gridleys of Task Group 31.2 had all been constructed before the war. These small destroyers, originally designed to accommodate no more than 175 men, now carried a crew complement in excess of 225. New weapons systems—as with the 20-millimeter Oerlikon and (for the Benhams) 40-millimeter Bofer antiaircraft guns—had also found residence aboard, while new electronics—as with variations of radar and automatic gun directors—were other necessary additions. In each case more space was consumed, stealing away what little comfort remained, while weight requirements were maximized, often to the verge of adversely affecting the ship's stability and performance. Managing such demands within such tight restraints was no small feat of engineering. And sustaining such innovation proved itself a never-ending challenge.

Moosbrugger clearly understood these challenges. He was well aware that, even as he was ashore preparing to receive orders for the next pressing mission, his teams back at Purvis were busily making final adjustments at integrating some of these latest mandates.

Due in large part to the Navy's recent poor performances—strongly evident during the early stages of the Solomons campaign, and especially at night—Fleet Adm. Chester Nimitz had in late November 1942 issued a tactical bulletin asserting an entirely new radar doctrine, to take effect by that year's end.[1] This new doctrine stressed a more efficient use of the existing radar variations and a more effective device for assimilating and communicating the gathered information, and with expediency between ships. This device was to be, as Nimitz initially coined it, the "Combat Operations Center," later to be re-designated as the Combat Information Center or CIC.[2] The admiral was to leave no room for misunderstanding; an allocation for the CIC and complete training for CIC teams were mandatory for all combat ships, regardless of their disposition. Such would again require the pursuit for space necessary at squeezing in yet more equipment and at a location that was centralized and of easiest access to the bridge. For the destroyer teams this was certain to be no small matter, and especially so for the older destroyers as in the case of the majority that were yet serving in the Solomons. Even when the space was finally determined, the rerouting of communications and the installation of required equipment did not happen readily, and training for making this package work exposed a whole other dilemma.

To assist his commanders with this new doctrine, Rear Adm. Mahlon Tisdale, who had succeeded Vice Admiral Ainsworth as commander destroyers in the Pacific Fleet, prepared two new handbooks that were designed to provide a standard for all his destroyers. Issued in June 1943, the *CIC Handbook* and *Radar Gunnery Notes* were to be the guidelines for destroyer commanders to use for both establishing their CICs and implementing their proper use. Both guides were very detailed and gave every effort at promoting the best possible use of this new tool. In the case of location and space accommodation, Tisdale offered suggestions, pointing out that "on most classes of destroyers the required larger space was found immediately below the bridge, though in one class it was necessary to use the division commander's cabin on the main deck."[3]

For destroyer commanders, regardless of the initial inconvenience these changes produced, the CIC was no hard sell; for the most part they welcomed the idea of centralized information and communications. In looking back to the past failures, most of the Solomons theater losses could be attributed to a confusion of communications and poor distribution of assimilated data. The CIC provided that one place of easiest access to the bridge where all data—sonar, radar, navigation, communications, gunnery, and torpedoes—could be quickly gathered, analyzed, and passed on, with recommendations, to the ship's command for the fastest possible response. It appeared that the CIC was certain to be a win-win institution with outstanding potential.

Tisdale also noted, however, that the CIC would only function as well as the men who were trained to work it. This included the commanders and the crews that were to use its processed information. In a clear notation of warning, the admiral added, "Not only must the C.I.C. itself be proficient, but the Commanding Officers and the weapon control parties must take fullest advantage of the information furnished by the C.I.C."[4] In other words, this information—regardless of how thorough—would mean very little in a complex combat situation if it was not acted upon with a quick, deliberate response.

In the case of Task Group 31.2, a force made up entirely of 1930s-era destroyers, the task of establishing the CIC was no easy feat and required considerable ingenuity on the part of these ships' crews. Lieutenant Southard, aboard *Lang*, described in detail the layout of his ship's newly improvised CIC. "The makeshift C.I.C.," he wrote, " . . . was part of the Captain's emergency cabin at the bridge level, behind the Captain's bunk (which had gimbals at each end to keep it level as the ship rolled). It contained a navigation and plotting board above the bunk, surface search master console (SG Radar), the sonar console, and the Air Search Radar console; also a fathometer. There was not much space; it was crowded. I had 5 (maybe 6) enlisted Petty Officers with me and an officer, console operators and telephone (sound powered talkers) to the bridge and gun director and torpedo director."[5] *Craven*, *Maury*, *Sterett*, and *Stack* all had similar arrangements.

Aboard *Dunlap*, since she was of the Fanning class, the CIC was set up differently. Lieutenant Olsen recalled, "Our CIC was in the Chart House one deck below the bridge. Here was a large plotting table, a large DRT (dead reconning [sp] tracer) and the SG and SC radars. The bridge [on *Dunlap*] did not have a PPI repeater, so the bridge had to depend on radar information from the CIC."[6] This arrangement was obviously a little less crowded and provided a better working environment for the operators, but its location was to prove just a bit disadvantageous to the bridge commanders, as Moosbrugger was soon to learn.

Training for the CIC also presented its own set of problems. Even as late as June 1943, schools for CIC training were still in the process of being established: one at Pearl and one at Noumea. In the meantime, it was recommended that officers and CIC personnel receive as much advanced radar and sonar schooling as time allowed. Again, the nearest shore-based school locations were at Pearl and Noumea. The demand for destroyers in the ongoing Solomons operations provided almost no opportunities for such specialized training. Most destroyer crews—as was the case for Task Group 31.2—were therefore forced to do the best they could with what was available. Learning by doing and hands-on instruction were often accepted practice in the South Pacific theater, where abrupt changes in doctrines and operational adjustments forced men to learn quickly. Fortunately for Task Group 31.2 there was a strong nucleus of experienced veterans, boasting expertise, knowledge, and a hardened determination at meeting just such a challenge and with success. This was the very type of combination that would soon pay great dividends and afford Moosbrugger and Simpson an unprecedented victory.

Regardless of these ongoing pressures to his command, Commander Moosbrugger appeared before Koli headquarters as a leader with a devout confidence that his team could ably respond to any mission given them. His only real concern was with his own right choices, and these he was sure to ponder throughout his future. Still, he displayed no reservation in his strides on this day, swiftly climbing the structure's few steps, whereupon he entered to be immediately directed back to Admiral Wilkinson's office.

Proceeding on, Freddie found the admiral's office door open, begging his entry. Just outside the threshold he paused, and through the opening he immediately observed that others were also present, as two other officers were seen gathered around a chart on a wooden table and engaged in a serious discussion with the admiral. Their conversation seemed intense, but it suddenly ceased, as all of their attention focused his way. They had been awaiting his company.

The admiral acknowledged Freddie's arrival with a silent gesture to enter. There was such simplicity to this command—even as Wilkinson was such a powerful presence, intellectually sharp and tactfully resolute—but it was commanding nonetheless. And so, Freddie made his way forward.

Having removed his hat from his head, Freddie approached the three men with his usual smile, curious to the measure of their import. A formal introduction then followed, and he extended his hand to the two officers who stood before him. The first gentleman Freddie knew. Comm. Alan P. Calvert he remembered as a lowerclassman at the academy, a graduate of 1924. But more so, Freddie knew Calvert as a destroyer commander, having had previous command of the *Craven*, leading her through her baptism of fire during the first raid against Wake Island in February 1942. Calvert also knew of Moosbrugger, remembering him from his days as skipper of *McCall*. Now Calvert was commander of Motor Torpedo Boat Flotilla One. The other officer was introduced as Flotilla One's intelligence officer, Lt. Comm. Henry Farrow. Freddie was less familiar with Farrow, but he had no doubt that this officer had significant importance to the gathering. And, as these initial introductions were now concluded, the meeting finally got down to the serious business at hand.

Redirecting everyone's attention to the nearby chart, a layout that represented the New Georgia/Kolombangara region of the Central Solomons, Wilkinson began his explanation for the meeting. He began with an update on the current situation, noting that the fight for New Georgia Island was progressing well but still ongoing. The hardest fighting was in and around Munda airfield, which was still being stubbornly defended by the Japanese, even though its future capture was assured. But the more immediate concern was wider ranging. Though the Japanese were indeed losing their grasp on the region, they had decided to commit to a formidable delaying action, hopeful that such an effort might slow American progress to such a point and incur such a cost as to deter any future efforts and eventually force a settlement. For this reason, the Japanese were staging troops ashore at Vila-Stanmore, on neighboring Kolombangara, in obvious preparations for the next foreseen American invasion. To aid with this effort, the Tokyo Express was once again actively engaged in ferrying the necessary troops and supplies to the region. Intelligence suggested that additional runs by the Express were imminent, and these could take place throughout any of the next several nights. In addition, enemy barge traffic throughout the region was also reported to have increased by a substantial margin, and was effectively maneuvering additional troops and supplies to other key defensive positions. The admiral then turned to Moosbrugger. "I want you to take two of your destroyers and join Commander Calvert's boats at sweeping Vella Gulf."[7] The admiral's message was clear; he wanted these runs of troops and supplies brought to a halt, and quickly. Wilkinson expected these sweeps to be nightly, and he hoped that they could begin as early as late evening on August 5.

Moosbrugger looked the chart over closely, studying the confinement of Vella Gulf. It was now obvious to him why the torpedo boat commanders were to be a part of the mission. Calvert had just recently moved his forward base to nearby Rendova and his boats had been patrolling Vella Gulf and the areas of Blanche Channel and Blackett Strait for most of a month. During this time, they had gained considerable experience in the region, having knowledge of enemy shore battery positions as well as familiarity with enemy destroyer and barge traffic and their tactics. Freddie wanted to know everything Calvert and Farrow had learned. So, as the meeting drew to its conclusion, he invited the two officers to join him on the following morning aboard *Dunlap* for a conference. There Simpson could also be in attendance; and from among this group a plan for meeting the admiral's set objectives could be finalized.

* * *

A thousand miles northwest of Moosbugger's meeting at Koli, Capt. Tameichi Hara was at this same moment in the midst of transport across Rabaul's Simpson Harbor. He was headed for a rendezvous with the destroyer *Hagikaze*, flagship for Capt. Kaju Sugiura. Hara had received a message from Sugiura earlier that morning, informing him of an important meeting that required his attendance. Joining Hara was Lt. Comm. Kimio Yamagami, the skipper of *Shigure* and a man who shared many of Hara's ideals.

The harbor on this morning displayed itself serene and peaceful—even despite an ominous presence of numerous warships—which allowed for a most pleasant passage of the sheltered anchorage. Both officers sat attentively in their boat, having their backs straight and eyes directed intently forward, while awaiting the journey's conclusion. Hara's face was stiff and grim, as he appeared noticeably anxious about the pending meeting. Both he and Yamagami had participated in the latest Tokyo Express to Kolombangara and had survived a late skirmish with several American PT boats. The aggressiveness of the torpedo boats had been somewhat unexpected and, had they been a bit better organized, should have proven quite devastating. Neither officer was overly eager at pursuing another, similar expedition, especially considering their fate was likely to be in the hands of some other commander. In addition, *Shigure* was badly in need of overhaul. Her steam turbines were nearly worn-out and her ability to make full speed was extremely diminished. Hara had hoped that his ship and crew could receive a short rest, and perhaps in the meantime his promised division might finally arrive, allowing him some future leadership leverage. He knew, however, that his superiors were determined to sacrifice as many lives as necessary in order to stop the American advance, and their demands were certain to override his own lowly considerations.

Once aboard *Hagikaze*, Hara and Yamagami received a warm welcome and were quickly directed to the meeting. Other destroyer commanders were already present, seated outside at a table and beneath the shade of a wide awning. The other commanders in attendance were Lt. Comm. Yoshio Yanase (*Kawakaze*), Lt. Comm. Masahiro Makoshi (*Hagikaze*), and Comm. Koushichi Sugioka (*Arashi*). Captain Sugiura motioned for Hara and Yamagami to join them. And the meeting was then brought to order.

Sugiura was a mild-mannered individual, who projected confidence but with an eagerness that gave Hara reason to doubt his rationale. It was obvious that Sugiura had high hopes of one day reaching the rank of admiral, and this was a red flag to Hara, who knew that such an ambition would require complete and unquestionable obedience to the whims of the naval hierarchy. Currently, orders passing through headquarters were being issued by distant planners, individuals who were miles from the combat zone and out of touch with the true conditions being experienced by commanders in the field. In such cases where the plan might prove unwise or even disastrous, Hara thought the logical and experienced commander would find reason and excuse for amending some finer details, making the plan more operationally sound, while still carrying out the given order. He did not, however, perceive Sugiura as this type of commander. What he was about to hear was to confirm his fears.

"Gentlemen," Sugiura began, "I am very happy to report that our last transport mission to Kolombangara was a complete success, thanks to your splendid co-operation. Both the Navy and the Army high command are gratified and have asked me to extend their appreciation to you. They have also ordered that the mission be repeated the day after tomorrow. *Kawakaze* will replace *Amagari* whose nose was bruised in ramming that torpedo boat [Lt. John F. Kennedy's PT 109]. I invite discussion and will welcome your opinions and suggestions."[8]

Hara noticed Yamagami squirming uncomfortably in his seat. He knew exactly what his confidant was thinking, for he too had heard the disturbing part of Sugiura's announcement and was also cringing at the prospect. Hara quickly glanced at the other commanders but, regardless of Sugiura's invitation for opinions, it was obvious that no one among the group was willing to challenge any part of the commander's statement. Sugiura was senior, but Hara held the same rank and expected that only he stood any chance at swaying some logic into the decision.

"Captain Sugiura," Hara addressed respectfully, "I understood you to say that we are to repeat the mission. Does that mean we are to conduct this operation in the same way as the last one?"[9]

In his clarification, Hara hoped that Sugiura would disclose some variances to the plan and not declare a complete repeat. Surely they would not use the exact same routes and times as before. But Sugiura wasted no time in confirming the worst.

"Yes, Hara," Sugiura responded. "We shall go through Vella Gulf and Blackett Strait again, and unload at the Kolombangara anchorage at 2330 [11:30 p.m.], exactly as we did the last time."[10]

Hara could not believe a commander would be so foolish. Sugiura's inexperience in the Solomons was showing profusely and his unwillingness to buck the system was obvious. Hara, however, was not quite ready to fold.

"Begging your pardon, Sugiura," Hara rebutted, "I do not think it wise to repeat the exact same formula again. This same procedure has already been used twice in Vella Gulf. Can't we vary the course somewhat this time? Blackett Strait by itself, with all those reefs and shoals, is unhealthy enough, without using the identical route for getting there again. How about feinting through Gizo Strait before sneaking into Blackett? Or how about just changing the timing by two hours either way?"[11]

Excluding Yamagami, who knew well his commander's bold outspokenness, the other commanders displayed a bit of shock at Hara's challenge. In the Imperial Japanese Navy, rarely did an officer openly criticize the logic of his superiors. But Hara had not gotten to his position by being quiet, but rather his rise to leadership was because of his boldness of intent and his expertise in tactical doctrines. Besides, he had the greater experience in the theater. But this did not seem to matter.

Sugiura paused a bit in his response, obviously taken aback by Hara's determined questioning of his position. Slowly, Sugiura began a lengthy explanation, but all Hara heard worth noting was, "I already have my orders."[12] There was no reason to extend the debate any further. The plan was to remain the same.

In order to smooth over their differences, Sugiura did offer that *Shigure*, Hara's flagship, take the van of the column, an important and honorable position of leadership. Again, shocking the other commanders, Hara refused. He politely pointed out that *Shigure* was suffering from engineering problems and that her ability to reach full speed was questionable, making her a potential hazard if swift maneuvering became necessary. For once, Hara was happy that his ship was inadequate, as she had offered him a good excuse for a refusal that he had made purely out of spite.

* * *

Back at Tulagi, the daylight hours of August 5 opened with a customary burst of brilliance. The morning sun reflected brightly across the surface of Purvis, instantly exposing every vessel nestled within the bay's protective barrier. As usual, the heat of the day followed quickly, rising to its brutal standard and aggressively attacking the outer decks and inner confines of each anchored destroyer. Veterans to this environment, the sailors of Task Group 31.2 appeared undeterred by these regional expressions of daily practice and pursued their normal duties as usual, efficiently and with utmost professionalism. They had grown accustomed to the work and to the discomfort. To these men this day was as any other, merely another twenty-four hours in the Solomons, as predictable as it was unpredictable.

This day, however, was soon to prove anything but usual. Not long after routine general quarters, a PT boat was sighted hurriedly approaching the *Dunlap*. The vessel's bow wave—the bright, white foam of water that rose high off the boat's bow to then quickly break away at forming a familiar broadening ripple—acknowledged an urgent advance; and its speed was to diminish only after having neared the destroyer, eventually to slow to a stop in its maneuvering alongside. This moment was not to pass without drawing the attention of the many sailors stationed nearby. No doubt this arrival held some critical importance, and they were all intensely curious as to its nature. Their nose for news rarely missed opportunity for new scuttlebutt, and certainly this was just the type of activity that could add potential hype to their ongoing speculations.

Meanwhile, from down alongside *Dunlap* an MTB officer was heard to call out, "Commanders Calvert and Farrow requesting permission to come aboard!"[13] *Dunlap*'s officer-of-the-deck stood at his usual vantage and quickly replied, "Permission granted!"[14] Calvert and Farrow immediately climbed the lowered gangway, pausing only briefly while saluting the destroyer's ensign before stepping onto its main deck. Then, without further ado, the two gentlemen were quickly escorted to the commodore's stateroom.

Simpson had arrived earlier, and he and Moosbrugger were already engaged in discussing the forthcoming mission. Both men were energetic about the mission, as was evidenced in their lively conversation, which was still ongoing when Calvert and Farrow finally made their presence known outside the cabin hatchway. The discussion paused and Freddie immediately beckoned the two guest officers to enter. Then he politely introduced both men to Commander Simpson. Handshakes were exchanged and some brief casual conversation ensued. Simpson had a gift for gab, often loud and profane but entertaining, and his wit stirred a few hearty laughs. A steward then arrived with a pot of hot coffee and a tray full of raisin cakes, a common hospitality to guests but one also indicative of a lengthy meeting to follow. Then Moosbrugger, having finally determined the formalities as concluded, called the meeting to order, and the planning resumed in earnest.

Poring over a chart of Vella Gulf and Blackett Strait, the four commanders gave lively debate to Wilkinson's directive, offering a variety of opinions and concerns. Commander Calvert had the latest intelligence related to the most recent Tokyo Express, which occurred right around midnight on August 2. The enemy force was noted as having consisted of four destroyers, traveling in a column, evenly spaced at about 500 yards. He continued his description by pointing to the chart, describing the enemy approach as having come from the north, around the eastern edge of Vella Lavella, to pass into Vella Gulf, to then enter Blackett Strait and on to their drop-off points near Vila Stanmore on Kolombangara. Simpson noted that this was the same night that he and Burke had taken their destroyers up "The Slot" to a position just north of the entrance to Kula Gulf, where they had hoped to catch this Express. Their choice of approach had, however, failed at intercepting the enemy. The MTBs, on the other hand, were in the correct position to make this contact, and were even to fire several torpedoes toward the enemy, but to no effect. One of Calvert's boats, the 109, under the command of Lt. John "Jack" Kennedy, was even then still missing and presumed lost to this action. Calvert then noted that, at Rendova, a memorial service was being planned for Kennedy and his crew even as this conference was ongoing (the commander was to learn later this very day that Kennedy and most of his crew were still alive and awaiting rescue). So, the caution was quite obvious; the Japanese were still proving extremely effective at night maneuvers, were quick to react, and deadly when confronted.

For several more hours the group of officers concentrated on where and how they should best engage an attack against the next assured Express run. Additional pots of hot coffee were brought to their aid. They discussed the known tactics of the enemy destroyers and the possible emergence of a cruiser. The possibilities of armed barges, unusual barge traffic, shore batteries, mines, submarines, and bombers all had to be considered within the framework of the plan. Moosbrugger was sure to factor in the weather as well. They couldn't afford to take anything for granted.

By early afternoon a plan had been agreed upon and the conference broke up. They would depart on the following morning, on August 6, to rendezvous at the Gizo Strait entrance to Vella Gulf. Calvert and Farrow departed, speeding back to their base to explain the details to the rest of the MTB skippers. Moosbrugger prepared to do the same with his task group commanders. But before he had a chance to call them together, he received yet another message from Wilkinson. There had been a change of plans. The new dispatch directed Moosbrugger as follows: "*Division A-1 (Dunlap, Craven, Maury) and Division A-2 (Lang, Sterett, Stack), depart Tulagi at 1230 6 August proceed to Vella Gulf via route south of Russells and Rendova to arrive Gizo Strait at 2200 and make sweeps of Vella Gulf avoiding mine fields. If no enemy contacts by 0200 7 August return north of Kolombangara at maximum speed to Purvis.*"[15] Wilkinson had obviously received some new information, and this warranted the necessity for a larger operation. But what was it? Surely Wilkinson would provide more. And no sooner had the first dispatch been read when a second dispatch arrived, this one ordering Moosbrugger to return to headquarters as soon as possible.

By this time, it was the middle of the afternoon. *Dunlap*'s crew was in the midst of being allowed a break from the sweltering heat, given an hour or so to enjoy some swimming in the bay. A gig had been posted as guard just outboard the ship, while a couple of sharpshooters stood on deck to ward away any unwanted intrusions by sharks. In the meantime, high-diving exhibitionists and water-flailing jokesters reveled at entertaining those who chose only to watch. One after the other, sailors—some stripped down to "bare asses"—took turns launching themselves off the destroyer's high decks to then smack into the cooling sea below. Swimming had become an excellent and widely used form of exercise among the fleet, as it was the easiest available and was perfect for allowing some timely release from a ship's sweltering confinement, not to mention that it provided a wonderful distraction from the stresses of war.

This afternoon of folly was typical of the exercise and was just reaching its climax—with the most dramatic exhibitions of diving spectacles yet to come—when Moosbrugger's order abruptly brought all revelry to an immediate end. The ship's speakers suddenly blared, "Station all special sea details . . . the ship will get underway as soon as possible."[16] Sailors reacted quickly, clamoring back aboard to gather up their discarded clothes and make ready at their posts. If there had been any doubts before, now there were none. Something very important was in the offing. Sherman noted, "It was evident to all hands that there was something brewing."[17] But, at this point, even Moosbrugger had no clear understanding of what.

Within a matter of minutes *Dunlap* was again on the move, steaming toward the exit of the bay and setting a course for Koli Point. This unexpected departure again caught the attention of the other task group sailors. The same phrase was vigorously repeated throughout each ship, "Something's up!" Scuttlebutt dramatically increased and anticipation levels became noticeably higher. Surely they were to hear something soon.

At Koli the dim light of evening was quickly fading into the darkness of night. Moosbrugger's gig reached shore and he anxiously escaped its hold to begin his march along the darkened path to Wilkinson's headquarters. His eagerness to learn of what had forced this new, profound change in the admiral's directive was difficult for him to hide. For this reason, his mind was wildly racing from one thought to the next, trying to anticipate what was about to be handed him.

When Freddie finally reached headquarters, he entered to find an administrative sailor awaiting him, and this young man immediately directed him to the admiral's office. Moosbrugger was quickly led through the small outer hall but noticed in passing that he was not alone, that there were some other gentlemen seated in wait nearby. Two of these men he recognized as fighter-director officers, but of the other two he was unfamiliar. The sailor opened the office door and pronounced, "Admiral, sir, Commander Moosbrugger." The admiral stood with one of his senior staff members, and he immediately beckoned that Freddie should approach.

The sage-appearing Wilkinson wasted no time at getting to his point. "Freddie," he began, "we have good reason to believe the Japanese are intending to reinforce the Vila-Stanmore area at around midnight of August sixth, using destroyers and possibly a cruiser."[18] Destroyer commanders (primarily Burke) had been hounding the admiral for some time for a crack at the Express. Now it was to be offered. "I'm ordering Calvert to keep his boats out of your way, on reserve status in Blackett Strait. Therefore, this operation is solely yours to direct. So, tell me, what do you propose to do?"[19]

If Freddie had been asked this very question twenty-four hours before, he would have likely stumbled with his response, unsure and well short of detail. But that was yesterday. Today he had with him a wealth of new information,

information that he would later refer to as "invaluable."[20] He was being offered the opportunity of a lifetime, the chance to lead a pure destroyer operation against the enemy, against the Tokyo Express no less, and he knew exactly how he intended to pursue it. Calvert and Farrow had already provided him with a great many observations on what he might expect from the enemy once sailing into Vella Gulf. This had been discussed in great detail at the earlier conference. The admiral had since provided the times and courses that were expected to be followed at meeting the enemy's advance. This had been given in the earlier dispatch. Of most importance, however, was Simpson's information, he having just that morning shared Burke's plan and how the former commander had intended to use it in his Kula Gulf approach, arguing in favor of using this same plan at Vella Gulf. Now that a similar opportunity was being offered to Moosbrugger, he felt well advised to adopt the Burke initiative, and this was the plan he offered to Wilkinson.

The admiral seemed well pleased with Moosbrugger's choice as he affirmed his approval with a positive nod, to then conclude his conversation with, "Your ships, Moose, you fight them as you see fit."[21]

Wilkinson had already promised fighter cover for the operation, just as he had already advised Freddie of the fighter-director staff awaiting him outside, the two officers who Moosbrugger had noticed earlier and who were to accompany his destroyers on this mission. Now that all the nuts and bolts of the operation had been thoroughly discussed, Wilkinson paused to invite the other two waiting gentlemen to enter into his office. He introduced these men to Moosbrugger as members of the press corps, war correspondents Pat Robinson and Art Burges. The press had long been begging for a ride with the destroyers into some action. Wilkinson advised Freddie that both reporters had been invited to go along on this mission. The admiral obviously felt that this was to be the opportunity to provide the press the very encounter—and hopeful positive outcome—they so sought. Without ado Freddie stretched forth his hand, pointed to the exit, and directed the two men to follow his lead.

Nervously waiting nearby, *Dunlap* remained committed to a back-and-forth pacing of the eerie Guadalcanal shoreline, obviously impatient for the commodore's return. The more that Moosbrugger's absence extended into the late evening hours the more the destroyer's officers and crew manifested their growing anxiety. Despite a fair amount of security, these waters remained hauntingly uncomfortable to traverse, and especially so at nighttime when visibility became so very limited.

The sky on this night was typical of the Solomons region, having become overcast and cloaked in an inky black that eyes found almost impossible to pierce. Under such conditions navigation required careful attention, or else the ship might risk the embarrassment of an accidental grounding. The threat of attack also remained a distinct possibility, as enemy submarines and airplanes still chanced a visit to the area on occasion, making alertness to such intrusions a constant necessity. Then too, there was the risk of mistaken identity, wherein some trigger-happy shore gunner or patrolling rookie pilot might mistake the ship for a Japanese intruder and take a pot-shot or two. There were still plenty of viable concerns worth the worry, and patrolling in the open anywhere in the Solomons, even in the semi-safe zones, often proved very disquieting.

Dunlap's slow and methodical rotations continued, even as the surrounding outer darkness was interrupted by the occasional passing of a friendly bomber, with its engines roaring and spouting a highly traceable blue flame exhaust while revealing a low approach to nearby Henderson Field. Otherwise, the stay, despite its risks, proved itself quite unremarkable, with but one exception; this being that when the commodore's gig returned, it did so with a surprising complement of passengers.

Certainly, if scuttlebutt had not already enough conjecture for the spreading, with this arrival aboard ship of press representatives, a new tidal wave of speculation now thundered its way throughout all the ranks. As might be expected, while being shown to their quarters, the two correspondents quickly found themselves the focus of every man's attention, with curious eyes watching their every move and incessant whispers following their every passing.

Once having returned to Purvis, *Dunlap* quickly settled in for the night. But there was too much excitement for many to sleep. The two reporter guests were almost immediately invited to the officers' wardroom for coffee, where all of the off-duty lieutenants and ensigns had already gathered, eager to inquire of the two gentlemen all that they knew—which was, quite frankly, much less than was hoped. Even so, the two reporters were besieged by an unending line of questioning.

Pat Robinson, it was quickly learned, was quite the veteran at covering the war. Considerably older and far more experienced than the more anxious-appearing Burges, Robinson was known as "The Dean" of the war correspondents. During his long tour in New Guinea, Robinson had met MacArthur in person and had witnessed firsthand a great many deadly actions. He had been a sportswriter before the war and rightly carried his play-by-play writing style with him as he described his many prolific observations for the enjoyment of his many readers back home. But Burges was no novice at covering this war either, as he too had spent a great amount of time traipsing through the mud and misery with the troops in the jungles, learning early on the many dangers that this new war brought. It was quickly obvious, however, that neither man knew much about Navy life or was well versed in naval terms. Robinson readily acknowledged to his captivated audience that about all he knew of the Navy was that there was a "captain-of-the-head" (a title often given to some screw-up who found favor as the ship's custodian over toilets), which drew a good sum of laughter.[22] Even so, this man's talent and flair for storytelling was equal to that of any old salt. He easily captured everyone's attention with his sharing of some of his wilder exploits while serving with MacArthur's troops on New Guinea (much of which Robinson had already fashioned into a book entitled *The Fight For New Guinea; General Douglas MacArthur's First Offensive*, Random House, 1943). Still, it was this upcoming mission that these officers had the most interest in learning about, and their questions to this theme were ever-recurring. Still, regardless of such determined interrogation, neither correspondent could provide the information that the officers and crew were truly hoping to hear. These two men just had not a clue of what to expect. "Admiral Wilkinson," Burges explained, "notified us on very short-notice of this opportunity to travel with the destroyers, telling us only 'that we might see a good show.'"[23]

* * *

Back at Rabaul's Simpson Harbor and shortly after his return to *Shigure*, Captain Hara set in motion the preparations for his ship's departure. He did so reluctantly. The conference with Sugiura had lasted nearly two hours, but the concluding details provided Hara with no sense of reassurance. He remained extremely suspicious of the plan and its potential for success. He was certain that a repeat of the previous Express route was a mistake. But he had done all he could do at persuading Sugiura otherwise.

The next several hours were to be very busy. Fuel tanks were topped off while crews made last-minute inspections of each piece of crucial equipment. In the meantime, boats—from which the supplies and troops destined for Kolombangara were to be brought aboard—arrived alongside Sugiura's destroyers. Hara stood motionless on the wing of *Shigure*'s bridge, observing without expression as 250 soldiers crowded onto his destroyer's outer deck. They could not know what awaited them. Hara hoped the journey would go well and that they would reach their destination safely—but he was obsessed with many doubts.

By midnight the preparations—as much as they were—were complete. The time to depart was set for 3:00 A.M. Sugiura, aboard *Hagikaze*, was to lead the way, followed by *Arashi* and *Kawakaze*, with *Shigure* as rear guard.

The sky on this night was overcast but the sea was calm, making the initial prospects for the passage to appear good. Intermittent rain squalls were expected, and these would be welcome cover for their advance, assisting the ships at eluding the eyes of the enemy, especially from the air. Hara had been informed by Sugiura not to worry so much about early detection by enemy planes, as he felt assured that their restricted range of 300 miles still applied, since they had encountered no such air activity in the previous transits. But Hara was far less certain. The Rendova airfield was most assuredly being used by the enemy by now, making the likelihood of farther-ranging air patrols of greater concern. Again, Hara felt Sugiura was taking too much for granted, adding to the risks of the mission, causing him to once again shake his head in frustration.

* * *

Morning at Purvis on August 6 awakened to the growling sound of Commander Simpson's gig preparing for departure from *Lang*, destined for a swift crossing of the bay's darkened surface on a direct approach to *Dunlap*. Earlier this morning Moosbrugger had sent an invitation to his second-in-command, requesting that he attend a private breakfast for the expressed purpose of reviewing Burke's plan one more time, discussing the necessity for any revisions before bringing the other commanders to conference. It was to be a crucial meeting—in more ways than one.

Simpson, for the most part, was well known for his brash outspokenness, a tendency that often rubbed his fellow officers the wrong way. The officers aboard *Lang* found him "abrasive" and "intrusive." Commander Wilfong, *Lang*'s highly disciplined skipper, often butted heads with Simpson, accusing him of interference in ship business and of circumventing the structured chain-of-command. Even so, Wilfong held great respect for Simpson's leadership. The commodore was widely recognized as one of the Navy's finest warriors, brilliant in battle and emboldened by challenge. Regardless of his reputation as a commander with personal motives, often mistrusted as self-serving, Simpson remained a critically important asset at achieving Wilkinson's directive. Therefore, Moosbrugger had good reason to cautiously display a sincere respect for the man. He was not to deny Simpson's credentials—he did indeed recognize Simpson as a gifted and brave leader, even despite his tendency at being self-absorbed and overly focused on his own destiny. Neither was Moosbrugger to be fooled by Simpson—it was obvious that Simpson's respect for Moosbrugger was low, just as his respect for Burke and Burke's plan was high. Freddie understood this, and he quickly determined a way to use this bit of understanding to his own advantage—gaining Simpson's loyalty simply by embracing Burke's proposal. Such was certainly no hard choice; after all, Burke's plan was well conceived and a perfect fit for the Vella Gulf mission; and Moosbrugger's positive response to Simpson's suggestion at using it did indeed play well with Simpson's ultra ego. For the short-term, at least, Moosbrugger had won a key bit of Simpson's confidence, and this would be all that he would need pursuant to a victory.

Winning Simpson's confidence was the easy part; winning a torpedo action against the Tokyo Express would be a far more difficult undertaking. Burke's plan was based on some study he had had of the Punic Wars and conceived while reading about one of that war's historically successful ground actions, that of a two-prong attack, precisely timed and alternating, that so readily threw the opposing side into such complete disarray and chaos as to cause his immediate destruction.[24] Recognizing its potential, Burke had quickly set to converting the tactic to naval terms and redesigning its application for explicit use by his own destroyer force. It was a plan that required two highly specialized teams, separately led, yet performing together in a planned sequence. It was an application that heavily reflected Burke's own vision of destroyer warfare, a type of operation that required leadership committed to a swift, emboldened offense, fearless in its approach and relentless to its objective. There could be no room for hesitation and/or second guessing.

Burke's plan, as it was designed, was to be executed under the cover of darkness and called for the ships to sail toward their objective in two parallel columns, each closely offset and at a protective posture of the other. They were to close the enemy on a head-on approach. Once in contact with the enemy, speed and positioning would then determine the best point for the next critical maneuver, when the two columns were to separate. The lead column was then to angle out for a parallel approach for the launching of torpedoes, while the secondary column was to simultaneously angle on a course aimed at crossing directly in front of the enemy's path, allowing this group to bring all their guns to bear while denying the enemy the same (a maneuver referred to as "the crossing of the 'T'"). If successful, the torpedo attack should cause the enemy considerable damage, create confusion, and draw his attention toward the lead column; this in turn was to allow the secondary column uninhibited opportunity for a near point-blank gunnery attack. The second attack was to inflict even greater damage and confusion for the enemy, with the effect of drawing his attention to the secondary column which, in turn, was then to allow the lead column opportunity to rush back in with its own gunnery. The crossfire to follow was designed to trap the enemy within a confined space, eliminate his ability at effective maneuvering, limit his capacity to fight back, and cause him total destruction. Moosbrugger would have likely seen this in boxing terms, referencing it as a series of well-placed jabs with the intent of knocking the opponent off balance, stunning him and allowing him no time for recovery, to then throw the knockout punch for the win.

There was a catch, however. For Burke's plan to truly have success, there was one very critical requirement, that of surprise. This was the key. If surprise could not be achieved, then the success of the operation would be placed in utmost jeopardy.

Gaining the element of surprise was certain not to be an easy chore. Even without radar the Japanese rarely missed locating their adversaries at night, regardless of the depth of darkness—and the possibility that a Japanese ship might even carry radar could never be dismissed. In addition, the Japanese had time and again proven themselves very quick to react, and they bore a reputation for unhesitant engagement with aggressively accurate gunnery and torpedoes, a very deadly combination for sure. Therefore, surprise was indeed crucial. Without it Moosbrugger's forces would likely find themselves divided, moving apart, and without the means to provide each other quick, effective support—a true recipe for disaster.

Despite the obvious risks, neither Moosbrugger nor Simpson displayed any appearance of reservation. Both men were eager to meet the challenge. They had complete confidence in their own abilities to lead and in their teams' abilities to perform. Any other plan was sure to hold similar—if not greater—degrees of peril. So, risk was somewhat a moot point. Moreover, this was their opportunity to prove the talents of an independent destroyer force in critical combat. No doubt, in comparison to some of the great sea battles already recorded in this war, this would be a small engagement. But it had such great potential, certain to raise morale and sure to advance the Solomons campaign to its conclusion—and perhaps it might even redirect the future of destroyer operations.

Once having concluded to their own satisfaction that the plan was indeed sound, Moosbrugger and Simpson quickly called for a conference on the matter. It was now time to reveal the objective and the plan to their commanders. Lieutenant Commander Iverson (*Dunlap*), Lt. Comm. Francis Williamson (*Craven*), Commander Sims (*Maury*), Commander Wilfong (*Lang*), and Lt. Comm. Roy Newton (*Stack*) were soon present and being handed their orders (Lt. Comm.

Frank Gould with *Sterett* was absent on patrol and was to rendezvous with the group in transit). The briefing that followed was concise and to the point. There was little time to waste; they were to depart at 11:30 a.m. (one hour in advance of Wilkinson's schedule due to *Maury* having an engineering problem that restricted her speed to 27 knots). The veteran commanders listened carefully to Moosbrugger, understanding fully what he expected of them and their officers and men. They were headed for assured combat, and they could afford no mistakes.

Meanwhile, the activities for the men aboard the destroyers of Task Group 31.2 quickly increased to a fever pitch. As the captains returned, they immediately handed down their orders for preparation to depart. There was to be no leisure on this morning. Fuel tanks were topped off, ammunition was inspected, and every piece of critical equipment was carefully scrutinized.

Aboard destroyer *Craven*, senior radio technician, First Class Radioman George Pritchett, recalled his orders from the ship's communications officer, Lieutenant (jg) Gaudy. "Mr. Gaudy," Pritchett wrote, "told me to work on the SG [surface search] Radar; to go over everything and if anything was even questionable to replace it. I was also to bring up anything [in the way of spare parts] I could think [of that might be needed] from the storeroom and [place it] in the transmitter shack. If the radar went down I was to get it back on the air as soon as possible." The urgency in Gaudy's voice combined with the increased shipboard activity was sure notice to the seriousness of the message. Pritchett concluded, "We were going into some kind of action."[25]

Indeed, every ship was suddenly alive with similar activities. Sailors swarmed about the decks of each vessel, expeditious in their efforts to complete every given assignment. Even ashore on nearby Tulagi—where supply requisitions from the destroyers were being filled with an unrestrained fervor—the increase in activity was so noted. The urgency was evident. Even Moosbrugger displayed impatience, sending an insistent plea to the base ordnance department, requesting speedy delivery of the new torpedo warhead extensions recently designed for the Mark 15 torpedoes, the American destroyer's most powerful weapon, a 21-inch diameter underwater missile that carried 660 pounds of Torpex explosive. Iverson had tried to acquire the new warheads when his ship was in Noumea, just prior to its move to Tulagi, but none were then available. *Craven* and *Maury* already had their torpedoes fitted with the enlarged warhead, a Torpex-filled extension that increased the torpedo's punch to nearly 900 pounds of explosives. Moosbrugger desperately wanted the same for *Dunlap*, and Tulagi had the extensions available—if only they could be acquired in the short time that remained before his ships' departures.

Without a doubt, of all its weapon systems, the torpedo was the destroyer's most lethal. This was the weapon that had given the destroyer its birthright and provided it with the power to effect its intended purpose, that of disposing of any seaborne vessel, regardless of size, speed, and/or strength. All other weapons were secondary, mere evolutions to the broadening roles given the destroyer. The torpedo remained the destroyer's primary weapon against ships. And, in the hands of a well-trained and experienced crew, no ship was safe from its deadly sting.

The Mark 15, however, had a crucial defect—it had a record of failure. It did not always detonate as it was designed. The Bureau of Ordnance had repeatedly tested and determined its torpedoes as "reliable" weapons, but in the field they were not performing up to their expectations. Time and again the American torpedoes were failing to detonate against their targets. In retrospect, the reasons behind these failures were multiple and complicated, encompassing an array of issues, including a fault in the Mark 15's depth-determining gyro, a miscalculation in its evolution of explosive weight, a weakness in its Mark 6 magnetic exploder, and even a flaw in its contact trigger. For more than a year these problems had persisted, but by August 1943, and despite some heavy suspicions as to the causes, it still remained unclear how they were to be resolved.[26] Moosbrugger, as did all commanders in the field, was well aware of the reports, but he too had no assured solutions. He now found himself in the position of preparing to lead destroyers on a major mission against the intrepid Tokyo Express with a problematic weapon that he relied on for success. This was a concern that he could dire afford to dismiss. He needed his torpedoes to work.

Moosbrugger had heard of the Navy's new Mark 17 torpedo and had inquired of them while in Noumea, but these had yet to be approved for use in the theater.[27] Certainly this new torpedo would have been greatly beneficial, as the newly designed Mark 17 was a patent improvement over the Mark 15 with both explosive punch and propulsion (carrying more than 1,000 pounds of Torpex explosive and driven by a more efficient hydrogen peroxide fuel), even as it also had new problems unique to its propulsion and retained some of the Mark 15's design flaws. Without any further options, Moosbrugger was assured of two things: (1) his torpedoes were lacking explosive punch and (2) their Mark 6 magnetic exploders were not working. The solutions, as he saw it, were twofold: (1) add the Torpex-filled warhead extensions and (2) disconnect the magnetic exploders and rely on the contact exploders only.

The decision to disconnect the magnetic exploders was highly popular. The Mark 6 was a close proximity fuse designed to be triggered by the magnetic field emitted by a ship's hull, causing the torpedo to explode directly under its target. The concept was German, originally used with mines during World War I, and it was a good design. The real issue was not so much the device itself as it was with the running depth of the torpedo. The underlying problem was caused by the poorly engineered positioning of the Mark 15's gyro, which allowed for the torpedo to run deeper than its setting, causing it to pass too far beneath the ship's hull to trigger the magnetic exploder. But this issue had not been fully determined at the date of Moosbrugger's Vella Gulf mission. Additionally, the Japanese had already developed a process of degaussing (demagnetizing) their ships' hulls, so when in use this altogether negated the effectiveness of the magnetic trigger. On the other hand, there was also a known flaw existing with the contact exploder, wherein it was susceptible to damage upon impact, though the failure rate of this device was very low in comparison to the Mark 6. Thus, the magnetic exploder was awarded all the blame for every previous failure. Wilber Fultz expressed this universal sentiment well. "We . . . got the word on our orders," he wrote, "[and] the torpedo gang went to work removing the 'Buck Rogers' crap out of the warheads and put them back on the old arming thing."[28]

The addition of the Torpex-filled warhead extensions was to be Moosbrugger's other resolution at correcting his torpedo deficiency problem, but, unknown to him, this was to add yet another issue. The additional explosive was to give the Mark 15 greater destructive power, but it also added nearly 500 pounds of weight. The unknown gyro issue was already causing failure at meeting the required depth settings and this extra weight was only to exacerbate the problem. Fortunately, there were a few keen individuals who did have some understanding of this issue. First Class Torpedoman James Fisher, acting chief torpedoman aboard *Maury*, already had some suspicions about the torpedo's errant running depth and quickly foresaw the problem with the extensions. "The new warhead extensions," he later noted, "made such a tremendous difference in the torpedo's weight that I figured that normal settings would cause the torpedoes to go beneath their targets. We had a prescribed setting for our firing calculations, but I was sure that they would run too deep with the new extensions."[29] Lieutenant Crenshaw had come to a similar awareness while waiting at Tulagi. "There was plenty of time to think," he wrote, "and after I had made sure everything was okay in [the] CIC and checked the gun battery . . . I started thinking about our torpedoes. I had seen with my own eyes at close range the torpedoes [mistakenly] fired at *Gwin* by *Ralph Talbot* [during the July 10 Battle of Kolombangara]. I had seen three of them pass under *Gwin*'s keel amidships, where they must have been drawing at least 20 feet. The only possibility was that the torpedoes were running deeper than set. Much deeper!"[30]

Then, in addition to his own torpedo woes, Moosbrugger faced yet another, even more worrisome unknown, that of the character of the Japanese torpedo. The Imperial Japanese Navy's best kept secret of the entire war was its 24-inch Type 93 "Long Lance" torpedo. The Long Lance was a deadly accurate piece of engineering not fully understood by American commanders and engineers till after the war's conclusion. It used oxygen for its propulsion and revealed almost no visible wake, making it nearly undetectable during its speedy approach. In addition, it carried a 1,000-pound warhead at speeds ranging from 36 to 49 knots with a maximum range of 43,000 yards. In comparison, on a good day the Mark 15 carried 900 pounds of explosives at speeds of between 28 to 46 knots with a maximum range of just 15,000 yards. More importantly, the Long Lance had excellent reliability. So, other than the consistent successes the Japanese had had with their torpedoes, Moosbrugger knew almost nothing of what he was facing.

In his conference with his commanders, Moosbrugger cautiously reiterated the importance of their covert approach, dependent on surprise for gaining the initial advantage. Even then, he could not have known just how greatly their future success was to hinge on this one element. Though Freddie rightly planned for every possibility—and he had the best team possible for the task—Sugiura's ships could still outfight him, even despite their encumbrance of troops and supplies. If stealth was in any way lost then likely so too would be any chance at victory. If torpedoes, being justifiably at question, were by any oversight allowed greater opportunity to fail, warning the enemy of attack, then so too was the mission to fail. There was no in-between. Perhaps unwittingly, Wilkinson's directive asked of Moosbrugger to accomplish the impossible: to achieve the perfect offensive maneuver, at night, and do so against the highly touted Tokyo Express. Surely some old fashioned "good luck" was in order. Even so, the veteran Moosbrugger knew better than to wager the future of this mission—or any other for that matter—on such well-wishing, even despite an appreciation for such a gesture. Victory, most assuredly, was to rely on talent, ability, and sound judgments, and not good fortune. Indeed, at Vella Gulf, the latter was to play almost no role at all.

Midshipman Arleigh Burke

Midshipman Frederick Moosbrugger

Arleigh with new bride Roberta "Bobbie" Gorsuch

Freddie's "flock": Dorothy, Edward, Dave, and Fred in 1943

Ens. Arleigh Burke aboard the *Arizona*

The *Mugford* as she appeared at the time of Burke's command

Lieutenant Commander Burke along with his officers aboard the *Mugford*. Standing right of Arleigh is Gelzer Sims, who would later lead *Maury* during the Battle of Vella Gulf.

The outspoken Henry D. Davison
as a midshipman

The *Craven* in 1943 and Lt. Comm. Francis T. Williamson

Wilber Fultz at the Isaacson Ranch, Fort Benton, Montana, in 1938

Wilber in 1943, right after Vella Gulf

Midshipman Albert R. Olsen

Even as a young boy, Olsen knew his destiny.

The Olsen clan. Seated (L to R) Anna, Hjalmar, and daughter Anna. Standing (L to R) are sons Charles, Clarence, Earl, Robert, and Albert.

Pemberton Southard as a midshipman (top left),
as the executive officer of *Lang* (top right),
and with Comm. John L. Wilfong (right).

The *Lang* on August 28, 1943, right after Vella Gulf while returning home

Pem and Jane (Duvall) finally had their "postponed" wedding at Charleston on September 12, 1943.

Russell S. Crenshaw Jr.

The *Maury* and Comm. Gelzer L. Sims

The *Sterett* and Comm. Frank G. Gould

Joseph D. Jeffrey

Harold E. Shear

The *Stack* and Comm. Roy A. Newton

Ralph Barber with his new bride, Virginia (Adair) Barber, in 1943

Ralph Barber as he appeared in 1944, still sailing with *Dunlap*

Gunner's Mate Charles "Chuck" Lee and Patricia Skinner on their first date, September 1942

Chuck Lee during a brief return to the States in 1943, a veteran of South Pacific combat

Dunlap in full dress in 1938

Dunlap leaders, front row (L to R) Lt. Vining Sherman, Lt. Comm. Clifton Iverson, and Lt. C. F. "Doc" Binder

Dunlap was one of only two Fanning class destroyers built.

Dunlap's officers and crew as photographed September 1943

Comm. Frederick Moosbrugger, C.O.
Task Group 31.2, aboard *Dunlap*

Rodger W. Simpson

Simpson aboard *Mahan* with early victories

Arleigh Burke in the Solomons

Adm. Theodore S. "Ping" Wilkinson Jr.

Adm. Gunichi Mikawa

Adm. Raizo Tanaka

Capt. Tameichi Hara

Capt. Kaju Sugiura

Shigure, the lone survivor of Captain Sugiura's group of destroyers

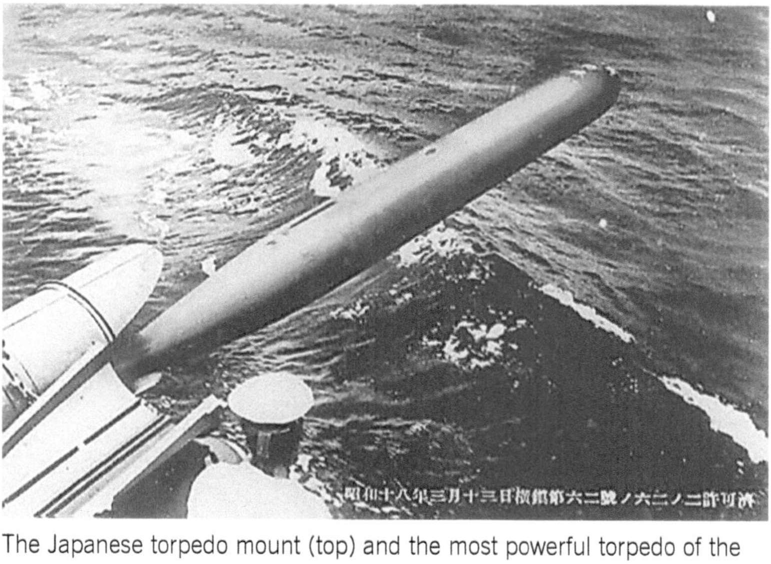

The Japanese torpedo mount (top) and the most powerful torpedo of the war, the "Long Lance" (bottom)

Craven's officers and chiefs on Noumea, January 1943—with Moosbrugger, Oliver, and Williamson (in rectangle) and Chief Torpedoman Mowrey (in circle)

Loyd Peters

James D. Oliver Jr.

Lt. Dan Gray (right) with Lt. Edward Eunson, *Lang*'s gunnery officer

War correspondent Pat Robinson (center) in New Guinea just prior to his move to the Solomons and his historic nightlong ride aboard *Lang* to and from Vella Gulf

Mitchell Sang (center) was the only American sailor to suffer an injury during the Vella Gulf action—a crushed hand at a 5-inch shell hoist at gun station #3 aboard *Lang*.

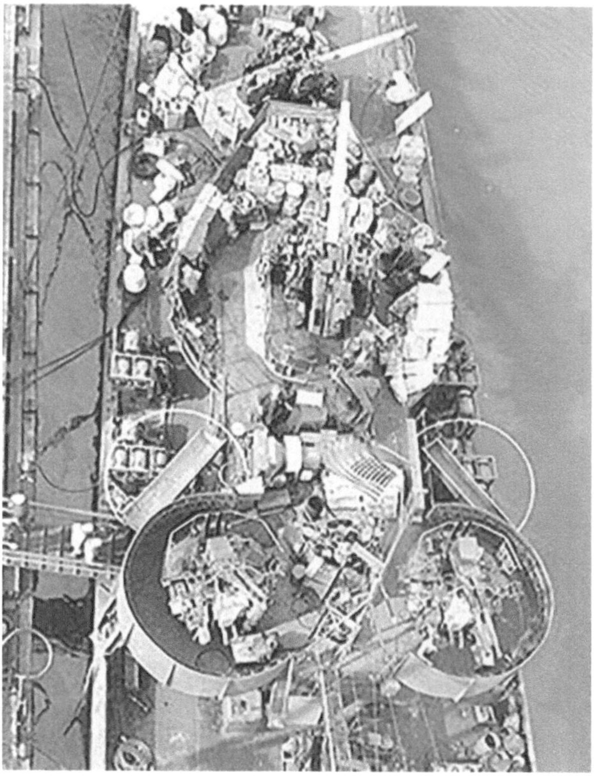

Above view of the after section of the *Lang* as seen in 1943, showing 5-inch guns #4 (upper), #3 (center), and the two twin-mounted 40mm guns (lower)

Starboard bridge wing of *Dunlap*, early 1944, having the three silhouettes of Japanese destroyers sunk at Vella Gulf

Crenshaw receiving the Silver Star

Olsen receiving the Silver Star

Commander Moosbrugger on September 10, 1943 after receiving the Navy Cross

Chapter Seven

All Ahead

Into Destiny's Darkness

As the deadline for departure quickly neared, Commander Moosbrugger took a moment to anxiously glance at the watch banded to his wrist. The time was 11:15 A.M. A boat carrying his requested torpedo warhead extensions was only now drawing near to *Dunlap*. This yard barge—a slow and cumbersome vessel—noisily churned the water, meticulously maneuvering close aboard the destroyer in its less-than-eager attempt to moor alongside. The cargo it held was well within grasp, but disappointedly so. Freddie turned to Iverson. "Send it back," he stated in disgust. "It's too late."[1]

The task group was committed to departing Purvis at 11:30 A.M., and Moosbrugger was to wager no delay for an additional amount of TNT for his torpedoes. The torpedoes were extremely crucial to the success of this mission, but so too was timing. Regardless of the need, the commander intended to sail into Vella Gulf on schedule. The torpedoes he had—though having a little less punch than he desired—would have to do. Time, however, was not a possession with which he cared to gamble. His ships' boilers were lit and up to steam. They were ready to go. He would order the anchors weighed and they would depart the Tulagi anchorage on time, just as had been planned.

Indeed, Lt. Comm. Roy Newton was by this same 11:30 mark already on the move, directing his destroyer, *Stack*, in advance of the others of the task group. The thirty-six-year-old Texan, a gangly man with a dimpled chin and sad eyes, had been in command of the veteran destroyer only since February, coming aboard while *Stack* enjoyed a rare moment stateside, at Mare Island for overhaul work. His initial arrival had not been well received by the destroyer's veteran crew, and it had taken him awhile to gain their confidence and respect. Newton, it was quickly noted, had a bit of a nervous character about him, and this trait became an immediate concern for those men who were to serve under him.

Nervousness, it was felt, was an indicator of potential indecisiveness, neither of which had a place in good leadership, especially in the South Pacific. Fortunately, by this August departure several months were already expired, having since allowed the captain opportunity to prove competency at his job, easing much of his crew's previous apprehensions.[2]

Stack's early departure was specific to orders given by the commodore, to leave first in order to catch up with the patrolling *Sterett*. Newton was to deliver Moosbrugger's sealed orders to *Sterett*'s skipper, Lt. Comm. Frank Gould.[3]

Gould, who had first come aboard *Sterett* as its executive officer in February of 1942, was known as a by-the-book type but whose leadership was fair. This captain understood what it took to command men, especially while at sea for long periods and experiencing extended absences from home and family. He had an overall concern for the well-being of his crew, and this had gained him considerable respect. Therefore, for Gould, the significance of Moosbrugger's sealed orders—which he surely did not take lightly—rated equal to that of *Stack*'s other cargo, a special allotment of precious bundles of newly arrived mail belonging to *Sterett*'s officers and crew.[4] Delivery of these letters and parcels had expeditious importance to the ship. (Mail did not come often in the Pacific and was always a great morale booster, and a crew's spirit was always an important factor toward success—not to mention, for some, it might be a final word from home, an offering that should never be denied.) Gould's men were knowingly going into battle and a letter from home was usually the perfect "pick-me-up" to sailors suffering the many uncertainties of the Solomons campaign. Surely the captain would make this delivery of his highest priority.

The rest of the task group (*Dunlap*, *Craven*, *Maury*, and *Lang*) followed *Stack*'s departure by only a few minutes. Moosbrugger, dressed in his khakis, sat in his chair at the bridge pilothouse, staring quietly across the distant seascape. The moment was subdued. Everyone was busy with his own individual tasks. The distinct vibrations of *Dunlap*'s powerful turbines could be felt across the entire plate surface of the ship's decking, noticeably so to the soles of the feet of each man aboard, notifying all of the commencement of this newest journey.

Speed increased and the destroyer's bow cut deeply into the water, leaving behind a traceable path of foam across the azure bay while leading as yet to some still mysterious and undisclosed destination. This was the beginning of what was certain to be many hours of tension-filled sailing. Many questions remained to be answered, and these, when answered, were sure to produce even more. It was this unknown, this uncertainty of what lay ahead, that taunted so many minds.

Aboard *Lang*, Commander Simpson stood his usual station on the ship's bridge posing his most serious stance. He appeared positively astute and attentive to the moment, quietly observing as Commander Wilfong directed the destroyer's course and speed. The forty-year-old Wilfong was a veteran skipper and widely known for his great skill as a ship handler.[5] Simpson would not dare interfere with such a specialist; make no mistake—even despite an often-disagreeable relationship—Simpson and Wilfong were completely professional, each respectful of the other's talents and completely united in their determinations to beat the pants off their Japanese counterparts. On this occasion both leaders were behaving at the top of their game, and this was a very bad omen for Sugiura's Express.

Also standing nearby, and with a curious eye to all, was the sandy-haired and slightly built Pat Robinson. Simpson had brought the tag-along correspondent aboard at his return from this morning's conference, and the two men had rarely since been seen apart. Robinson, it was observed, did not seem predisposed to roam about the ship much, nor was he to mix with the crew.[6] Instead, he seemed more intent at having the best observation possible for coverage of his story, and Simpson, who obviously sought a good deal of Robinson's attention, was obliged that the correspondent got his wish. Wilfong could have objected. No doubt he was not overly fond of having a guest on his bridge, yet he appeared willing to put up with the observer's presence—for as long as he did not interfere with any of the operations.

Back aboard *Dunlap*, and once well outside the bay, Moosbrugger finally turned to Iverson and gave an approving nod. Iverson then picked up the mike to the ship's public address system. "Attention, all hands," he began. "This is your Captain. This destroyer task group has been given orders to seek and destroy a suspected run of the Tokyo Express, expected to take place tonight somewhere off the southwest coast of Kolombangara. This is to be a night torpedo and gunnery action against enemy destroyers and possibly a cruiser. Enemy snoopers and gunboats are possible. Be alert." A similar transmission was given aboard the other ships.[7]

A few minutes later the destroyers entered Savo Sound, and Moosbrugger ordered the column into a serpentine "S" maneuver (this maneuver, having its origin accredited to Simpson, was given by most all passing American warships as a hallowed salute to all of the many ships and men already lost in these waters).[8] The moment was solemn and thought provoking, intended as a memorial to the dead and a reminder to the living that this is a terrible war that forgives no mistakes. For some—as with Lieutenant Olsen—this was a personal reminder that old scores needed to be settled and that long-sought opportunities for revenge do find an offering, even if precariously so. Indeed, a deadly confrontation with the enemy was brewing, and no longer were they sailing bound to the defense of other ships or being restricted in their pursuit. This time they were hunters seeking a trophy. This time they were free to engage the enemy as they saw fit. And the men of Task Group 31.2 were as ready as any could be at completing such a task.

Young Lt. Joseph Poitevin, a native Iowan and naval reservist serving aboard *Craven*, would later admit to "a bit of apprehension." This was to be his "first significant encounter with the Japanese." He therefore had good reason to feel some anxiety. He knew the history of the recent nighttime engagements against the Imperial Japanese Navy—as these losses were no secret. But he "didn't feel any great fear . . . . This . . . was offset by my confidence in the *Craven* and its experienced crew, as well as . . . the other five destroyers in our group, that had survived a year and a half of tough war . . . in the South Pacific."[9]

Years after the fact, veteran after veteran, regardless of the destroyer and/or position they served, spoke of this moment with unanimous agreement to Poitevin's single sentiment of "confidence." They were all confident in their leaders, their training, and their abilities at meeting any challenge. They were equally confident in each other, knowing the performance of every man would be crucial. And they were confident toward success. They were indeed "confident," but, as Poitevin, they could not help but also be just as admittedly anxious.

Lieutenant Davison noted the reality well. "Hell," he stated emphatically, "there's not a man alive that doesn't get very apprehensive every time there is a prospect of action. Sooner or later you learn that if you get hit, you get hit, and fluffing off on the job isn't going to put any armor anywhere, make fires any cooler or shrapnel any gentler."[10] In other words, you deal with the fears and you do your job.

Lieutenant Olsen would surely have agreed with Davison, as he clearly understood the tendency of all men to be fearful of the unknown. The Solomons campaign had always presented itself as a deadly arena that left day-to-day survival in question. He expected to see—even feel—the anxiety. During this departure, however, the reactions by some of the crew were even a bit surprising to him. He found the sailors aboard *Dunlap* were taking this new mission with an unprecedented level of seriousness. "In the afternoon," Olsen wrote, "while making our approach, a few of the men were carrying small Bibles and one group did gather behind gun mount #1 to talk and sing a few hymns. I had never seen this happen before."[11]

The group passed Savo Island in the early afternoon, and it was here that *Sterett* and *Stack* were seen to rejoin the formation.[12] The task group was now complete. Moosbrugger immediately ordered the force to a pre-determined antiaircraft formation, a circular configuration that was to allow maximum gun coverage during the daylight hours. *Lang* moved to the van of the circle, while *Maury*, *Craven*, *Sterett*, and *Stack* took stations along the rest of the outer ring. In the center was *Dunlap*, designated as primary fighter-director, having one of the two fighter-director officers aboard.[13] *Maury* remained the secondary fighter-director. All defensive precautions were now in place and the force proceeded forward, semi-secure and watchful.

The rest of the officers were by this time clearly informed of the objective and the plan. The proposal was well received. Moosbrugger's adaptation of Burke's plan was both operationally sound and unique—even in spite of the risks of night engagement. Lieutenant Davison reflected his approval of Moosbrugger's choice. "He didn't head us up the Slot but instead set a course that passed south of the Russels [*sic*], on up by Rendova, past the chain of islands guarding Kolambangara [*sic*], and south of Vella Lavella through Gizo Strait into Vella Gulf. The snoops [enemy reconnaissance aircraft] would be patrolling the main drag like nobody's business, but two would get you five they wouldn't figure on us coming up the back way. Hell, we had always used the Slot, hadn't we? If all went well, we could be sitting on the front porch when Hirohito delivered the groceries. If all didn't go well, we would have a few busy minutes with more than an even chance of ending up like the *Helena* and a few others that hadn't fared so well.[14] If we could stop the reinforcement, though, whatever the cost, the end would justify the means. At War College they call that 'calculated risk.'"[15]

* * *

Still overtly concerned about Sugiura's own determined "calculated risk," Capt. Tameichi Hara stood quietly at his usual spot on *Shigure*'s bridge, rigid with thought and endeavoring to go over in his mind every possible scenario that might confront him in the hours to come. So far, the journey had been unremarkable. The sea was calm. The sky was mostly cloudy yet obliging of some momentary sunshine. There were distant squalls noted, but nothing else was worthy of distraction.[16] All was quiet. They were well within the protection of their own air cover and outside the usual patrolling of the enemy (excepting that of submarines), and the dangers were to this point minimal. In other words, the mission was proceeding just as it had been planned—though Hara had his doubts that it would remain so.

By 4:30 p.m., Sugiura's column had safely reached Buka, continuing their passage south, on course and on schedule. All appeared as before, to be going well. Suddenly, Hara was shaken from his deep personal thoughts—there was some excited commotion coming from the wing of the bridge. A lookout was pointing skyward, reporting an enemy plane seen ducking into some nearby clouds. An instant later *Shigure*'s radioman announced having overheard an outgoing message, coded "Urgent," suspected as being sent from the very same plane.[17] The column had been spotted, Hara was certain. Sugiura was notified of the development, and Hara expected the division leader to surely make some type of adjustment to compensate for the enemy awareness. But no changes were made. Hara looked at Yamagami with profound disgust. He could not believe Sugiura's audacity, bordering on stupidity, seemingly inviting enemy intervention. "It grieved me," Hara wrote later, "to see our same speed of advance and course maintained, even after we had been sighted by the enemy. I gritted my teeth and followed along."[18]

* * *

At 5:30 p.m., Moosbrugger was handed a dispatch. It read in part, "*Report from Black Cat plane* [a Catalina PBY long-range patrol] *#1 of Flight 15. Japanese force sighted at latitude 04° 50' South, longitude 150° 40' East, course 190° True, speed 15 knots. Estimate time to Vella Gulf 2400* [12:00 midnight]."[19] This was the confirmation that Moosbrugger had been hoping for.

Wilkinson had assigned six Black Cats to Task Group 31.2, each tasked with the explicit purpose of searching for this enemy Express. Most of the flights had, however, encountered bad weather or developed radar problems, interrupting their patrols—but not plane #1, and it had hit paydirt. Freddie now knew that the enemy Express was indeed real and headed his way, just as Wilkinson had prophesied and just as he had planned for. He could barely contain his enthusiasm. Everything was moving along perfectly. Still, he knowingly remained a long way from victory.

Having the Black Cat report in hand, at 6:00 p.m. Moosbrugger confidently ordered his ships to form into a single column (*Dunlap* in the van, followed by *Craven*, *Maury*, *Lang*, *Sterett*, and *Stack*, in this order) with each vessel spaced at intervals of 500 yards.[20] The group then marched forward, presenting an impressive line that was bent on completing its mission and with a readiness to meet whatever challenge the enemy might send its way. Indeed, the hunt was on and—even despite an acknowledged high degree of apprehension—the crews would be sorely disappointed if they did not find their prey.

Word of the spotted enemy ships spread quickly throughout each of the preying destroyers, stirring a great many personal conjectures about what might be encountered in the hours ahead. The talk remained, to this point, positive.

Aboard *Sterett*, Lieutenant Jeffrey arrived in the wardroom for dinner, entering to a great din of ongoing discussion. He sat and quietly listened, somewhat amused but equally concerned by what he heard. "The new officers fervently hoped we would run into the whole Japanese Navy," he noted, "[while] the older and more experienced quietly prayed that any engagement would be short, with a minimum of casualties to our forces."[21] No doubt Jeffrey could empathize with the excitement being generated by the pending action, especially by those who had yet to experience the true horrors of open sea combat. He, however, still had vivid recollections of *Sterett*'s earlier encounter with enemy forces at night. That meeting, he remembered all too well, had not been so pleasant. This meeting, he understood, could end equally the same—though he truly prayed it would not.

Aboard *Craven*, Gunner's Mate 3rd Class Carl Lanz stood his post at the helm, nervously steering the ship.[22] He also displayed some of the same evolving anxieties. *His* greater anxiety, however, was not so much for any pending action—though this too surely occupied his mind—as it was instead for avoiding some silly mistake at the wheel. Following the lead of *Dunlap* might appear as a simple task, but in truth it was quite trying, requiring many adjustments. The ship's captain, Lt. Comm. Francis Williamson, kept close watch of his ship's progression, and such rigid oversight could certainly play havoc with the nerves of any already anxious helmsman. But Williamson was a caring and careful leader, who proved never to be so overbearing with his supervision.

A Rhode Islander and a veteran destroyer officer, Francis Williamson had the distinction of having come from a very close-knit family, a family that (similar to the Olsens) had sent into service six commissioned brothers, of whom he was the first. A highly respected leader and a good friend to Moosbrugger, he was known for having a pleasant, almost fatherly demeanor. Lanz fondly recalled Williamson, adorned in his khakis, sitting in his captain's chair and calmly coaching the men around him. "We talked about steering the ship in column, which is hard to do because of the wake from the forward ship. He advised me not to over steer."[23] Williamson's good nature had its usual calming effect on Lanz, and his anxieties settled for the moment. But this night was just beginning, and this captain was sure to have his hands full at trying to ease all the apprehensions along this journey.

Since leaving Purvis, Moosbrugger's task group had maintained an average speed of 25 knots, keeping its advance steady, and was enjoying the cooperation of calm seas. Time, to this point, had passed by rather quickly and the progress was good. Each tick of the clock was bringing the American force closer to destiny's door, and each milestone of its pre-assigned course was one step nearer to revealing the true mettle of its leadership and crews. Jeffrey remarked, "To the north we could see the Russell Islands, over which floated lazy, golden cream-puff clouds set in a bright blue sky. Ahead to the west and low on the horizon was an ominous line of storm clouds."[24] How could he not but wonder if this was a sign, a sort of premonition of the thunderous battle to come.

By 6:24 P.M., the sun was setting low on the horizon. Orders were given to "darken ship" and "prepare for maximum speed."[25] So far everything was proceeding as planned—Moosbrugger was maintaining his schedule and he continued to display his confidence toward success. The influx of critical information was readily available to the bridge, and nothing to this point gave reason for any undue concern.

As was expected, the new CICs were very busy. Olsen, Southard, Crenshaw, Davison, and the rest of the CIC crews were regularly distributing to their respective commanders the ranges and bearings of the nearby islands, using radar, dead reckoning, and soundings. Here it needs to be noted, however, that radar ranges and bearings had to be received with a bit of caution, as actual island shorelines were well below the radar's line of sight. Accidental grounding was of real concern—as such an event would surely end the mission, not to mention place the ships at great peril. For this reason alone, Moosbrugger was to make several trips from the bridge to the chart-house directly below, personally checking that his intended track-line was being meticulously followed.

Meanwhile, the crews of each of the ships continued their preparations. Most ominous of these provisions were those of the medical departments. Aboard *Dunlap*, Pharmacist's Mate Ralph Barber had been assigned to the aft repair party, and there he was busy setting up an operating table and first-aid station in the crew's head. His preparations caught the attention of many passing sailors, and he could sense their alienation to his activities.[26] No doubt this was all so very new to him. He had been aboard the destroyer for only thirteen days. He had never even witnessed any of the ship's guns fired, and especially not in hostility. That the others around him were anxious was obvious, but he did not fully comprehend this anxiety. He did understand that they were heading into enemy territory and that there was a likelihood of casualties, but at this point the seriousness of this matter had not fully registered with him. This was for him just like a drill—like all the other drills he had been involved with before, that of training and not reality. Besides, he had seen many casualties at the hospital on

Noumea. It had not yet occurred to him that *his* life was at risk. Soon, he would understand fully.

Barber's boss and ship's doctor, Lt. C. F. Binder, a most professional man, did understand the seriousness of the matter. Once having thoroughly checked all of his preparations, he immediately approached the CIC to report to his good friend Olsen. Olsen was very busy but quietly paused upon seeing the doctor approach. "Everything in sickbay is ready," Binder stated matter-of-factly and in a monotone voice.[27] Olsen nodded, silently acknowledging his friend's information. The doctor's report was brief but spoke tons, jolting Olsen to a new sense of reality—this was the first moment of this mission that he would truly assess the genuine possibility for casualties. His job in the CIC now revealed itself to be even more critical.

On board *Sterett* the ship's doctor, Lt. Harry Nyce, took a different approach to his job. After checking his supplies and finalizing his preparations, he made a concerted effort to wander the ship and to engage in jolly conversations with the men, hoping some humorous stories might still their nerves and lift their spirits—this being the best medicine he could possibly prescribe to them before assured combat. Jeffrey would later note of Nyce, "Destroyer doctors had an unenviable position. They either died a thousand deaths from the boredom of professional disease or had so much business that one medico could cope with it only through superhuman strength."[28]

Regardless of what might await them, Moosbrugger's ships continued along their path, determined and steadfast. So far there had not been a single interruption at meeting their schedule. The group's progress had been uninhibited. But at 7:58 p.m., *Dunlap* suddenly began to slow. There was a bit of a scramble on the bridge at seeking the cause of the problem. In response, engineering reported that a shot of water into the steam had tripped out the main throttle. Iverson immediately contacted *Craven* by TBS (Talk Between Ships), notifying Williamson of the trouble while hoping to avoid any accidental collision. This glitch, however, proved very short lived, as *Dunlap*'s excellent engineering department had learned from their lessons in the past and soon had the problem fixed and their ship back up to full speed. In fact, less than thirty seconds elapsed with the correction, affecting no negative impact to Moosbrugger's important schedule.[29]

Fifteen minutes later, in a separate incident, a lookout on *Dunlap*'s bridge wing calmly pointed out what appeared to be a searchlight bearing 262 degrees True. The initial thought was that the light was originating from Simbo Island, but a navigational check proved it to be too far south. Moosbrugger determined the light, wherever its origin, to be too distant to be of immediate concern and it was therefore ignored (a dispatch on the following day would reveal this light as having originated from a flare accidentally discharged by a friendly plane).[30]

By 7:30 p.m. the task group was heading northwest toward Gizo Strait, designated "Point Option," the entrance into Vella Gulf. Gizo Strait was a narrow passageway, treacherous and confining, unfriendly to ships in daylight let alone at night. Moosbrugger ordered "General Quarters" and set the material condition "Able," the highest condition of readiness. All non-essential functions were now to be secured, except freshwater and flushing systems which were temporarily left in operation.[31] There was no doubt that this juncture would be critical.

They were now closing in on enemy territory. The surrounding sea and sky were quickly being consumed by darkness. It was also beginning to rain. As a result, visibility steadily decreased and lookouts were forced to strain their eyes to see even a mile distant. Again, Moosbrugger would have to depend on navigation from Iverson and his CIC.

In the meantime, the men of *Dunlap*'s crew scurried about the ship's darkened decks, each one endeavoring to reach his individual GQ stations and with the greatest possible haste. They knew this was no drill—this was serious business, requiring a serious response. "This wasn't the home grounds any more," as Lieutenant Sherman so noted, "we were a visiting team." The lieutenant, just like every other man aboard, seemed well prepared. "I checked my life jacket and my helmet, and I put the little tin of emergency rations which my Aunt Marguerite had sent me, together with an extra clip of 45-caliber cartridges, into my pocket. And with an oilskin raincoat thrown over my shoulders like a cloak, I went out on deck to check the repair parties with Ensign Paul Stevens."[32]

With similar expediency, Torpedoman 2nd Class Robert Wallick quickly gained his post, located at the torpedo director and firing mechanism just outside the bridge pilothouse. Arriving with him was Torpedoman 2nd Class Ed Hawkins, the director operator. Both men settled into their key position with just the type of swiftness they had practiced drill after drill. Wallick slipped on his talker's set—a headset and phone that allowed him to communicate with the torpedo batteries below amidships and the ship's CIC. He then fastened the oversized, gray helmet that fit snugly over the phones and listened for the confirmations from the torpedo crews. With all confirmations complete, he then reported, "Torpedoes, manned and ready." Having then finished his prerequisites, Wallick curiously turned for a gaze into the pilothouse. He was curious to see what was happening with the commanders, and he was obviously impressed with his observation. "Most men on the bridge were regular navy and very experienced," he would later write. "Captain Iverson was very active, scoping with his glasses . . . and really in control. Moosbrugger was calmly sitting in the port side wheelhouse chair, looking very confident."[33] Such was a very reassuring view, for sure.

Aboard *Sterett*, Lieutenant Jeffrey strapped on his web belt, holstering his .45-caliber automatic pistol, grabbed his life jacket, and quickly headed for his GQ. "I stepped out on the deck and into the blackest night I ever saw. Through the opaque void I [climbed] upward—more by familiarity than by sight—to the gun director, the highest battle station on the ship."[34] No doubt as he pursued his post he was once again reminded of that deadly dark night off Guadalcanal, when nine months earlier through the flash of gunfire and explosions he first saw that massive steel pagoda, that towering superstructure of the enemy battleship bearing down on his ship from out of nowhere. This night, however, promised to be different. This night, if all went as planned, the Americans would have the advantage, rewarded with overwhelming victory—so he truly hoped.

Lt. Dan Gray, aboard *Lang*, grabbed his life jacket and quick-stepped out of his compartment for the main deck. As damage control officer, he and the men under him were to prepare for the worst. "I remember saying a little prayer," he noted somberly. "[Though my] emotions were more of anticipation and excitement . . . I [was] sure a little fearful . . . because [this] was [my] first major operation."[35] His most immediate hope was that this first action would not abruptly end in tragedy, and be his last.

Aboard *Stack*, Lt. Harold Shear had a task similar to Gray. Shear was in charge of his destroyer's forward damage control party. "My responsibility was to control the damage if we were hit," he noted. This was not a pleasant thought, this possibility of being hit, but it was reality, and regardless of how unnerving, could not be discounted. "The damage control central was right at the machine shop, which was at the top of the forward engine room hatch on the main deck. I had my group of damage control people there, petty officers and machinist's mates and boatswain's mates who could take care of any damage."[36] Obviously everyone hoped to avoid any such need.

On *Craven*, Torpedoman 2nd Class William Haden and Chief Torpedoman Lyle Mowery settled into their respective positions at Torpedo Mount #2. Haden was the phone talker, and once all the crew was present, he notified his counterpart at the director, Torpedoman 1st Class William Lewis, "Mount Two, manned and ready." Afterward, they waited. "We sat at our station in the wind and rain." But this was not a meaningless wait. There was purpose. This night they were almost assured a contest with the enemy and "we were out for blood," Haden concluded.[37]

Gunner's Mate Chuck Lee reached his GQ station at *Lang*'s 5-inch gun mount #3 and quickly prepared for placing the weapon into action. Arriving with him was a broad-shouldered, 6-footer of a fellow by the name of Mitchell Sang. Coxswain Sang, a blond New Yorker with a known ill-temperament, was the projectile loader, having the task of picking up the heavy 50+ pound 5-inch projectile from an elevator lift and placing it onto a tray before the gun's breech. Chuck would then ram the projectile and its accompanying powder into the breech for firing.[38] When engaged, this process would be repeated over and over for as long as needed—or until the gun was put out of action.

Firing at night was tricky, however. Unlike the concealed mounts of *Lang*'s forward two 5-inch guns which had some lighting, gun #3 (as well as #4) was an open mount. In the darkness it was hard for the crew to see. They worked their tasks mostly by instinct, taught from hours upon hours of drill. There was one distinct advantage to the open mount, however, and this was that it did allow its crew to have full view of all that was going on around them—and on this night they were sure to get quite a show.

The former Montana cow hand, Wilber Fultz, found his anxieties to be just as high as everyone else. His GQ was first powderman for *Craven*'s 5-inch gun #2. He and the five other men who made up the gun crew were all housed within the gun's heavy steel outer shell, tightly huddled within its claustrophobic darkness. They were ready for action but, momentarily, there was nothing for them to do except wait. It was not a comfortable feeling, corralled inside the steel housing, not knowing what to expect or when. Easing some of their confinement, one of the men had opened the outer hatch, automatically switching off the dim lighting but allowing some fresh air to flow inside while providing some visible access to the outside. Still their stress continued to build. To pass the time they talked among themselves. "We had plenty to talk about," Fultz wrote. "We were concerned and somewhat scared but . . . talking [about it] . . . was a big help." Furthermore, he acknowledged that they knew every change of their course. Information about their progress flowed freely over the phones, as Williamson continued to do everything within his means to ease the anxieties of his crew. "Our Cap the Old Man was a good man," Fultz added. "[He] said the crew should know what was going on; as we would all get there at the same time."[39]

Back aboard *Dunlap*, Fire Controlman Loyd Peters was also making his way to his GQ, located at the gun director. Before leaving his compartment Loyd overheard a curious discussion between two other sailors. One handed the other a piece of currency and said, "Here's the five dollars I owe you." The other replied, "But you just borrowed it last night." The first then responded, "Yes, well, if I don't get killed tonight I want to borrow it again tomorrow."[40] It was a bit humorous—and then a bit not.

Joining Peters in his pursuit was friend and fellow fire controlman, Joe Baldwin. These two men knew exactly how to react. They had practiced this scenario many times before. Their climb to the director was instinctive and made with great haste. Once reaching the station the two eagerly pulled themselves up through the director's upper hatches to peek above its steel housing. This was the highest post aboard ship, and they both hoped it might provide an optimum view of all that surrounded them. But the darkness refused to oblige. A combination of the low overcast and intermittent showers hampered their efforts to see even beyond a few feet. They could see almost nothing. If not for its phosphorescent wake, even the ship's bow was itself close to hidden. Truly it was an eerie moment, almost foreboding—and its depression was not easily overcome. After a few quiet moments Baldwin turned to Peters. "I wonder where we'll be this time tomorrow?" "I don't know," Peters responded meekly, continuing his lonely stare into the outer darkness. There was another long pause. Baldwin then concluded, "Hell, I wish it was this time tomorrow."[41]

* * *

Having entered Bougainville Strait at 9:00 p.m., the southward advance of the Japanese destroyers continued to progress without any overt sense of jeopardy.[42] Darkness had since collapsed around these ships, cloaking their movements from any nearby enemy coast watchers as well as further sighting from the sky. The threat from enemy planes was now extremely diminished, and the darkness was received as a friend. Sugiura, therefore, stood stalwartly on *Hagikaze*'s bridge with unbent confidence, ordering his ships to change course to 140 degrees True and increase speed to 30 knots just as his plans had predetermined.[43] Obviously, there was to be no deviation from his original directive. Sugiura's most immediate concern, it appeared, was keeping to his schedule, nothing more. Outside of the enemy plane previously reported by *Shigure*—a sighting the commander flatly ignored—the journey remained quiet. Soon his ships would be entering Vella Gulf, and there, he suspected, only enemy torpedo boats might try some type of offensive action. For this he would be watchful. Otherwise, he truly doubted there would be any other interference from the U.S. Navy. Even the torpedo boats, despite their testiness, had rarely proven any serious obstacle to the Express.

Aboard *Shigure*, however, the atmosphere on the bridge was far more ominous. It was obvious at this point that Hara had little confidence in Sugiura's leadership. Frustration was written all over his face. Yamagami expressed a similar demeanor. Both commanders silently stared forward, across their destroyer's bow and into the darkness beyond. The enemy had to know they were coming. Hara doubted the Americans would let them pass without some serious attempt at stopping their mission. If Sugiura expected otherwise then, in Hara's mind, he was a fool. But, for *Shigure*, there was no other option. Regardless of what might lie ahead, Hara was duty bound to follow Sugiura's lead. Perhaps the gods would be with them. Perhaps too Sugiura would be lucky and this same plan would indeed work for a third time. But Hara was far from hopeful.

* * *

Moosbrugger's ships also continued on course and on schedule. By 9:00 P.M. the task group was proceeding between Ganongga and Gizo Islands, making speed at 25 knots.[44] Eighteen minutes later the course was changed to 000 degrees true, due north and in line to pass through Gizo Strait, the last threshold before entering Vella Gulf.[45]

"Point Option," the entrance to Gizo Strait (Latitude 8° 03' South—Longitude 156° 41' East) was safely reached at 9:59 P.M. Moosbrugger ordered the column to slow to 15 knots and to begin a "careful" search of the area.[46] The strait was the perfect spot for an ambush, and Moosbrugger intended to keep up his guard.

Again, the CICs became the focus of activity. Navigation through the strait was done mostly by radar and sonar soundings—both were also searching for signs of the enemy. Lookouts strained to see anything out of place or that might interfere, but they could see very little. At least knowing that Calvert's MTBs were all stationed far to the northwest, in Blackett Strait, was of some comfort—if any small craft were located, they could be readily assumed as enemy and fired upon immediately. But, momentarily, navigating the treacherous reefs was Moosbrugger's greatest concern.

Dunlap's lead was critical, but every ship was responsible for its own safety in this transit. Quartermaster 2nd Class Richard Allison should have already been at his GQ post at *Craven*'s helm, relieving Lanz, but it had been requested that he remain in the CIC to assist with the navigation, at least until the ship had successfully traversed the strait. Allison had been aboard *Craven* since before the war and had considerable experience with navigation and was well respected for his abilities. He would later note, "Our charts of the entire area were of very poor quality. They were 1820 survey—British Admiralty Survey. Very little upgrading had been done to them. All had disclaimers '*Use With Extreme*

Caution—Errors Of Up To 4 Miles May Be Experienced.'"[47] Navigating this region during the day was challenging enough; at night it was almost unthinkable. Poor charts and poor visibility in this maze of reefs would have been certain disaster without the highly skilled personnel possessed by Moosbrugger's task group. Still, even experience and expertise were not enough to fully guarantee success or to overcome all the anxieties of the crews.

Seaman 1st Class Clyde Conner was at his GQ in the ammunition room of the #4 5-inch gun aboard *Dunlap*. Stationed deep inside this after section of the destroyer—confined within a dimly lit compartment and surrounded by high-explosives—these moments passing through the strait played havoc on his nerves. Conner and the rest of his gang could feel the screws shudder as they slowed and knew that they were at a very crucial avenue. "The scariest time was when the ship was going [through Gizo Strait]. The distance . . . was quite narrow, leaving little room to maneuver." Conner knew that here they were sitting ducks for enemy attack. What if the enemy destroyers were waiting for them, sitting just outside the exit of the strait? There would be no place for Moosbrugger's ships to go—no way to unmask (to turn broadside and reveal) their guns and torpedoes or be able to fight back. They would be trapped. "I was wound up tight," Conner added. "Being in the ammo locker we were not privy to much that occurred topside, so we were [all] totally relieved to hear there was no contact with enemy ships."[48]

Conner was far from alone at having such initial fears. Lieutenant Davison expressed the experience in the best possible terms. "Like on all jaunts into enemy held areas, you at first expect all hell to break loose from thousands of shore batteries, submarines, mines and what not the minute you stick your nose in. It's not a nice feeling—a basket of butterflies in the stomach, a very dry throat, moist palms—but there's not one thing you can do about it but sit there and take it and hope that you're all set to do your job when the time comes."[49]

These brief minutes of passage seemed like hours, but by 10:11 p.m., the destroyers of Task Group 31.2 had all safely entered Vella Gulf.[50] Everyone breathed a great sigh of relief—but the biggest challenge was yet to come.

Aboard *Craven*, Allison had finally been released from his duty in the CIC and was now occupying his position at the helm, and "with considerable relief."[51] Lanz was equally thankful. He welcomed Allison's arrival and quickly headed for his own GQ, amidships, as gunner for the starboard 20-millimeter machine gun.[52]

Allison then noted that he was immediately "advised that all course changes would be from the 'Flag' on the *Dunlap* and transmitted by way of our TBS using the 'Lovers Code,' i.e., Love = 000° (North), Option = 060°, Victor = 120°, Easy = 180°, Roger = 240°, and Sugar = 320°."[53] He was to listen closely for each signal and respond accordingly.

At 10:16 P.M., the group was passing Liapari Island to starboard. Here Moosbrugger ordered the group to dispose in a line of division columns.[54] Simpson in turn ordered *Lang* to lead the rest of Division Two (A-2 or DesDiv15) at forming on a bearing of 150 degrees True and at a distance of 4,000 yards off the starboard quarter of Division One (A-1 or DesDiv12).[55] All ships of each division were to remain at intervals of 500 yards and maintain the current speed of 15 knots, keeping their visible wakes to a minimum.

Ten minutes later the moon set. The night was now at its darkest. The sky above remained overcast, with a ceiling of around 4,000 feet. Surface visibility remained low, extending at times from between 3,000 and 4,000 yards, and this was often interrupted by frequent rain squalls. But the wind was light and the sea was smooth, making the sailing somewhat pleasant at least.[56]

Allison made mention of what he felt was the task group's greatest advantage. "We could see in the dark," he wrote. "We had most of the entire gulf on our 'SG' radar. We could see our sister ships, *Stack*, *Sterett* and *Lang* to the southwest. [Our] position [was] in the center of the gulf. We were aware that Commander Calvert had his MTB squadron covering the 'Slot' north of New Georgia. We were ready." He later added with a bit of afterthought, "The possibility that the enemy might have radar [providing them with the same advantage] never entered my mind."[57]

Aboard *Lang*, Lieutenant Southard was extremely busy, attentive to his given tasks of overseeing the ship's makeshift CIC. The confinement here was hot and claustrophobic. He carefully managed the information being gathered, both with the navigation of the reefs and the radar searches for the enemy. So much about this mission depended on the job given him. He had little time to think of anything else—though, while heading into almost assured combat, he could hardly help but give some momentary thought to Jane. A full year had passed since the two had been together. Only through letters had they been able to communicate to one another—though she had assured him that she was loyally awaiting his return. She still planned on being his wife. Truly he hoped not to disappoint her.

Southard's thoughts of home were very brief. As much as he would have liked, he could not afford the time for his mind to waver from the many tasks ongoing in the CIC. He was continually checking each calculation for navigation and each sweep of the radar. Suddenly he heard the familiar boom of

Commodore Simpson. "Lieutenant Southard!" the commander called, turning his focus toward the CIC. "Yes, sir!" Pemberton quickly responded, peering curiously through the hatchway. He could see Simpson standing beside Wilfong, who seemed oblivious of the commotion and continued to scope the outward distance with his glasses. "What the hell's the matter back there?" the commodore shouted. "I want us closer to that island. We can't stir 'em up from out here." At 10:56 p.m., Moosbrugger had ordered a course change to 000 degrees True, in order that Simpson's ships might sweep the western shore of Kolombangara for enemy barges. If located, the barges were to be marked on the grid and bypassed until the entire gulf had been thoroughly swept for enemy shipping. If the Express was not located, then they would return to destroy the barges. Simpson's ships mounted the 40-millimeter Bofers, which were ideal for barge busting. If there were barges around, he wanted to know.[58]

"But, sir, I don't recommend that," Southard strongly advised. He suspected that to move any closer to the shore was asking for trouble. "The charts we are using are just too unreliable to chance such a move." Simpson appeared frustrated and it was obvious he didn't much appreciate Pem's recommendation. He stood waiting for Southard to acquiesce, but the lieutenant was adamant. Noting the tenseness of the moment, Wilfong finally turned to join in on the discussion. "He's right," the captain intervened in a firm tone. "If Lieutenant Southard says it's too great of a risk, then we should listen." Simpson gave Wilfong a cool stare, knowing he had already overstepped his bounds with the captain. He paused and then withdrew his request. "Very well, Lieutenant. You're the navigator. Stay the course." Wilfong, who was surprisingly diplomatic about the commodore's navigational interference, looked at Southard and gave an approving nod—he was glad Pemberton had stood his ground.[59]

Meanwhile, Moosbrugger continued his close supervision of the operation. He and Iverson assisted with the searches, peering through their glasses while sweeping the darkness for signs of anything unusual. Both men appeared calm but, in truth, they were just as anxious as every other man aboard.

Moosbrugger looked at his watch again. The time was 11:15 p.m. If the Japanese ships were still on schedule, then the radar should soon be picking them up. Three minutes later the bridge phone lit up as it buzzed for attention. Iverson quickly lifted the receiver from its bulkhead location and placed it firmly to his ear. Moosbrugger focused his attention on the captain's face. "It's Olsen," Iverson announced. "He has a contact, bearing ninety degrees true, distance four thousand sixty yards."[60]

Wow! The contact was close, almost within visual range. How could the radar not have picked them up before now? The portside lookouts immediately shifted their focus toward the bearing. There was nothing. This was not acceptable.

Moosbrugger's frustration was apparent. He departed the bridge in a huff and ran down the ladder to the CIC. "What do you have, Lieutenant?" he demanded upon his entry.[61]

Olsen was standing over the shoulder of Radarman 3rd Class Dean Savage, the ship's most respected radar technician. Both men kept their eyes glued to the radar scope, observing its sweep. "Contact's moving at zero degrees true, speed sixteen knots," Olsen pronounced. "It's a good one, sir," Savage added.[62]

Moosbrugger moved closer, intent at making his own observation. He wasn't sure; it just didn't feel right. He was about to break Burke's first rule of swift engagement, but he felt he had a good reason. "Have you requested a confirmation, Lieutenant?" "No, sir," Olsen replied. "Get me a confirmation." "Yes, sir."[63]

Olsen turned to Radioman Walt Farmer. "Farmer," he commanded, "send out to *Craven* and *Lang*—'have contact, bearing ninety degrees true, distance four thousand. Can you confirm?'"[64] The radioman responded in the affirmative.

In the meantime, precious seconds passed. Each tick of the clock was crucial. If the contact was indeed good, there would be little time to react. "Sir," Farmer finally responded, "It's *Craven*. They report only a slight indication." "What about *Lang*?" Olsen queried. "Just a minute, sir." There was a brief pause. "*Lang* reports 'no contact.'"[65]

"It's a side lobe," Moosbrugger announced with some relief, referring to a phenomenon whereby certain atmospheric conditions caused the radar to reflect off a shadow of its own ship.[66]

Savage looked up to Olsen with near disbelief. It was right there on the scope. The blip was too clear for a side lobe. "Sir," Olsen interjected. "Are you sure, sir?" Moosbrugger gave the lieutenant a thoughtful stare. "Change course," he suddenly ordered. "Take us to thirty degrees true, increase speed to twenty-five knots." "Yes sir," Olsen responded.[67]

Aboard *Craven*, Torpedoman Haden sat listening to his phones. He suddenly perked up. "Hey, Chief," he called out to Mowery. "*Dunlap* is reporting a contact." "Yeah?" Mowery responded, with some low-key interest. "Yeah." Haden answered. Then after a slight pause he added, "And we're chang'n course." "Yeah?" Mowery again responded, continuing his almost lethargic expression. "Yeah," Haden confirmed, displaying his confusion. Mowery rightly suspected, however, if it was something worth real concern, they would soon know. Until then, there was no reason for excitement.[68]

The movement in course and speed was indeed quite noticeable, and it immediately caused a rise in tension throughout the entire task group. Silently, sailors gave each other a momentary look of concern. Their eyes met and their lips noticeably tightened. It appeared this might be it, the moment they had long been expecting.

Back aboard *Dunlap*, Moosbrugger, Olsen, and Savage continued to devote their complete attention to the radar screen. As *Dunlap* began to increase speed and make its turn, so too did the contact, and with a simultaneous pattern. "Side lobe, Lieutenant," Moosbrugger affirmed, giving Olsen a light slap on the back. "Yes sir," Olsen conceded. Freddie then relaxed his stance and ordered, "Return to our previous course and speed. Contact the other ships and tell them to disregard the report, contact false." Olsen nodded. "Yes sir."[69]

Moosbrugger departed the CIC feeling vindicated and especially relieved. He was thankful his initial evaluation had been correct. The CIC team had done everything right, but hasty acceptance of how the contact first appeared could have been devastating. If he had reacted too quickly—assuming the enemy was indeed out there somewhere—he would have no doubt alerted the opposing ships to his presence and lost the element of surprise. If he had been wrong—well, it could have been just as bad.

* * *

Several miles to the northwest, just northeast of Vella Lavella, Sugiura continued to direct his destroyers on a south/south-easterly course. Everything remained quiet, but there was no lack of vigilance among his officers and crews. His lookouts eagerly searched in all directions, yet the darkness was so intense that almost nothing was visible. Only the dim outline of Vella Lavella's volcanic peak appeared to stand out.

Aboard *Shigure*, Captain Hara stood nervously scouring the outer darkness while continuing his ardent display of frustration with the whole situation. The extra load of troops and supplies in combination with his destroyer's worn condition were finally taking a toll. The ship's power plants were unable to keep up. *Shigure* was now lagging 1,000 yards behind the rest of the column.[70]

Unsure of what should be done, Lt. (jg) Yoshio Tsukihara, Hara's navigation officer, approached the commander and questioned, "Sir . . . Shall we use the overboost to gain back our lost five-hundred meters?" To this point Hara had acted with discipline, but no more. He suddenly erupted with vent-up anger. "*No!*" he shouted. "This is good enough! To hell with the prescribed five-hundred-meter distance! Don't overboost the engine!"[71] Tsukihara, who was profoundly taken aback by his commander's piercing response, nodded with near apologetic affirmation and quietly melted back to his station.

Hara would later note his nervousness. "Kolombangara," he wrote, "loomed to starboard [he surely meant Vella Lavella, as at no time prior to the engagement was Kolombangara to his starboard], its towering volcanic peak overhung with ominous clouds. To port I could see nothing but blackness, from which anything could emerge at any moment. It made my spine creep."[72]

Back aboard *Hagikaze*, Sugiura had his lookouts desperately searching for any sign of the enemy. Having had previous encounters with the American torpedo boats, it is almost certain that these were at the height of his concern.[73] To defend his column from any such attacks, it appears that Sugiura had ordered his ships to train their weapons at staggered intervals. Lead ship, *Hagikaze*, trained to port, *Arashi* to starboard, *Kawakaze* to port, and *Shigure* to starboard. He must have suspected, rightly, that if an attack did materialize, it would be sudden and allow little time for his ships to react. It was therefore justifiable to surmise that by at least having a portion of its weapons already pointed in the right direction that the unit could at least have some swiftness of response—a strategy not too unlike that of Moosbrugger, with his two staggered columns.

Hara, however, did not think well of Sugiura's arrangement. His patience with the unit commander had ended. At around 11:25 p.m., Hara suddenly began shouting orders. "Stand by for action! Aim all guns and torpedoes to port! Set gun range at three thousand meters! Set torpedoes to run at two-meter depth, angle twenty degrees! Double the lookouts!"[74]

Excitement raced throughout *Shigure*. Officers and crew alike scrambled to fulfill the orders of their irate commander. During the ten minutes that followed, Hara nervously peered through his glasses into the unrelenting darkness.[75]

A few additional minutes passed. Suddenly the voice tube sounded forth the familiar voice of *Shigure*'s torpedo officer, Lieutenant Doi. "Sir," Doi barked. "May I turn the tubes from portside back to their original starboard position?" Hara was thoroughly confounded by the request and immediately displayed his rage. "*No!*" he retorted. "*No*, Doi, for heaven's sake, *no!* Starboard visibility is so good we can see the reefs of Vella Lavella! To port we see no more than two thousand meters, and we don't know where the enemy is! Stay trained to port and be ready for action any moment!"[76] Regardless of how quiet the night displayed itself, Hara's gut told him not all was as it appeared.

* * *

The atmosphere aboard Moosbrugger's ships remained as tense as ever. If they were to meet the enemy, then they would surely meet him soon. Visibility continued to be very limited. Lookouts were often seen to lower their glasses and rub their eyes from the strain. If the enemy was indeed out there—and they believed that he was—then they must locate him first, or else, suffer the consequences.

After many hours of anxious sailing, Task Group 31.2 was now at the most critical juncture of its mission. They would soon meet the enemy in combat—or they would go back home empty-handed. Either way, the men were ready to get on with what was in store.

On *Dunlap*, Radioman Pritchett exemplified the status quo. He gave one last check of the CIC instruments. His job was to fix anything about the electronics that should fail. The recent false radar blip had given him some reason for concern, but every meter showed the equipment to be functioning properly. Convinced that everything was okay, he ventured a moment to step outside. "I prayed my Rosary," he wrote later.[77] Whatever happened next, he would leave to Divine providence.

Chapter Eight

Execute

The Moment of Truth

With midnight nearing, the destroyers of Task Group 31.2 continued on their cautious yet uninterrupted northerly advance. Crews of each ship anxiously searched the gulf for its many hidden dangers, all while surrounded by a veil so purely black that eternal nothingness appeared as its only revelation. This night was so ungodly quiet, so akin to a terrible foreboding. Concerned eyes grew weary at their constant probing, peering into the depths of this darkness that refused to yield anything. The silence was wretched, the unknown gut-wrenching, and the pressure of duty immense. Nerves were as taut as the stays of the ships. Surely the enemy was out there, somewhere, but where? Who would find who first? To whom might the advantage be given? How many casualties might they expect? And such inescapable apprehensions were only in their adolescence.

Having concluded his business in the CIC, Moosbrugger raced his way back up the ladder to *Dunlap*'s darkened bridge. The climb was hardly of notice to him, yet his heart pounded heavily from the exertion, like a thundering kettle drum rumbling within his chest. Raw adrenaline pumped wildly through his veins, jolting his body to a speedy recourse. He knew action was nearing. He had to be ready. His mind became consumed with the numerous projections, calculations, and options available to him. The slightest mistake, he knew, could prove damning. The greatest weight of responsibility was his, and it grew heavy on his shoulders. He entered through the bridge hatchway, displaying a stoic expression yet determined with his approach. Again, the nearby phone buzzed for attention. Iverson quickly reached for the receiver, this time handing it directly over to Freddie. "Moosbrugger," the commander anxiously acknowledged. He listened. Olsen's now familiar voice was once more heard to respond, ringing out in a barely controlled excitement, "Sir, we have a new contact, bearing three five nine degrees true, range twenty-three thousand nine hundred."[1] The time was 11:33 P.M.

With a slight grin displayed upon his lips and a faint glimmer shown in his eyes, Moosbrugger's expression suddenly pronounced some measure of satisfaction. This bearing and range were more to the order of his expectations. The distance was good. There was time for proper procedures. "Get me a confirmation, Lieutenant," he ordered. "Yes, sir," Olsen replied.[2]

Seconds later, aboard *Craven*, Williamson received *Dunlap*'s newest inquiry. "*New contact, bearing three five zero degrees true, range nineteen thousand seven hundred, course one eighty, speed twenty-five. Can you confirm?*" Williamson immediately called back to his CIC for the verification.[3]

Lieutenant Davison, who had just finished a routine review of all the various operations of his combat center, responded to Williamson's inquiry with great expediency. He quickly rejoined the radar operator, eager for the confirmation. Both men closely examined the dim green-cast screen before them. There was nothing. The bright scoping representing the radar's beacon displayed no capture of suspicious activity. Disappointed, the lieutenant was about to reply in the negative . . . and then . . .

"Captain!" Davison shouted, suddenly seeing a blip, a small dim spot briefly illuminated within the sweep of the scope. "Looks like I might have something. Sir, I'm checking the short scale. Yeah, we're searching now; I think we've got him . . . course one eighty speed twenty-five. That checks with us."[4]

Williamson immediately responded back to Moosbrugger, "*Affirmative, I have contact, course one eighty speed twenty five.*"[5] *Dunlap*'s radar now displayed two distinct blips on its screen. Surely this was it. This had to be the Express they had been sent to find and destroy.

Finally assured of a legitimate target, Moosbrugger calmly ordered, "Division One, prepare to fire full port torpedo broadside—come to new heading three three five degrees true."[6] He looked at the face of his watch. The time was 11:38 p.m.

Aboard *Craven*, Torpedoman Haden suddenly straightened his stance once more. His headphones were again alive with news. "Hey, Chief," he called out to Mowery, "they're reporting another contact." "Yeah?" Mowery responded, once again displaying no immediate concern for alarm. Haden's excitement did not waver but continued, and with even greater energy. "Yeah . . . Four ships. Range nineteen thousand yards." Finally, the chief's interest began to be tweaked. "Yeah?" he repeated, his voice now cracking with a little more enthusiasm. "Yeah!" Haden acknowledged with additional volume. "Prepare to fire full port tubes!" he repeated from his phones. Obviously, there was no denying this command. Chief Mowery's eyes opened wide and his body began to animate.

"All right, men," he yelled, "this is it! We've got four! Insert the primers! Let's line'm up!"[7]

Likewise, aboard *Maury*, acting Chief Fisher busily directed his teams with equal enterprise. Despite the restraints of darkness, the destroyer's port mounts cranked outward with all due speed. Fisher's crews performed just as they had been trained. His torpedoes were soon in firing position and the chief displayed his confidence; he had personally set the speed and depth of each of his eight torpedoes, and he was certain his adjustments were to provide his "fish" the greatest possibility toward success. On *Maury* the torpedo depth setting was off standard, and—though known only to a very few—this one difference was likely to prove the most dramatic deed of the night.

With regard to his initial orders, Moosbrugger had specified that all torpedoes were to be set for intermediate speed and to the standard "depth of 5 to 9 feet." But this was the depth that both Fisher and Crenshaw had earlier concluded was allowing the torpedoes to run too deep, and especially so now that they were mounted with the added weight of the new warhead extensions. For this reason, on *Maury* an arbitrary decision was made to reset the torpedo depths to the minimum, to that of 5 feet. Permission from Moosbrugger for the change was neither requested nor granted. (How high up the chain of command was responsible for this decision is even today a bit unclear. What is clear, however, is that Moosbrugger was not notified of this change or of the concern that led to the decision. It is not known how he might have reacted had he been informed.) Regardless, Fisher had final responsibility for completing these adjustments, and he did so with all due confidence that this was the appropriate action.

Elsewhere among TG 31.2 the preparations for battle continued at an excited pace. Within the various CICs the TBS was a chatterbox of information. Reports were being regularly sent and received throughout the group. From *Craven* to *Dunlap*, "I have three targets." From *Dunlap*, "We have four."[8] Aboard *Lang*, Simpson kept a close monitor of each new development. He kept his commanders thoroughly informed and cautioned them to hold their line close to the Kolombangara shore. Meanwhile, within the cramped confines of his CIC, Lieutenant Southard continued to oversee each piece of this critical information. Ranges and bearings were being called out at thirty-second intervals—19,000 yards, 17,500 yards, 16,000 yards, etc. "We tracked the targets," he noted, "kept the bridge and gunnery and torpedo officer informed of ranges and bearing . . . everything worked just like we had practiced and trained."[9]

This same type of efficiency was also noted aboard *Maury*. Lieutenant Crenshaw was to write, "[The CIC reported to the] Bridge that the target was a column of four ships. The lead ship appeared bigger than the other three. [Lieutenant] Medler was plotting the ranges and bearings each minute, the PPI sweep being momentarily halted for accurate measurement. Acker was the ship's best radar operator and doing great. Bean was plotting the ranges and bearings on the Air Plot to check Medler's solution."[10] In effect, the CIC team was working just as it had been designed.

Back aboard *Craven*, Davison's enthusiasm for his job grew proportionately to the excitement within his CIC. Range to the targets was now 15,000 yards and closing. He passed the information on to the bridge. Then he called up to his gunnery officer, Lieutenant (jg) Jim Oliver, to confirm the preparations for the 5-inch batteries. "What do you get, Jim?" By this time the fire control radar had already been coaxed to its targets. "One eighty speed twenty-five . . . We're ready!" Oliver responded. Davison paused to peer once more at the radar screen—the distance was continuing to close. Returning his attention to Oliver, he further instructed, "Hold it until I give you the word. We'll try the fish first. Let me know if there are any changes." There was another brief pause, and then with afterthought Davison curiously inquired, "Can you see him?" Oliver, who had been searching through the infinity for hours—so much so that his eyes were now having difficulty responding to any additional sweeps—persisted with his efforts at locating the enemy. The impenetrable cloak before him refused to reveal anything. "Hell no," he finally responded, "it's pitch black up here."[11]

Davison kept an unfailing monitor of every report while maintaining his open communication with Oliver. He was certain that if any important changes should occur that the junior lieutenant would be first with the news—as his confidence in Oliver was high. "Jim had come aboard in San Francisco one July afternoon back in '42, a pink cheeked youngster just out of the Academy. He was as smart as they come and had assumed more than his expected load—so much more, in fact, that when I became Exec, he was the logical one to take over my old job as gun boss. During the year he had been aboard there had developed between us an excellent relationship characterized by understanding and mutual respect. I knew his way of doing things, and he seemed to be able to sense what I wanted done, and get it done, before it was necessary to give orders. It was an intangible thing but invaluable in this sort of business."[12]

Meanwhile, the forward-most position with the most vantage, *Dunlap*'s pilothouse was full of energy. Iverson was continually giving out orders, keeping his lead ship on course, meeting the yet unseen adversary on a quickly shrinking parallel approach. His CIC was now reporting the enemy ships using a shallow zigzag course, 165 degrees and 180 degrees True, at speeds of between 25 and

30 knots. The captain turned to his torpedo officer, Lt. (jg) R. L. Gilbert. "Gil," he commanded, "use target course one seven six degrees, speed twenty-seven."[13]

At the port wing of *Craven*'s bridge, Torpedoman Lewis stood at the ready, at his post right next to the ship's torpedo director. His position provided an optimal view of the outlying gulf, but still the distant void produced nothing for the eyes to see.[14] His targets were at this point only numbers, computations given to him by the torpedo officer. He had already set the firing solutions. Now he waited, concentrating on his preparations to close the circuits on the firing panel that led to the electrical firing keys on the tubes.

Torpedoman Haden, Lewis's comrade on the phones, was only a few feet below and very busy at his own rite. His task, though practiced many times over, was proving difficult. It was so dark he could hardly see his instruments, and the red filtered flashlight he was using was of little aid. He was having difficulty keeping the torpedo battery's pointers matched to the calculations given him from the bridge. Still he persisted. When the word finally came to "Stand-by to fire," Haden made one final adjustment and then switched on the mount's ready-light. His preparations were all complete. Control of *Craven*'s "fish" now belonged to Lewis.[15]

Moosbrugger stood near Iverson, still appearing very confident while calmly listening to each bit of new information passed his way. He stared silently into the depths of the darkness beyond. Nothing could be seen, but he knew the Express was out there, swiftly closing from the opposite direction—now closing at a combined speed in excess of 45 knots. *Dunlap*'s radar had captured every movement of the enemy, and so far he displayed no obvious knowledge of the American presence. But was he aware? Were his torpedo and gun crews poised for immediate action? Were his torpedoes already in the water, speeding beneath the surface toward their targets? These questions and more surely raced through Moosbrugger's analytical mind even though, at this point, such could be allowed little bearing on his immediate actions. He and his ships were already committed to an offensive effort and he must now follow through. He patiently waited. Displaying no fear, he carefully assessed each passing second of the clock's hand while projecting an assurance that he would know when the time was right to act.

Suddenly, with almost a psychic-like confidence, Moosbrugger broke his silence. "What's the track angle?" he queried. "Two ninety," Lieutenant Gilbert acknowledged. Freddie gave another quick glance at his watch. The time was 11:40 P.M. This was it, the moment for action. Everything he, his officers, and his crews had trained for now centered on this one unequivocal instant in time. He ordered, "Execute!"[16]

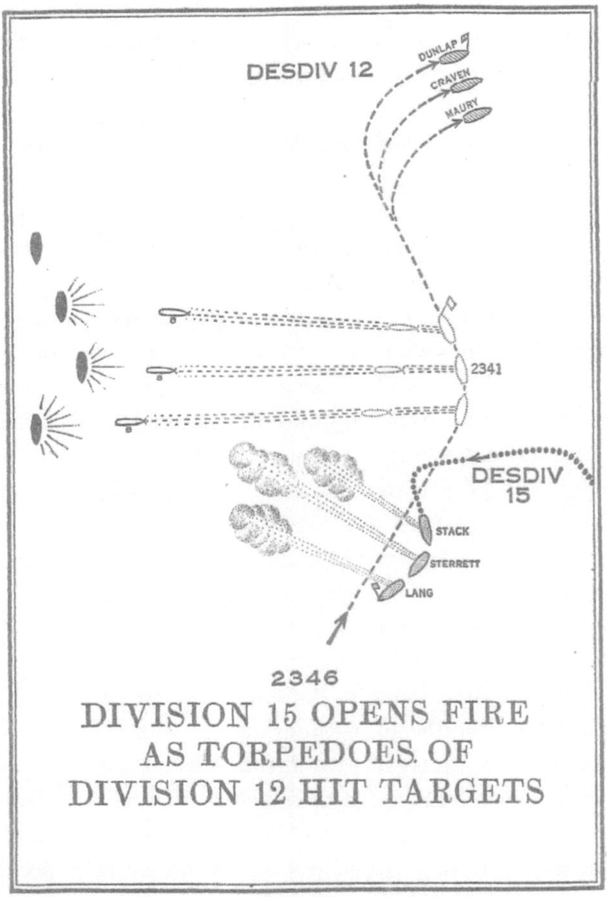

Simplified chart from an October 1943 Naval Intelligence Combat Narratives Report on Action at Vella Gulf of August 6-7, 1943. Denotes action at 11:46 P.M. (2346 hours).

Their progress had been so quick. Lieutenant Olsen noted just how thoroughly amazed he was by how speedily everything up to this point had transpired. "The thing that impressed me the most was the extreme rapidity of events. From [the] initial detection at 23,900 yards at 2333 [11:33 p.m.] to a firing point about 4500 yards from the target took only seven minutes. During this short time the torpedo mounts were trained to port and torpedo speed and depth settings were checked. Information was passed from Combat to the Torpedo

Officer on enemy course and speed and bearing. This data was entered into the torpedo director and the director generated a torpedo mount train angle. The Commodore was kept fully advised concerning our approach to the firing point. I believe he was monitoring the track angle at the director. When the track angle was 90 degrees and we were close to the firing point he gave the order to fire torpedoes."[17]

Fire Controlman First Class Patrick Gaither was at *Craven*'s gun director, accompanying Lieutenant Oliver and manning the director range keeper. This moment, while confined to the swelter of the enclosed director, was so very "tense." Gaither later wrote, "Every man [was] doing his job with no conversation." They were well informed and knew action was imminent. "We could keep up with what was going on by telephone and vocal orders from the bridge, and [were] aware of the range to our target." The enemy ships were so close, so unbelievably close. The range was by now less than 5,000 yards. Gaither wondered "if the skipper was going to make a point-blank attack." The others with him were equally concerned. So it was, upon hearing the orders for the torpedoes to be released, that they enjoyed some initial sense of relief.[18]

At his station, Haden listened intently to his phones as Lewis began punching the firing switches. "Fire one, fire two, fire three, fire four . . . Lewis was so excited," Haden later recalled. "He was like a boy with a new toy." Meanwhile, Haden followed the firing sequences, wooden mallet in hand, ready to manually strike the individual primers "just in case the bridge control was not functioning . . . but it was."[19]

In all, twenty-four torpedoes were successfully launched from Moosbrugger's column of three. There was not a single misfire. The torpedoes escaped their tubes with minimal effort and their nighttime ignition produced almost no visible flash (all of Moosbrugger's destroyers mounted new flash suppressors at the torpedo tubes, a last-minute addition the commander would later note that "functioned effectively"[20]). The first phase of the attack was now complete. Surprise appeared to have been achieved. Now they awaited the answer to a far greater question: Would these torpedoes hit their targets?

Upon hearing Moosbrugger's order to "Execute," Lieutenant Davison instantly pressed down on the knob of his stopwatch. There was a hush in the CIC, almost a breathless moment as the hand of the timepiece began its critical rotation. Davison moved back to check the radar scope. Four very distinct targets were now only 4,000 yards distant—almost within visual range—and still no evasive maneuvering was detected on their part. He felt his muscles tighten under the stress. "Judas, if we miss," he spoke under his breath, "they'll see the wakes and then. . . ." [21]

Not one of the enemy ships had yet been spotted by any of the lookouts—outside visibility remained less than 4,000 yards. Each ship of Moosbrugger's division reported their torpedoes away, running "hot, straight and true."[22] The time was noted in the log as 11:45 P.M. Freddie immediately ordered, "Division One, execute upon receipt, Turn Nine," a full 90-degree turn to starboard—a maneuver designed to clear any enemy torpedoes.[23]

At this very same moment, Simpson ordered his division to change course to 270 degrees True and then to 190 degrees True, respectively, taking his ships in column to port on a course to pass across the bow of the approaching enemy vessels. So far the operation was being executed exactly as it had been planned. Only the results remained to be seen.

* * *

At 11:45 P.M., Sugiura's column—persisting with its uninterrupted southeasterly course and even as *Shigure* now lagged 1,500 yards—remained surrounded by the opaque darkness and was very much unaware of any nearby threat. Posted lookouts were diligently searching in all directions, but without notice of anything hostile. No doubt these veteran sailors were nervous, yet they would display no obvious lack of confidence. They knew what to look for, and they knew their optics were of a superior quality to that of any other navy, a combination that in the past had even gained them advantage over enemy radar. They had good reason to feel optimistic—even despite the high risks of their mission. If the enemy did appear, they felt assured that they would see him first. This advantage, they truly believed, would surely ensure any opposition a speedy demise.

Meanwhile, the unabated search continued, though nothing beyond a pure darkness could be seen. Perhaps the enemy had chosen not to give challenge, or perhaps he was waiting in the wrong place. Hara could only hope for such good fortune, but he truly doubted such likelihood. These doubts would soon prove fully warranted. "White waves!" the portside lookout, Petty Officer Yamashita, suddenly screamed. "Black objects . . . Several ships heading toward us!"[24] The warning energized an instant burst of excitement, nearing pandemonium on *Shigure*'s previously inanimate bridge.

The bells of general alarm were quickly sounded, relaying their familiar notice to all hands. This was exactly the type of enemy action Hara had feared. His eyes opened wide. "Full starboard helm!" he yelled. The helmsman reacted swiftly, immediately spinning the wheel as far to the right as it would go, desperately demanding the ship to turn quickly. The destroyer jerked and leaned noticeably to port in its response. All eyes were now focused on the spot where Yamashita pointed. Hara grimaced. "Launch full port torpedoes." His orders were reactionary, pure defensive logic in the effort to preserve his ship and crew. He hoped he was not too late.[25]

Aboard *Hagikaze*, alert lookouts had also sighted the enemy ships. Sugiura, as had Hara, responded quickly by sounding the general alarm. He scoped the distant darkness with his glasses, hoping to make out his adversary. An immediate second warning, a report from Commander Sugioka (*Arashi*), identified the objects as "torpedo boats." This was what Sugiura had been expecting, and he prepared to react accordingly. Then a third warning, this from Commander Yanase (*Kawakaze*), reported a sighting "to starboard"—momentarily diverting Sugiura's attention away from the critical quarter. The timing was unfortunate, but he could not disregard the warning. He had, after all, prepared for attack from either side. This was indeed a likely tactic to be used by the torpedo boats, and he pursued the possibility. *Hagikaze*'s lookouts quickly swept their glasses to the west, yet they saw no sign of the enemy. Yanase's report was obviously false. Frustrated, Sugiura immediately turned his attention back to port. But the lost seconds would prove damning.[26]

Meanwhile, Hara remained committed to *Shigure*'s evasive maneuvers. The destroyer struggled at making any better speed, but Yamagami's veteran crew was able to coax the best from their ship's old worn-out engines. She vibrated heavily and groaned with stress but finally succeeded with entering the hard right turn. Heavy black smoke poured from her stack, purposefully created in the hopeful effort to hide their escape. Torpedo crews had in the meantime—since already having their batteries trained to port—successfully launched a full salvo of all eight of *Shigure*'s deadly Long Lances. The massive torpedoes swooshed from their tubes in quick succession, splashing into the sea to speed off in the direction of the enemy, though their aim was only a guess. Hara nervously waited. He took a moment to glance toward the rest of the column. Its course remained unchanged. "Damn! Damn!" he exclaimed.[27]

* * *

Within the tight confinement of *Craven*'s CIC, Davison continued his close observation of the radar. The hand of his stopwatch ticked loudly, almost thunderous as the seconds continued to pass. He, as well as the others around him, nervously anticipated some sign of success, but there was nothing. The blips on the scope remained unchanged. Surely the torpedoes had not missed, not at such close range, not all twenty-four.

Davison peered nervously at his watch. It was past time. He then glanced over to the radar. There was still no change. Thinking the worst, he reached for the phone and called up to Oliver. "Jim," he yelled, "stand-by. It doesn't look good." There was a brief pause. "Roger," Oliver finally responded with noted disappointment. Then, his voice cracked excitedly, "Wait! There they go! I just saw a dull red explosion! There's another . . . and another, and two more! We got'em, we got'em . . . we got'em! They're blowing up all over the place! The cruiser's on fire . . . look at that! They just had the biggest damn explosion I've ever seen! Gees, I wouldn't miss this for anything! Stick your head out and take a look! If you don't, you're going to regret it the rest of your life!"[28] The time was 11:49 P.M.

Aboard *Dunlap*, the bridge was quiet. Moosbrugger stood silently staring in the general direction of the enemy ships. The time seemed to pass ever so slowly. Nothing happened. He too began to doubt. Then he saw it, a dull red explosion, then another, another, and yet another even bigger. His jubilation could hardly be kept in check.

Just outside the pilothouse hatch, Torpedoman Wallick, who had shifted from his director to a nearby pair of thirteen-power observation glasses, was still wearing his phones when upon seeing the distant flashes he shouted a gleeful "hurrah" into the receiver. The transmitted message was heard all around, and men were seen popping out from everywhere trying to see the show.

"Look at that! Look at that!" Moosbrugger yelled as he ran outside the pilothouse. In his excited haste the commander tangled his feet in Wallick's phone cord, stumbled, and nearly fell, giving the surprised torpedoman a quick jerk to his neck. Both men were okay, however, and neither allowed the incident to long divert their attention from the spectacle of the burning ships. Indeed, their recovery was almost instantaneous, as they were eager not to miss a single moment of the distant display.[29]

Still perched high atop *Dunlap*'s gun director, Peters and Baldwin continued with their uninterrupted observation of the distant darkness. They had heard Moosbrugger's orders, and they had seen the torpedoes slip from their tubes into the darkened sea. The night had suddenly become so uncommonly quiet, so much so that the thumping of one's own heart became the only proof of existence—even the crash of the ship against the sea seemed silenced. The tension was nearly unbearable. Peters heard a noise below and curiously leaned over to find the source; the war correspondent, Art Burges, was quickly climbing up the ladder to reach a position on the director platform, obviously seeking a more commanding view. Now they would all endure the same long wait.

"After we had fired [the] torpedoes," Peters noted, "I thought they had all missed. It seemed like it took forever."[30] He and the others around him nervously anticipated something to happen, but all remained quiet—too quiet. Fears began to mount that something had gone terribly wrong. Hearts raced with uncertainty. Then finally, and to everyone's greater relief, the explosions began.

"When the first one hit," Peters wrote, "it looked like someone lit a match. Then the sky lit up like the fourth of July. There were explosions and fires. One ship exploded [this would prove to be *Kawakaze*]. It looked like the bow went up and then nose dived down."[31]

Peters gave Baldwin a glancing smile. They had seen enough. The first stage of the attack was obviously a success, but there was more to come. The two men dropped back down into the confinement of their director and settled into their individual operator seats—they were certain that their role would soon follow, as it surely would.

With his task at the torpedo battery complete, Haden rushed back to his secondary station at *Craven*'s fantail, to the depth-charge racks. Once there, he paused to stare out across the port quarter—the region where he expected to see the explosions. He was as anxious as anyone to see the results of his fish. But there was nothing—only an undisturbed black void met his searching gaze. "It seemed like ages before [the torpedoes] reached their marks," he recalled later. The wait was despairing, but then the explosions began—one, two, three, and four in rapid succession. Haden smiled and everyone around him cheered. This was their inspiring moment of retribution. "Remember Pearl Harbor!" Haden cried aloud.[32]

Coxswain William Lazarz, who anxiously stood his post as pointer at *Craven*'s 5-inch gun #2, expressed a similar reaction. "I guess I expected to see hits right away," he explained. But the distant darkness yielded nothing. Like most others, he too began to think the torpedoes had missed. "That was the longest four minutes of my life. That's when I really got scared." He felt as though his heart was about to explode. "Then I saw a red flash, then another, and another." The fears Lazarz had only seconds before realized were instantly transformed into elation. The heavy pounding of his heart was now induced by excitement, fueled by the apparent success of the attack. "I forgot all about being scared," he concluded. He and his fellow gunners gave out a brief, excited cheer. Then they prepared for business.[33]

* * *

From *Hagikaze*, the alarm for pending action had been sounded and every sailor in the Japanese column was by now alertly manning his post, nervous yet ready for immediate action. Sugiura's officers and crews were tough veterans, men very familiar with the Solomons and fully cognizant of the persistent dangers of the region. They knew to expect the unexpected and were prepared to react accordingly. These were some of the Imperial Navy's best, well-trained young men who were as well versed in modern warfare as they were with ancient tradition. They had pledged their honor to defend to the death their families, their beloved Nippon and, of even greater importance, their godlike emperor, Hirohito. Surrender, for these men, was not an option. Victory was their only edict, nothing less. This night they were as determined as ever to bring defeat to their enemies. After all, nighttime tactics were the expertise of the Japanese sailor, were they not? The darkness had always before been their friend, aiding them in victory. The Americans had always performed poorly at night. Why should they expect this fight to be any different?

Perhaps these sailors did indeed boast a good deal of confidence, but the soldiers crowded around them were feeling far less secure and readily displayed their unified discomfort. They were anxious and woefully out of their character, surrounded by an opaque sea as sinister as death itself, facing an enemy threat and having their fates contingent on the menial protections that their host ships might provide. There was no escaping their feeling of insecurity and helplessness. They were literally there for the ride, unable to affect the outcome. So they waited, each huddled among a crowd, while praying for deliverance yet fearful of none.

Back aboard *Hagikaze* the search for the enemy continued. There remained some momentary confusion as to the sightings, frustrating the efforts of the lookouts, and this caused considerable disarray. Sugiura, however, continued to display a calm command of the situation. But just as he turned his attention back to port, the commander was immediately confronted by a terrifying spectacle. Four distinct torpedo wakes, the slender trails of foaming phosphorescence ominous evidence of the deadly underwater missiles, were seen speeding directly for his ship. Lookouts screamed out concurrent warnings, "Torpedoes!" They pointed frantically, expecting to energize action. Sugiura's face turned pale. "Hard-a-port!" he shouted to the helmsman. But it was too late.[34]

Hagikaze's structure strained at the effort to turn quickly. The helmsman spun the wheel as far to the left as it would allow. It was not enough. The destroyer could not maneuver fast enough and was heavily jarred by simultaneous torpedo hits, two tremendous blows—one striking the fire room—that brought the vessel to a shuddering and painful stop. The explosions were deafening, and the deadly fires they spawned would spread quickly throughout the ship's interior, racing from one compartment to the next while incinerating many men in their progress. Sugiura and others on the bridge were thrown forward and slammed hard against the steel bulkhead, left bruised and bleeding but alive. They were all slow to recover, stunned by their initial trauma, but each finally managed to pull himself to his feet—then to be confronted by a horrifying view of death and destruction.

A quick evaluation revealed the severity of their situation. The ship was without power and at the mercy of the currents and the distant enemy. The sea was already dotted with many bodies, some living and some dead, soldiers and sailors, men either blown overboard or taken by fear at trying to escape the carnage of a sinking ship. Many wounded and dead littered the decks, their bodies twisted in hideous forms. The ship groaned with the sounds of agony. Those men who remained capable, heroic sailors and soldiers alike, fought desperately at containing the damage—despite little hope for success. And the horror of this night was only just beginning.

Aboard *Arashi*, Sugioka frantically screamed out his orders, hoping to save his ship. "Hard to port!" he yelled. "Brace for impact!"[35] Torpedoes were on their way, cutting a path straight toward his destroyer's exposed port side. At Sugioka's desperate call the helmsman frantically maneuvered the rudder, but the disabled *Hagikaze* was in his way. The helmsman found himself suddenly trying to avoid a collision, forcing the destroyer back into the paths of the torpedoes. There was not enough time for any other maneuver. He could not avoid the destruction. No less than three well-directed torpedoes slammed into the destroyer. The resulting explosions were massive, sending a huge ball of fire rocketing skyward, lighting the darkened sky for miles. Within seconds the whole ship was a blazing inferno. The bridge was wrecked. Sugioka's bleeding body lay still, his life ended by the initial blast. Wounded men, who had no chance at escape, were now doomed to burn alive. The living tried to abandon ship, leaping overboard in the hope of swimming to safety, but even the sea was aflame. Almost none were to survive.

On *Kawakaze*'s bridge, Yanase stood frozen in shock. The exploding ships were his first warning of the torpedoes. His lookouts—perhaps still focused to starboard—had not seen the approaching threat. His next sensations were that of a bright, hot flash and a deafening roar. The entire forward section of his destroyer instantly disappeared before his very eyes. A monstrous wall of saltwater followed, crashing over what remained of the ship, reaching even above the heights of the bridge—a wave created when the destroyer, sheared of its bow, plunged hard against the sea's surface, forcing its mangled hulk to a sickening and brutal stop. Two torpedoes had struck the destroyer well forward amidships, one reaching deep into the forward magazine, setting off a ton of stored munitions that instantly obliterated almost everything forward of the bridge. The force of the blast was nearly beyond description, killing every man forward—incinerating their fragmented forms—while leaving many others severely wounded and in a hideous state of desperation. Still, even despite such a terrible plight, *Kawakaze* remained afloat, critically damaged but with some power remaining and void of out-of-control flames—the wall of seawater had smothered most fires and allowed those men in charge of damage control to concentrate on other matters. For Yanase, at least, there remained some small hope that his ship might be saved. But even this bit of optimism would soon disappear.

Aboard *Shigure*, Hara witnessed the terrifying explosions but was far too occupied to stop and ponder the fate of Sugiura and the rest of the column. His crew had successfully launched eight torpedoes at the distant enemy ships, but these were without true targeting. In the meantime, *Shigure* made decent speed while still initiating its hard turn to starboard. Hara was hopeful his actions were enough at avoiding a similar catastrophe, but it was hope with very little optimism.

"Torpedoes!" a lookout screamed, pointing off to port. Hara's eyes widened. Sure enough, three foaming wakes could be seen streaking straight for his ship. His worst fears were realized. Hara stood helpless at his post, watching as the first torpedo passed just 22 yards ahead of *Shigure*'s bow. The second would pass even closer, clearing the bow by only a few feet. The third appeared to be right on target.[36]

"Brace for collision!" Hara shouted. He grasped the nearby railing, so tight that his knuckles turned white. Others around him stiffened themselves in preparation for the hit. Everyone waited with grim expectation—but, amazingly, nothing happened. A dull thud was all that was noted, nothing more. Apparently, the torpedo had malfunctioned.[37]

Hara gave a quiet sigh of relief. The commander knew that he had been very fortunate. But such luck could not be guaranteed to continue. It was now time to get his destroyer out of harm's way. He ordered the helm to continue the hard right-turn, then to proceed on a new course due north and with the best possible speed. Hara looked at his watch. The time was 11:47 p.m. He would later write, "Those two minutes [between 11:45 and 11:47 P.M.] . . . were the most breathtaking ones of my life."[38]

Throughout this time Yamashita had maintained his dedicated search. During the torpedo scare he had briefly lost sight of the enemy ships, but he had since relocated what he thought was their distant wakes. He suddenly shouted, "Torpedo explosion! Enemy ship hit!"[39] During this observation he had seen a brief flash off to the east and was thoroughly convinced that his initial evaluation was true. The timing appeared correct, and the report caused an instant uproar of cheers to pass throughout *Shigure*. Everyone unequivocally accepted the petty officer's assessment. Surely they had exacted some form of revenge upon their adversary. (In reality, however, none of Moosbrugger's destroyers were touched. Hara would later suggest that the explosion had been caused by one of his torpedoes striking the wake of one of the American destroyers. But none of Moosbrugger's ships reported any such explosion. More than likely the explosion—if there was one—occurred when one of the torpedoes struck one of the many reefs off the Kolombangara shoreline.) Accurate or not, Yamashita's report did provide *Shigure*'s crew with some much-needed boost in morale as well as a bit of vindication for their perceived dishonor. The enemy had surprised them, and so completely so as to woefully force them into a hasty retreat. This was not the way of the Japanese warrior. This was an action of disgrace. This presumed success, however, this torpedo strike against the enemy—as even Hara was soon forced to consider—might indeed open the door to their returning to the fight. Surely they should try.

* * *

Torpedoman Wallick—having since recovered from his whiplash—returned to his curious survey through the ship's powerful optics. His view of the distant carnage was very good and he was delightfully impressed. "It appeared," he wrote, "as if two ships were blown to pieces and a third, which appeared to be a cruiser, was enveloped in a mass of flames. . . ."[40]

Perhaps due to the expectation that a "cruiser" was to be a part of the enemy force and/or partly due to the true disparity in size of Sugiura's destroyers, nearly everyone throughout Moosbrugger's command believed the burning silhouette they witnessed on this night was that of a cruiser. Even Moosbrugger believed this to be true. Within the bright hues of the distant inferno the enemy ship was observed from various angles, and its identification seemed undeniable—it was too large to be a destroyer, therefore, it had to be a cruiser. Obviously, a victory over such a vessel was electrifying, charging the American crews with renewed vigor. Everyone was eager with his logic. (It would later be proven that this ship was the destroyer *Arashi*, but in the meantime—and for many weeks to follow—the mistaken identity continued.)

From aboard *Craven*, Fire Controlman Second Class Patrick Lynch observed, "Shortly after we fired our fish, there were several explosions and in the flames I saw two ships. One appeared to be a destroyer which sank immediately following a flaming explosion amidships [it is most likely from Division One's angle of view that this ship was *Hagikaze*, though it did not sink immediately as thought but was instead hidden behind the flaming remains of *Arashi*]. By this time, flames were pouring out of the other ships; I could see a cruiser in the flames and one destroyer [*Kawakaze*] to the right of it."[41] (It needs to be noted that all evidence appears to show that from the line of sight of Moosbrugger's division that Sugiura's ships were nearly lined up abreast of one another, with *Arashi* having moved a little past the powerless *Hagikaze*, and *Kawakaze* almost due south of *Arashi* by likely no more than a couple hundred yards. The line of sight from Simpson's division, however, displayed *Kawakaze* to the left of *Arashi*, while *Hagikaze* was hidden behind the flames of *Arashi*.)

Yeoman First Class Martin Hullender, also aboard *Craven*, had his own view of the distant chaos. "I am an eye witness to only three ships," he explained, "one of which I think was a heavy cruiser [*Arashi*] and two destroyers. One destroyer [*Hagikaze*] appeared to be larger than the other [*Kawakaze*]. The smaller of the two destroyers was foolishly steaming around the burning ship when I last saw her."[42]

Another aboard *Craven*, Lt. John "Joe" Poitevin, stood his station near the after 20-millimeter gun mount, awed by the distant display of pyrotechnics. His view was a little less distinct than others with higher observation; still he had little difficulty at believing that the blazing ship was a cruiser. "Our first sight of the Japanese ships came when the torpedoes hit them, and the resulting explosions lighted the area. Since I had no binoculars, my naked eye view . . . was only that of an exploding ship in the distance, and partly obscured by smoke. And as the 'word' came out that this ship was possibly a 'cruiser,' I could easily concur, as it seemed . . . to be a 'large' ship, easily larger than a destroyer."[43]

Regardless of the true composition of the Japanese column, there was no doubt that it had sustained massive punishment. The explosions from the initial hits were quite violent and the fires were unprecedented.

Ralph Barber—who after completing his medical preparations had moved up to the weather deck just aft of the #2 stack and between torpedo mounts #1 and #2—saw the explosions clearly and compared the flames to those he had seen in Birmingham's steel plants with "the blast furnaces in full force."[44]

Wilber Fultz noted with his cowboy perspective that the "cruiser" was "burning real good" and her structure "was red hot like a branding iron." "Nobody could [have] lived through that," he concluded.[45]

The explosions were even visible many miles away. Calvert's torpedo boats—still patiently patrolling Kula Gulf—reported to Rendova of seeing the "loom of battle" and "three tremendous explosions."[46] Not too far away, a friendly photo-reconnaissance plane flying over Vila, on Kolombangara, also saw the explosions, reporting "four fires which appeared to be on the shore of Vella Lavella."[47] These reports were forwarded to Wilkinson at Koli, but weather prevented the plane from having a closer look, and further word of what was transpiring was not immediately forthcoming. Japanese shore batteries on Kolombangara were also privy to the engagement, but they could not readily make out Moosbrugger's ships in the darkness nor were they certain that the exploding ships were their own. Beyond those directly involved, the battle and its status remained a mystery.

Even despite the obvious aspects of the distant carnage, there was no certainty that the American ships were out of harm's way. The capabilities of the enemy were most assuredly diminished, and greatly so, it was believed—though to what degree was unknown. The Japanese navy had always before proven itself quite resourceful and determined. It could never be underestimated. If these ships had a way of responding, they surely would. Lieutenant Shear prepared his repair party for the worst. "Listen," he wisely pointed out, quelling the enthusiasm of his men, "we're going to get some of that stuff back, so you'd better be ready for it."[48] And he said this not just to regain order; he truly believed it to be true.

* * *

Hara was in a quandary, equally torn between rationale and honor. *Shigure* had so far managed to evade the enemy torpedoes and was presently on a north by northwest heading, safely on course to soon be beyond the deadly reach of any enemy gunnery. Still, it was quite obvious to him that the majority of his officers and men wanted to return to the fight, and especially so after hearing Yamashita's encouraging report. The enemy was clearly thought to have been wounded. Perhaps now the odds were a bit more even. But Hara was not so sure, and he was determined not to react in wanton haste.

"Have you heard anything from the rest of the column?" Hara questioned, directing his attention to his radio operator.[49] In the distance the commander could see the burning wreckage of at least two ships, but which ones he could not be certain. Perhaps another of Sugiura's column had also evaded the torpedoes. If so, then there was indeed an opportunity to confront the enemy.

"Sir," the radioman replied, "I have heard only a brief message from both *Arashi* and *Kawakaze*, and they only reported being hit by torpedoes. I have heard nothing from *Hagikaze*."[50]

Hara stood silent. The strain of the situation displayed heavily on his face. The enemy had executed the attack brilliantly. Never before had he witnessed such precision from the Americans. His own choices were few. *Arashi* and *Kawakaze* were most assuredly out of action. Sugiura and *Hagikaze* might be okay, but this was in doubt. If, however, the flagship had indeed survived, to rejoin it could allow the opportunity for a strong response against the American attackers. At the very least the two ships might provide some assistance to the many Japanese sailors who were now forced to struggle in the open sea—this even despite *Hagikaze* and *Shigure* being already filled to capacity with soldiers. Moreover, to abandon the region without a fight would have all the implications of cowardice, blanketing Hara's command in shame. On the other hand, to rush blindly back to the region just for the sake of honor and without hope of any positive effect would likely gain them nothing but a suicidal death. Some aboard would have surely preferred the death. Hara, however, recalled the wise words of his grandfather: "Never seek an easy death, for that would be against the true spirit of Bushido." He struggled for a decision. Nothing seemed to aid him. His lookouts had lost visual contact with the enemy. He did not know where the enemy was or what he was up to. He did not even know what the opposing force was comprised of. To return to the area of the sinking ships would be a tremendous risk. But perhaps it was a necessary one. Hara suddenly stiffened his stance. "Helm!" he ordered. "Turn us about! Reload the torpedoes! Prepare for battle!" He then turned to his trusted radio operator. "Keep trying to contact *Hagikaze*. Let me know the moment you hear anything."[51]

* * *

In an instant *Craven*'s combat center had transcended from muted silence to thunderous jubilation. No longer was the compartment's stifling confinement of any deterrence to the animations of its residents. Victory had surely been achieved, and the celebratory congratulations were already well underway. Lieutenant Davison, however, was quick to quell such overzealous enthusiasm.

Regardless of every temptation to revel as the others, he refused. The work of the CIC was far from over. He reminded his team of the gunnery assured to follow and how it was imperative that they remain focused, alertly tracking and accurately conveying the enemy's dispositions until his every threat was completely eliminated. Presently, all four Japanese ships remained captured on the radar's scope, and this was clear evidence that some danger persisted. Then, as if timed to bolster Davison's caution, the radar operator suddenly exclaimed, "Sir, one's getting away!"

The occupants of *Dunlap*'s bridge were equally caught up by the initial torpedo success, and their resonated excitement was not so easily suppressed. There was a profound difficulty returning to the business at hand, especially while such a grand display of burning ships so boldly illuminated the nighttime sky. Such distraction was inescapable, even for Moosbrugger, who remained in awe of the totality of the destruction. Then, with instant recall to reality, the bridge phone suddenly began its familiar buzz. The revelry was interrupted. Iverson quickly grasped the receiver. "Sir," Olsen was heard to say. "*Craven* is reporting one enemy ship as attempting an escape . . . we cannot confirm."[52]

Iverson informed Moosbrugger of the report; but without a radar repeater on the bridge, they could not readily see for themselves.[53] Three ships were certain to be heavily damaged and sinking—this had been witnessed visually. The fourth was also presumed damaged, but to what extent they could not readily be certain. It was reasonable that the one unseen vessel was still under power. If so, it was indeed likely that it might try to flee the scene. Even so, Moosbrugger was unable to affirm Williamson's report. He still believed all four ships to be exactly where *Dunlap*'s CIC had them located.[54] Freddie, therefore, determined not to risk chasing a shadow. Besides, Simpson's ships were in a far better position to begin the initial mop-up phase of the operation, and Moosbrugger was determined to rely on Division Two's gunnery for stopping any strays.

Simpson did indeed have his ships right where they should be, preparing to cut directly across the bow of the Japanese column. His guns and torpedoes were poised for action, awaiting orders to commence fire. And the expressions—as with the tensions—were to be no less dramatic.

With expectation of a long, busy night, Lieutenant Jeffrey had wisely packed a light late-night snack, a quickly manufactured cheese sandwich which he hoped would ward away any pending pangs of hunger. It was now nearing the midnight crucible, and his thoughts soon turned to the tasty wrap held in his pocket. *Sterett* had for the most part become a quiet ship, steeped in deafening uncertainty—even the lieutenant's own director crew had unusually little to say.

The tensions had increasingly built ever since their entry into the gulf and were now at their climax, churning at the gut and drying the throat. Jeffrey would wait no longer. He finally determined that this was the moment to eat away his concerns. He carefully unwrapped the sandwich, gave it a quick inspection, and then placed it to his lips for one nice-sized bite. Then, as if on cue, the phones instantly came to life—the approach of enemy ships was confirmed by radar, and the CIC was quickly giving out bearings and ranges. Jeffrey's eyes suddenly opened wide, and all his energies eagerly diverted to preparing for action. Without additional thought he quickly tossed his precious snack over the side and began the processes for coaxing his guns to point to their intended targets.[55]

Word spread rapidly that Division One had fired their torpedoes. *Sterett*'s fire control radar was quickly coaxed to the same targets. Jeffrey's guns were at the ready. With equal expediency, *Lang* and *Stack* also had their batteries set to fire. Simpson eagerly ordered the column to port, aiming to interdict the path of the enemy approach. The execution was flawless. Now they would wait—wait for the success of the torpedoes and subsequent orders sure to follow.

As with Moosbrugger's command, Simpson's men also found the lapse of time between the torpedoes being fired and their initial strikes to be agonizingly slow. "I was sure they had missed," wrote Jeffrey. For the lieutenant—as with the many others—the hands of the clock appeared to have stopped. But the enemy ships were still approaching and at a high rate of speed, forcing the lieutenant to question why they were not ordered to fire. His answer came when "two simultaneous red flashes tore into the night." The torpedoes had found their mark. "The lead enemy ship," he went on to describe, "a destroyer, sank almost immediately [*Hagikaze*, however, did not sink as first thought but to Division Two was merely hidden behind the eruption of *Arashi*]. The second was a cruiser that burst into brilliant flame."[56] The thrill of this moment was indescribable, a vision so etched into the subconscious mind as to never be forgotten. This, however, was only the beginning.

Aboard *Lang*, Lt. Dan Gray continued his observations from the destroyer's main deck, persistent with his duties while overseeing the readiness of his damage control specialists. He too had been notified of the torpedoes fired by Division One, having his access to the CIC through the ship's phone circuits and talker who relayed each crucial message. "We had contacted the enemy exactly at midnight as planned," he noted.[57] Somewhere beyond his eyesight the enemy ships were racing forward, aware or not. For Gray this moment was unprecedented, for he had never before been so close to the enemy, and his emotions were at this point in a bit of distress. He was somewhat uncertain of how he should react, as he struggled between confidence and fear. None of this would matter, however, when the "explosions and huge flames suddenly appeared."[58] The excitement of the success was so grossly consumed by the explosive shock and the mind-numbing display of destruction that his every emotion was briefly paralyzed. The brightness of the distant flashes seared into the retina of his eyes, capturing the image as a snapshot that would never fade. His shouts of jubilation surpassed his gasps of awe—a great victory had surely been awarded them and it appeared deeply one sided. Even so, there remained reason for caution, for the conclusion was in no way affirmed.

Gunner's Mate Chuck Lee had a similar view. "All of a sudden there was a huge explosion with flames lighting up the sky. Torpedoes had hit at least [three] of the enemy ships. The first one . . . was emitting flames and more explosions, hundreds [of] feet into the air. The other two were burning furiously." But he and the others of the gun crew had little time to marvel at the distant spectacle. "In seconds, the order came down to 'commence rapid firing.'"[59] And the roar of the 5-inch guns instantly took precedence.

Still actively confined within *Lang*'s cramped combat center, Lieutenant Southard was far too busy to seek even a brief view of the fireworks on display outside. He was tempted, but he would not dare a peek. He could hear joyous shouts coming from the bridge and was attuned to the many graphic descriptions coming from all over the ship, confirming the initial success—and this would, for the moment at least, have to suffice. "My only choice was to remain in the CIC . . . alert to whatever should show up and keep the skipper informed."[60] His team had no time to revel as the others. Southard knew Simpson's aggressive style. He knew, too, of Wilfong's passion for speed and delivery. Neither would withstand the enemy any opportunity for recovery. Most assuredly, this action was but at its threshold—and, despite its victorious conclusion appearing every bit in hand, to presume that this fight was over could prove very much a mistake. The veteran in Southard knew never to underestimate the will of the Japanese sailor. The enemy could be allowed no quarter, and he knew Simpson would give him none.

Chapter Nine

Commence Fire

Finishing the Deed

Simpson wasted no time at delivering his command to fire. Only moments before, he and his lethal band of destroyers—all patiently poised for action and eager to claim a piece of the victory—stood slyly in the darkness and completely hidden from the enemy. Having now clearly witnessed the first blow, and determined to provide a proper and prompt dispatch of the Japanese adversary, at 11:46 P.M. the commander gave his order. "Commence fire!" he sternly pronounced.[1]

The responding reports of the 5-inch guns were immediate. The simultaneous blasts of *Lang*'s main batteries instantly jarred the flagship sideways, notifying all aboard that they were indeed entered into the fray. The eruption of the guns was with such profound unison that their cumulative blast nearly deafened every unprotected ear, and their joint concussion painfully jarred the bones of every man stationed nearby. The intensity of the rapid-fire that followed sounded remarkably comparable to that of machine guns. The reoccurring patterns of the blasts were so quick it heated the gun barrels to a glowing deep red and blistered the thick gray paint used to protect them from the elements. The surrounding air was soon consumed with the putrid odor of sulfur and filled with a black expanse of smoke, originating from the flashless powder ignitions and growing heavier with each explosive discharge. Shell casings quickly littered the outer gun decks, left to roll freely with each sway of the ship and either forced into one another with a heavy brassy clang or sent reeling past the gunnels to a silent departure into the sea. With each motion of the destroyer there was heard the shrill singing of electric motors and hydraulics, as continuous efforts at keeping each gun on target were rigorously maintained. All the while, round after round blasted outward to arch its way on a destructive course, intent at delivering death to any unfortunate soul standing in their path. The duel of the cannonade had begun.

The most obvious target was the second enemy ship, the heavily damaged and terribly burning "cruiser." Under radar control, *Lang*'s 5-inch guns were drawn to focus their first volley here. *Lang*'s gunners, as expected, were at the top of their game—notable hits aboard the opposing ship were almost instantaneous, as new fires and explosions were quickly observed. *Sterett*'s main batteries followed suit, firing volley after volley into this same burning hulk. The distant pyrotechnics initially started by Moosbrugger's torpedoes were now intensified even further, as flaring eruptions shot brilliantly into the distant sky. Observers readily reported additional hits with additional explosions, yet the stubborn enemy vessel refused to sink.

From *Lang*'s 5-inch mount #3, Chuck Lee worked with as much deliberate haste as physically possible, yet he was barely able to shove one round into his gun's breech when it was ready for the next. There was little time to observe the true results of his weapon's accuracy, and even then the growing concentration of smoke from the firing obscured the better part of his view. Only occasionally did he catch a good glimpse of the explosions and fires erupting against the distant backdrop of darkness. For the moment, his sole duty was to perform his job to the perfection of his training, effected through all those many accumulated hours of continuous drilling that had been so loathed. Now those drills were paying dividends. With each additional round fired, his confidence grew all the more, ever so thankful for those individuals, like Chief Leonard Wood, who had taught him so well.

Mitchell Sang, the muscular coxswain feeding the heavy 54-pound projectiles onto Lee's ramming tray, was equally unending with motion and devotion to duty. There was no cessation to his efforts—even despite his painful injury. Indeed, the darkness, smoke, and excitement hid the grimace on his face and the blood pouring from his crushed right hand. The wound had occurred just as the gun's second salvo released and Sang reached for the next shell being elevated by the hoist from the handling room below. This hoist mechanism had a notorious reputation on all ships and had claimed a number of hands and fingers over its lifetime. Lack of good vision combined with the rush of effort and the motion of the ship once again brought injury to another of its victims. In his haste, Sang grasped for the shell just a bit too early, briefly catching his right hand between the hoist and its guide. The excruciating pain was instantaneous, as was his reaction to pull away. His powerful jerk released his hand but ripped a 1-inch gash between his first and middle fingers. All of his fingers were badly mashed and blood gushed from the wound, menaced even more by an acute throbbing that increased with each beat of his heart. He risked further injury by continuing, but he did not hesitate. He did not slow the speed of his motions at all, and none of the others working with him would know of his injury till long after the gunnery ceased. He would report to sickbay only after the ship departed the area, over two hours later.

Two minutes into the barrage, the firing suddenly paused. Observers on *Lang*'s bridge had noticed sporadic gun flashes, believed to be originating from two twin-mount guns of another of the enemy ships, projecting from the darkness just to the left of the burning "cruiser." Simpson immediately ordered his destroyers' guns to "Cease fire" and for fire control to search for the new target. Within seconds the radar had locked onto the belligerent opposition and all four 5-inch guns adjusted to the coordinates. At 11:49 p.m., Simpson again gave the "commence fire" order, and the successive volleys resumed.[2]

As before, *Sterett*'s gunnery quickly followed suit, adjusting to the new target and joining *Lang* with pinpoint accuracy. The targeted ship was identified as a destroyer (*Kawakaze*), and hits from both *Lang* and *Sterett* were immediately observed to impact the region of the enemy vessel about amidships. Small explosions were noted, and fires were soon seen to spread all along the vessel's main outer deck. Sporadic—though terribly ineffective—gunfire from the enemy destroyer continued, as brave gunners did their best to ward away their attackers, even in spite of their ship's doomed state.

On board *Stack*—though two minutes into the opening of the gunnery—Captain Newton had yet to order his main batteries to open fire. His gunners were impatiently waiting, hoping to add to the enemy destruction, but the order they were expecting was not readily forthcoming. The ship's torpedo officer had reported a "good target near the burning enemy ship."[3] Though this target was not immediately identified, Newton elected first to allow his torpedomen their chance. He ordered the starboard torpedo battery to fire on the new target. The response was met with great expediency, as all four starboard tubes instantly released their menacing missiles into the darkened sea. The ship immediately lurched noticeably to port in acknowledgment of the discharged weight. A spread of four foaming trails was then observed to disappear into the infinity beyond.

With his torpedoes now successfully sent stealing toward their mark, Captain Newton finally gave the order for his 5-inch guns to "open fire."[4] The initial target, as with *Lang* and *Sterett*, was the burning "cruiser," and *Stack*'s gunners responded with all able haste. But, realizing that the other two division destroyers had since diverted to a new target, Newton quickly ordered his batteries to the same adjustment. *Stack*'s gunners were just as quick with this response, and so the woes of the second enemy ship (*Kawakaze*) increased.

The effect of this gunnery was unprecedented. From high atop his director's perch, *Sterett*'s gunnery officer, Lieutenant Jeffrey, had the ideal view and was totally awestruck by the sight. The distant spectacle, the expanding fires, series of dramatic explosions, and constant cascading of red-hot shrapnel, was incomparable to any of his previous experiences. The destruction was even more intense than any of what he had witnessed at the Battle of Guadalcanal and far more one-sided. At Guadalcanal, the confusion of the actions and the enemy's deadly response had been a fearful contest. Here, however, everything was working just as it had been planned. This was so unbelievable. He wanted to cheer at the top of his lungs, but the shock of the success imprisoned his voice. He was so energized, so emotionally charged, but there was no time to accurately display it. Furthermore, Jeffrey thought better of jinxing the operation with any premature accolades of celebration. He rightly knew that this action was not yet concluded.

Indeed, pursuant of the surprised enemy, all three destroyers kept up their steady barrage of high-explosive 5-inch shells, sending each and every round arching outward to their targets with the highest degree of accuracy. To the bitter shock of their opposition, the precision of the American gunnery was phenomenal, as few rounds were to land without adding some misery to the stymied Japanese ships. Furthering the woes of the enemy even more, from deep within the flaming mass another large explosion was suddenly noted, believed to have been a direct hit from one of *Stack*'s four previously launched torpedoes. So far, this action was being executed with complete perfection and just as it had been planned. The only glitch came at 11:51 p.m., when at the firing of its ninth volley *Sterett*'s No. 1 gun had its breech jam, ending its usefulness for the duration of the operation—though this would prove to be of no negative effect to the impending outcome. If the enemy was to escape this night it was to take far more than a single misfire to advance the miracle.

* * *

Aboard *Kawakaze*, Captain Yanase eagerly sought a way to save his crippled ship. He still had propulsion, but—with the destroyer's bow missing—making any good speed and maintaining decent maneuverability was impossible. Furthermore, to move forward forced more water into the exposed holds of the ship and hampered his repair parties' attempts at stopping the leakage. He still had power to his two after 4.7-inch main batteries, gun #2 (a single mount), and gun #3 (a twin mount), and might have no choice but to fight. Unfortunately, he had no clue as to the makeup of his adversary or where he was located, nor did he have any communications with the remaining ships of the column. *Arashi*, he knew, was a total wreck and out of action. He knew too that *Hagikaze* had also sustained major damage from at least one torpedo strike, but that was all. Of *Shigure* he knew nothing.

Yanase determined to try and move away some distance from *Arashi* and her ominous light. It was quickly apparent, however, that the enemy—now certain to be surface ships—was already targeting the area with gunfire. More explosions and shell splashes were observed all around the burning *Arashi*. Splashes around *Kawakaze* (though more likely only flying debris from the exploding *Arashi* rather than shells from Simpson's gunners) indicated to Yanase that he too was being targeted. His gunners were ordered to return fire. They obeyed, firing blindly into the distant darkness, hopeless—short of some great stroke of amazing luck—of hitting anything while instantly divulging their exact location to the enemy.

Within seconds the American gunners zeroed in on *Kawakaze*'s position, dooming her. A hail of high-explosive 5-inch projectiles quickly followed, and many well-directed rounds instantly struck the crippled destroyer portside amidships. There was no place for the poor soldiers still crowding her decks to hide, and the carnage was massive. Helpless men were ripped apart by each blast, sending bodies and body parts flying through the air in a gruesome display of pyrotechnics. Fires quickly erupted, spreading across the main outer deck as well as interior decks below, chasing the surviving men aft and into the sea. The wounded could not escape—their screams could be heard over the din of gunfire and explosions. Damage control parties tried to extinguish the blazes, but without success—the intense shelling hampered their every effort. *Kawakaze*'s gunners continued to return fire, but they had no exact target and could only guess as to what direction and distance to fling their own deadly rounds. The end was surely near.

Yanase knew his ship had no chance of survival. There was no escape. Shipboard communications were no longer functioning. Fires were out of control. The bridge could no longer affect the outcome. Enemy shells continued to hammer his wrecked destroyer with impunity, and he could only watch. The reflected light of his ship's flames drew even more hits. The wheelhouse reeled with each jarring explosion. Holes were ripped in the portside at the waterline, fatal wounds that instantly allowed tons of seawater to rush into the vessel's interior compartments. The destroyer leaned heavily to port, farther and farther, until its roll was unstoppable. Those few men still able quickly abandoned their stations for an escape into the surrounding sea. Yanase, grieved by this embarrassing loss, remained on the bridge, determined not to leave his position of command. Within seconds the deed was done—*Kawakaze* was fully capsized and rapidly settling beneath the waves, taking Captain Yanase on a joint descent to their eternal resting place. The time was 11:59 p.m.

* * *

On *Dunlap*'s bridge, Moosbrugger continued to direct his own force in combat. The enemy ships had been completely blindsided by his tremendously effective torpedo attack. Still, they remained on the surface, and this he could not allow. The matter was not yet concluded. "Course one eighty," he ordered.[5] The change was to take them due south and again along the coast of nearby Kolombangara. All three ships quickly responded and formed in a line opposite of their initial approach, with *Maury* now taking the van. The time was logged as 11:52 p.m.

Off to the southeast, the eruptions from the enemy "cruiser" continued, lighting up the distant darkness with its unruly blaze and unending fireworks. This was the most obvious target, but radar revealed that two distinct targets remained, with another enemy ship (*Kawakaze*) located just slightly to the east. Just three minutes into his new course Moosbrugger ordered his division to "commence fire" at this new target.[6]

Waiting inside *Dunlap*'s dimly lit #4 handling room, Seaman Clyde Conner finally received the anticipated order to begin passing ammo to the 5-inch gun positioned directly above. Fear and expectation had been aplenty in his claustrophobic hold, where he and three others were anxiously confined and blind to all the happenings outside. So far, the only initial knowledge that these men had of the ensuing engagement was relayed to them through the phones, and this was of little aid at relieving the stress that so fully beleaguered their nerves. When the torpedoes finally hit and the announcement of the success was finally given, Conner and the others with him breathed a great sigh of relief. "We were elated," he noted.[7] Each man was even allowed a quick peek outside the escape hatch, there to see the burning "cruiser." But the engagement was, at this early stage, far from over. Orders were soon received for the 5-inch guns to open fire, and it was instantly clear that more was yet needed to close this action. Anything could still go wrong.

Despite his concern, there was little time for Conner—or any of the others for that matter—to consider the negatives. As soon as the gunfire ensued, it was all business. "We were too busy to be scared," he wrote. "My function was to place a powder canister on the hoist, send it up to the ready room and then place a projectile on the hoist. This routine . . . continued . . . rapidly . . . and the concentration required was such that one had no time to think."[8]

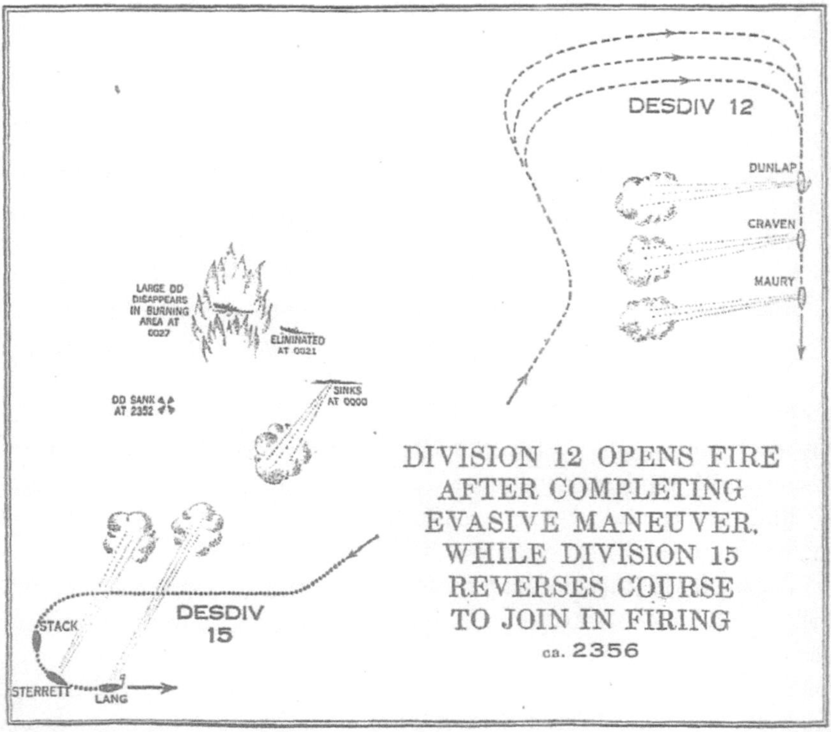

Simplified chart from an October 1943 Naval Intelligence Combat Narratives Report on Action at Vella Gulf of August 6-7, 1943. Denotes action at 11:56 P.M. (2356 hours).

The first salvo blasted from Moosbrugger's three ships in one near simultaneous effort. A thunderous jolt, felt heavily throughout each ship, confirmed to every sailor aboard that the gunnery duel had now begun.

Aboard *Dunlap*, combat rookie Ralph Barber had never before experienced the firing of the 5-inch guns. Their eruption sent a chill up his spine, as he sensed instant panic racing throughout his body. He noted of this opening barrage that "although we were firing to starboard, burnt cork from the ammo casings drifted down the port side of the ship. This . . . indicated to me that we had been hit."[9] It would take a few long seconds for him to figure out otherwise, and happily so.

So far, every execution of Moosbrugger's plan appeared to be without flaw. But this quickly began to change. The extreme jar of the initial volley of cannonade was instantly responsible for knocking *Maury*'s SG radar off-line.[10] Sims no longer had his advantageous view of the gulf, and he quickly reported this loss to his boss, Moosbrugger. It was a serious issue, but not one that seemed detrimental to this stage of the operation. Freddie aptly determined to continue the shelling without pause.

From his own position on the bridge, Moosbrugger had a good view of the cannonade. Tracer rounds were seen to arch across the darkness on their way to their intended recipient. Hits were immediately observed on the distant target. Simpson reported over the TBS that Division Two had previously diverted its fire to this same target, and from his position numerous other hits were observed within the crossfire. Everything appeared well in hand, but at 11:57 P.M.—just as *Kawakaze* and Captain Yanase began their joint slide to the ocean's bottom—Olsen suddenly interrupted the ongoing observation to notify the bridge that *Dunlap*'s SG radar had also gone down. One minute later Williamson reported *Craven* as having lost its SG as well and of having to cease fire to make the repairs.[11] Moosbrugger was now blind, without the electronic eyes that had provided him such an initial advantage. Beyond the brightly burning flames of the "cruiser," he could see nothing. Moosbrugger needed his SG and he needed it *now*!

In *Dunlap*'s CIC, Olsen stood quietly, anxiously overseeing Savage, as the radarman quickly removed the panel to his radar console, peering in to a small darkened interior that revealed only a maze of glass tubes and wires. Outside, despite the radar's loss, the gunfire continued and the console jarred heavily with each new volley. A battle lantern was brought to aid Savage as he searched for the problem, hoping for a quick solution. Despite the pressure, the radarman displayed nothing short of calm confidence. A few anxious seconds later and the console suddenly flickered back to life. The scope regained its illumination, and its sweeping hand once again displayed what remained of the enemy force. Savage stood with a smile, and Olsen gave him an approving slap of his back. Then the lieutenant phoned the bridge. "SG is back on line!" Savage had fixed the console in only two minutes.[12]

Moosbrugger and Iverson gave out a unified sigh of relief. Iverson then made a mental note to be sure to commend Savage for his expedient effort. Throughout this episode, Moosbrugger had opted not to cease fire from *Dunlap*—depending on the targeting estimates to be given out by the batteries' fire-control for accuracy—even despite the ongoing negative effect that this was to have with correcting the radar issue. The commander was determined at keeping the Japanese off balance, caught in the crossfire between his and Simpson's ships, offering them no possibility of escape. Indeed, the effectiveness of this gunfire, while not having the benefit of the radar coordinates, would seem in serious doubt. But when the radar sweeps did resume, they quickly revealed that Lieutenant Holmquist's ongoing calculations were almost spot on, nearly perfect targeting. Iverson was to add the gunnery officer to his growing commendations list. He was truly thankful for the profound professionalism being exemplified by his crew. Of even greater importance, however, the radar displayed no other intruders elsewhere in the region and currently showed only one blip remaining in the area of the enemy ships. With this reassurance, Moosbrugger suddenly ordered, "Cease fire!"[13]

In the preceding minutes, aboard *Craven*, Captain Williamson and Lieutenant Davison were forced to deal with the ongoing frustrations of correcting their own radar issue. The jar from the systematic and unified eruptions of their destroyer's 5-inch guns was also responsible for the disabling of its SG radar, also to cause loss of the electronic vision of the gulf. Like Savage on *Dunlap*, Radioman Pritchett quickly attacked the problem, but the correction did not come quite so readily. Pritchett's initial attempt to reset the machine did not work and, with his bag of spare parts in hand, he began a hurried trace of the console's electronics, searching for what was likely nothing more than a loosened tube. Meanwhile, Williamson could do little, other than wait and watch from his vantage on the bridge, as gunfire from *Dunlap* and Division Two continued to hammer away at the remaining enemy ships.

Minutes ticked by and the nerves of the captain grew unusually on edge. The whole division remained blind, having only the distant flares from the burning ships as evidence of the current location of the enemy. Like Moosbrugger and Iverson, Williamson was begging for his radar. More minutes ticked by. Finally, the captain heard Davison call to him from behind, "Sir, SG is back up!"[14] Williamson was noticeably relieved. Once again, all essential information was freely flowing to him from the CIC, and he now had a clear grasp of where the remaining enemy ships were located. He quickly turned to order his batteries to resume their cannonade, but was just as suddenly interrupted by the TBS report from Moosbrugger ordering all gunnery to cease. A second later the TBS cracked with additional lively chatter, this time from *Stack*, providing a confirmation that another enemy destroyer (*Kawakaze*) had been sunk. Despite the material malfunctions, the American ships were still very much in control, and everything continued to promise nothing short of complete victory.

During this same episode, Captain Sims and Lieutenant Crenshaw were still confronting their own radar issues, though with a bit of a different approach to their blindness. *Maury*'s first salvo had caused the SG radar to overload, forcing its relay to automatically trip to the "off" position. Resetting the circuit was as simple as the push of a button, but Crenshaw ordered his radar technician, Radioman Horatio Seymour, not to reset it just yet. Sims, like Moosbrugger, was determined to keep his batteries in action, and so Crenshaw did not want to risk that the continued jarring might cause any permanent damage to the SG set. Besides, the FD (Fire Control) radar was still functioning and had the enemy target locked. The 5-inch salvos continued to fire effectively. But then it was learned that both *Dunlap* and *Craven* were also operating without their SG. This bit of news changed the situation dramatically, and Sims immediately ordered his guns to "cease fire." Someone needed eyes on the gulf to make sure no other enemy intruders were sneaking in. At the conclusion of the fifth salvo, *Maury*'s 5-inch guns fell silent. Then, with Crenshaw's permission, Seymour immediately hit the reset button, and the SG resurrected to new life.[15]

The radar renewed its sweep of the surrounding area. Little had changed. Momentarily, only two blips (*Arashi* and the sinking *Kawakaze*—with *Shigure* escaping, hidden by the background of Vella Lavella, and the electronic signature of *Hagikaze* hidden within the widespread debris of *Arashi*) were all that remained of the enemy column and—outside Moosbrugger and Simpson's divisions—the gulf was still empty of all other traffic. Any direct threat to the American vessels appeared moot.

Confident that the other ships could now handle the gunnery, Captain Sims determined that *Maury* should become the designated eyes for the rest of Division One, and he notified Moosbrugger of his intent. For the duration of any additional cannonade, *Maury*'s guns were ordered to be still, allowing its SG unhampered effort for its function and undisturbed sweeps of the gulf. Obviously, *Maury*'s proud gunners were not fond of being denied further participation in the one-sided shootout, but the captain's orders had been given and with wise precaution.

Exactly at midnight all gunnery temporarily ceased. The only target now remaining, or so it appeared, was the remains of the burning "cruiser." With the guns of both American divisions now silenced, the opportunity was given for some momentary study of the distant burning hulk, seeking some identification of the type of ship that so stubbornly refused its fate. After a close observation through his glasses, Simpson reported over the TBS to Moosbrugger that "the burning ship is a three-stack cruiser."[16] Iverson peered through *Dunlap*'s powerful optics. Though he could not make out any clear identifying features, he reported to Moosbrugger that there was "a hell of a lot of fire" and that the ship was indeed "a great deal larger than a destroyer."[17] From his own advantageous position, Gunnery Officer Holmquist "could clearly see and identify the after gun turret of the type mounted on a Kuma or Natori class cruiser. Three stacks and a high bridge structure forward, also features of a Kuma or Natori, were visible."[18] Moosbrugger concluded the target must indeed be an enemy cruiser.

With curious afterthought, and while still having his gunnery officer on the horn, Iverson inquired of Holmquist if the reporter, Art Burges, was still at the gun director platform, catching all of this historical handiwork. Surely the correspondent had a commanding view and was making many notes of the ongoing action. Being in the easiest position to observe, Peters stood up to look. Burges was nowhere to be seen. Peters then lowered himself to his seat. "Not there, sir," the sailor responded. "He's not here," Holmquist reported back. Where could he have gone?

Iverson ordered a quick search for the missing press rep, and nearly every occupied area was checked. No one had seen the man. How could they have lost their VIP guest? Hopefully he had not fallen overboard. The search was continued and, finally, after several additional minutes had passed, Burges was found, sitting by himself within the seclusion of the wardroom. The initial blast of the 5-inch batteries had frightened him terribly. He had seen the torpedo strikes, he explained, and that was enough for him. He preferred the safety of the ship's interior over that of the exposed gun director platform, especially during the firefight stage, and he refused to budge, even when invited to the bridge.[19]

Meanwhile, Moosbrugger's division continued its slow march to the south. On *Maury*, Captain Sims kept a close watch as his helmsman directed the destroyer along Moosbrugger's prescribed course. The darkness remained intense and continued to yield very low visibility. Each destroyer was by now back to being separated by about 500 yards, with *Maury* in the lead, nearing the coastline of Kolombangara. A portside lookout suddenly reported seeing gun flashes off of the destroyer's port bow. Sims quickly moved to the bridge wing portside of the pilothouse for a closer view. Almost immediately he saw the tiny flashes resonating in the distant darkness, and he suspected coastal guns on Kolombangara were trying to make their range. His more immediate concern, however, was that with the course they were now traveling *Maury* would soon be moving directly in-between the island and the burning "cruiser." His destroyer would then be silhouetted as a perfect target for those determined enemy coastal gunners. Sims quickly returned to the pilothouse and notified Moosbrugger by TBS of the situation, hoping for a quick course correction.[20]

Moosbrugger acknowledged Sims's concern in the "affirmative," and at 12:03 A.M. he ordered a course change to 310 degrees True, taking the force on a track that would pass just a few thousand yards north of the "burning mass" (*Arashi*).[21] Having made this change in direction, Moosbrugger was now determined that his force should take up a defensive position near the northwest entrance to the gulf. There he would prepare to intercept any new enemy force that might try and come to the aid of the wounded enemy vessels. In the meantime, the commander's gunners were to continue intermittent fire into the one brightly burning hulk that remained—that of the presumed enemy "cruiser." And the gunnery did resume—though, even with additional confirmed hits, this vessel still refused to sink.

At 12:05 a.m., Moosbrugger again ordered a change of course, this time to 000 degrees True, turning his force due north. This order was intended as an "execute upon receipt," but the transmission was confused and was received by both *Craven* and *Maury* as an "execute to follow." As a result, both ships delayed their turn and this was to cause considerable distance to expand within the formation. A precious few seconds passed before the errant transmission was corrected. Visibility remained very low and the miscommunication led to the destroyers of Division One losing temporary sight of one another, leading to a loosely separated column that took several minutes to tighten back together.[22]

At 12:07 a.m., to add even more alarm to this moment of confusion, from high atop *Dunlap*'s director platform, Gunnery officer Lt. (jg) Carl Holmquist reported a splash in the water just off the ship's starboard bow. It was thought that this splash was a near miss, believed to be from a 3-inch shell.[23] They were taking on gunfire! No one on the bridge had seen the splash, but the report could not be dismissed. Previously, there were reported gun flashes observed coming from the area of the enemy ships, but the only vessel thought remaining was surely incapable of such offense. Perhaps the gunners on Kolombangara were responsible. This shell, however, was close, and shore guns would have been reaching out to their maximum range. Radar disclosed no other intruders in the region. Therefore, provided the shell splash was real, it must have been one last "Hail Mary" from some determined Kolombangara gunner, for no enemy ships of significance remained. Moosbrugger remained confident of complete victory.

* * *

To the north, however, Hara was once again directing his only slightly injured destroyer, *Shigure*, south—unknowingly proceeding with a heading that was on a near collision course with Moosbrugger's temporary out-of-sorts division. Hara's decision to turn back had not been made easily and was full of risk.

Even despite many additional efforts to contact Sugiura, no friendly radio transmissions had been received, and this was an ominous silence. Meanwhile,

Shigure's crew alertly searched for the enemy both to the south and southeast regions of the gulf—though, outside of *Arashi*'s wildly burning hulk, there was nothing to be seen. There was no sign of the enemy ships. Even so, Hara was no fool. He knew these ships remained a threat and were likely searching diligently to find him. To avoid their detection, he hugged the coast of Vella Lavella, seeking to use the island to mask *Shigure* from the probing enemy radar. So far, the maneuver appeared to be working.

Continuing her approach, *Shigure* had by 12:10 a.m. reached a point less than 3 miles from *Arashi* and was closing. Suddenly a tremendous explosion erupted in the distance directly forward. It was a blinding display of pyrotechnics, a great flash that mushroomed upward by hundreds of feet and quickly expanded into a giant semicircle, this to be followed by a super-sized umbrella-like cascade of flares and flaming projectiles. The ensuing concussion could be felt even at *Shigure*'s greater distance. Hara immediately queried his radio operator, hoping he had by now heard something, anything, from at least one other ship. But the airwaves remained eerily still. The signs were most disparaging.

Hara was once again forced to reevaluate his situation. He assumed the worst—it now appeared that his destroyer was the lone survivor of Sugiura's doomed column. To complicate matters, *Shigure*'s helmsman had only moments before reported to Hara that the destroyer's steering was sluggish and slow to respond. It was reasonable to conclude that the previous strike of the dud torpedo had somehow damaged the ship's rudder control. Hara knew to turn back north would be a tremendous blow to his crew's morale, but he must consider it. The enemy's composition and location remained completely unknown to him. *Shigure*, only slightly damaged but overburdened with troops and supplies, was no longer in fighting trim. The rest of the force appeared destroyed. Hara turned to Yamagami and shook his head in bitter frustration. The situation was untenable. He had to decide quickly whether to retreat. He knew he would surely be damned if he did and just as surely damned if he didn't.

* * *

Aboard *Lang*'s bridge, Simpson, now flaunting his broadest, most sinister smile, openly displayed his great pleasure with the progress of the ongoing operation. Between his habitual uses of profanity, he eagerly pointed out every successive hit delivered to the doomed enemy, this abbreviated discourse often congratulatory to the planning, its command and execution. With each new explosion, his eyes gleamed even brighter in the reflection of the distant flames and ongoing destruction. Unlike Burges, Pat Robinson bravely maintained his station near

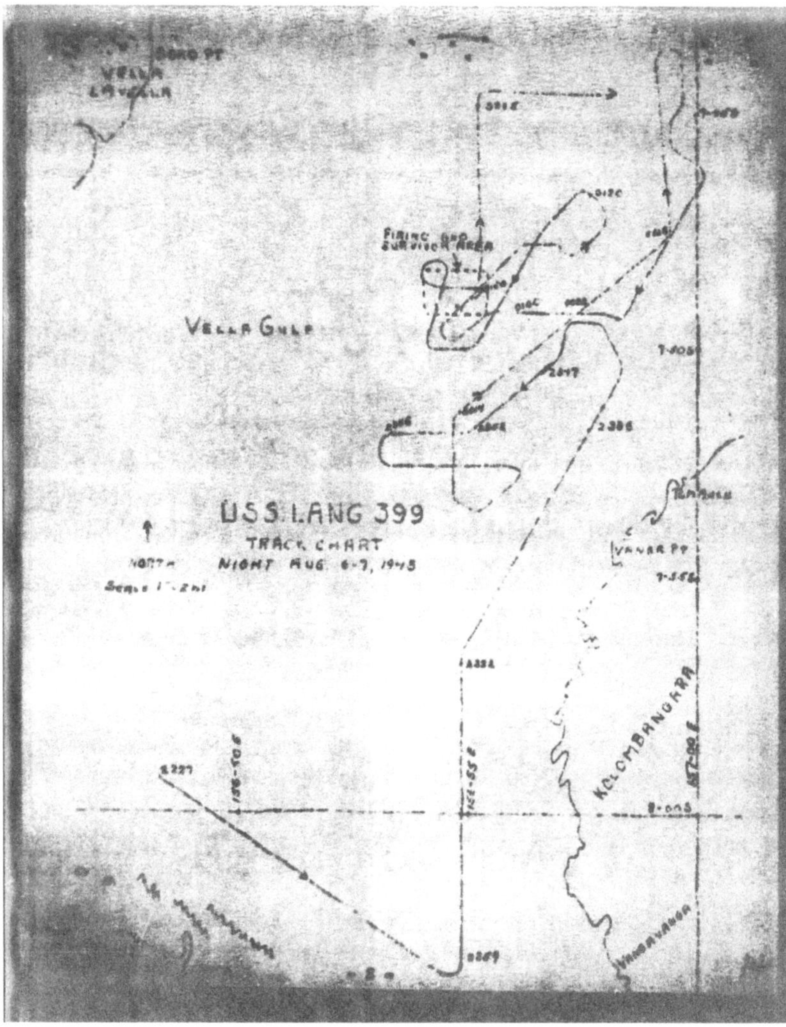

Detailed track chart from the August 15, 1943, USS *Lang* Action Report for Vella Gulf on August 6-7, 1943.

the commodore, keeping detailed notes of the action while soaking in every proud comment that Simpson willingly tossed his way.

Meanwhile, Wilfong, who stood his most serious stance, wavered little from the important task of directing his ship. Dismissing much of the boasting going on beside him, he focused only on the completion of the tasks within his assignment. From behind, Southard, who maintained his lengthy confinement within the CIC's tight configuration and who refused concession to its swelter, fed forward every bit of the incoming intelligence. Outside, the gunnery continued, though its level of intensity had now lessened and its targeting was directed only at the remains of the burning "cruiser." The radar, though a bit upset by all the debris and large area of flames, was working properly and revealed no other targets. It, therefore, appeared—to everyone—that no other enemy ships remained and that the engagement was nearing its definite conclusion.

In the distance the great concentration of flames continued its brilliant illumination of the night sky. The display had been ongoing since the opening moments of the engagement, and even despite unprecedented punishment the burning "cruiser" still stubbornly maintained its buoyancy. Every attempt to sink it had so far been resisted. That it should remain on the surface was a bit frustrating, but it was a dead ship, nonetheless. Then, at 12:10 a.m., an enormous explosion rocked the entire area. Originating from near the center of the inferno, the massive blast erupted with the highest degree of violence. The concussive power of the explosion, a super-heated wave seen as a translucent bubble against an opaque background, instantly expanded into a huge glowing dome that just as quickly dissipated into the outlying darkness. From within its center a pillar of fire and debris rose in excess of 600 feet into the air, to then mushroom widely outward and cascade back to the ocean's flaming surface, increasing to nearly double in size the area previously consumed by fire.

Sherman noted, "Then, flaring up into the night from the 'guts' of the Jap cruiser like a great fiery asterisk, came an explosion, the granddaddy of them all, which seemed to reach right up and grab the sky itself, and it clung there belching from minor explosions, within the big one which flared off into the night from this swirling, bellowing mass of fire. The force of that explosion shook us as though we'd been hit."[24]

"Cease fire!" Simpson quickly ordered. There was no immediate need to waste any further shelling. Surely the "cruiser" was finally obliterated. It was now time to evaluate the situation. The commander intended to allow his radar an undisturbed moment to search the region for any remaining targets. As directed, the invisible sweeping probe reached out across the darkness and on through the region of smoke and flame, seeking any prey. Seconds passed as an electronic impression reflected its visions on the console screen, but without conclusion—the immense debris field was causing too much interference. The intensity of the distant flames even obscured any attempt at a visual evaluation. Even so, it seemed unlikely that any ship could remain afloat after such an explosion, but for the short-term any confirmation of the sinking was to remain elusive.

To the northwest, Moosbrugger continued to lead his column on a course 310 degrees True toward Vella Lavella, attempting to block any enemy approach from the north. The explosion aboard the "cruiser" had captured much of his lead ship's attention, but not for long. A starboard side lookout suddenly screamed a warning, "*Torpedo, close aboard!*" The destroyer was immediately thrown into a desperate frenzy. Iverson reacted to the warning swiftly and without any hesitation. "Turn nine zero degrees! Increase speed to thirty-three knots," he ordered. The response from the helm was equally as swift, as the wheel spun hard to starboard. *Dunlap* turned sharply, leaning heavily to port in the execution. Meanwhile, every capable eye searched the sea's surface for the menacing torpedo trail—but none was seen. If it existed, it had obviously passed by with a harmless drive. Iverson, therefore, ordered his ship to return to its original course and speed.[25]

There remained a serious concern, however. If the torpedo was in fact real, from where had it originated? No other outstanding targets appeared on radar, except for the obvious blip that was the burned-out hulk of the "cruiser," and surely this vessel no longer had such capabilities. But at 12:17 A.M., a *Lang* lookout excitedly pointed to the sudden appearance of yet another ship. Amazingly, another enemy vessel moved slowly in-between Simpson's ships and the field of flames, boldly revealing itself to the division's anxious gunners. The silhouette was undeniable—a destroyer (*Hagikaze*), displaying itself very much intact and with only a minimal amount of physical damage, had somehow survived all the previous gunnery and torpedoes. It did not appear to be under power, yet it was slowly moving, obviously adrift to the currents.

Regardless of its state, at less than 5,000 yards, this target was impossible to miss, and Division Two gunners were quick to respond to Simpson's order to "commence fire." The gunnery was fast and extremely accurate. *Lang* fired off the initial volley, with one round striking the destroyer solidly on the forecastle. *Sterett*'s gunners, but a half-second behind, blasted a three-round volley (less gun #1) with surprising deadly effect. All three 5-inch shells slammed the destroyer squarely amidships, one penetrating to a vulnerable magazine. A violent explosion erupted. The whole topside of the destroyer appeared to disintegrate, and an instant later this ship was standing upright with its bow pointed skyward. Within seconds the doomed enemy destroyer was gone, having disappeared into the Deep Six—so quick that neither *Stack* nor any ship of Moosbrugger's division had even time to engage.

* * *

Sugiura turned to *Hagikaze*'s skipper, Commander Makoshi, appearing embarrassed and most apologetic for his blunder. He had obviously led his force squarely into an American trap. His own flagship remained powerless and beleaguered by a steady intake of seawater, both being effects of the previous torpedo strikes. Damage control parties had successfully extinguished most fires aboard and were making some headway at shoring-up the weakened bulkheads, but engineering was having no success at all at restoring even minimal propulsion to the destroyer. Without power the ship was doomed, faced with a situation that was completely hopeless.

The violently exploding *Arashi* was close aboard, and its massive amounts of spilt oil and gasoline had ignited the surrounding ocean into a fiery death trap. *Hagikaze*'s silhouette was being reflected from within the brilliance, assuredly exposing her to the enemy. Shell splashes were observed all around, and Sugiura was sure that they were being targeted, even though remarkably few new hits had so far been received. The origin of the shelling remained impossible to tell—all observation was blinded by the burning *Arashi*. Even if the enemy location was known, it would have been of little aid. The intense heat and amount of flying shrapnel made any exposure to the outer decks a deadly prospect. And without power, any meaningful defense was impossible. Most assuredly, *Hagikaze*'s life expectancy could be measured in mere seconds.

Finally, a 5-inch shell found its mark, exploding violently against the forecastle just forward of the superstructure. A shower of sparks erupted from within the detonation. Sugiura, Makoshi, and the others on the bridge reacted quickly, ducking below the splinter shields, seeking protection from the superheated blast. Bits of shrapnel instantly pinged off both the exterior and interior bulkheads, but both Sugiura and Makoshi were unscathed by the flying steel. The two officers then began a slow return to their feet. They were nearly upright when another barrage of 5-inch shells suddenly slammed the destroyer amidships. The entire ship reeled from these concentrated hits. Sugiura and Makoshi were thrown back to the deck, dazed and disoriented. A secondary explosion erupted and a brilliant white flash followed. The power of this blast ripped *Hagikaze*'s decking and shattered her framework, opening her hull to a massive flood of seawater. The end had finally come. Within seconds the destroyer was gone, sent plunging through the surface of a fiery sea and on to its eternal grave in the depths below.

Sugiura regained consciousness finding that he was in the water and surrounded by a mass of burning debris and hundreds of floating bodies, both living and dead. How he had gotten free of the ship he did not know, but Makoshi was also nearby, suffering the same experience and very much alive. The two officers, as well as the many others who survived, were now at the mercy of the sea. Rescue appeared unlikely—*Shigure* was the only ship that Sugiura did not readily know of its fate. Even if Hara remained nearby, Sugiura knew there was little chance he could safely effect any operation at gathering up such a number of survivors. Indeed, as the commander closely observed his surroundings amidst a hellish surface, his vision was one of only despair. The fiery sea was full of men, those living thrashing for survival. There was little hope except to try and swim for one of the nearby islands. So, the long night of terror was destined to continue.

* * *

It finally appeared that the engagement was reaching its conclusion. Additional sweeps by Moosbrugger's radar showed no signs of enemy activity to the north or northwest. A menacing little squall obscured much of the Vella Lavella coastline and so effectively interfered with the radar probe into that region as to be blinding, but the commodore doubted that anything had escaped their trap. All initial reports had confirmed all four enemy ships originally captured by radar as having been sunk. This left nothing to escape. Moosbrugger's greatest remaining concern was merely to be watchful for the sudden approach of any additional enemy ships. But this clearly seemed not to be happening.

Meanwhile, to the southeast, Simpson—whose gunners were temporarily at rest—remained poised to engage anything left of the enemy that might raise its ugly head. Like Moosbrugger, however, he was unable to locate any new targets. Outside of the large area of flaming sea (located just a few thousand yards to his northwest) and Moosbrugger's division (located a farther distance in the same direction) the gulf appeared completely void of all enemy activity. But remarkably, after some further observation, it was indeed affirmed that the burned-out hulk of the "cruiser" was still afloat and was apparently doggedly determined to remain that way. How this vessel continued to sit on the surface defied all understanding, but somehow it was still there—scorched, disfigured, and silent but very much still there. At this point, Simpson had had enough of this stubbornness. It was finally time to put this carcass to rest, once and for all. The bellicose commander determined that he would finish the job with a spread of six torpedoes, two from each of his three ships. "Inform Commander Division One—am firing torpedoes into remains of cruiser—request Division One clear line of fire."[26] Simpson needed to give Moosbrugger time to clear his own ships of any possible paths that the torpedoes might take. The message was sent by TBS and provided all the warning necessary.

On *Dunlap*'s bridge, Moosbrugger was quick to acknowledge Simpson's transmission. To his own division he ordered, "Change course to zero nine zero degrees. Follow upon receipt." Two minutes later Moosbrugger was sending Simpson the "all clear."[27]

Simpson's ships were by now steaming to the northeast, passing almost due east of the burning remains of the last Japanese ship still known to be afloat, that of the suspected "cruiser." The coup-de-grace to the operation was now at hand. With their port torpedo batteries cranked outward and lined up on target, the three destroyers under Simpson's command prepared to fire. At 12:22 A.M., the order to "execute" was given, and six Mark 15 torpedoes hit the darkened sea on path to their intended target. The seconds ticked by, soon to be interrupted by another large explosion, followed by two to three smaller blasts, each erupting from the confines of the drifting derelict. Simpson immediately requested a report from his radar. The screen showed itself entirely empty of all enemy ships. The engagement, swift and direct as it was, had finally reached its conclusion.

To the north, Moosbrugger continued to direct his division with astute confidence. At 12:32 A.M., with assurance that any danger from Simpson's torpedoes had elapsed, he ordered his ships to a new course of 060 degrees True. But, just as this new order was being acted upon, a nearby lookout again shouted out an abrupt warning of "*Torpedo*!" Iverson reacted quickly. "Left rudder! To two one zero degrees! Speed to twenty-five knots!" the captain shouted. *Dunlap* turned with a violent shift, cutting sharply into the surface of the sea while leaning hard to starboard. The wheel was kept hard over, till the turn was complete. In the meantime, a visual search for the belligerent torpedo was pursued—but there was no confirmation of its existence. Again, the report was deemed false.[28]

Reaching the designated 210-degree course, the helmsman straightened the ship. By now Iverson knew the danger had faded, but he also realized that the evasive maneuvering had greatly separated *Dunlap* from the division's other two ships. Visibility remained very poor and his lookouts could no longer see either *Craven* or *Maury*. Iverson ordered the speed reduced and immediately requested from Olsen a range and bearing of *Craven*'s position. A moment followed. "*Craven* bearing zero three four degrees, range thirty-three hundred," Olsen responded.[29] Iverson then contacted Williamson by TBS, notifying him of the unexpected maneuver and change in course. Rather than *Dunlap* changing course again, however, Moosbrugger ordered *Craven* and *Maury* to join up. Together they would then return to the area of the burning debris and pick up a prisoner for interrogation. At 12:35 A.M., Williamson notified *Dunlap*, "I have you in sight."[30]

* * *

Aboard *Shigure*, Hara displayed a countenance that resonated with complete frustration. He was deeply troubled, struggling with how to proceed. His lone destroyer, he was sure, faced incredibly poor odds if it continued along its present course. Burdened with an excess of troops and supplies, engines taxed and struggling, and steering sluggish and ill-handling, there was little doubt that for *Shigure* to pursue this contest would lead only to a catastrophic end. To turn away, however, was a decision assured at having its own set of terrible consequences. To return to base, having no serious damage and without some evidence of having at least wounded the enemy in action—and in an action that had claimed three of the Imperial Navy's finest destroyers—was certain to stir a good deal of controversy and criticism. Of even greater concern, such a decision would surely devastate the crew's morale and subjugate them to a tremendous amount of ridicule and embarrassment. Still, Hara's choice seemed all too clear—he had little option but to retreat.

Hara turned to his radio operator, pleadingly inquiring one more time if any word, even if just the faintest of signal, had been received from any of the other destroyers. The response was brief and non-argumentative. "None, sir," the radio operator answered with regret.[31] With this answer, Hara knew no true justification remained for continuing his approach. Any effort at confronting the enemy or at attempting rescue was surely to be futile. There was no reason to place his ship and crew in any further jeopardy. *Shigure* must turn around.

Before turning about, however, Rabaul needed notification of what had happened, an unenviable task for Hara. He did not know how Rabaul would respond. Nevertheless, he ordered his radio operator to send headquarters the sad news of the loss and of *Shigure*'s desperate situation, requesting further instruction. The delay between messages was agonizingly slow, and this gave greater concern that *Shigure*'s actions were being viewed with considerable disfavor. A few more minutes passed and finally a reply was received. "Return to base. Ask Kolombangara to rescue survivors."[32] This brief response, despite its authorization for retreat, was in no way reassuring to Hara and his future. No doubt he would have a lot of explaining to do, especially as to how he and his one ship had escaped, unscathed and with guns unfired, when three companion warships were lost in such dramatic fashion. Quite frankly, he wasn't so sure that he understood this himself. Later he would write, "The enemy had ambushed us brilliantly . . . The hits on *Arashi* and *Kawakaze* were phenomenal. Never before had I seen such marksmanship from the enemy. We had been taking altogether too casual a view of his torpedo technique . . . It was the most astounding torpedo success in history."[33]

Chapter Ten

Scenes of Victory

God This is Awful

The burning wreckage that highlighted the darkness was a powerful display. Deep orange, pulsating glows rising up from a low, dense covering of black smoke—that only periodically revealed its source of unruly flares of red flame—lit a path across the broad surface of sea in a manner that awed the senses of every observer. The view was surreal, dreamlike. From every angle of observation, from outside stations and from open hatchways, men gazed at the distant spectacle. They appeared paralyzed by the hellish scene, unable to speak to its magnitude or to fully grasp its meaning. The engagement had been so amazingly short, so shocking with its brevity that it was hard for many to believe it was truly over. The recent boom and jar of the cannonade still rang fresh in every ear, but only as a residual reminder of the intensity of the climaxing gunfire that had only moments earlier so shattered the peace. Smoke of burnt powder and thunder of exploding shell had since dissipated into the darkness like a fleeting memory, almost as though they had never existed. The only sound of prominent character to remain, boldly pronouncing itself within the cascading wind, was that of a high-pitched melody, singing its way through the tautly stretched stays. Beyond some minor vibrations created by the engaged turbines and screws, the deck plating was still, indicating all gunnery had ceased. The battle had indeed ended. The enemy was destroyed. Their mission was a success. It all seemed far too easy. "Damn good job," a lone sailor finally forced his previously stunned lips to proclaim.[1]

Once again Frederick Moosbrugger checked the hands of his watch. The time was 12:34 A.M. Radar aboard every one of his ships had at this moment confirmed the same remarkable message; no enemy ships remained. Like others, he mused at the decisiveness. This was surely among the most spectacular feats in the history of naval warfare. Burke would surely be proud, as his plan had worked perfectly, just as it was intended. Complete and unequivocal surprise had been achieved. Timing had been without flaw. Every ship, every officer, and every sailor had performed to the peak of their expectations and exactly as they had been trained. Torpedoes and gunnery had functioned with the highest degree of accuracy. The enemy had been caught so completely unaware as to pronounce his doom from the very outset, and he was never allowed even the slightest opportunity for recovery.

Frederick Moosbrugger—as every other member of his team—was thoroughly convinced that he had managed a most amazing victory, an unparalleled "clean sweep," and without a single enemy-inflicted casualty to his own force. He did not know of Hara and *Shigure*'s escape. In truth, the commander rightly suspected the possibility that one enemy ship might have gotten away, would even admit so later, but initially chose to commit to the more absolute scenario. On September 16 he would proclaim to correspondents, "We hit them so unexpectedly and so hard they didn't have a chance. None of them got away and we had no damage."[2]

Simpson would write a similar conclusion: "The complete surprise of the torpedo attack and the large oil fire started on the cruiser apparently disorganized the enemy. One destroyer apparently went alongside the cruiser to rescue personnel, while another was taken under gunfire immediately and sunk. After several minutes one destroyer did attempt gunfire and probably fired torpedoes, but it was smothered in gunfire and sank. The last destroyer when backing clear of the cruiser was seen by Division A-2 [Destroyer Division 15] and destroyed by gunfire."[3]

Sherman affirmed this sentiment. "On the bridge we were as stunned as we were exalted. In a few short minutes four Japanese men-of-war had been totally destroyed in a manner so violent and final that when I first awakened the following morning the events of that night seemed to linger in my weary head like a dream."[4]

* * *

Regardless of how it may have initially appeared to Moosbrugger and Simpson, one of their targets had indeed escaped. *Shigure* and Hara had managed to evade the wrath of the destructive American torpedoes and the determined eyes of searching enemy radar. Just how this had happened was not so readily understood, and certainly not by any of *Shigure*'s own personnel. The American trap had been so well conceived and so perfectly executed that escape seemed nothing short of a miracle. By rights, *Shigure* deserved no better fate than that of any of the rest of Sugiura's force—had it not been for one unimagined aid, that being the poor performance of this ship's ailing power plant. Hara had earlier shown some reserved appreciation for this engineering problem, as it had so conveniently offered him an excuse for refusing Sugiura's conference setting gesture of conciliation; now he had equal reason at being thankful for this same component, as it was the one element likely most responsible for his destroyer missing the worst of the midnight chaos. Indeed, the ship's lack of power, and nothing other—leaving her lagging behind the rest of the column by more than a thousand yards—was the most crucial factor for her not being counted among the casualties.

So, by 12:39 A.M., Hara was successfully directing his lone destroyer north by northwest, escaping Vella Gulf at best possible speed. But, as fortunate as this may have been, it was a transit made with great misgiving. This bit of success, though by no means meaningless, neither conveyed itself as a particularly rewarding moment nor brought any sense of immediate relief to the commander, his junior officers, or crew. Among them, there was little exhibition of raw emotion. Morale, just as Hara had feared, rapidly sank into a dire state of deep depression. The bridge where he stood was solemn and quiet, void of all conversation. There were no random discussions, no vocalized reflections of the night's harrowing experience. No one appeared to venture into any reasoning for the terrible loss. A few of the men did lowly grumble at having been forced to such a humiliating retreat, though their volume was never to reach their commander's ears—even despite his understanding of such talk. Otherwise, every voice remained still. Duties returned to being the primary focus for everyone, and were thus intentionally allowed to overshadow all other concerns. Evaluations of what had occurred earlier were set aside for later—as usual, there was sure to be ample opportunity for hindsight and second guessing. For now, too many dangers persisted to dwell on anything other than the present. Indeed, daylight would soon be upon them, and they needed to be as far from the reach of enemy airpower as possible. No doubt, they would be hunted, and—if not for Moosbrugger and Simpson's overconfidence that all enemy shipping had been sunk—perhaps even found.

Left behind, Sugiura floated among all that remained of his once proud force. It was a scene right out of hell itself: a sea dancing in hideous orange flames, conjoined by a littering of all variants of flotsam and manned by all sorts of human debris. The surface of the water, heavily coated in a mixture of thick putrid oil and gasoline, treated the commander harshly, blistering his exposed skin and stinging his unprotected eyes—but he lived, which was far more than could be said for a great many others who had been with him this night. Despite their irritation, Sugiura forced his afflicted eyes to open, hopeful of finding something for his immediate encouragement. It was not to be.

The sight that greeted the commander proved to be even more painful. The dreadful light cast from a great dappling of enduring fires revealed body after body, so numerous he could not count, men both living and dead, floating across an immense surface of a sea that surrounded his every circumference. Screams, so terribly voluminous and wretched, were heard to resonate from the wounded and dying who were obviously suffering horrific agonies. He could not escape their torment, nor could he escape his own burden of shame for such unnecessary loss. He prayed for it all to end, but no such relief was forthcoming. Just as the bedeviled souls around him, he was trapped in a misery that would haunt him for much of the rest of his existence.

* * *

At 12:32 a.m., another change of course was meticulously penned in *Lang*'s log, noting that Simpson's three destroyers were heading in a linear formation back to the area of the fiercely burning debris. They were returning to review their handiwork. But what the commander and his force found proved unlike anything they had ever before witnessed.

The sea ahead of their approach was on fire, the breadth of which none had ever before experienced. Great clouds of black smoke hung low across the entirety of the water's surface. The sickening "stench of burning oil, wood, diesel, paint and flesh" soon permeated the air, quickly invading the nostrils of all who sailed into this hellish realm.[5] At a speed of nearly 20 knots, *Lang*'s bow—as did *Sterett* and *Stack*'s—cut swiftly forward and into a most alarming surface. Even before it was thought possible, the ships were racing through large amounts of flotsam. The area was so expansive and its scope so broad that for it to have derived from just "four" ships seemed unbelievable. Hundreds of bodies, both living and dead, suddenly appeared, extending as far as the night allowed the eye to see. Almost instantly, the prop wash at the fantail darkened from the effects of blood. Many unfortunate survivors were being sucked directly beneath the ships and into their props, shredding the bodies of men into a chum that became instant lure to hungry sharks.

The immense number of survivors was so completely unexpected that there was no way of avoiding them. The sea was carpeted with human bodies, and by the time they were seen they were already enveloped around the ships. Turning one way or the other might have saved some but just as assuredly doomed others. Pat Robinson noted the moment accordingly, "Over the rail I could see hundreds of Japs in the glow cast by the burning ships. Some probably burned or wounded were screaming in agony. 'God this is awful,' the skipper said as our ships ploughed through the Japs, the propellers cutting many to ribbons."[6]

To the north, Moosbrugger's three ships were experiencing a similar situation. Assured that the gulf was now clear of all enemy traffic, at 12:35 A.M., Freddie ordered his ships back south—with the intent of rejoining Simpson to then depart Vella jointly by way of a northern route around Kolombangara, just as Wilkinson had originally ordered. This southern trek would be by way of the shortest passage, taking his three ships through the region of the burning debris, therefore requiring the approach to be made with considerable caution and a curious amount of vigilance.

Throughout this approach, visibility—as it had throughout the operation—remained very restrictive. A light rain had been sporadic and was falling once again, hindering good observation even further. Moosbrugger's approach to the debris field remained quite deliberate and slow, intent at avoiding any inopportune damage to his own ships—for there were sure to be some floating hazards. Even so, no remarkable obstructions were initially recorded. However, just as was to occur with Simpson's group, the silence of this trek was soon interrupted by a great din of voluminous groaning and moaning, periodically highlighted by the piercing sound of horrific screams.

Within the low orange glow of the intermittent fires, numerous bodies could be seen floating nearby. But, in a dramatic difference to Simpson's initial pass, Moosbrugger's ships were all traveling at a slow speed, encouraging the possibility of immediate rescue. Freddie was determined to take at least one prisoner for interrogation. Obviously, he would not risk an attempt at bringing many of the survivors aboard, as the Japanese were just too unpredictable and could prove too dangerous to his ships, yet he was willing to take on a few. But success for this part of the operation—unlike the previous engagement—would not be so easily met.

Indeed, every initial attempt at rescue failed. The silhouettes of Moosbrugger's ships were apparently recognized by the surviving Japanese as American and, despite the assured agony that many of these men were enduring, every anguished lip turned completely silent. The Japanese who were within sight were seen to swim quickly in the opposite direction or just duck beneath the surface of the water in order to avoid capture. None would give up willingly.

Davison wrote of the approach: "When [the 'cruiser'] had gone at last, we proceeded over to the patch of blazing oil that marked her grave and slowly circled it, looking for survivors and some clue as to the identity of the ships we had dispatched. . . . We saw one group of survivors but as we approached they dove under water and refused to be picked up. We left them to reap the doubtful benefits of their decision."[7]

Meanwhile, the hand of the clock continued its uninterrupted pace, quickly advancing toward the 2:00 a.m. deadline. Several minutes were consumed in this initial pass, though ample time still remained before departure of the task group would be required. Moosbrugger decided a second effort was warranted, hopeful that another try might bring greater success. Just then, however, an urgent message from Sims was received over the TBS, giving the commander good reason to reconsider.

Maury, as Moosbrugger already knew, had a menacing feed pump problem, an untimely issue that had been plaguing the destroyer ever since her departure from Tulagi. *Maury*'s engineering department had babied the apparatus throughout the mission, managing to keep any additional deterioration to a minimum. But the various recent maneuvers in combination with the added jar from the brief cannonade had finally taken their toll on the mechanism, leaving it with a life expectancy of mere minutes. At 1:11 a.m., the No. 2 main feed pump blew its seals and ceased to function. All power was shifted to the No. 1 main, and this feed pump was also in danger of being lost.[8]

At 1:15 a.m., Sims reported his ship's engineering casualty to Moosbrugger. At best, the captain expected capacity for maximum speed of 27 knots no longer than another hour.[9] He would then be forced to use his ship's cruise feed pump, having a maximum speed of 22 knots, and this pump was also in question. That would leave *Maury* with only her emergency feed pump and a prayer in reserve, providing the destroyer a maximum speed of only 12 knots and likely leaving her well within the range of enemy planes by sunup.[10]

Moosbrugger knew he could not risk staying in Vella Gulf any longer; he needed to get *Maury* to safety and could not waste another minute at doing so. At 1:18 a.m., he ordered the second pass through the debris aborted. His division immediately headed north at 22 knots, beginning what was sure to be a long and uncertain trek back to Purvis.[11]

In the meantime, Moosbrugger notified Simpson of the situation and ordered Division A-2 to stay behind for an extended period and try to gather a prisoner before leaving.[12] Wilkinson's original 2:00 a.m. deadline still stood, and was not to be surpassed. Regardless of the outcome, Simpson was at that moment to order his ships out of Vella to rejoin the other division at the best possible speed.

Simpson received Moosbrugger's order to try and pick up the prisoner and he responded without waver, quickly giving the command to turn about. And *Lang*, *Sterett*, and *Stack* turned quietly in the night for yet another approach to the area of flaming sea.

Since having already made one dangerous pass through this region, the sailors aboard these three ships were far less certain about the justification for a return, and they looked at one another with a bit of confusion and mounting concern—as not only were their ships turning back toward the Japanese debris field but they were also slowing, and dramatically so. No one could understand such a motive. What was worth such a hazardous venture? Then the ships' intercom systems crackled with the announcement, "Attention! All hands! This is your captain speaking. We are to return to pick up a prisoner. There is to be no unnecessary talking. This is an order. Stand by."[13] "*Stand by?*" What was the commodore thinking? "*No unnecessary talking?*" "*Pick up a prisoner?*" How crazy was this?

The extreme nature of the darkness, the impenetrable pitch that had so enveloped Vella, remained true to its most eerie demeanor. There were no stars, no moon, and no horizon to be seen. Visibility was less than 2,000 yards. Even so, and despite some light rain, the sea remained remarkably smooth. Sailors stood fast at their stations, nervously staring across the blackened infinity and toward what remained of the once raging fires. The approach continued even as the pace slowed further. Since their first pass the flames had dissipated considerably, and visibility along the region was far more degraded. Survivors could, however, still be seen bobbing around in the water, though in far less numbers than their previous experience—a factor likely attributed to the group's first destructive pass. The groaning and wailing had also changed, replaced by some sort of chant, noted by some to sound like a repetitive "Kow-we."[14] This din even caused Captain Wilfong to believe incorrectly that his crew was responsible for the overt noise. Thinking that his own men were sending out some call of intimidation to a helpless enemy, he immediately ordered everyone to "Pipe down!"[15] But the haunting sound continued, even as the ships came to a complete and daring stop.

The destroyers' turbines fell silent and their screws were stilled. On *Lang*, Lieutenant Gray and his repair party hurriedly tossed lifelines and a cargo net over the starboard side of the destroyer at amidships. Commander Simpson then ordered that no survivors should be allowed aboard except at this one station. On *Stack*, Lieutenant Shear and his party went through the same riggers with the same orders. Likewise, the repair party on *Sterett* began a similar response.

Meanwhile, all the crews waited, quietly as ordered yet anxious with each idle minute.

Lieutenant Jeffrey noted, "We were all uncomfortable about lying dead in the water, an easy target for any lurking sub."[16] Indeed, the ships were all being silhouetted by the remaining fires, and this was not an ideal position in an area that remained under enemy control. One lurking enemy submarine could play havoc with the whole lot of them.

"Why was the ship ordered to stop?" Chuck Lee questioned. "Our thought was that the ship could be in [great] danger, as literally hundreds of survivors were in the water. We never picked up any survivors as most of us did not trust the Japanese. They could have been suicidal or devious with other methods to harm us."[17]

Indeed, the Japanese were not to be trusted. Many were likely still armed. Some might have grenades on their person, which—if the grenade remained functional after a thorough soaking of saltwater—could cause tremendous damage and death aboard the confined spaces of a destroyer. With the exception of the officers, who did carry sidearms, destroyer sailors likely carried nothing more than a knife for a weapon. Allowing even one of the Japanese to come aboard was a risk—certainly a risk that none was fond of taking. They had just won a great victory, and they had done so without a single casualty. Why gamble with such unnecessary peril? In most every man's view it was now time to make a speedy passage to friendlier waters, not a time to linger in enemy territory, offering him some chance to intervene with some effort at revenge.

Nevertheless, even as the hand of the clock pursued its unrestricted tick, the three destroyers of Simpson's division remained stationary, resolute at fulfilling Moosbrugger's orders. All they needed was one survivor, and then they could be on their way. The task seemed simple enough, but it proved to be anything but. In some cases a few survivors did come close. On *Lang*, one survivor even managed to grasp the screw guard at the fantail to begin his climb aboard. He was nearly upright and out of the water when a lone sailor (a man said to have just recently learned of his own brother's death at another Pacific engagement) suddenly rejected his approach. Seeing the Japanese survivor make his way on deck—and at a spot not authorized—the sailor instantly picked up an empty powder casing and, while holding it high overhead, tossed it with all that was within him. The weighty piece of brass, with its trajectory on target and velocity increased by the aid of a timely gust of wind, slammed the unsuspecting Japanese squarely in the face, knocking him directly back into the darkened sea, never to be seen or heard from again. There would be no others. Though additional survivors came near, none could be enticed close enough to the designated pick-up area at amidships. Still—despite the sailors fast losing patience with this highly unpopular duty—the allowable time for fetching a prisoner had yet to expire.

The rescue effort continued as ordered. But, in spite of this persistence, every quiet effort at coaxing a survivor near enough for capture proved entirely unsuccessful. Many anxious minutes passed, and the results remained negative. Then—regardless of the orders to the contrary—some sailor aboard *Lang* finally reached his limit with the lack of Japanese cooperation. As another survivor came into view, an anonymous voice suddenly blurted, "Get over here, you son-of-a-bitch!" At the sound of the English-speaking voice, a whistle was heard to blow, instantly resounding from somewhere far out in the darkness.[18] Again, the night turned eerily quiet. The chanting immediately ceased, as did all moaning and groaning from the wounded. Simpson and Wilfong were now assured that any further chance at capturing a prisoner had ended. It hardly mattered; the 2:00 a.m. deadline was nearly upon them. The time had come to depart the area. They would leave the survivors to their own fate and, as previously ordered, head for safer waters.

Back to the north, *Maury*'s status continued to change minute by minute. Moosbrugger kept his ships moving at the best possible speed, which began at 27 knots, even as it was obvious that such momentum could not be sustained. *Maury*'s No. 1 main feed pump was straining terribly and, despite every effort from engineering to nurse the ailing mechanism along, it was sure not to hold.

In the meantime, *Maury*'s chief machinist's mate, John Goss, worked in tandem with Chief Watertender Bill Tomilson at trying to repair the No. 2 main. As these two huddled around the device, a saltwater hose was brought to bear. There was hope that a spray of the cooling liquid on the hot feed pump might allow it to be safely opened. When, however, the packing nuts were loosened, searing hot steam escaped from the cover—the result of a leaky valve—scalding the hands of both chiefs. In obvious pain, these two determined men continued with their efforts and successfully removed the old packing. With it, they planned to salvage enough usable material, to be added with some other leftovers from a previous overhaul, to engineer a fix that would last at least a few additional hours.[19]

The seriousness of *Maury*'s issues was obvious, but Sims displayed every confidence in his engineering department, knowing if there was a way to correct the problem, they would surely find it. When Chief Goss appeared on the bridge to report the status of the pumps, Sims rightly suspected that Goss already had a plan in place for the repair. He therefore showed no surprise when Goss spoke of the ongoing efforts to get the No. 2 main back on line, and only nodded his approval.[20]

There was no further delay. Even with his blistered hands beginning to turn white, Goss refused aid and lingered on the bridge only long enough for making his comments before returning to continue with his repairs. He knew time was of the essence. If *Maury*'s propulsion was to fail, it was not going to be due to any lack of effort from Goss or any member of his team.

Meanwhile, Moosbrugger kept his line of ships on the march. He was receiving regular updates from Sims and had constant awareness of *Maury*'s situation. The news was not wholly unsettling just yet.

It was also by this time that several minutes had since passed the 2:00 A.M. deadline, which added some reassurance to the commander that at least Simpson should now be racing to rejoin his force. Soon all of his ships would be reunited, and together they could make fast for the safety of Purvis. But, even with the greater security of their union, Moosbrugger still had no assurances that his ships were to encounter no harm. Obviously, many concerns remained.

By 2:09 A.M., and since having given up on the capture of any enemy survivors, Simpson was indeed directing his three destroyers on course to rejoin the rest of the task group, just as had been ordered and just as Moosbrugger was expecting. This was of obvious relief to every crewmember, as in their minds this departure was already way past due. To his own ships Simpson's orders were simple and direct—make full steam, at a speed of 30 knots, and depart Vella Gulf by way of a northern route past Kolombangara.

Left behind were the only visible residuals of the recent victory, the glowing pulsations of the few remaining fires. With each mile gained the orange cast of the dying flames faded, slowly consumed by the southern horizon until the night was once again overpowered by an opaque darkness. To the northeast there appeared the dim but growing silhouette of Kolombangara Island, dark and sinister, where enemy eyes were likely still searching for the American ships and anxious shore gunners were hoping for a chance at a lucky shot. The commander intended to offer no such opportunity. Somewhere ahead of him were the destroyers of Moosbrugger's division, most assuredly at this moment to be nearing 25 miles distant. It would surely take Simpson's ships some time to catch up, but at least they were headed the right direction.

This journey north proceeded quietly and without the slightest bit of interruption. Even so, opportunity for any meaningful rest remained elusive. Simpson ordered his crews to "stand-to" at their GQ stations, as—regardless of their great victory and positive direction—not all threats were yet passed. None of the task group was clear of enemy territory and, therefore, any lack of vigilance was sure to be a foolhardy venture—the Solomons campaign had so aptly proven that such indiscretion would only invite tragedy. So, the wary watches continued.[21]

The men of Task Group 31.2 stood alert. Despite this night having been long and tiring, there appeared to be no lingering effects on the ongoing performances of the crews. An overdose of adrenaline had been pumped into and through the throbbing veins of every sailor, and noticeably so. Energy levels remained electric. The previous excitement that this action had produced refused to dissipate even the slightest. Long after their departure from the arena of battle, these men were still slapping each other on the back and congratulating each other for their fine efforts. This had been a special night, and everyone knew it. Such an unprecedented victory was a stimulant not often experienced within these confines of warfare, and these men were sure not to dismiss any such inoculation. The lack of sleep and strains of combat did not seem to register. Every man, for the most part, enjoyed an unending emotional high, jovial, festive and completely dismissive to his own exhaustive state, leaving their weariness to catch up later—as it surely would.

Once finally having some time to think over the whole affair, Loyd Peters would note with a good bit of thanksgiving, "I [was just] glad to get out alive."[22] Others were a little more varied with their expressions. "We were all highly elated!" stated Olsen, who had received a hearty "pat on the back" from Moosbrugger.[23]

"Elated" seemed to be the correct adjective, as numerous others used this same expression to describe their own feelings for the moment. Barber noted the enthusiasm that he witnessed as "jubilation."[24] "The results were tremendous," wrote *Dunlap* boatswain's mate John Huber, "so most everyone was in high spirits."[25] Another *Dunlap* sailor, Shop Keeper 2/c Glenn Allen, concluded a paragraph about the battle in his diary with "A good time was had by all."[26] Pem Southard wrote that of himself and the others around him "a feeling of relief and accomplishment prevailed" and "given the responsibility and motivation [we had] produced some pretty good results."[27] Lieutenant Gray fully concurred; "There was a great feeling of pride," he noted, "excitement and of course relief that we were still alive and had done so much. . . ."[28] Even so, the mission remained incomplete, as the ships were still some distance from safety. They had a good ways to go to be back in home waters and, for this reason alone, there remained obvious concern.

The desire for security could find no greater stage than that evidenced aboard *Maury*. Still aided by Chief Tomilson, Chief Goss stood thoroughly focused with his ongoing task, pursuing his intense effort at trying to salvage enough packing to repair the destroyer's No. 2 feed pump. The hands of both men looked dreadful, blistered and peeling, yet both refused to stop their work for any medical treatment. Both men knew time was against them, as the No. 1 feed pump was deteriorating rapidly and would surely not last much longer.[29]

At 2:39 A.M., the fears were proven accurate, as the No. 1 pump suddenly expired, spilling an immense and blinding amount of steam into the engineering compartment. The destroyer's forward momentum decelerated, and noticeably so. Speed fell quickly, down to 20 knots before the cruise pump could be brought on line, allowing the destroyer to pick up the pace a bit, back up to a sustained 22 knots. It was an acceptable rate, but just how long the cruise pump could handle this pressure was a question few wished to ponder.[30]

Ever since *Maury*'s departure from Vella, Sims had been keeping Moosbrugger abreast of his situation with regular reports over the TBS. Upon learning of the latest feed pump casualty, he regrettably notified the commander that his ship's situation had now turned critical. The three ships had just passed the northernmost point of Kolombangara, but they remained far too close to the menacing enemy airbase at Rabaul for any sense of comfort. Moosbrugger had been preparing for just such likelihood and quickly countered by ordering a defensive antiaircraft escort to be provided the ailing *Maury*. *Dunlap* was to take position just off *Maury*'s port bow, while *Craven* was to do the same off her starboard, and both ships reduced their speed to keep pace with the slower division mate. Crews remained at general quarters, and radar searches took precedence over every other precaution. The enemy was sure to send his air force out for revenge, and Moosbrugger had no intention at being caught flatfooted. But, for as long as the 22-knot pace could be kept, there still remained good reason for optimism.

This promise, however, was far from secure. If progress was slowed any more, by daylight Moosbrugger's division would still be within the reach of the enemy bombers, and *Maury* would then be a sitting duck for attack.

Meanwhile, Chiefs Goss and Tomilson stubbornly continued their efforts at correcting their ship's engineering woes. Suddenly Goss gave out a positive shout, announcing their success, the two having finally manufactured a suitable packing for the No. 2 pump—and it certainly came none too soon. Just as had been deeply feared, the cruise pump also failed. It had lasted only fifteen minutes. Again, the destroyer began to slow. The emergency feed pump was quickly engaged but—unless the engineering of Goss and Tomilson was truly a success—this mechanism was just as likely to fail and was all that stood between a reduced speed of 12 knots and an even slower—and far more dangerous—tow.[31]

Though his hands were by now painfully blistered, it was Goss who carefully cradled the precious packing while rushing back to the No. 2 feed pump, fronted by Tomilson, who cleared the way. Even as hot steam continued its escape from the faulty valve, neither man hesitated to begin the reassembly of the disabled equipment. With the aid of additional saltwater spray, the packing was reinserted, the cover carefully replaced, and the bolts retightened. Then, as everyone nervously stood by, waiting for the pressure within the pump to build, there was complete silence. Would the packing hold? The pressure dial began to climb, higher and higher, finally reaching its desired level, and a cheer suddenly arose from within the compartment. The packing was indeed holding. The fix Goss and Tomilson had engineered was working.[32]

Goss happily reported to Sims that the No. 2 feed pump was back on-line and functioning properly. This was great news, to be sure. Sims's faith in the talent of Goss and the rest of his engineering team had paid off. This was truly another proud moment for his ship. The time was 2:55 a.m. "All ahead flank," the captain ordered. And the destroyer's momentum began to increase, back to 22 knots, even up to 25.[33]

Moosbrugger was notified of *Maury*'s engineering success, and he sighed in relief. It now appeared that the mission would indeed be safely completed and with a timely return to Purvis. As another positive note, *Maury*'s slowing had allowed Simpson's division opportunity to catch up and much more rapidly than previously expected. Division 15 passed the northernmost point of Kolombangara at 2:44 a.m. and was currently lagging only a few thousand yards behind. It was now almost certain that the task group would sail back to Tulagi as one unified force, victorious and unscathed.

Without further incident, Moosbrugger's electrified task group began its passage of "the Slot," cruising southeast atop a smooth sea at 25 knots. These early morning hours were typical of the Solomons, highlighted by a tropical yet somewhat cooling blast of salty air that rushed mightily across the outer decks of each destroyer. As a welcomed feel to the soles of every foot, the deck plating of each ship vibrated to the deep, soothing growls of the turbines in their pursuit for distance. All else was still, and thankfully so. The only anxious moment to follow came at 3:57 a.m., when radar picked up the approach of an unidentified aircraft, provoking the lookouts to a renewed vigor for focus and giving gunners a nervous twitch of their trigger fingers—but the plane proved friendly and the moment passed only as a brief notation in the logs.[34]

Having this bit of concern aside, Moosbrugger finally determined that the time had come to allow his victorious crews some well-deserved rest—at least until the approach of sunrise, when the mandatory dawn GQ would force everyone back to their respective stations. "Secure general quarters," he commanded.[35] It was a welcomed order. The crews had been actively manning their GQ stations in excess of eight hours, and very tense hours at that. There was "a very 'loud quiet,'" Quartermaster Allison noted among those men aboard *Craven*. "Most of us had been up since 0600 [6:00 A.M.] the day before and were very tired. . . ."[36] Still, the "adrenaline high"—having been produced earlier this night—maintained its strong influence, negating the effects of exhaustion for most men, as few opted to use this moment for sleep.

Indeed, no one seemed willing to concede this amazing night to history, not just yet. The galleys and wardrooms were quickly filled to capacity, as ham sandwiches and hot cups of coffee were readily passed out and eagerly consumed—all while additional conversation and comparisons of the previous action inspired a whole host of new stories.

The "Snipes," those men who had been confined to the lower engineering decks, eagerly sought out those who had witnessed firsthand the outside scenes of the one-sided battle. The accounts they received were dramatic and required no embellishments. Machinist's Mate Ferdinand Yannotti, aboard *Craven*, listened to each story and swelled with pride at each telling. "It was like payback," he wrote, "for the sneak attack on our shipmates on Dec. 7, 1941 . . . I'm thankful for being a part of that."[37]

That hundreds of men had died a horrendous death this night made little to no initial negative impression on the mindsets of any of the victors. Killing was just one of those inescapable aspects of war. It was called "survival," a part of that old axiom "kill or be killed." But revenge also played an undeniable role as well. Captain Wilfong's earlier pronouncement of "God this is awful" was certainly not the most prevalent sentiment among the men, for even Wilfong felt very positive about the events of this night, especially considering that he too had experienced the Japanese attack at Pearl.[38] Davison, the "trade school boy" and professional "naval officer," wrote little of his own innermost emotions other than a single word of "proud."[39] But he too surely thought of his lost comrades still entombed within the sunken remains of *Arizona* and gave a silent salute to avenging their untimely demise. Olsen no doubt thought of his brother and rested a little easier this night knowing that he had played such an important role at stopping the "Tokyo Express," the very group most responsible for Earl's death. His coconut cup had not long to wait for its triumphant moment—for many toasts were surely in the offing.

These perceptions might seem harsh, but they were not wrong. The Japanese *were* a brutal enemy, deceitful and inhumane, repetitively evidenced by many previous acts. Furthermore, it was they who had aggressively started this war and "dastardly" so. Therefore, there was almost no remorse and little—if any—pity for the lives lost. "After Pearl Harbor, the Battan [*sic*] death march and beheading [of] American officers (captured American flyers of Doolittle's Tokyo raiders), I was glad to help send a few thousand of them to their reward," later wrote Carpenter's Mate Gene Hansen of *Craven*.[40] Lieutenant Shear gave a little more brief but similar assessment of such warfare. "You don't worry about killing people," he stated simply.[41] Torpedoman Haden concluded the matter by stating in proxy for everyone, "We felt real good about it all."[42]

Perhaps, however, it was Gelzer Sims who defined the circumstances of warfare in the better terms. A few days following the action, Sims confided to Crenshaw, "the picture of those poor Japanese sailors struggling in the black oil in the light of the raging flames [is] etched permanently in [my] mind. [I] was glad to see the hulls of their ships shattered as they had shattered ours, but the men in the water were different. They were enemy, defeated in fair battle, but they were also sailors, shipwrecked and dying."[43] There could be no more powerful statement.

Of far greater impact to morale, however, was the understanding of the way with which the victory had been won. Moosbrugger and his men had knowingly confronted the enemy—a highly experienced and proven enemy at that—and defeated him at his own best game, a nighttime torpedo and gunnery action. Night action had so far been the nemesis of the U.S. Navy, and a successful night torpedo action was before this date nearly unheard of. Moreover, this victory had come without Moosbrugger's force receiving a single enemy-inflicted casualty. How simply amazing was this. How gratifying it was to be returning with such a story to tell. In warfare, no experience could surmount it, nor would it ever.

Even so, any celebration remained just a bit premature. With the anticipated appearance of the morning sun, once again there rang the traditional alarm demanding these sailors to return to their designated GQ stations. This was expected. Routines would not change, even in the midst of victory. But unlike any previous times, this morning's exercise met a renewed energy and without any display of the usual misgivings. Eyes were bright and faces were beaming—at least in the initial moments. Truly this was a new day—one of the most promising that these sailors had experienced in a long while—and they embraced it wholeheartedly.

Aboard *Maury*, smiles were even a bit broader. Their destroyer was once again back up to full-speed and in fighting trim. Chiefs Goss and Tomilson were fully responsible. Since finally having their hands treated in sickbay, bandaged and issued shots of "medicinal whiskey" for dulling the pain, they were again returned to their engineering duties, where they resumed repairs on the other pumps. By dawn, all pumps were back on-line and at the ready if needed.[44]

Such fortitude was of the truest example of the type of men these destroyer sailors were, each so determined and unfailing as to give any commander the confidence he required to enter any type of action, press against any foe, and to stand tough against any and all odds. Truly this was a defining moment, but it was not without some residual stress. This morning was only just a beginning to this day. They had not yet reached safety, and many concerns still remained.

Moosbrugger was indeed watchful for the unexpected. To the east the sun could be seen peeking above the horizon, imposing its extra warmth upon each of the ships while offering its nonpartisan support to any would-be attackers.

Sailors manned their stations, waiting for these critical moments to pass. As daylight grew brighter, the eyes of the men began to squint, suppressed by the sun's brilliance and with sudden acknowledgment to their own true exhaustion. Weariness was finally beginning to overpower their earlier inoculation of energy. It was now 6:53 A.M. and, just as their struggling eyelids were about to lose their battle with fatigue, a well-defined group of distant specks were suddenly noticed appearing within the background of a brightening blue sky.[45]

A warning was immediately sounded, "*Bogies approaching!*" These were planes, but whose? They were flying from the east, but this was no true indicator of identity. Adrenaline was once again sent charging through every vein, quickening the beat of each heart and surging each mind to a whole new attentiveness. All eyes were at once reawakened and instantly refreshed with a renewed alertness. Men hesitated their breathing, anxiously hoping, praying that this was not some ominous sign of perhaps the feared retaliatory Japanese air assault they had so tried to avoid. An uneasy quiet instantly settled along every ship. The seconds passed as minutes. Lips tightened and muscles tensed. Then a shout was heard to arise from among the crowd. The word spread quickly, followed by an echoing of thunderous cheering. The renewed revelry was the grateful response to the exclamations of "*they're friendlies!*" Wilkinson's promised air cover had arrived.[46]

Marine (Vought F4U) Corsairs, with their familiar gulled wing silhouettes gleaming in the early morning sunlight, were soon circling above, given over to the direction of the fighter-director officers aboard *Dunlap* and *Maury*. What a beautiful sight these planes were too. While in a combat zone, little provided a greater sense of security than that of seeing these flyboys hovering in the sky above. Untold times they were to save a sailor's bacon (his posterior), and no doubt their aid would be called upon on many more occasions yet to come. On this morning it mattered not at all that the talents of these fighter pilots were of no immediate need; all that was truly important was the reassurance of just knowing that they were nearby, ready if the need should arise. So, as general quarters were secured once more, sailors were finally able to relax, able at last to close their eyes in true rest, calm their nerves with a nicotine fix, and/or just enjoy the birth of another new day and say to one's self, "We survived one more."

* * *

Captain Sugiura also survived to see the sunrise—but his ordeal had so far been horribly unpleasant, and was far from over. The surviving men of his command had had no hope of a friendly rescue at sea. They would fend for themselves or perish. Vella Lavella was the closest landmass, and so this became their chosen destination of escape. Their swim would be extremely long and tiring. The wounded and hurting were aided by others of better condition, hoping this assistance would be enough to see them all to shore—for many it would not. Rain peppered them as they slowly moved across the oily surface of the sea. Finally, after more than twenty-four hours of agonizing approach, the ablest of the men finally reached the sandy beaches of the island, and there they collapsed in exhaustion.

Sugiura and Commander Makoshi were among the numbers of haggard and hurting men to reach the objective, but their condition was too worn for bringing immediate leadership and organization to the scattering of survivors. At least they were on friendly territory, as Vella Lavella was still under Japanese control. And the American ships were sure to have long departed the area by now. Thus, there was no sense of urgency. They could do nothing till daylight anyway, so they rested.

Once dawn did arrive, Sugiura was finally able to evaluate his situation a little more clearly. A full day had passed since his initial debacle at sea. The long hours in the water had taken an even greater toll of his command, as many victims weakened by burns and wounds had been doomed to perish. Those survivors who reached land were strewn for miles up and down the shoreline. Of these, some were fortunate enough to be grouped into large parties but most were of small gatherings of less than a dozen or so, making organization of the whole impossible.

Sugiura had no way of knowing the exact number of men to reach the island. (It was later determined that of the 1,520 sailors and soldiers estimated aboard the three destroyers that were sunk, only 310 survived—but this number was based only on those successfully located and returned to Rabaul some twelve days later. More could have initially survived only to have perished in the jungles. And some of Sugiura's men were still found wandering the island after the American occupation in late August.)[47] Their location was at best a guess. The captain had no charts, though he was certain that no Japanese base camps were located anywhere nearby—as the Japanese had invested only a handful of troops in the island's occupation. The village of Barakoma lay to the extreme south of the island and Horaniu was to the extreme north. He had surely landed somewhere about the center of the island's eastern shore. Either way, a trek to safety was sure to be a long and difficult journey through jungle, and this without ready supplies of food or water. Further survival did not appear all that promising.[48]

As ordered, Hara had sent a message to Kolombangara requesting immediate rescue efforts to be made, and search parties were indeed sent to locate what remained of Sugiura's men. But it was to take days to locate the bulk of the survivors and to return them to safety. Certainly, Sugiura's pitiful groups were to have no easy time in the interim.

Hara would later see Sugiura, just shortly after his return to Rabaul. "It pained me to see Sugiura . . . emaciated and ashamed," Hara wrote as a final notation to an end of a horrible chapter for the once "invincible" Tokyo Express.[49]

With Sugiura's return, the true extent of the tragedy would finally be known. He and others of the survivors were to share their horrifying experiences with Rabaul's commanders, and their testimonies were all quite grim. The attack had been lightning-fast and without any opportunity for recovery. Somehow the Americans had managed to master the night torpedo/gunnery engagement, and with devastating results. Such acknowledgment could no longer be dismissed. All future Express reinforcement runs were indefinitely suspended. Slowing the American advance now looked to be impossible. The reality was that the Solomons could no longer be held—and Rabaul was surely in danger of being next.

* * *

All cheering aside, Moosbrugger had no immediate comprehension of the true extent of his one-sided victory. That his task group had stopped the Tokyo Express, and done so flawlessly, was a certainty; but just how this success would change the whole outcome for the rest of the Solomons campaign—even the war—was yet to be understood. Perhaps this aspect of his victory was not even relevant for the moment. Just the knowledge that he and his men were returning as the victors, with everyone and everything intact, was his most profound understanding and his only momentary boasting. All he would rightfully declare was that this was their day to celebrate. Tomorrow—as he so aptly understood—would be just another day at war in the deadly contest that was the South Pacific, without promise of anything other. So, Task Group 31.2 raced back to Purvis, bursting at the seams with its good news, hopeful that its sharing would at least lift the spirits of all who might hear—as it surely would, and with far broader scope than any could have initially imagined.

The six ships of Task Group 31.2 sailed proudly toward Tulagi with crews determined that this return should stand out above all others. A special signal, one denoting their success, was required. From the "mastheads" of each ship brooms were hastily hoisted high, there to sway magnificently in the breeze in noticeable unison.[50] "Clean sweep" had become a significant expression with relationship to this recent victory at Vella Gulf, and the hanging brooms were meant to boast the magnitude of this success—that they had indeed swept away the enemy and as easily as with the swipe from a bristled broom. Aboard *Lang*, Shipfitter Denver Fleming proudly placed this in perspective, penning in a stanza of his poem, "The Mighty *Lang*": "*The brooms were at the yardarm, the whistle it did blow, the Mighty Lang had scored again, and we let the whole fleet know.*"

Moosbrugger no doubt rallied behind this exercise of pomp, as he was just as anxious to testify to his team's excellent performance as anyone aboard. Indeed, he intended to do so personally, to Admiral Wilkinson especially—and he would not have long to wait.

At just a few minutes past 9:00 a.m., a dispatch was received—Wilkinson was calling—ordering Moosbrugger to report to fleet headquarters at Koli Point, just as soon as possible. The amphibious force commander wanted nothing less than to hear firsthand of this amazing action, and certainly Moosbrugger was eager to oblige.

Freddie quickly made his preparations to depart, ordering Iverson to direct *Dunlap* on a new course, a heading to the north shore of Guadalcanal. As the other fighter-director officer was aboard *Maury*, Moosbrugger simply ordered Sims to take over as guide back to Tulagi—Simpson would have full tactical command. Signal flags were raised. "Disregard my movements," these colorful banners read while waving briskly at the yardarms. *Dunlap* then separated from the others and peeled away to the starboard, cutting her bow sharply across the surface of the sea in the direction of Koli.[51]

The rest of the task group continued on; but this journey, too, was nearing its conclusion. The high ground of Florida Island stood close by, as back through Savo Sound the ships passed while pressing on to the nearby anchorage. How wonderful Purvis appeared to them. How secure of a feeling it was for this victorious band to know that they had truly made it back, safe and sound. Moosbrugger's proud line of veteran destroyers (less *Dunlap*) gracefully entered the bay at just a few minutes past 11:00 A.M. What an amazing twenty-four hours it had been. "It was always great to come back. Yes sir!" Davison wrote.[52]

Chapter Eleven

Well Done

Summation of Victory

Frederick Moosbrugger received nothing less than a hero's welcome at Koli. Handshakes, salutes, and repetitions of "*Well done*" were continuously given by a whole host of notables.

At Wilkinson's headquarters, Freddie eagerly detailed the operation for all who were there to listen. The admiral was ecstatic, eagerly commending Freddie in terms that he would surely appreciate. "You pitched a shut out in a big-league game . . . no hits, no runs, no survivors," Wilkinson loudly applauded. A dispatch stating the same was then sent to every ship of Moosbrugger's victorious troop.[1]

Having long complained of the Navy's inability to break the enemy's supply lines, General Harmon marked the victory with his own grateful and genuine appreciation. To Moosbrugger he messaged, "To you thanks and highest admiration for [this] splendid action [of] your force."[2]

With his own shared intelligence playing a critical role in the outcome—even as some of his own officers and crews were witness to the distant explosions that had so brilliantly brightened the Vella skyline—Commander Calvert was as eager as any to convey his thoughts. "Heartiest congratulations on a job beautifully done," he transmitted to the reception of each of the task group destroyers.[3]

Of even higher regard, Admiral Halsey—who was obviously thrilled to hear of this outstanding performance—sent his own personal commendation. "Well done Moosbrugger and Task Group Thirty-one point two," he expedited with communiqué. "Your crafty and devastating attack on the enemy's surface force bespeaks the utmost professional skill, splendid state of readiness and relentless fighting spirit. You and your outfit added new glory to destroyer traditions."[4]

Moosbrugger could not have been prouder, even as—with all due humility—he made perfectly clear to whom he owed all this reward. To those who had served him so well, he acknowledged, "My heartiest congratulations to all hands on a beautiful job last night. You showed what a tough bunch these destroyer sailors are."[5]

Three days later, delayed but very much as enthusiastic, a messaged response was received from General MacArthur, sent from his headquarters in Australia and forwarded by Halsey. It read: "Please express to the commander and all ranks and ratings of the task force engaged, my admiration for their brilliant action in Vella Gulf. It is but further evidence of the magnificent fighting capacity of our naval forces."[6]

* * *

There would be no similar rolling accolades for the surviving Japanese. *Shigure*'s forlorn return would not receive even a pittance of the greeting experienced by Moosbrugger and his men. Hara and his lone destroyer reentered Rabaul's spacious harbor on the evening of the 7th, welcomed only by subdued darkness and quiet indifference. The moment was solemn and disconcerting. Even Hara, who was usually stone of face, could not hide his woeful expression. The commander suspected, justifiably so, that his career was surely in jeopardy and probably nearing a premature and undeserved end. Regardless of the region's tropical climate, there was sure to be a cool reception awaiting him ashore.

Others aboard the destroyer were equally concerned, as their embrace here appeared just as much in question. *Shigure*'s officers and crew felt greatly disparaged, displaying their most profound embarrassment for having been forced to such a shameful retreat. The recent ordeal had horribly shaken the confidence of all aboard. Even so, the security of the harbor was not entirely lost, not to everyone. The destroyer's smothering mass of hitchhiking soldiers (many of whom were by this time ill of the sea and suffering the great discomforts of overcrowding) embraced this promise of solid ground with unabated expressions of relief. Their pitiful journey had finally ended. What might happen next was for fate to decide.[7]

As anticipated, Vice Adm. Tomoshige Samejima, current commander of the Eighth Fleet, ordered Hara to report to his headquarters for a debriefing. This was no eager moment, as Hara fully expected to face a truly belligerent round of very tough questioning. His detailed account of this devastating loss, in addition to his explanations for his own actions, were surely to be heavily scrutinized. Hara knew there would be no worthwhile defense available to him for what appeared as such a cowardly retreat. He presumed no quarter would be shown him, and that perhaps he might even be blamed and reprimanded for the failure. He prepared for the worst.

Later that morning, Captain Hara warily disembarked *Shigure* and proceeded by boat to Rabaul City, where Admiral Samejima's headquarters awaited his arrival. The journey was itself a bit unsettling. There was rampant confusion ashore, nearing the point of panic. The disarray found here was profound and a clear reflection of the current strategic situation. The overall news was bad, very bad. Munda, on New Georgia, had fallen to the Americans on the 4th, and the island was now fully conceded as lost. Kolombangara was assuredly the next expected step for the American advance. But—once dealt the terrible loss at Vella Gulf—this ground also looked to be hopelessly indefensible. The cost of Sugiura's defeat was a measure of more than the negative sum of lost ships and men; it was a tactical depression too staggering to overcome. The fleet's remaining destroyers were too valuable to risk in any other similar ventures. It was therefore a certainty that—at least for the short-term—there would have to be a moratorium placed on all future Express reinforcement runs. The thousands of troops remaining on Kolombangara, as well as the other smaller contingents remaining in the Central Solomons, would have to fend for themselves. This, in effect, meant that—short of some miracle—the Central Solomons could no longer be held. (The only redeeming miracle the Japanese were capable of—which was no small feat—took place from September 27 through October 6 with the complete evacuations of over 10,500 men from both Kolombangara and Vella Lavella and with the loss of only one destroyer—versus one American destroyer lost and two others severely damaged.)

At Rabaul's headquarters the atmosphere appeared even less optimistic. Hara walked in to find a bewildered staff stumbling about their duties, looking as though they were in some dispirited trance. The captain's arrival was hardly noticed as he passed through the host of aides and trudged onward to his appointed meeting. He then paused just outside the admiral's office doorway. Samejima was found quietly waiting inside, and he immediately beckoned Hara to enter. Strangely, the admiral showed no initial animosity, but welcomed the captain with a humbled, seemingly even apologetic demeanor. Such was an unexpected reception, to say the least. Samejima then sat down at his desk and prepared for the report to be given. Without interruption the admiral listened as Hara explained all that had happened at Vella, given at least in as much detail as the captain had understanding. When the accounting was concluded, Samejima gazed forward in momentary silence. Hara awaited the admiral's response, still expecting some type of stinging rebuke. However, when the response was given, Samejima spoke no ill criticisms. Instead, the fleet commander astonished Hara by personally assuming full responsibility for the loss. It had indeed been a foolish mistake for him to have sent these ships on the very same routes and times as the previous two missions, even despite the earlier successes.[8] Hara was stunned, and he emitted an instant sigh of relief. He had been vindicated of the matter—even as his own personal anger for the failure remained steadfast. This preventable mishap of judgment had not only caused tremendous loss of life and material but had also driven morale to a whole new low. The repercussions, Hara knew, would likely have an irreversible effect on the war, and perhaps even doom any last bit of hope at stopping the increasingly more powerful American advance. The Solomons were thought to be the most critical arena for forcing an early settlement to this war; now this appeared lost for certain.

Afterward, Hara returned to his flagship, and he did so determined not to appear the defeatist. Having retained his command was certainly for Hara a principal encouragement worthy of high note, but for the officers and crew of *Shigure* much more would be needed, especially if their spirits were truly to be rekindled in some positive manner. Hara knew the men of his command were painfully discouraged. Somehow, he needed to rebuild a strong sense of confidence among them, providing them direction that was both clear and constructive. The captain expected, and rightly so, that *Shigure* would soon be called back into the thick of the fight. For this reason, everyone aboard needed to be at the peak of readiness, especially if they were to have any chance at surviving. Such would surely be a monumental challenge, but Hara appeared ready to tackle the effort.

To begin this healing, Hara gave *Shigure*'s crew the next day off. The men were all allowed their leave, one third of the complement at a time. This was the first true break these men had had since having arrived back in the South Pacific.[9] Certainly it was well deserved too. Despite the recent loss, Hara knew that Yamagami's men had performed like the veterans that they were. Their every action had been expeditious and fully capable—victory at Vella Gulf was just not meant to be.

Among the most respected of performances was that of young Petty Officer Yamashita. Before allowing him his leave, Hara called this bewildered sailor to his quarters for a personal chat. There the commander immediately commended the petty officer for his timely actions. Hara knew no medals would be awarded, not after such an unprecedented failure. So, with a few kind words, appreciatively acknowledging Yamashita's fine example and critical role toward saving the ship, the commander presented his own silver watch as reward.

Awed by the offering, Yamashita initially refused it, humbly stating that he was not worthy. Worthiness, Hara quickly explained, was for he to decide, and he had already decided. "Take it," he insisted. Yamashita reached out and accepted the prize, saluted the officer, and then departed with a glow of utmost pride.[10]

Ironically, later that evening Yamashita returned, and with him came evidence of just how trying Hara's efforts would be, and of how truly difficult it was for a Japanese to endure any type of humiliating defeat. The petty officer's uniform was torn, his face bruised and bloodied, and his eye blackened. Hara witnessed the return and confronted the young petty officer, calling for an immediate explanation. Yamashita lowered his head and reported with embarrassment that he had "fallen." But Hara knew better. It was obvious that the young man had been beaten. Demanding the truth, the petty officer was finally forced to confide that he had indeed gotten into a fight while ashore. Yamashita went on to explain that during his visit to a local bar—where after having consumed a good amount of strong drink—he began to show off the watch that Hara had given him. The response was not as he expected. Another man, unassociated with *Shigure*, remarked of how shameful the destroyer's retreat had been and that he had no respect for the petty officer or any so-called gift of honor. Another piped in and referred to *Shigure*'s officers and crew as "bums." Immediately feeling the need to defend his own honor, as well as that of his ship and shipmates, Yamashita threw a punch, resulting in a hard-fought scuffle between the men. This was the real reason for his wounds. But the petty officer quickly explained, his opposition had received punishment of equal consequence.[11]

Hara shook his head. He was not at all happy with the explanation. "You should have ignored them," the disappointed commander reprimanded. "Do you think *Shigure*'s action was wrong?" "No, sir," the petty officer quickly responded. "Your judgment was absolutely right." Hara quickly interjected, "Then fight the enemy, not your own countrymen." The conversation was thus ended and Yamashita sheepishly melted away.[12]

Hara obviously understood, perhaps even expected, the confrontation met by his proud petty officer. Though he would not express it, the commander was likely even a bit pleased with the intensity of pride displayed by Yamashita. But there was a more important battle to win, and the opponent was American, not Japanese. This was the understanding that Hara intended to get across. It *was* understood too. Despite the embarrassing loss at Vella Gulf, it was this action more so than any other—as later noted by the commander—that was most responsible for the greater unification of *Shigure*'s crew. This ship and the men who served aboard her would go on to fight in many more actions, and both would do so with the utmost effect and honor.[13] Surely nothing could say more of the character or type of men that Moosbrugger's force had met on that dark August night. Such made their victory even more amazing.

* * *

On August 9, the Associated Press led off the war news segment of its Mackay Radio broadcast with this highly energetic announcement: "*American naval forces in an hour long night battle sank a Japanese cruiser and two destroyers and probably sank a third destroyer after intercepting the four warships carrying supplies to the enemy garrison at Vila, Kolombangara Island, General MacArthur announced in his Sunday noon communiqué. The Americans suffered no losses. . . .*"[14]

On the following day, Pat Robinson's graphic play-by-play description of the engagement hit newsstands back in the states, allowing his privileged readers a glimpse into the South Pacific fight as otherwise rarely given. The article's byline read: "U. S. Squadron sees Japs first in narrow waters and foe dies quickly without a chance." Robinson's details were picturesque and as fast-paced as the battle. "The victims burst into high-flung flame and for the next 46 minutes a lurid orange glare illuminated a large area as sheets of fire licked along the sea," he wrote. "Repeatedly, white balls of fire shot out of the glare as more torpedoes and shells hit the wallowing Jap vessels . . . We raced through flame flecked seas at tremendous speed firing all the time . . . [seeing] tracer bullets landing on the burning Jap ships, a beautiful but awesome sight."[15] This veteran correspondent's excitement was in no way hidden, and this served to add even greater emphasis to the success experienced by Moosbrugger and his men.

If Art Burges recorded anything in print about the battle, it is not readily found. Even if it exists, it would not likely carry the firsthand detail of Robinson's. Burges spent nearly all the engagement in Dunlap's wardroom. In fairness, this was his first experience aboard a destroyer at sea, and directly into heated combat at that. Wilkinson's "good show" was just a bit more than he was prepared for.

For sure, the Vella Gulf action was no small matter, and it provoked a great swelling of pride among the men of Moosbrugger's task group—just as with the whole of the South Pacific command. Indeed, this victory cannot be overstated. There was reason for the great array of accolades that followed. Obviously, for the U.S. Navy's destroyer fleet, this engagement enlightened everyone to the destroyer's formidable impact when allowed to be properly used, and others, as Burke and his newly formed Destroyer Squadron 23 (most notably known as the "Little Beavers") were to soon underscore. But, foremost, this sound defeat of the Japanese resupply efforts in the Solomons meant that the Japanese hold here was over—and it appeared to all but ensure the future defeat of Japan altogether. No one doubted that the road to Tokyo was still long and full of pitfalls, exacting a high price on both sides, but the conclusion was at the very least being glimpsed. Long pressured by his most trusted commanders to do so, Admiral Halsey was now convinced that an island-hopping campaign would be fully successful. His previous hesitation had been centered on having strong Japanese bastions, as Rabaul and Kavieng, precariously at his rear, with continuous airpower capability at attacking his flank and important supply routes. Now that he had proof that the Japanese resupply of these fortresses could be controlled and isolated, areas like Rabaul could be left to wither on the vine, given over to a decimation by bombers without the need of a costly investment of additional time and waste of precious manpower necessary for subduing by ground invasion. This was a big deal, and it was clearly understood right up to the top levels of both the U.S. and Japanese leadership. Perhaps no small engagement had greater repercussions. The celebrations were truly justified. But this victory would also stir some rather surprising and disconcerting residuals.

By the morning of August 8, the heated action of Vella Gulf had long since ended, and the destroyers under Moosbrugger's command now stood quietly at their respective moorings in Purvis Bay. Here they awaited their next assignment. Activities aboard each of the ships had returned to normal, and crews were once again tending to their routine duties, albeit with a renewed sense of vigor.

Aboard *Lang*, Captain Wilfong stood on the bridge with his usual oversight, watchful as this day unfolded. The morning began in typical fashion. Then, from out of the corner of his always vigilant eye, the captain spied the stealthy approach of two unannounced figures, each seemingly closing his position with purpose. The commander's mind was mostly occupied with the business of his ship, overseeing what needs remained in the preparation for the vessel's next mission, yet this advance could not be ignored. He turned slowly, as with only slight curiosity, and found himself suddenly confronted by both Commander Simpson and his tagalong war reporter friend, Pat Robinson. The two gentlemen brandished broad smiles, giving greetings that appeared overtly interested in the captain's well-being, which instantly gave rise to Wilfong's suspicions—as he fully trusted neither man. In his hand, Robinson held a large piece of rolled-up parchment, and without speaking to its meaning he slowly began to open it for full display. Wilfong's expression remained serious as his eyes danced back and forth from Simpson to Robinson and finally to the unrolled parchment.

The sheet was quite colorful and commanded notice, brandishing along its right side the silhouettes of one cruiser and three destroyers, while along its left were four Japanese naval ensigns, and at the bottom was a beautifully crafted American eagle bracketed by furled American flags. The artwork was indeed quite spectacular, but it was the center subject that more effectively captured the greater attention of Wilfong. At the heart of the parchment was a photo of President Roosevelt, torn at length and nearly in two, applied to the paper in the shape of a V.[16] The captain's face reddened and his lips tightened. He recognized the photo as the one that had long found its home in his destroyer's wardroom, the very one that had been presented to the ship by the president following a trip with him to Panama and Cocos Island in 1940. The president's hand-inscribed notation was still clearly visible, "To the Captain and Crew of the USS *Lang*, my escort ship," signed "Franklin D. Roosevelt."[17]

Below this photo a new inscription had been added, and with beautifully applied calligraphy it read: "*On the night of 6-7 August, the U.S.S. Lang with Task Group 31.2 intercepted in Vella Gulf a Japanese force consisting of one cruiser and three destroyers rushing troops to their sorely pressed forces in New Georgia. With a well-executed gun and torpedo attack the Japanese force was destroyed and sunk. The U.S. force achieved no damage to ships or personnel. Except, the shock of gunfire tore this picture from its mooring and damaged the inscription. The Officers of the U.S.S. Lang respectfully request of their commander-in-chief a replacement. (Signed) Cmdr. Rodger W. Simpson, U.S.N., division commander and Cmdr. John L. Wilfong, U.S.N., commanding.*"[18] Simpson's signature was already boldly applied, but the document still awaited the same from Wilfong.

The captain's outrage was immediate. Wilfong had seen the photo shortly after the action and, while it was true that the gunfire had caused the framed photo to fall to the wardroom decking, breaking both its frame and protective glass, the photo itself had remained undamaged. He glared at the two men, knowing that this was nothing more than a publicity stunt, purposefully crafted to embellish a story that absolutely needed nothing more to add to its magnitude. He suspected Robinson was responsible for the plot but knew Simpson had fully endorsed the venture; and he was right.

Robinson admitted to having first seen the fallen photo just shortly after the action, when he had arrived in the wardroom for coffee and with the intent at gathering additional comments from the junior officers about the previous battle.[19] Upon seeing the fallen photo, however, Robinson—whose keen eye for news never closed—quickly conceived of the idea for his story's elaboration and was shortly thereafter approaching his new friend Simpson for support. Always watchful for his own greater interest, the commodore obviously thought highly of Robinson's idea and eagerly embraced it as a very worthwhile scheme. He ordered the photo removed and then commissioned one of *Lang*'s more artistic sailors to follow Robinson's instructions for the specially prepared parchment. Afterward, as he assured the reporter, they would take the scroll to Wilfong, request the captain's signature, and then the document would be fully ready for delivery.

But Wilfong wanted nothing to do with the overzealous project. He instantly accused both men of destroying ship's property and refused to sign the document. Embarrassed by this refusal, Simpson called the captain aside and demanded his cooperation. Regardless, Wilfong would not budge, threatening even to file a report on the matter while defiantly keeping his signature to himself. It appeared that the captain's patience with the commodore's insistent meddling and constant circumventing of the chain of command had come to an abrupt end. This stunt, in his view, was nothing more than a fabrication, a lie, and one that he was unwilling to accept.

Aboard *Lang*, the once tropical atmosphere suddenly cooled to a most uncomfortable level; the Solomons had for *Lang*'s crew never before felt so frigid. For hours the two officers kept their big guns unmasked, each refusing to back down with each equally determined at having their own way. But Wilfong was just as equally observant to the needs of his ship and, once having realized how this impasse was negatively impacting the effectiveness of his command, he rightly concluded that this was one battle not worth the extended fuss. There were far more important things for him to focus his attention on, and, after finally feeling that his point had been thoroughly pressed, he begrudgingly gave in and signed his name to the troubled parchment.[20]

It was during this event that the divide between Simpson and Wilfong purportedly reached its ultimate expanse—and it promised never again to shrink. The parchment however, even despite the trouble it stirred, did indeed find a successful route to the White House. In an Associated Press article entitled "Warship Wants FDR Photo" and dated September 1, Francis McCarthy (an AP correspondent who had during this time visited aboard the *Lang*) wrote, "President Roosevelt was asked today for a personally autographed picture of himself to replace one in the wardroom of a destroyer attached to a light task force which sank four Japanese warships on the night of Aug. 6-7." The article went on to explain the story behind the photo, even detailing the parchment scroll and its inscriptions. It then concluded by stating, "The Vella gulf battle was the second engagement in which Commander Simpson's flagship emerged without loss or damage." So, in the end, Simpson got his added bit of sought-after attention, Robinson was able to enhance his already remarkable story (detailed in his own International News Service article entitled "Vella Gulf Victory Made Murder by Clean Surprise"), and the officers and crew of the *Lang* did indeed receive a replacement photo from a very appreciative President Roosevelt.

But controversy was not yet ended. Another tiff came on the evening of this same day, when Moosbrugger invited all of his task group commanders to accompany him ashore to Tulagi. This event was intended to be celebratory, to share in drink, both in toast to their recent victory and to congratulate Iverson for reaching his thirty-fifth birthday. The group gathered at the Tulagi Club, and here a round of drinks was quickly passed out and downed. A lively and impassioned conversation soon followed, eventually leading to a discussion of how many and what types of ships had been destroyed during the recent operation. The views of these commanders were quite varied on this matter. But it was Simpson, with his usual boasting and overpowering personality, who took to causing another flap, this time in a heated exchange with the man-of-the-hour, Iverson.

Since every one of the skippers had a differing opinion as to the number and types of ships sunk, Simpson felt obligated to correct them all by loudly pronouncing his own statement of fact. "All four had been sunk," he claimed authoritatively, "and at least *two* were light cruisers." Iverson laughed aloud. He thought Simpson's claim to be ludicrous. "There were only three, none of which were cruisers," Iverson barked back. Simpson seemed incensed that anyone would even dare challenge him, and he immediately entered into further argument with Iverson, creating a standoff that quickly required Moosbrugger's personal intervention. Becoming the broker for a peaceful settlement, Freddie took the middle road. "There were definitely three ships sunk," he stated flatly, "*possibly* four and one *might* have been a cruiser." The debate thus drew to a quick close as so too did the festivity, leading the officers to return quietly to their respective ships.[21] Even so, this discussion proved never to be quite so conclusive, as the debate over the numbers and types of enemy ships sunk at Vella Gulf was destined to continue for many more years to come. Momentarily, however, a far greater war waged, and this still took precedence.

Even for the victorious Task Group 31.2, the fight was far from over. On the morning of August 9, Admiral Wilkinson again directed Commander Moosbrugger to lead his now famous force (less *Maury* and *Stack*—replaced this night by *Gridley* and *Wilson*) back to Vella Gulf. It was suspected that the Japanese were intending to send a new reinforcement effort to Kolombangara, and the admiral was adamant that the Tokyo Express not catch new life from any bit of success.

That Hara had escaped Moosbrugger's original trap remained at this point in time an unknown. It was likely for this reason that both Moosbrugger and Wilkinson were feeling just a bit overly confident. Suspecting that the Japanese were still in the dark as to his methods, Freddie was fully determined to execute the very same approach as he had used on August 6-7, lagging his timing by only a mere thirty minutes. In retrospect, however, his determination was not only flawed but could have proven most disastrous, especially had Hara returned as one of his opponents—certainly a likely scenario. Fortunately for Moosbrugger, on this night the Tokyo Express refused to show itself. Following the advice of Hara and other Japanese destroyer commanders, Rabaul's leadership temporarily suspended all future Tokyo Express reinforcements. The stealthier submarine I-boat force and Daihatsu armed barges, though far slower, less convenient and even lesser effective, were left to struggle with the supply issues on their own. There was little more the Imperial Japanese Navy felt capable of doing.

Those soldiers, Marines, and airmen trapped on the remaining islands would be expected to fight on the best they could, sacrificing themselves in the attempt to slow the American advance so Japanese forces could be reconsolidated and replenished for another stand elsewhere—which would now be on Bougainville Island, in the Western Solomons. But even this effort was not to fare so well, and Moosbrugger's next success would again prove to be the bearer of more bad news for the Japanese.

Indeed, even as Moosbrugger's second Vella visit did not—as it was hoped—capture any additional Japanese surface ships for destruction, it did manage to interrupt the Imperial Navy's supply train even further. Like his first trip into Vella Gulf, Moosbrugger's two divisions quickly dispersed into their two offset lines of northerly approach. Once again Simpson's ships hugged the coastline of Kolombangara, making note of barge sightings along their passage. Once assured that the Tokyo Express would not be appearing, Moosbrugger had his ships retrace their advance to engage the earlier bypassed Daihatsus. Several of these barges were relocated, and Simpson's division—now in the van—took a good number of these under direct fire.

The 40-millimeter guns of *Lang*, *Sterett*, and *Wilson* were most effective, eliminating several of the region's remaining small surface transports, further depleting the enemy's ability to move troops and supplies in the Central Solomons (one brief firefight did draw a spirited reply of gunfire, but caused only some superficial damage to *Lang*, and without harm to any of her crew). The number of barges actually destroyed or damaged is not known for certain. This night was once again inky black, and a good evaluation of the results was impossible. Storekeeper 2nd Class Glenn Allen, aboard *Dunlap*, noted in his diary that the group "sank 8 Jap barges" on this mission.[22] Moosbrugger's official report stated that five barges were taken under fire and that four of these were thought to have been sunk.[23] Regardless of the true number, this action was but a further pronouncement to the Japanese that their past dominance of the night had indeed ended.

Though certainly not with the excitement of three days before, Moosbrugger's return was still seen as a success, and would set the stage for many new changes to come. Foremost among of these changes was the disbanding of his task group, as most of Moosbrugger's band of destroyers and their crews finally received the news that they had so been longing for. They were being relieved.

The newer Fletcher class destroyers were by this time reaching the Solomons region in growing numbers, and this was allowing the older veterans of the campaign, as with the Benhams and Gridleys of Task Group 31.2, to be given a chance for some real rest. *Stack*—since having been away from the States less than six months—remained in the Solomons region for several additional months, participating in the November raids against Rabaul. *Sterett* also remained in the Solomons, but for only another month, as by October 8 she was enjoying a cordial greeting at Sydney, Australia, where her complement was thereafter relaxing to many fine amenities. For *Lang*, *Maury*, *Craven*, and *Dunlap* the news was even more welcomed. Each of these ships was to begin their own individual treks back to the West Coast for scheduled overhauls. They were all going home.

Dunlap—with Moosbrugger still aboard—arrived back at Noumea on the morning of September 7. Here the crew learned of their good fortune, that in two days they would depart in a direct route for San Diego. Glenn Allen would write with understatement in his diary, "Everybody was in a good mood."[24]

At Noumea, *Dunlap* spent "a few days alongside [a] tender" before departing for the States.[25] The ship and crew had been serving in the South Pacific for nearly a year now, and obviously everyone was very anxious at getting started toward home. But there was a last-minute glitch. Admiral Halsey sent word to Moosbrugger and Iverson that while they were at Noumea he wanted to personally decorate them with the Navy Cross, to be awarded at a special ceremony before *Dunlap* sailed. Halsey's headquarters was on the island, so this did not initially seem to be of any inconvenience. However, the admiral first wanted to get Wilkinson's approval for how the citations read before he would present them. This did present a problem, as Wilkinson was back on Guadalcanal—or so it was thought.

The issue was not with Moosbrugger, as he would not be sailing with *Dunlap*, but for Iverson it was quite a quandary. Any delay would surely not sit well with *Dunlap*'s crew. Iverson certainly did not want to be the reason for a late start. Fortunately, Wilkinson was already on his way to Noumea. Still, getting the needed approval for the citations would not happen readily or without some extra effort. Iverson explained, "Moosbrugger got word that Wilkinson was on Noumea, and he asked me to go ashore with him to get . . . approval of the draft citations. We finally located [the admiral] in the early afternoon, but we did not get to see him as he was taking a nap. [Freddie] was told to come back about 4:30 [p.m.], which he did. [He finally] got the approved citations which he then delivered to Lt. Commander Stassen, who was [the] Admiral's [Halsey's] Flag Secretary." The two officers were then told to be present for Halsey's staff conference on the following morning at 9:30 a.m., when the presentations would be made. Moosbrugger's perseverance looked to have everything back on track—though not just yet.[26]

Later that afternoon, Moosbrugger and Iverson stopped by the South Pacific Club for a few drinks before returning to the ship. Freddie was not known as a heavy drinker as—despite his father's proprietorship of a saloon—he usually avoided alcohol altogether. Many of his acquaintances never knew him to drink at all. There was obviously some good reason for this. Iverson explained that in truth Moosbrugger "loved to drink but knew once he started . . . he didn't want to stop. For this reason, he very seldom went ashore and when he did he would always caution me to get him back to the ship before dinner."[27]

On this occasion there appeared to be no threat to the usual plan. But once arrived at the SoPac Club, Freddie was unexpectedly met by an old academy classmate, an old friend whom he had not seen for years. The two quickly began to reminisce, and before long Iverson was being ignored entirely. Despite every effort to get Moosbrugger back to the ship in a timely manner, Iverson was unable to convince the commodore that he should leave. Finally, by 6:00 p.m., Iverson determined that any further delay on his part would serve no good purpose, so he headed back to *Dunlap* on his own, leaving Moosbrugger behind. The commodore had promised that he would follow shortly.[28]

That evening, Moosbrugger was still absent the ship. Iverson waited up for a while but was already asleep when, at 11:00 p.m., he was awakened and told that "the Commodore had fallen overboard." Sure enough, during his attempt at a stealthy return, Freddie had slipped and fallen off the destroyer's gangway and into the water below. "He was really swacked," Iverson noted. On-duty sailors quickly pulled Moosbrugger back aboard, and Iverson took care to see that the commander was taken to his quarters and put to bed. But how was he to get the commodore ready for the early morning meeting with Halsey? This was sure to be a difficult task. At sunrise, Iverson immediately set his and Moosbrugger's stewards to work at getting Freddie prepared for his morning appointment.[29]

At 7:30 A.M., the stewards had the commander's best uniform laid out, with a hot breakfast and large pot of hot coffee waiting. Then the real struggle began. Just getting the commodore awake was the first obstacle, which took some time. Helping him to get dressed took additional minutes. Nothing went smoothly. Finally, after several doses of strong black coffee, Freddie looked to be ready for going ashore. Though still some distance shy of sober, Moosbrugger managed to arrive at the staff meeting on time and with at least an appearance of sobriety. And, with Iverson as close escort, Freddie took his seat and awaited the ceremony to begin.[30]

As expected, when Halsey arrived, the first order of business was the presentations to Moosbrugger and Iverson. The two were called up front and the admiral began by reading the citations. Of Moosbrugger he stated: "The President of the United States takes pleasure in presenting the Navy Cross to Frederick Moosbrugger, Commander, U.S. Navy, for extraordinary heroism and distinguished service in the line of his profession as Commander, Destroyer Division Twelve, during a surface engagement with enemy Japanese forces at Vella Gulf, Solomon Islands, on the night of 6-7 August 1943. Conducting a perfectly coordinated attack on Japanese forces, Commander Moosbrugger skillfully disposed the units of his destroyer division for maximum fire power and efficiency, which resulted in the annihilation of the entire force of one cruiser and three destroyers. He brought his ships through the engagement without loss or damage. Commander Moosbrugger's inspiring leadership and the valiant devotion to duty of his command contributed in large measure to the outstanding success of these vital missions and reflect great credit upon the United States Naval Service."[31] He then took the medal from its box and pinned it to the front of Freddie's blouse. A salute and shake of the hand followed, as did a "thank you, sir" from Freddie. Halsey then leaned close and spoke softly, "I'm glad you could make it." There had been no hiding his true condition from such a veteran commander. Then the admiral moved on to Iverson for a similar presentation. All was well.[32]

On September 16, the United Press reported on Admiral Halsey's presentation of the Navy Crosses to Commander Moosbrugger and Lieutenant Commander Iverson, noting their key roles in the victory. The headlines read in large bold print: "Vela [*sic*] Gulf victory called one of war's most decisive battles; full story is told." In the opening paragraph the article clarified the message even further, stating, "The American destroyer flotilla which defeated a Japanese task force in Vela [*sic*] Gulf without suffering a single hit won one of the 'most decisive' battles of the war for surface craft, Captain Francis X. McInerny [the spokesperson for Admiral Halsey] said today."[33]

Truly, there seemed to be no question that the Vella Gulf victory had indeed been a "decisive" win and with historic proportions—but it was but a single victory in a long war that seemed far from any short conclusion. For those war-weary sailors sailing the war-torn Pacific, the only meaningful victory would be the one that would completely end this conflict and allow them a lasting return to their families and homes. This, Vella Gulf was not—though it surely was a huge step in the right direction, rewarding most of its victors a brief but very welcomed break in the action and a timely stateside visit with loved ones.

Lang, *Maury*, *Craven*, and *Dunlap* each made their own individual journeys eastward, excitedly pressing toward the security of home waters and the promise of seeing family once more. Energy levels increased and broad smiles became more and more prevalent with the passing of each successive mile. How wonderful it felt to be going home, even if for only a few days. Just to get back to civilization, to hear the old familiar sounds, to smell the old familiar smells, to walk again along the crowded city streets and or to lie in the green grass of a rural valley, gave new priority to every menial task. Everyone wanted this trip to conclude quickly and without any waver. There was a wish for flank [maximum] speed, to press the ships hard at reaching their goal with record time, as plans were being made and men were more than ready to execute their leaves. After all, the ships were all scheduled for overhaul, so why not use what the tired old turbines had left in them to expedite the journey. Surely the skippers concurred, but only to full speed would they press, even as they too felt the strong tug for enterprise.

When *Lang* arrived back at San Francisco—passing beneath the Golden Gate Bridge on September 4, 1943—a boisterous cheer echoed throughout the ship. They were home at last. Pemberton Southard gave out a thankful sigh and smiled; he had already charted his next course well in advance of this moment. Once securely moored, Pem immediately requested his leave from the destroyer, and via plane and bus he quickly headed off to Charleston for his long-awaited reunion with Jane. What a happy occasion this was, a tearful and joyous embrace of what would surely be a momentous venture in life.

Pemberton Southard and Jane Duvall were married on September 12—a full year later than originally planned, but finally their day arrived. They had a brief but blissful honeymoon in New York City, and then Pem and Jane proceeded on by train to San Francisco, where "she set up housekeeping with another *Lang* Navy wife" and he rejoined *Lang* for another eight months of combat at sea.[34]

Pem permanently departed *Lang* while the destroyer was at Pearl preparing for the Marianas campaign and returned to the states in June 1944, having new orders for reassignment as the officer in charge of the Pre-commissioning Fire Control School at Norfolk, Virginia. This was a fortunate time, allowing the lieutenant and Jane several secure months at being at one another's side. But in March 1945—the same month that his son, Joe, was born—Pem's vacation from the war ended and he returned to the Pacific. The lieutenant stepped into his next important role, that of executive officer aboard the newly commissioned destroyer *Myles C. Fox* (DD-829).

As theorized by Pem, it was this commissioning that brought about an interesting chapter in World War II history. "In March 1945," he later noted, " . . . I wrote a letter to Hirohito, Emperor of Japan. I told him that I was Executive Officer of the USS *Lang* (DD-399) which had sunk three of his destroyers in the night action at Vella Gulf in August 1943. I was now coming back in a new Radar Picket Destroyer to sink more of his ships, shoot down his planes, and assist in the bombardment and landing on the shores of Japan. If he was real smart . . . he would immediately surrender to the United States of America. . . . As the *Myles C. Fox* was steaming . . . part of a large carrier task force, en route to the invasion of Japan, Hirohito surrendered. It wasn't the 'A' bomb—he had received my letter."[35]

Charles "Chuck" Lee, the resolute gunner who had found an honored home aboard *Lang*, was just as eager as Southard with his return to San Francisco. Chuck had a like-minded determination. More resolute than ever, Chuck Lee disembarked his destroyer for the streets of the city with a mission. He intended to search out the pretty Patricia Skinner for another try at her hand. Finding her phone number, he called her up, requesting that they meet. Surprised by the call, Patricia excitedly agreed. They went out for a movie, and their romance almost instantly sparked anew. Chuck had every intention of marrying this girl, but before he could formally ask her, *Lang* was called back to the South Pacific. With no other choice, he popped the big question in a letter. This time Patricia responded in the affirmative, agreeing to be his girl, and his alone.

Chuck's excitement was beyond description. He had experienced two great victories in less than two months. How simply grand was this. Of course, the union did take some time, as Chuck was not able to return to the States until April of 1944. Even then the war was still ongoing and his stay promised to be short, making a formal church wedding impossible. For this reason, their vows were given in the local city hall, on May 4. It had been a long time coming, but Chuck and Patricia were finally mister and missus, the Lees.

Ralph Barber's return to the States came on September 25, with *Dunlap*'s safe arrival at San Diego. After an almost reverse transit of his initial trip into the South Pacific, Ralph was back on American turf. He immediately headed for his hometown of Birmingham, where Virginia was waiting. This was another momentous reunion. Without further delay, on September 30, 1943, they had their long-awaited wedding. For once Ralph's plans went exactly as he imagined; he and Virginia were man and wife.

After a brief honeymoon in Long Beach, California, Ralph returned to *Dunlap* for the duration of the Pacific war, while Virginia awaited his promised return. The sailor who had initially shown little fondness for ships and the sea had found his preference aboard a destroyer. *Dunlap* had done him well. And he would indeed make it back home, safely returning to Virginia's side on September 19, 1945.

Dunlap sailor, Loyd Peters, was also very grateful to be home. Despite his initial thought, the Navy had turned out to be not quite as "romantic" as he initially visualized. The uncertainty of war had changed this for sure. But the Navy did indeed provide the "steady job" he had hoped for, despite its many risks. And *Dunlap* had kept him safe, providing him with ample welfare and many good friends for the journey. He even managed to make it back home in time for Christmas—though not till 1945. He was only four years off from his 1941 letter.

Craven's Wilber Fultz, the fed-up cowboy from Montana, welcomed his return too, and with a whole new perspective. He still loved the Navy and was very proud of being a part of the recent Vella Gulf victory, but the Montana plains that he had so eagerly left behind only two years before no longer seemed so foreboding. Ranch life now looked a whole lot better to him—so at the war's end and upon receiving his discharge he happily returned to Fort Benton and rejoined his father at work once more. The cowboy sailor had learned in the South Pacific a whole new appreciation for home.

For these men, as well as for other veterans of the action, Vella Gulf was indeed a momentous event and is a very proud moment in their lives. It could well be said that it was life-changing. These were "exciting times," noted Albert Olsen many years after the fact.[36] Vella Gulf is arguably the most perfectly fought engagement in naval history and (outside perhaps that of the ambush and shooting down of Admiral Yamamoto and his staff) no other action of similar size and duration had a greater impact on the conclusion of the Pacific war. It can also be argued that this engagement—in concert with the great victories at Midway and Guadalcanal—was a true turning point of the Pacific war. Certainly, if the tide was not fully turned here, it was given a momentum it otherwise did not have. For it was at Vella Gulf that the U.S. Navy finally overcame its distrust for radar and its fear of the night. It was here that the destroyer navy was finally offered the opportunity to display its true mettle, and it did so with far greater effect than even its advocates expected, flinging the door wide open to future similar actions. It was here, too, that a confidence of overall victory became reality, and the Pacific military leadership finally felt free to fully endorse its plans for bypassing Japan's stronger island bases (as Rabaul), allowing these fortifications to wither away from forced neglect, in pursuit of weaker, more favorable targets.

Therefore, it was at Vella Gulf that the Imperial Japanese Navy faced its inevitability, that of its own future ineffectiveness at providing even minimal support for its shrinking perimeter outposts. No longer did the Japanese navy rule the night, nor would it ever again. Just as had been feared by the Japanese leadership, Moosbrugger's victory did indeed echo the decisive end to the war. And it was all due to the right group of men, coming together at the right time and with the right purpose. Perhaps nothing states it better than a simple line inscribed many years later by Pemberton Southard; when the U.S. Pacific Fleet was at its most desperate moment to take full control of the sea and the war, tasked to stop the Tokyo Express and end Japanese dominance of night action, "we rose to the occasion."[37]

Chapter Twelve

Final Notes

Debates, Controversies, and Conclusions

Moosbrugger's great victory at Vella Gulf, even in spite of the many years that have passed, continues to be an important topic of study as well as the beneficiary of many honors. Not only did the surviving veterans thoroughly enjoy sharing their own reminiscences of the battle, but so too did the historians (professional and amateur) who spoke with them about this matter. This has led to numerous articles being written about this engagement over the years, each in exclamation of this action's important role in naval history. The Naval Academy has also chosen to give careful honor to the battle, as study of the action has been used as required criteria for many of its graduating classes of cadets. Adding further to this legacy, two ships have since been christened with the name of *Vella Gulf* (the CVE-111, commissioned April 9, 1945, and decommissioned December 1, 1970, and the CG-72, commissioned September 18, 1993, and decommissioned August 8, 2022), just as the three commanders—Burke, Moosbrugger, and Simpson—were each honored with destroyers christened after them (Arleigh Burke would even have an entire class of destroyers named for him). Still, even in spite of such recognition and scrutiny, many of the finer details of this engagement have remained untold, and over the years this has caused some unsettling controversies to appear.

Almost before the battle was ended, the great debate over the number and types of ships sunk began, and this discussion continues yet today.

For a good many veterans of the action—since more than half of the participants on that night were not in a position for good observation—there was little choice but to accept the historical ruling, that only three ships were sunk and that all of these were destroyers. But for those veterans who did have a good view of the action, such convincing proved dramatically more difficult. Few of these men, whether officer or enlisted, ever fully accepted the official record. To their dying day, these individuals have argued that the ship they witnessed explode that night was far too large to be a destroyer. "If that ship was a destroyer it was the biggest destroyer I ever saw," stated *Lang* gunner's mate Kenny Arthur some sixty years after the fact.[1] And this would prove to be typical of the affidavits provided time and again with regard to this one question.

All of the initial reports, even by Moosbrugger and Simpson, were in agreement that four ships were sunk in the action and that one of these four was "a cruiser." Within hours of the battle, *Dunlap*'s Glenn Allen penned matter-of-factly: "This was our biggest [night] yet. Battle of Vella Gulf. Made a torpedo attack on 1 cruiser (Jap) and 3 Jap destroyers. Sank them all."[2] But in a report produced in 1944—the result of interrogations of some Japanese survivors of the action—there was stated something dramatically different. The Japanese survivors, all captured on Vella Lavella, testified (even to the name of the ships) "that all four of the ships were destroyers" and "that one of the destroyers had escaped."[3] This information forced the Navy to change its official conclusion to then claim that Moosbrugger's force could only be conclusively accredited with sinking three enemy destroyers while heavily damaging a fourth. But Capt. Tameichi Hara's own story even refutes this, as he claimed (with the exception of the dud torpedo strike against *Shigure*'s rudder) that *Shigure* escaped completely untouched.

Based on its full post–August 1943 war history and an outstanding record to boot, it is impossible to debate that *Shigure* not only survived annihilation at Vella Gulf but also escaped without the knowledge of Moosbrugger and his force. Hara's own survival is a testament to this escape, and his record of the events gives a very good accounting of the Japanese side of the debacle. His story unmistakably affirms that only four Japanese destroyers were involved.

Still the controversy over the existence of a "cruiser" has persisted. Even despite the extreme darkness of the night and the action being both fast and furious, there is no detracting from the fact that the flames produced during the battle appear to have clearly projected the silhouette of this vessel, and it displayed itself very much larger than a destroyer. This in combination with this ship's initial identifiers and its ability to absorb great punishment impressed upon every observer that it had to be a cruiser, and they would be hard-pressed to be convinced of anything other.

There were, however, some early hints that these initial observations were indeed suspect and incorrect. Moosbrugger wrote in his reports that in order for the descriptions given at identifying the cruiser to be correct that "either the

Japanese had a new type of cruiser or the cruiser was a heavy cruiser with the after control tower mistaken for a stack."[4]

The heated debate that took place at Iverson's birthday gathering on Tulagi was another indicator of doubt. In his own official report, however, Iverson noted—somewhat to the contrary of his early argument with Simpson—that "[from] the relative size of [the] radar 'PIPS' the cruiser was believed to be leading the formation followed by the three destroyers. The second 'PIP' on the screen, while not as large as the first one, was considerably larger than the remaining two, and it is probable that this was a larger destroyer than the third and fourth ships in the enemy column."[5]

Japanese reports of the action remain uniform, including the more detailed account given by Hara. These all affirm that *Hagikaze* not *Arashi* was leading the column, but that it was *Arashi* which had its fuel tanks rupture and burst into the inferno as witnessed by Moosbrugger's ships. So, if Iverson's report is to be considered accurate, then it was *Hagikaze* that the Americans initially identified as a "cruiser"—later to be changed to *Arashi* when this ship was observed to erupt into flames. All further reports and observations purported the vessel fully engulfed in fire as "the cruiser," and this ship was identified by the Japanese as *Arashi*. That the Americans identified this ship as a "cruiser" was determined by several identifiers, including length or size, number of stacks, positioning of superimposed gun turrets, aircraft catapults, and the ability to withstand punishment. All of these observations were reasonable at concluding that the burning vessel was indeed a cruiser—but it is just as reasonable to conclude that they were all wrong.

The lead ship, *Hagikaze*, was also reported by many observers as "the destroyer" that was sunk almost immediately, accounting for the first tally—a contradiction to Iverson's radar conclusions and a false report that actually led to the final count of ships sunk as four (as *Hagikaze* was counted twice). This ship was reported to have been struck solidly by torpedoes to then disappear from radar. Though *Hagikaze* was indeed struck by two torpedoes amidships, igniting fires in her engine rooms and bringing the destroyer to a dead stop, she did not readily sink as initially reported. The second destroyer in the Japanese line, *Arashi*—even despite the heroic effort of her helmsman—could not avoid both the oncoming torpedoes and collision with the damaged *Hagikaze*, so she was maneuvered around the injured destroyer to her own detriment. No less than three torpedoes hammered this ship, causing a tremendous explosion and fire which temporarily masked *Hagikaze* from view—giving the false impression to both visual observation and radar that *Hagikaze* had indeed sunk. It was at this point that the initial identification of *Arashi* as a cruiser was reported. But it was this explosion and subsequent fire that were likely responsible for causing an optical illusion, furthering misidentification of *Arashi* as a "cruiser." *Hagikaze*—thought to be sunk—was at this point closely parallel to the starboard side and likely just slightly abaft of the disabled *Arashi*. It is even possible that the initial explosions on *Arashi* ripped this ship into two separate sections and that both the forward and after sections were still afloat and apart by several feet. The resulting fuel fire covered not only the two sections of the ship but also the water's surface surrounding them, making it appear as though it remained intact and much larger than it truly was. In the background there was also the silhouette of *Hagikaze*, which could easily explain the added smoke stack. Since both destroyers were of the newer Kagero Class, they were indeed larger than most destroyers and did carry superimposed gun turrets, as reported. If it could ever be proven that *Arashi* had indeed split into two separate floating sections, this too could explain her supposed resilience under fire. The seas on this night were relatively calm and there was little current to cause the two sections to separate quickly any great distance. Most gunfire was aimed at *Arashi*'s more vulnerable amidships—and should the two sections be separated by only a few yards as suggested—then these rounds were likely only falling into the sea without effect. The fact that more explosions were observed, on a ship already totally engulfed in flames, was of little proof that additional major hits were truly being acquired. Only the reported observation of catapults (which originated from only one source) cannot, other than being mistaken, be explained.[6]

Moreover, this also explains—as radar continued to show only three "pips" immediately following the torpedo strikes—why it was later assumed that all four ships were sunk. Hara had so successfully maneuvered *Shigure*, using covering black smoke and a quick hard starboard turn close-in toward Vella Lavella (caught only momentarily on *Craven*'s radar), as to completely mask this vessel from all further visual and radar observation, making his escape perfect. Therefore, *Shigure*'s presence and escape went without further notice for the rest of the night. But *Hagikaze*—already thought to be sunk—was now being counted as the fourth ship.

In retrospect, and just as affirmed by the final official version of facts, it can only be concluded that three destroyers out of a combined force of four destroyers were actually sunk at Vella Gulf, and that no cruiser was present. Perhaps, as more and more mapping and modern-day exploration of World War II Pacific war shipwreck sites continue, what mystery remains of this issue will one day be more fully explained. If *Arashi* is indeed one day located and found to be in two separate sections, perhaps then the mystery can be fully resolved. Until then, this question will remain.

But this is not the only controversy to exist. In addition to questions concerning the makeup of the Japanese column, there is yet another valid question: Who should receive the most credit for the success of the initial torpedo strikes? Did one of Moosbrugger's ships have more hits than the others? And, if so, how could this have happened?

As was the normal targeting procedure, on this night *Dunlap* targeted the third and fourth ships of the Japanese column, *Craven* targeted the second and third, while *Maury* targeted the first and second. Each ship fired eight torpedoes. Per Moosbrugger's initial directives, torpedo depths were to be set at 5 to 9 feet.[7] *Dunlap* fired the standard non-modified Mk. 15 torpedo while *Craven* and *Maury* each fired Mk. 15s with the new warhead extensions. If the later found gyro issue of the Mk. 15 played its assumed role, four of eight torpedoes fired by *Craven* likely ran too deep to be greatly effective.[8] *Dunlap*'s torpedoes, whether running at the proper depth or not, could be assumed to be directed at neither of the two lead enemy warships. *Maury*'s torpedoes, on the other hand, had two distinct independent actions occur that may have provided the true punch and success so key to Moosbrugger's greater victory. And, as it turns out, neither of these actions was with the commander's knowledge or control.

Sims wrote in his report that his torpedoes "were fired in full salvo with [a] two degree spread." Torpedo speed was set at "intermediate" with the depth setting at "five feet."[9] Five feet was the minimum setting and matched the conclusions reached by both Crenshaw and Fisher with regard to the deep running issues of the flawed and over-weighted Mk. 15s. Curiously, both Crenshaw and Fisher claimed full individual responsibility for the minimum setting, and resolutely so.

Fisher stated that he had changed the settings "on his own, without knowledge of anyone," and only disclosed this after the battle had ended. According to Fisher, he had initially made this change on August 2, while Arleigh Burke was still aboard and just prior to departure for the Kula Gulf incursion. Burke had not ordered the setting change but was notified of it and concurred with Fisher's decision. Since the enemy was not met that night, the torpedoes were not launched. The settings were not changed. Prior to the August 6 departure, "no order was received to change the settings," Fisher recalled.[10]

Crenshaw, on the other hand, claimed that he was the one responsible for ordering the change, conferring with Captain Sims of his decision in the very late moments of the preparations. "There is no doubt," stated Crenshaw, "that I went to the captain, discussed this matter with him, and then went to the torpedo battery to have all torpedoes set at the minimum depth setting. I have no recollection of discussing the matter with Fisher beforehand. He may well have drawn similar conclusions concerning the problems as I had. As to the actual setting of the torpedoes, Fisher and his men would certainly have done the actual setting."[11] Despite Crenshaw's assertions, Fisher claimed that he "personally reset the depth for *Maury*'s torpedoes—without authorization to do so." He went on to state that he "did not inform (the) captain of the change because (he) knew (Sims) could not approve it, as he would follow the standard (depth)."[12]

The fact that Sims acknowledged the "basic depth setting, five feet" in his report does not completely clarify this controversy, as there is no indication in the report why he altered from Moosbrugger's prescribed 5 to 9 feet settings and no recommendations from Sims are found in the report for this important change. Regardless of who was responsible (a controversy likely never to be fully resolved), this decision was not only wise but surely key to the success of the operation; and it does appear to have been done without the initial knowledge and approval of Moosbrugger.

In addition to *Maury*'s unique torpedo depth setting, there was another factor that inadvertently occurred, also adding considerably to the operation's success. Sims noted in his report that "[the] actual bearing of the target at [the] instant of firing was 318° T, but due to [a] communication lag the salvo was fired on target bearing 321° T. Luckily, this lag caused [our] spread to enclose the entire formation."[13] At this instant *Maury*'s eight torpedoes, each set at a minimum 5-foot depth, running at intermediate speed and at a 2-degree spread, were on course to hit all four enemy ships (had *Shigure* been at its prescribed 500-yard interval rather than its actual 1,500-yard lag). It can therefore be safely assumed that the two torpedoes that struck lead ship *Hagikaze* came from *Maury*'s salvo. Under the circumstances, it can also be safely assumed that of the three torpedoes that hit *Arashi*, that one or more of these were also from *Maury*. It is even likely, considering the proximity of these first three destroyers and the timing of their hits, that one or both of the two hits made against *Kawakaze* can also be attributed to *Maury*. According to Albert Olsen, a claim later made by one of *Dunlap*'s crew argued that their ship had actually targeted ship #1 versus the usual doctrine of targeting #4, though this was without substantiation from any other source. Olsen had studied this claim thoroughly. He later wrote, "There appears to be no way to determine whose torpedoes hit what. I do not remember shifting targets . . . There is little doubt in my mind that *Craven* and *Maury* spreads sunk ships #1, #2, and #3. In retrospect, it is unlikely that the torpedoes of *Craven* and *Maury* could be so far off target to hit #4. Since #4 was lagging and the [post examination] showed a hit on [ship #4's] rudder [with additional] torpedo wakes that missed, I think [it] is logical that *Dunlap* was on target #4."[14] Therefore, the torpedo that apparently struck *Shigure*—which has its own unique controversy—appears to have come from *Dunlap*. In retrospect, it is entirely possible—perhaps even likely—that *Maury* had five to seven of the eight torpedo hits so counted this night.

Such evaluation is, however, only speculative, will likely never be affirmed, and should not dismiss the equal possibility that *Craven* and *Dunlap* also had successful hits of their own. In reference to *Maury*'s likely key role, Russell Crenshaw stated reflectively that "[as] for the five (more likely seven) torpedo hits on the three leading Japanese destroyers having been fired by *MAURY*, I have always thought so, but there is no way of proving it. Certainly, as evidenced in the ship's Action Reports, our ship was more concerned with the details of the torpedoes and their settings."[15]

At this point, it is also important to note that the success of this action was entirely due to a team effort. Burke's plan, in order to work, required that both teams of destroyers execute their roles perfectly and, so doing, complement each other's efforts. The torpedoes alone (outside of *Arashi*) did not complete the job, not even of ending the full threat of Sugiura's force. The destructive gunnery of Simpson's division was fully responsible for finishing off *Hagikaze* and *Kawakaze*, neither of which may have sunk without this added punch. Therefore, as evidenced through this historical record, it is correct to credit Burke's plan, as adopted and adapted by Moosbrugger, key for placing these two teams of American destroyers in the perfect position for all the advantage in a combat situation. And when the leadership and men of these teams executed their parts of this plan with the precision and perfection that was so ardently displayed, there was little chance afforded the Japanese to escape.

But what of the one that did get away? What of the torpedo that struck the rudder of *Shigure*? Hara claimed that this torpedo was "a dud." About the damage it caused he went on to explain, "It was not until *Shigure* went into [dry-dock] four months later that we found in the rudder a hole nearly two feet across. An American torpedo had passed right through it without exploding."[16] This brief description, however, only added to the controversies and even brought considerable question to Hara's overall story.

Torpedoes do not spin and cannot bore through steel like an armor-piercing shell. Many knowledgeable veterans and naval historians alike were astonished to read Hara's claim. A dud torpedo might severely damage, even rip away a rudder, but not pass through it only to leave a perfectly round 2-foot hole. Such was impossible. Therefore, it is reasonable to think that Hara—perhaps to bolster his own defense of leaving the action—was being disingenuous with his descriptions. Even so, *Shigure* did without question manage to escape, damaged or not. The rest of Hara's story appears correct and concurrent with all other aspects of the engagement, and this remains the only detailed account ever given from the Japanese perspective.

Without a doubt, however, the greatest controversy was raised in 1997, when Harold Shear (the former damage control officer aboard *Stack* who by this date was a retired admiral, having a long career with many important positions, including vice chief of naval operations) made the extraordinary claim that Rodger Simpson had ordered the depth charging of the Japanese survivors at Vella Gulf. During an interview with Paul Stillwell (Director, History Division, U.S. Naval Institute), Shear volunteered, "Now, this is a pretty dirty story that I am going to tell you. The commodore [Simpson] said, 'Okay, we're not going to let these men get ashore. They're within swimming distance of the beach. We're going to take care of them.' So we went through those masses of men dropping depth charges—pattern after pattern."[17]

When asked about his reaction to this order, Shear responded, "The depth charges were released from the bridge. We had a manual release, triggered release from the bridge. I didn't drop those depth charges, but I saw the men, and I knew exactly what was going on . . . There were thousands of men [in the water] . . . many, many hundreds . . . We made a very determined effort to get prisoners aboard, but even if we had, I don't think it would have made a difference . . . We probably would've gone ahead with that action anyway. I don't think you'll find that written up in books very much."[18]

Stillwell then asked Shear if this decision by Simpson had been "good?" Shear answered quite emphatically, "Yes, absolutely, absolutely, because we were in a hell of a fight down there in the Solomons. . . . there was no sense in letting several thousand [Japanese] get ashore, with or without their weapons."[19]

Though likely not intended, Shear's claim instantly darkened the legacy of both the Vella Gulf operation and the leadership of Commander Simpson. Furthermore, since this official allegation had come from such a reputable and celebrated naval commander as Admiral Shear, it could not be readily dismissed. But was this correct?

In the official after-action reports submitted following the Vella Gulf engagement, Simpson did indeed write: "When the survivors refused to be rescued, ComDiv A-2 [Division 15 commander, Simpson] should (here the author draws emphasis on Simpson's word "should") have destroyed them with depth charges."[20] Captain Wilfong concurred, writing in his recommendations, "Drop depth charges in the area where enemy survivors are swimming."[21] No doubt both commanders felt justified to make these statements because the survivors had been offered ample opportunity to surrender but had refused, leaving them as a hostile and perhaps armed force fully capable of returning to combat. Even so, these statements appeared only as recommendations. Nowhere in the reports of any of the commanders is there any confirmation that this depth charging actually occurred.

In 1998 and more descriptively so in 2000, John W. Ballantine, a former ensign and radar officer aboard *Lang* at Vella Gulf, made a remarkably similar accusation as that of Shear. In a letter to the author, he described his recollections of the action and wrote almost in passing of "Japanese in the water" and "our use of depth charges on them."[22] When asked to clarify his statements more thoroughly, Ballantine detailed the following: "I was . . . serving as radar officer near the bridge. The incident I observed, with some horror, occurred I would now guess at 2 or 3 o'clock A.M., when the action was pretty well completed . . . many Japanese were in the water . . . [At this time] my attention [was drawn] to the fantail from which the depth charges were being dropped. The battle being substantially over, I was on deck near the bridge, just outside my radar station. Needless to say, it was a jarring experience to me, a lasting acquaintance with the horrors of war . . . As to where the command [to drop depth charges] came from, I have no knowledge. I thought from [Simpson], who was a pretty severe gentleman. Nor do I have any remembrance of any particular discussion of the incidence, i.e. it seemed to be accepted as part of the game, perhaps correctly. . . . I think it is something none of us like to dwell, hence the ease of forgetting."[23] And so, Shear's controversial charge appeared to have support. Still, the question remained: Did this depth charging actually take place?

Former gunner's mate Charles Lee, who was at station that night near the depth charge racks on *Lang*, responded to these accusations with complete denial. "At no time did I see any type of underwater explosive device used in this area by the U.S.S. *Lang*. A depth charge would have created quite a mountain of water and would have killed or injured many in the water . . . I can't imagine any person would resort to a depth charge attack in this situation."[24]

Dandridge Gray affirmed Lee's recollection. "I was surprised on the subject of . . . the depth charging of the Japanese survivors. As Damage Control Officer, I was on the main deck during the battle and afterwards. I think I had a fairly good observation post . . . close to the depth charges. I saw nothing that appeared that the charges were going off, and I certainly heard nothing of that nature. I would categorically deny that this ever happened! I suppose it could have been discussed on the bridge or in the C.I.C., but I never heard one suggestion or discussion about it."[25]

Pemberton Southard was aghast at such an allegation. "*No depth charges* were dropped on any Japanese survivors at Vella Gulf, August 1943," he disputed stoutly. "There were no Bridge releases of depth charges. Phone talkers, Bridge to depth charge racks on [the] stern, told them when to roll one—fire 'K' guns, etc . . . . rack talker had to report 'ready' before the charge left the ship. Someone, torpedo men usually, had to remove a safety bar across [the] back of each rack. Someone had to put powder charges into each 'K' gun to launch it away from the ship. Each 'K' gun had to be reloaded by hand—I believe 8 to 10 600 lb. depth charges were in each rack on the fantail. A pattern could be several [depth charges] on a good contact—usually 4 [600 lb. charges] + 'K' guns. When . . . expended, it takes some time to get more from the depth charge below deck storage—hoist them all—get them charged with hydrostatic [fuses] inserted and onto racks. [At] Vella Gulf in the middle of the night, black—no lights—turning, slanting and [sea] spray, 'pattern after pattern' is ridiculous. No one on *Lang* [beyond the accounting of Ballantine] heard any underwater explosions; and believe me—'pattern after pattern' would have [been] heard. The depth charge settings would have to be on shallow for personnel and there would have been a lot of water going skyward. Plus the ship's speed would have to be high, my guess is 20 [knots] or more, so as not to get concussion damage. [Furthermore] . . . I do not believe [Shear] had any contact with Simpson. Simpson rode *Lang* not *Stack* and we anchored separately. His quote [of] Commodore Simpson . . . is hard to believe. . . . If my memory serves me—all [of] the depth charge talk occurred while returning to and at Purvis Bay, after the battle was long over—wardroom talk. I doubt if [Commodore] Simpson would have allowed any depth charging unless he was ordered to do so. And he was not. [As for Ballantine, we] were all at General Quarters stations, including Ensigns. They don't go wandering where their 'attention is attracted.' There were no depth charges dropped. No notes were ever taken but most thought dropping depth charges [on survivors] was a 'no-no'—like shooting an aviator parachuting from his airplane. Dropping charges didn't enter anyone's mind till well after the battle was over and we had left that area. It did get in the final action report but I believe [it was] forgotten after a few days."[26]

So, the debate continued. Certainly, the seriousness of this allegation could not be dismissed, especially considering that one side or the other of these statements—from equally honorable and reputable men—had to be mistaken. Proving or disproving any similar type of accusation is difficult. In this case, however—beyond Shear and Ballantine—no other veterans of the action have so far been found who remember anything remotely close to any depth charging of helpless Japanese survivors. Shear was correct that no mention of this has ever been referenced in any books, and perhaps for good reason—as there is, to date, no physical evidence to support that this ever happened.

On the contrary, all of the evidence available discredits it. None of the official reports note it, outside mention of such action in the recommendations section, which is acknowledged. Pat Robinson, an embedded reporter aboard the *Lang*, wrote nothing of this—and not even his short friendship with Simpson would have likely overridden his tangent for such graphic detail. More importantly, Hara does not mention in his narrative any occurrence of depth charging and—though he was not personally witness to these final moments following the action—he did speak with Sugiura afterward, giving him access to the accounting if it were true. Additionally, Japanese POWs from Vella Lavella, who were later interrogated about the Vella Gulf action, reportedly mention nothing of any depth charging. Surely, if this depth charging were true, the survivors would have made claim. Of even greater point, however, is the evidence of the disposition of Simpson's force in those final minutes before departing Vella. As alluded to by Southard, the ships would have to have been traveling at a rather fast pace in order to drop depth charges safely.[27] In the minutes prior to their departure, they were either traveling slowly (under 10 knots) or completely stopped, and time afterward did not allow for any lingering long enough to drop "pattern after pattern" of depth charges and still meet the deadline set by Wilkinson and as ordered by Moosbrugger. Furthermore, Simpson's ships throughout the operation remained in a linear formation, with *Lang* in the van and *Sterett* and *Stack* following, separated by no more than 500 yards. With this type of formation, dropping depth charges (if even just by *Lang*) would at any speed have placed the other ships at considerable risk. Certainly, no disrespect is intended to either Shear or Ballantine, as they obviously were both sharing what they honestly believed to be true, but given the available evidence, their accountings must be concluded as being confused and incorrect.[28] The logical conclusion is that *no* depth charges were dropped on Japanese survivors at Vella Gulf nor were the recommendations to do so in the future ever acted upon. There is just no existing physical evidence to provide anything to the contrary.

And, finally, there is the question of who should receive the greater credit for the success of the action, the planner or the executor? Arleigh Burke—while still at Noumea—obviously had feelings of envy when he first heard the news of Moosbrugger's Vella Gulf victory. Not only had this great triumph been achieved by a fellow commander and academy classmate, but also with use of Arleigh's own former command and only three days following his being forced to leave it behind. Vella Gulf was the very type of action that Burke had so desperately sought. No doubt his earlier disappointment was revisited. But ever the professional, Arleigh wasted no time at adding his own congratulations to Moosbrugger's growing list of commendations. His sentiments were both sincere and direct, even as they hinted of some self-gratification. "Dear Moose," he penned. "Your battle the other night will go down in history as one of the most successful actions ever fought. It was splendidly conceived and marvelously executed. . . ."[29] Having read the report in detail, Arleigh was convinced—as would later be affirmed—that Freddie had somehow learned of his own plan and had modified it for use at Vella Gulf. The noted comment of "splendidly conceived" was but a slight hint to his old classmate that he understood how the victory had been achieved.

But Moosbrugger never pretended to be responsible for the plan; only for its execution and its end results did he ever take credit. In retrospect, the victory at Vella Gulf opened the door even further for Burke, just as it extended greatness to both his and Moosbrugger's legacies.

So, what has become of these victors and vanquished of the Vella Gulf action? Who survived the war and who did not? Obviously, there is a large roster of men, both American and Japanese, who participated in the battle, and it would be impossible to record each individual history. For the most part, however, the number of Japanese who initially survived the action was perhaps only a fifth of their original number, and far fewer of these would survive the war. On the American side, an amazing 100 percent of the combatants survived—with Mitchell Sang having the only injury recorded during the engagement—and, with very few exceptions, all of these men would go home to their families at the end of the war. Even the six ships of Moosbrugger's command (*Dunlap*, *Craven*, *Maury*, *Lang*, *Sterett*, and *Stack*) would all survive the war, enduring numerous other important engagements to successfully return to the States at the conclusion of hostilities. Perhaps no other group of veteran warships and crews could boast such good fortune.

Shortly after the Vella Gulf victory, Arleigh Burke's command over Destroyer Squadron 12 ended, and by October he stood in command of Destroyer Squadron 23, a group soon to be more prominently known as the "Little Beavers." By this time Nimitz's decision to bypass certain Japanese strongpoints (the "leap-frogging" strategy long favored by Halsey, Wilkinson, and MacArthur for expediting the push toward Tokyo, and another of the reasons why these three were so overtly excited with Moosbrugger's Vella Gulf success) was leading to the battles for Bougainville (the last of the Solomon Island crucibles before moving on to the Admiralties, successfully bypassing and cutting off supplies to Rabaul and Kavieng, leaving these to wither away in the months to follow). This move, in turn, forced the Imperial Japanese Navy to rejoin the fray, and proved to be the last direct duels with Japanese surface warships till the opening of the Philippine operations in late 1944. It was during this approach to Bougainville that Burke's destroyers were thrown headlong into the melee and finally the determined commodore got his due, in two victorious night torpedo actions at Empress Augusta Bay (where Captain Hara and *Shigure* were once more a part of the opposition and who were again to escape) and Cape St. George. The battle at Cape St. George was even reminiscent of Vella Gulf, as it was again a purely destroyer versus destroyer action that left the Japanese fleet shy of three more of these valuable assets and without loss to the Americans. It was another nearly perfect action.

Burke's future list of achievements is equally significant. He finished out World War II as chief of staff for his old friend and mentor Marc Mitscher, serving with the carrier fleet till the capitulation of Japan. By this time, Arleigh was already a legend. He would go on to serve numerous leadership roles in the Navy, concluding this service as chief of naval operations (1955–1960) and retiring in 1961. Of all of his titles, however, none was more endearing to him than that of "31-Knot Burke," renowned as the greatest destroyer commander ever. Arleigh died at Bethesda Hospital on January 4, 1996. Throughout the seventy-two years of his life, Arleigh's most enduring fan, his beloved Bobbie, stood loyally at his side, both in good times and bad. True to form, one and a half years later, on July 4, Bobbie Burke followed her man to his next important station.

Frederick Moosbrugger closed out his service in World War II as commander over the deadly destroyer pickets at Okinawa, protecting the fleet from a firestorm of "Divine Wind" kamikaze pilots. Among the many ships to serve under his command during this volatile episode were *Lang*, *Sterett*, and *Stack*, three of his old Vella Gulf vanguard. After the war, Freddie's Navy career was maintained as advancements placed him in many new positions of authority, among which were commander of Destroyer Flotilla One and superintendent of the U.S. Naval Postgraduate School at Monterey, California. His retirement came in October 1956, with the rank of vice admiral.

Curiously, Moosbrugger never spoke much about the war or his role in it, even to his most immediate family, nor did he boast about his exceptional naval career. He did on occasion speak highly of Arleigh Burke and of his old friend Clifton Iverson, with whom he kept in touch after the war. Mostly, however, he quietly resigned to civilian life, playing the stock market and an occasional mean game of checkers. His darling love, Dorothy, preceded him in death in 1966. Freddie died on October 1, 1974, still his reserved self, and still a bit of a mystery to those who sought to know him. At the time of this writing, he is survived by only one of his sons, Edward, who lives in Santa Monica, California—Dave, the youngest, who lived in California, passed away on December 15, 2012; and the elder son, Fred, who lived in Maryland, passed away on October 1, 2013. Edward wrote most appropriately, "My father had a combination of courage and analytical ability. He knew how to plan and had the courage to act."[30] At Vella Gulf he did both.

Rodger Simpson, the controversial and colorful right-hand man to both Burke and Moosbrugger, remained true to his character right up to the end of the war. In spite of his perceived self-serving pursuit of publicity, he was at the forefront in acknowledging the talents of those who served under him. Shortly after the Vella Gulf action, he wrote, "The complete understanding of all possible situations encountered by the Division Commanders and Commanding Officers is largely responsible for the success achieved. Each knew what he was supposed to do and capably carried it out. . . . The three ships of Division A-2 are regularly assigned to Destroyer Division 15. The Division Commander is very proud of their first action as a unit."[31]

Still, Simpson never quite warmed up to Moosbrugger, and always felt that Burke would have been the better leader at Vella Gulf and therefore rightly deserved the victory. He wrote Burke shortly after the action, "You probably know by this time that Moosbrugger used your plan almost verbatim. . . . I got them accepted. . . . Thanks a million. The result was too easy. . . . I am looking forward to the time when the stakes are a lot higher and I can follow you in."[32] This admiration for Burke was no big secret, and neither was his lack of warmth for Moosbrugger.

Simpson was truly a naval hero worthy of the recognition. During his command of Destroyer Squadron 12—while in the fight to win the Bismarcks—Simpson's "gallantry and intrepidity" won him the Silver Star. Most notably, however, as the war was nearing its end, he was given responsibility for both planning and organizing the rescue of over 7,000 Allied prisoners of the Japanese, expediting their extraction before their captors could execute upon them any additional last-minute harm. For this effort he was awarded the Legion of Merit.

Rodger W. Simpson was indeed a man for his time. He retired from the Navy in 1951, a rear admiral, and died at the young age of sixty-six in 1964.

For his part in the Vella Gulf engagement, Pemberton Southard received the Silver Star. As expected, the Navy remained his choice of career. During his thirty years of active service he made seventeen moves, taking on the responsibilities of several staff and command positions (including plans officer for Commander Amphibious Group Two, C.O. and professor of naval science of the NROTC unit at Princeton University, chief staff officer for the Fleet Training Group Guantanamo Bay, and C.O., Fleet Training Center, Newport, Rhode Island) to then retire at the rank of captain in 1971. Pemberton and Jane then took up full-time residence in South Carolina, where they lived out the rest of their lives. The Southard-Duvall marriage that began in Charleston on September 12, 1943, encompassed sixty-three wonderful years. Sadly, Jane passed away on December 4, 2006. Despite his loss, Pemberton promised to carry on, to "Corpen [headed for] 90 then Corpen 100."[33] He exceeded the ninety, but his heart could go little more. On October 24, 2008, Pemberton Southard departed on his final journey—there was to be no additional two-year separation from Jane.

Not only at Vella Gulf did Albert Olsen successfully avenge his brother's death, but he also served Moosbrugger, Iverson, and *Dunlap* with the leadership necessary for making that victory a reality. For his fine efforts he too was awarded the Silver Star. But his leadership success did not end here. Afterward, as skipper of the *Hutchins* (DD-476), he led his command of officers and men through two critical invasion operations, at Iwo Jima and at Okinawa, having his destroyer credited with shooting down several enemy planes during the great kamikaze raid on April 6, 1945. He would later serve during both the Korean and Vietnam Wars (commander of USS *Hank* DD-702 from 1949 to 1951, flag secretary to CinCPacFleet 1953 to 1956, commander of Destroyer Division 172 1957 to 1960, commander of USS *Paul Revere* APA 248 1960 to 1961, chief of staff to the commander of Carrier Division 17 1961 to 1962, commander of Destroyer Squadron 7 1962 to 1963, director of Field Support Activity 1964, and finally commander of Naval Station San Diego 1966 to 1968). Olsen had a lifetime of commendable achievements (in addition to his Silver Star, he would later be awarded the Legion of Merit, Bronze Star, and the Vietnamese Distinguished Service Medal) well worth the boasting—though he was mostly content to "toast" old victories, heroic brothers, and the young Scandinavian sailor who ventured to start it all for him. Albert R. Olsen Jr. retired from the Navy as a captain. He passed away at the age of ninety-one on October 31, 2015.

Russell Crenshaw Jr. retired from the Navy as a captain in 1967. His naval skill and engineering ability are among the most renowned in the world. In 1955, his published work *Ship Handling* became for many world-class navies the "bible" for learning this important proficiency. He would later author additional books, including a narrative of *Maury*'s part in the Solomons crucible, entitled *South Pacific Destroyer* (Naval Institute Press, 1998), which includes a superb chapter on the Vella Gulf action. His engineering leadership was responsible for the successful introduction of two highly important surface-to-air missile systems, the Terrier and Polaris Systems. While serving at the Pentagon, as director of the Anti-Air Warfare Division, he oversaw the development of many of the Navy's weapons systems. In 1964, he was assigned to the staff of the secretary of defense, where he remained until his retirement and subsequent founding of his own engineering consultant firm. For his part in the Vella Gulf action, Russell Crenshaw Jr. was awarded the Silver Star. After retirement, he resided in Maryland, where he passed away on February 4, 2017.

Henry D. Davison, the straight-talking lieutenant of *Craven*'s CIC, wrote an unpublished article about the Vella Gulf action, which he titled "Grossly Underbid." In it he concluded, "we entered Purvis . . . with brooms at [the] mastheads and a proud list to starboard," noting the operation's success as a clean sweep and with all portside torpedoes away.[34] Davison was certainly proud of being a part of this action. For his leadership at Vella Gulf, he would also receive the Silver Star, and this he proudly added to the Purple Heart he was awarded for wounds received at Pearl Harbor. Davison's service in the Navy lasted long after the war ended, as he taught a term at the Naval Academy and subsequently served at several other impressive command positions. His retirement from the Navy came in 1963, as commander. He spent the next twenty-one years serving as a tenured instructor at the Department of Engineering Technology, St. Petersburg Junior College, St. Petersburg, Florida—where he lived with his wife, Betty, and where together they raised their two daughters. "Hank" (as he was best known to family and friends) Davison died February 19, 1999.

Harold Shear, the cadet known as "The Admiral," did indeed acquire the rank, and a four-star admiral at that. A renowned submariner, Shear's service in the Navy spanned forty-two years, wherein he held such positions as commander-in-chief of U.S. Naval Forces in Europe and vice chief of naval operations. He retired in 1980 as commander-in-chief of Allied Forces in Southern Europe.

After a lengthy illness, Adm. Harold Shear died at his home in Connecticut on February 7, 1999.

Shear's academy classmate, Joseph D. Jeffrey, retired from the Navy as a commander in 1964. Jeffrey would later assist his former boss, Charles R. Calhoun, with research for his book *Tin Can Sailor* (Naval Institute Press, 1993) and in it is given Jeffrey's splendid accounting of the Vella Gulf action. For wounds received at the naval Battle of Guadalcanal, Jeffrey was awarded the Purple Heart. Tragically, Joseph D. Jeffrey died at his home in Maryland in the spring of 2007 of a massive heart attack, just hours after his wife, Gina, had died from a massive stroke. He was eighty-seven.

Even before the war ended, Vining Sherman published his own excellent account of the Vella Gulf action, simply titled *The Battle of Vella Gulf* (U.S. Naval Institute Proceedings, January 1945). His story is full of great detail, displaying a recollection that is both vibrant and fresh. He also painted two wonderful paintings of the action, using his artistic gift to record the battle. These paintings were then presented to his old boss, Capt. Clifton Iverson—but both were later lost in a tragic house fire. Vining Sherman retired from the Navy as a captain in 1965. He is still known for his artistic talents, having not only painted and sketched many wonderful landscapes but also devoted much of his time as an art instructor. At the time of this writing, the author has lost all contact with Vining. His last residence was Vero Beach, Florida. No obituary for him has been located. If still living, his age would be 109, making him possibly the only living veteran of the Battle of Vella Gulf remaining.

After the war, Dandridge Gray decided he liked the West Coast better than the East and so he made his permanent home in California. Here, he and his wife, Joan, raised their family. Dan returned to his prewar occupational roots, in business, though he never forgot his experiences aboard the *Lang*. He would later state that his "pre-war life had been good . . . and I was happy . . . and [this] luck seemed to carry over to the *Lang*"—just as it continued for him in his days after.[35] Dandridge Gray was certainly no "90-day Blunder" as he once called himself. He was successful and still smiling throughout his life—and very much appreciative of his "lucky" association with one of the most fortunate ships of the war, the USS *Lang*. Dandridge Gray passed away on February 24, 2014.

Charles "Chuck" Lee remained aboard the *Lang* until June 1945. He then returned to the States and was discharged shortly after the war ended. Chuck and Patricia were finally rejoined to experience the marriage they had begun more than a year before. They established their permanent home in San Francisco. In 1950, Chuck began his next choice of careers—another having considerable risk—becoming a member of the renowned San Francisco Fire Department. The work suited him well. For thirty-two years he served the city and the department, retiring in 1982 as battalion chief, director of training. A fully tenured teacher and as an aside to his firefighting duties, Chuck also taught (part-time for twenty-eight years) Fire Science classes at the local city college. For Patricia and Chuck, the wartime romance that began in 1942 turned into a marriage that lasted seventy exciting years. Certainly, the Lees exemplified togetherness and love that by today's standards is a rarity, and both maintained an unwavering devotion to one another throughout it all. Their story is even highlighted in the Larry King book, *Love Stories of World War II* (Crown Publishing, 2001, pages 107–113). Charles Lee passed away on April 13, 2014, to be followed by Patricia on March 1, 2022.

Ralph Barber never became a doctor. Instead, he re-enlisted for four years in the active Naval Reserve and used the GI bill to go to school to become a pharmacist. He received his diploma and license in 1949 and quickly began his career. He eventually partnered with another individual at co-owning a drugstore. It was during this time, however, that Ralph became interested in an opening with the Federal Bureau of Narcotics, and he applied for the position. He was sworn in as an FBN agent on October 15, 1954. He remained with this agency through three subsequent mergers, as he eventually became an agent for the Drug Enforcement Administration. He retired in 1975.

Despite the obvious dangers of his occupation, Ralph's old high school sweetheart and wartime bride, Virginia, loyally remained at his side and was always his most avid supporter. Theirs was indeed a happy life, raising a family together, seeing the world, and sharing life with friends. Sadly, on July 16, 1998, just two months shy of their fifty-fifth wedding anniversary, Virginia passed away. The relationship was once again forced to go long-distance. In the meantime, Ralph maintained an active life, keeping close to his family and becoming instrumental in the leadership of the continuing yearly gatherings of the *Dunlap* crew reunions. The sailor, who initially had little love for the sea and ships, never forgot the little destroyer that brought him back from war in one piece. Nor did he forget his promise to Virginia, as Ralph Barber returned to his sweetheart's side on September 18, 2016.

Loyd Peters's stay aboard *Dunlap* lasted until the ship was decommissioned on December 14, 1945, when he finally headed home for his long overdue Christmas holiday. His time in the Navy lasted until he was discharged in 1947. He then joined the Naval Reserve and was called back to active-duty status on January 1, 1951, to serve an additional sixteen months during the Korean

Conflict. Eventually, Loyd returned to Kansas, married, and raised a family. Much like his shipmate and friend, Ralph Barber, Loyd maintained a close relationship with all of the former crew of the *Dunlap*, active in nearly every reunion. In retrospect, his naval experiences may not have been quite as "romantic" as he initially expected, but they were surely memorable and provided for him a treasure-trove of unforgettable friendships. Loyd Peters passed away on Valentine's Day, February 14, 2009.

Wilber Fultz often stated that his "years in the Navy were [among] the greatest experiences of his life," and he truly enjoyed sharing these experiences with so many of his friends and family.[36] The older brother who had joined the Navy with Wilber served most of his wartime service stationed in Australia, and he too came home to his family and friends. Wilber's younger brother, whom he had worked to help support, joined the Marines and was twice wounded in the Pacific, though he also managed to make it through the war alive. Just as he and his brothers had discussed it, they did indeed see a vast amount of the world—though not exactly as they had envisioned. Still, the experience was very worthwhile, teaching all three boys a great deal about life and living. For Wilber, he learned that home is still home, no matter how hard the life had seemed. So, he returned to Montana where once again he settled back into the saddle. In 1950, he married Helen Belle, and together they raised a family of three boys and one girl (one son was tragically lost to a severe asthma attack in 1988). Wilber Fultz passed away on March 16, 2001, just three months after celebrating his fiftieth wedding anniversary.

After the Vella Gulf action, Kaju Sugiura returned to Japan, where he served briefly at the Yokosuka Naval District. On December 1, 1943, he was given command of the heavy cruiser, *Haguro*. Just as his ambition dictated, Sugiura did indeed manage to become an admiral, promoted to rear admiral on May 1, 1945, while still in command of *Haguro*. He would not, however, survive the war. On May 16, during an engagement with British warships off Penang, Malaysia (the Battle of Malacca Strait), *Haguro* was sunk. Not content to survive another loss while under his command, Kaju Sugiura went down with his ship. As an added honor, his rank was thus posthumously promoted to vice admiral.

Tameichi Hara would be among only a small number of Japanese Vella Gulf veterans to survive the war. While still aboard *Shigure*, Hara faced the wrath of Arleigh Burke and his "Little Beavers" during the Battle of Empress Augusta Bay, where again he and his ship managed to escape. (Later, without Hara aboard but while still carrying his fighting spirit and good fortune, *Shigure* participated in the Battle of Surigao Strait, October 24-25, 1944, where she again made good her escape, as sole survivor of Admiral Nishimura's doomed Southern Force. *Shigure*'s superior luck finally ran out on January 24, 1945, when she was torpedoed by the American submarine *Blackfin* just off the Malayan coast and sunk.) Hara was shortly after relieved of his command of Destroyer Squadron 27, and he reported to Yokosuka Naval Station on December 27, 1943, where he began to instruct at the Torpedo School. Almost a full year later, on December 22, 1944, the demand for experienced combat commanders placed him back at sea, as captain of the light cruiser *Yahagi*. By April 6, 1945, the American invasion of Okinawa was well into its sixth day, and to counter the effort the Imperial Japanese Navy sent in its last big ship, the super-battleship *Yamato*, with *Yahagi* and eight destroyers as escort, to do battle. "The Ten-Go Operation," as it was named, was a one-way suicide mission, intended to blast its way into the thick of American shipping, sink as many transports as possible, and then beach the ships to be used as steel fortresses. But the force never reached its goal. American planes located the group during its passage and sank *Yamato*, *Yahagi*, and four of the escorting destroyers before they could do any harm. Hara lost his ship but survived the sinking. He returned to Japan to prepare for the defense of the homeland, instructing unconventional defensive tactics to young men (dressing them as women and priests to give them some advantage against American invaders). The war ended before the tactics could be used. Afterward, as a civilian, Hara returned to sea, commanding a merchant ship. His book, *Japanese Destroyer Captain* (Bantam Books, 1961) is among the best for an inside view of the Japanese navy during World War II, and in it is the only Japanese accounting given of the Battle of Vella Gulf. Tameichi Hara died in 1980. His grandfather would surely have been proud, for Tameichi was indeed a samurai of the highest order.

* * *

"Thus ended the Battle of Vella Gulf in a perfect American victory."

(Tameichi Hara, 1961)

Notes

Chapter One: Commanders: Leadership in the Making

1. Potter, *Admiral Arleigh Burke*, 4–5. This was a time when corporal punishment of children was an accepted form of correction, and Arleigh's father gave little quarter to irresponsible acts and/or lies for covering up such irresponsibility, meting out such discipline in good measure when his children gave him reason.
2. Potter, *Admiral Arleigh Burke*, 4–5. Clara had Arleigh well on his way to reading by first grade, and her challenges to him thereafter made him a very well-read student of literature by the time of his graduation.
3. Potter, *Admiral Arleigh Burke*, 6.
4. Potter, *Admiral Arleigh Burke*, 7.
5. Potter, *Admiral Arleigh Burke*, 7.
6. Potter, *Admiral Arleigh Burke*, 7.
7. Potter, *Admiral Arleigh Burke*, 8.
8. Potter, *Admiral Arleigh Burke*, 8.
9. Potter, *Admiral Arleigh Burke*, 8.
10. Potter, *Admiral Arleigh Burke*, 8.
11. Potter, *Admiral Arleigh Burke*, 8.
12. Potter, *Admiral Arleigh Burke*, 9.
13. Potter, *Admiral Arleigh Burke*, 9.
14. Potter, *Admiral Arleigh Burke*, 9.
15. Edward Moosbrugger email to author, October 28, 2004.
16. Edward Moosbrugger email to author, October 28, 2004. Jacob was born near Lucerne, Switzerland, in 1865, but shortly after this date his family moved to Wurttemburg, Germany. According to family history, Jacob was baptized in Germany three days after his birth in Switzerland. As a young adult Jacob moved to Philadelphia with two of his brothers. It was here that he met and eventually married his wife, German-born Rosine Maier, in 1892.
17. Edward Moosbrugger email to author, October 28, 2004.
18. Phone interview with Dave Moosbrugger, September 22, 2004
19. Edward Moosbrugger email to author, October 28, 2004.
20. Phone interview with Edward Moosbrugger, September 29, 2004.
21. In a phone conversation with the author on April 10, 2008, Elaine Turner (Frederick Moosbrugger's niece and Moosbrugger family historian) noted that she believed this

appointment was awarded from A. Lincoln Acker, who was the Republican representative for Philadelphia County at that time.

22. Potter, *Admiral Arleigh Burke*, 21.
23. Potter, *Admiral Arleigh Burke*, 22.
24. Potter, *Admiral Arleigh Burke*, 35.
25. Potter, *Admiral Arleigh Burke*, 42–43.
26. Potter, *Admiral Arleigh Burke*, 42–43.
27. Potter, *Admiral Arleigh Burke*, 46.
28. Following the conclusion of the First World War there were numerous concerns over the buildup of naval power. Great Britain, in particular, had great interests around the world and wanted to retain its naval dominance at preserving its colonial infrastructures. The United States and Japan were also growing in naval strength and worldwide influences. France and Italy too had strong naval forces and interests around the world commanding their concerns. Despite these nations being allies during the First World War, they had considerable distrust in each other's intentions for the future. One answer it seemed was to restrict naval construction in a way that would preserve the status quo. The Washington Conference in 1921 initiated the first naval limitation treaty, restricting tonnage and types of ships to be constructed by each naval power. This treaty was then, with some additional tweaks, reaffirmed at the London Conference in 1933. Unfortunately, there were loopholes within the treaties that allowed many nations to cheat. Only the United States seemed to follow the treaty to its strictest points, causing a future weakness in U.S. Naval forces that could easily be argued as the cause for the early disadvantages with the Japanese Pacific Fleet. Adding the Great Depression to the mix only compounded these issues as, due to the extreme loss of revenues, financing for naval construction was also severely slashed.
29. Potter, *Admiral Arleigh Burke*, 43–44.
30. Potter, *Admiral Arleigh Burke*, 44.
31. Potter, *Admiral Arleigh Burke*, 46–47.
32. Potter, *Admiral Arleigh Burke*, 51.
33. Potter, *Admiral Arleigh Burke*, 51.
34. Potter, *Admiral Arleigh Burke*, 52.
35. Potter, *Admiral Arleigh Burke*, 53.
36. Potter, *Admiral Arleigh Burke*, 53–54.
37. Withington, *Lucky Bag of 1923*, 70.
38. Withington, *Lucky Bag of 1923*, 70.
39. USS *Moosbrugger* (DD 980), "About the Destroyer's Name."
40. Chief of Naval Operations, *Dictionary of American Naval Fighting Ships, Vol. V*, 52.
41. Chief of Naval Operations, *Dictionary of American Naval Fighting Ships, Vol. V*, 52.
42. USS *Moosbrugger* (DD 980), "About the Destroyer's Name."
43. Chief of Naval Operations, *Dictionary of American Naval Fighting Ships, Vol. VII*, 316–17.
44. Frederick's two older sisters, Sophie and Mathilde, had also prematurely died in the 1920s. "So my father lost both parents and two sisters before he was age 30," noted Edward Moosbrugger in an October 28, 2004 email to the author.

45. Edward Moosbrugger, Email to author, October 28, 2004.
46. "Republican China"; and Ienaga, *Pacific War 1931–1945*, 58–67.
47. USS *Moosbrugger* (DD 980), "About the Destroyer's Name."
48. Chief of Naval Operations, *Dictionary of American Naval Fighting Ships, Vol. I*, 152.
49. USS *Moosbrugger* (DD 980), "About the Destroyer's Name."
50. Chief of Naval Operations, *Dictionary of American Naval Fighting Ships, Vol. VI*, 179–80.
51. USS *Moosbrugger* (DD 980), "About the Destroyer's Name."
52. Edward Moosbrugger, Email to author, October 28, 2004. According to family history Frederick and Dorothy were first married by the justice of the peace in Chester Co., Pennsylvania, but they were later married in the Catholic Church. Frederick was Lutheran and Dorothy was Catholic. Their sons were raised in the Catholic faith.
53. USS *Moosbrugger* (DD 980), "About the Destroyer's Name."
54. Chief of Naval Operations, *Dictionary of American Naval Fighting Ships, Vol. III*, 374–75.
55. Chief of Naval Operations, *Dictionary of American Naval Fighting Ships, Vol. III*, 374–75.
56. USS *Moosbrugger* (DD 980), "About the Destroyer's Name."
57. USS *Moosbrugger* (DD 980), "About the Destroyer's Name."
58. Morison, *History of United States Naval Operations in World War II, Vol. III*, 43.
59. Morison, *History of United States Naval Operations in World War II, Vol. III*, 46–47.
60. Morison, *History of United States Naval Operations in World War II, Vol. III*, 43.
61. Potter, *Admiral Arleigh Burke*, 54–55.
62. Potter, *Admiral Arleigh Burke*, 54–55.
63. Potter, *Admiral Arleigh Burke*, 54–55.
64. Potter, *Admiral Arleigh Burke*, 54–55.

Chapter Two: Pearl Harbor: Reality Strikes Home

1. Cohen, *East Wind Rain*, 19, 64, 263, 295. 2,403 deaths occurred as a result of the attack, of which 1,177 were aboard the *Arizona*. Another 1,178 individuals suffered wounds. Nineteen ships were sunk or seriously damaged; 188 planes were totally destroyed and another 159 were damaged. The Japanese losses amounted to five midget submarines and nine crewmen (one, Ens. Kazuo Sakamaki, survived and was captured—Japanese POW #1) and twenty-nine planes with fifty-five crewmen.
2. Roosevelt, address to the nation, December 8, 1941.
3. Davison, "Grossly Underbid," 1.
4. Davison, "Grossly Underbid," 1.
5. Davison, "Grossly Underbid," 1.
6. Nease, "Henry Donald Davison: USS Arizona Survivor Stories."
7. Nease, "Henry Donald Davison: USS Arizona Survivor Stories."
8. Morison, *History of United States Naval Operations in World War II, Vol. III*, 109. "*Arizona* lost almost four fifths of her complement—47 officers and 1056 men killed or missing, 5 officers [of whom Davison was one] and 39 men wounded . . ." This number given by Morison of the dead would later be revised to 1,177.

9. Nease, "Henry Donald Davison: USS Arizona Survivor Stories."
10. Fultz, Written response, January 20, 1998.
11. Helen Fultz, Letter to author, May 22, 2004.
12. Helen Fultz, Letter to author, May 22, 2004.
13. Helen Fultz, Letter to author, May 22, 2004.
14. Wilber Fultz, Written response, January 20, 1998.
15. Wilber Fultz, Written response, January 20, 1998.
16. Wilber Fultz, Written response, January 20, 1998.
17. Chief of Naval Operations, *Dictionary of American Naval Fighting Ships, Vol. II*, 203.
18. Morison, *History of United States Naval Operations in World War II, Vol. III*, 120–21.
19. Cohen, *East Wind Rain*, 97–98.
20. Radios picked up an unexplained plea, "Do not attack me," from a Bombing Squadron Six plane. "This is six baker three [6-B-3] an American plane," the call continued. This transmission was confusing to everyone who heard it. No one could make sense of the plea. Then the same pilot signaled he was preparing to crash-land in the ocean. Nothing more was heard.
21. USS *Moosbrugger* (DD 980), "About the Destroyer's Name."
22. Early 1942 letter transcript provided to author in Edward Moosbrugger email, October 28, 2004.
23. Edward Moosbrugger, By phone, September 29, 2004.
24. Kyle, "One Man's Navy Family," 27.
25. Olsen, Letter to author, October 1, 2004.
26. East Carolina University, *Biographical Sketch of Russell S. Crenshaw, Jr. (USS Maury)*.
27. Crenshaw, Letter to author, May 12, 1999.
28. USS *Lang* (DD 399) Log Report, Sunday, December 7, 1941.
29. Novak, *USS Lang—Fifth Anniversary*.
30. Southard, Letter to author, July 29, 2004.
31. Southard, Letter to author, June 2004.
32. Southard, Letter to author, June 2004.
33. Southard, Letter to author, June 2004.
34. Southard, Letter to author, June 2004.
35. Southard, Letter to author, June 2004.
36. Southard, Letter to author, December 1998.
37. CBS radio transcripts for December 7, 1941.
38. Barber, Forwarded letter to author, originally a biographical history developed for Ralph's daughter, Pamela, undated.
39. Barber, Forwarded letter to author, originally a biographical history developed for Ralph's daughter, Pamela, undated.
40. Barber, forwarded letter to author, originally a biographical history developed for Ralph's daughter, Pamela, undated.
41. Barber, forwarded letter to author, originally a biographical history developed for Ralph's daughter, Pamela, undated.

42. Arey and Tower, *1942 Lucky Bag*, 64.
43. Arey and Tower, *1942 Lucky Bag*, 205.
44. Sherman, "The Battle of Vella Gulf," U.S. Naval Institute Proceedings, January 1945, 61 (inset).
45. Sherman, "The Battle of Vella Gulf," U.S. Naval Institute Proceedings, January 1945, 61 (inset).
46. Peters, Email to author, March 1, 2007.
47. Peters, Letter to author, May 17, 2004.
48. Potter, *Admiral Arleigh Burke*, 55–56.
49. Potter, *Admiral Arleigh Burke*, 54.
50. Potter, *Admiral Arleigh Burke*, 54.
51. Roosevelt, address to the nation, December 8, 1941.
52. Though damaged, the *Nevada* was the only battleship in the harbor to make steam and get underway. The gallant effort, however, did not succeed. Once the Japanese saw it was trying to make an escape, their bombers concentrated attacks on the ship hoping to sink it in the narrow channel of the harbor's entrance, blocking its future use. Numerous bombs found their target and the damage became serious. Seeing that the ship was in danger of sinking, the captain directed the big battleship into the shallows south of Ford Island, where she was grounded and fortunately saved.
53. Edward Moosbrugger, By phone, September 29, 2004.
54. Edward Moosbrugger, Email to author, October 28, 2004.
55. Edward Moosbrugger, Email to author, November 4, 2007.
56. While five Japanese two-man submarines were deployed from larger submarines outside the harbor, only one was thought to have been successful at getting in. This one was sighted, attacked, and sunk by the destroyer *Monaghan*. For decades after, it was believed that no other midget submarines were successful at entering the harbor and at contributing to the attack. The Japanese, however, continued to promote that one other of the submarines had in fact entered the harbor and successfully torpedoed one of the battleships. This notion was consistently dismissed by historians. However, in 2009, an underwater expedition reexamined remains of a midget submarine initially found in 1994 among a debris field 5 miles south of the harbor entrance. This submarine was in three intentionally cut sections, having its torpedoes missing, but was exhibiting the distinctive figure-8 net cutter on its bow used solely for the Pearl Harbor attack. This immediately brought the discussion back to the forefront. In brief, it was determined that this was indeed the fifth midget, that it appears to have indeed fired its two torpedoes, and (considering the debris found with it) had afterward settled on the bottom in the West Loch of the harbor, where for some reason it could not escape. It was surmised that, following the May 1944 explosion of several LSTs in the West Loch, salvage crews later scooped up the submarine with the other debris and discarded it in the ocean dumpsite outside the harbor. Additionally, a well-known Japanese aerial photo, taken during the attack, does appear to show a midget submarine briefly bucking to the surface after firing its torpedoes, with these directly aligned at targeting the *West Virginia* and *Oklahoma*. It has also been determined that one of the torpedoes that struck the *Oklahoma* caused considerably more damage than the other torpedo strikes, indicating a larger explosive payload

indicative of the 800-pound warheads of the midget submarines. Despite such evidence, the debate continues.

57. Edward Moosbrugger, Email to author, October 28, 2004.

CHAPTER THREE: GUADALCANAL: GATEWAY TO HELL

1. Edward Moosbrugger, Email to author, October 28, 2004.
2. Davison, "Grossly Underbid," 1.
3. Hoyt, *Glory of the Solomons*, 23.
4. Potter, *Admiral Arleigh Burke*, 56–57.
5. Morison, *History of the United States Naval Operations in World War II, Vol. V*, 182–83.
6. Potter, *Admiral Arleigh Burke*, 57–58.
7. Davison, "Grossly Underbid," 3.
8. Morison, *History of the United States Naval Operations in World War II, Vol. VI*, 212.
9. Olsen, Follow-up phone interview, September 29, 2004; Kyle, "One Man's Navy Family," 28.
10. Olsen, Follow-up phone interview, September 29, 2004.
11. Olsen, Follow-up phone interview, September 29, 2004.
12. Kyle, "One Man's Navy Family," 28.
13. Calhoun, *Tin Can Sailor*, 48.
14. Calhoun, *Tin Can Sailor*, 74–96.
15. Calhoun, *Tin Can Sailor*, 74–96.
16. Calhoun, *Tin Can Sailor*, 95–97.
17. Calhoun, *Tin Can Sailor*, 119.
18. Sherman, "The Battle of Vella Gulf," U.S. Naval Institute Proceedings, January 1945, 61.
19. Crenshaw, *South Pacific Destroyer*, 23.
20. Pihl and Johnson Jr., *Lucky Bag of 1921*, 109.
21. USS *Simpson* (FFG 56), *About the Ship's Name.*
22. USS *Simpson* (FFG 56), *About the Ship's Name*; Chief of Naval Operations, *Dictionary of American Naval Fighting Ships*, Vol. IV, 195.
23. Joint Army-Navy Assessment Committee, *Japanese Naval and Merchant Shipping Losses*, 34.
24. USS *Simpson* (FFG 56), *About the Ship's Name.*
25. Chief of Naval Operations, *Dictionary of American Naval Fighting Ships*, Vol. IV, 195.
26. Chief of Naval Operations, *Dictionary of American Naval Fighting Ships*, Vol. IV, 196.
27. Southard, Letter to author, July 29, 2004.
28. Barber, A portion of an autobiography made for his daughter, Pamela, and forwarded to the author, undated, 3.
29. Barber, A portion of an autobiography made for his daughter, Pamela, and forwarded to the author, undated, 3.

30. Barber, A portion of an autobiography made for his daughter, Pamela, and forwarded to the author, undated, 3.
31. Barber, A portion of an autobiography made for his daughter, Pamela, and forwarded to the author, undated, 3.
32. Barber, A portion of an autobiography made for his daughter, Pamela, and forwarded to the author, undated, 3.
33. Lee, Written response, September 12, 2004.
34. Lee, Written response, September 12, 2004.
35. Lee, Written response, September 12, 2004.
36. Lee, Written response, September 12, 2004.
37. Lee, Written response, September 12, 2004.
38. Lee, Written response, September 12, 2004.
39. Lee, Written response, September 12, 2004.
40. Lee, Written response, September 12, 2004.
41. Lee, Written response, September 12, 2004.
42. Lee, Written response, September 12, 2004.
43. Lee, Written response, September 12, 2004.
44. Peters, Email to author, March 1, 2007.

Chapter Four: The Tokyo Express: "Hellova Nuisance"

1. Tanaka, *Japanese Navy in World War II*, 54.
2. Sherman, "Battle of Vella Gulf," U.S. Naval Institute Proceedings, January 1945, 61.
3. Tanaka, *Japanese Navy in World War II*, 55.
4. Tanaka, *Japanese Navy in World War II*, 61.
5. Tanaka, *Japanese Navy in World War II*, 61.
6. Tanaka, *Japanese Navy in World War II*, 60.
7. Tanaka, *Japanese Navy in World War II*, 61.
8. Tanaka, *Japanese Navy in World War II*, 68–69.
9. Tanaka, *Japanese Navy in World War II*, 69.
10. Tanaka, *Japanese Navy in World War II*, 69.
11. Tanaka, *Japanese Navy in World War II*, 69.
12. Hara, *Japanese Destroyer Captain*, 165.
13. Hara, *Japanese Destroyer Captain*, 165.
14. Tanaka, *Japanese Navy in World War II*, 72–73.
15. Hara, *Japanese Destroyer Captain*, 10–11.
16. Hara, *Japanese Destroyer Captain*, 12.
17. Hara, *Japanese Destroyer Captain*, 17.
18. Hara, *Japanese Destroyer Captain*, 35.
19. Hara, *Japanese Destroyer Captain*, 166.
20. Hara, *Japanese Destroyer Captain*, 103.
21. Hara, *Japanese Destroyer Captain*, 185.
22. Hara, *Japanese Destroyer Captain*, 181.
23. Hara, *Japanese Destroyer Captain*, 181.

Chapter Five: Tulagi: The Gathering

1. Sherman, *The Battle of Vella Gulf*, U.S. Naval Institute Proceedings, January 1945, 63.

2. Davison, "Grossly Underbid," 2.

3. Davison, "Grossly Underbid," 2.

4. Morison, *History of United States Naval Operations in World War II, Vol. V*, 10.

5. Potter, *Admiral Arleigh Burke*, 79.

6. This quote is an author's paraphrase of a more in-depth yet non-detailed conversation between Wilkinson and Burke. Potter, *Admiral Arleigh Burke*, 83–84.

7. This quote is an author's paraphrase of a more in-depth yet non-detailed conversation between Wilkinson and Burke. Potter, *Admiral Arleigh Burke*, 83–84.

8. Crenshaw, *South Pacific Destroyer*, 199.

9. Crenshaw, *South Pacific Destroyer*, 199.

10. Iverson, *Some Observations on the Battle of Vella Gulf*, 4.

11. Iverson, *Some Observations on the Battle of Vella Gulf*, 1.

12. Hailey, "Lure of the 'Tin Cans,'" *New York Times Magazine*, May 16, 1943.

13. Hailey, "Lure of the 'Tin Cans,'" *New York Times Magazine*, May 16, 1943.

14. Hailey, "Lure of the 'Tin Cans,'" *New York Times Magazine*, May 16, 1943.

15. Gray, Letter to the author, May 25, 2004.

16. Gray, Letter to the author, May 25, 2004.

17. Fultz, Written response, January 20, 1998.

18. Lee, Written response, September 12, 2004.

19. Barber, From an autobiographical essay written to his daughter, Pamela, copied and forwarded to the author, undated.

20. Roscoe, *United States Destroyer Operations in World War II*, introduction, xvii–xviii.

Chapter Six: The Mission: Facing the Challenges

1. Commander in Chief, Pacific Fleet, *Pacific Fleet Tactical Bulletin No. 4TB-42*, November 26, 1942.

2. Commander in Chief, Pacific Fleet, *Pacific Fleet Tactical Bulletin No. 4TB-42*, November 26, 1942.

3. Commander Destroyers, Pacific Fleet, *CIC Handbook for Destroyers Pacific Fleet*, June 24, 1943, preface.

4. Commander Destroyers, Pacific Fleet, *CIC Handbook for Destroyers Pacific Fleet*, June 24, 1943, preface.

5. Southard, Written response, December 1998.

6. Olsen, Written response, January 29, 1998.

7. Wilkinson, author's reconstruction of events and dialogue of Admiral Wilkinson as described in Commander in Chief, U.S. Fleet, *Information Bulletin No. 11, Chapter 58, Battle Experience Naval Operations Solomon Islands Area 12 July–10 August 1943: Night 6-7 August 1943, Battle of Vella Gulf Between Task Group 31.2 and Japanese Light Forces*, 2.

8. Hara, *Japanese Destroyer Captain*, 183.

9. Hara, *Japanese Destroyer Captain*, 183–85.

10. Hara, *Japanese Destroyer Captain*, 185.

11. Hara, *Japanese Destroyer Captain*, 185.

12. Hara, *Japanese Destroyer Captain*, 185.
13. Dialogue given as it was [and is] Naval protocol.
14. Dialogue given as it was [and is] Naval protocol.
15. Commander in Chief, U.S. Fleet, *Information Bulletin No. 11, Chapter 58, Battle Experience Naval Operations Solomon Islands Area 12 July–10 August 1943: Night 6-7 August 1943, Battle of Vella Gulf Between Task Group 31.2 and Japanese Light Forces*, 2.
16. Sherman, *The Battle of Vella Gulf*, U.S. Naval Institute Proceedings, January 1945, 64.
17. Sherman, *The Battle of Vella Gulf*, U.S. Naval Institute Proceedings, January 1945, 64.
18. Author's reconstructed dialogue of this conversation based upon the following sources: Commander in Chief, U.S. Fleet, *Information Bulletin No. 11, Chapter 58, Battle Experience Naval Operations Solomon Islands Area 12 July–10 August 1943: Night 6-7 August 1943, Battle of Vella Gulf Between Task Group 31.2 and Japanese Light Forces*, 2; Morison, *History of the United States Naval Operations in World War II, Vol. VI*, 213; Roscoe, *United States Destroyer Operations in World War II*, 233; U.S. Navy, Office of Naval Intelligence, *Combat Narratives. Solomon Islands Campaign*, 3.
19. Author's reconstructed dialogue of this conversation based upon the following sources: Commander in Chief, U.S. Fleet, *Information Bulletin No. 11, Chapter 58, Battle Experience Naval Operations Solomon Islands Area 12 July–10 August 1943: Night 6-7 August 1943, Battle of Vella Gulf Between Task Group 31.2 and Japanese Light Forces*, 2; Morison, *History of the United States Naval Operations in World War II, Vol. VI*, 213; Roscoe, *United States Destroyer Operations in World War II*, 233; U.S. Navy, Office of Naval Intelligence. *Combat Narratives. Solomon Islands* Campaign, 3.
20. Commander in Chief, U.S. Fleet, *Information Bulletin No. 11, Chapter 58, Battle Experience Naval Operations Solomon Islands Area 12 July–10 August 1943: Night 6-7 August 1943, Battle of Vella Gulf Between Task Group 31.2 and Japanese Light Forces*, 2.
21. Author's paraphrase of a paraphrased reconstruction of dialogue as given by: Morison, *History of the United States Naval Operations in World War II, Vol. VI*, 213.
22. Sherman, *The Battle of Vella Gulf*, U.S. Naval Institute Proceedings, January 1945, 64.
23. Sherman, *The Battle of Vella Gulf*, U.S. Naval Institute Proceedings, January 1945, 64.
24. Potter, *Admiral Arleigh Burke*, 83.
25. Pritchett, Written response, June 2, 1998.
26. Rowland and Boyd, *U.S. Navy Bureau of Ordnance in World War II*, 90–130.
27. Commander in Chief, U.S. Fleet, *Information Bulletin No. 11, Chapter 58, Battle Experience Naval Operations Solomon Islands Area 12 July–10 August 1943: Night 6-7 August 1943, Battle of Vella Gulf Between Task Group 31.2 and Japanese Light Forces*, 17–18.
28. Fultz, Written response, January 20, 1998.
29. Fisher, By phone, August 28, 1999. (In an in-person interview that took place with the author on August 8, 2008, Fisher noted that initial settings were prescribed differently for various opposing ship types—battleships, cruisers, destroyers, etc.—and his recollection was that 12 feet was the usual setting for destroyers.)
30. Crenshaw, *South Pacific Destroyer*, 207.

CHAPTER SEVEN: ALL AHEAD: INTO DESTINY'S DARKNESS

1. Commander in Chief, U.S. Fleet. *Information Bulletin No. 11, Chapter 58, Battle Experience Naval Operations Solomon Islands Area 12 July–10 August 1943: Night 6-7 August 1943, Battle of Vella Gulf Between Task Group 31.2 and Japanese Light Forces*, 17–18.
2. Shear, Interview transcript as given to Paul Stillwell, *Reminiscences of Admiral Harold Edson Shear*, 77–78.
3. USS *Dunlap* DD 384 Action Report, 2.
4. USS *Dunlap* DD 384 Action Report, 2.
5. Southard, Letter to author, June 2004.
6. Southard, Written response, December 1998.
7. Gaither, Written response, February 1998; Lazarz, Written response, January 2, 1998; Rivera, Written response, January 8, 1998.
8. Morison, *History of the United States Naval Operations in World War II, Vol. VI*, 214.
9. Poitevin, Written response, January 2, 1998.
10. Davison, "Grossly Underbid," 3–4.
11. Olsen, Written response, January 29, 1998.
12. USS *Dunlap* DD 384 Action Report, 2.
13. USS *Dunlap* DD 384 Action Report, 2.
14. Davison's reference to *Helena* was in noting the previous month's action in nearby Kula Gulf, also against the Tokyo Express, wherein the cruiser *Helena* was sunk by three well-placed Japanese torpedoes.
15. Davison, "Grossly Underbid," 3.
16. Hara, *Japanese Destroyer Captain*, 187.
17. Hara, *Japanese Destroyer Captain*, 187.
18. Hara, *Japanese Destroyer Captain*, 187.
19. U.S. Navy, Office of Naval Intelligence. *Combat Narratives. Solomon Islands Campaign*, 4. The word *True* in ship headings throughout refers to true north, as opposed to magnetic north.
20. USS *Dunlap* DD 384 Action Report, 2.
21. Calhoun, *Tin Can Sailor*, 119–20.
22. Lanz, Written response, January 9, 1998.
23. Lanz, Written response, January 9, 1998.
24. Calhoun, *Tin Can Sailor*, 119.
25. USS *Dunlap* DD 384 Action Report, 2, 9.
26. Barber, Written response, January 5, 1998.
27. Olsen, Written response, January 29, 1998.
28. Calhoun, *Tin Can Sailor*, 120.
29. USS *Dunlap* DD 384 Action Report, 9.
30. USS *Dunlap* DD 384 Action Report, 14.
31. USS *Dunlap* DD 384 Action Report, 2.
32. Sherman, *The Battle of Vella Gulf.* U.S. Naval Institute Proceedings, January 1945, 66.
33. Wallick, Written response, February 12, 1998.
34. Calhoun, *Tin Can Sailor*, 120.

35. Gray, Written response, December 11, 1998.
36. Shear, Interview transcript as given to Paul Stillwell, *Reminiscences of Admiral Harold Edson Shear*, 75.
37. Haden, Untitled/undated essay written a few days after the battle.
38. Lee, Written response, September 5, 2004.
39. Fultz, Written response, January 20, 1998.
40. Peters, Email to author, June 6, 2004.
41. Peters, Email to author, June 6, 2004.
42. It should be pointed out that for some unexplained reason Captain Hara, in his *Japanese Destroyer Captain* narrative, denoted time differences of as much as two hours in comparison with Moosbrugger and the other American destroyer timetables. In this case Hara referenced 7 P.M. whereas Moosbrugger referenced 9 P.M. To avoid confusion, American logged times are referenced in this narrative.
43. Hara, *Japanese Destroyer Captain*, 187.
44. USS *Dunlap* DD 384 Action Report, 3.
45. USS *Dunlap* DD 384 Action Report, 9.
46. Commander in Chief, U.S. Fleet, *Information Bulletin No. 11, Chapter 58, Battle Experience Naval Operations Solomon Islands Area 12 July–10 August 1943: Night 6-7 August 1943, Battle of Vella Gulf Between Task Group 31.2 and Japanese Light Forces*, Iverson and Moosbrugger, 5; U.S. Navy, Office of Naval Intelligence, *Combat Narratives, Solomon Islands Campaign*, 5; USS *Dunlap* DD 384 Action Report, 3, 9.
47. Allison, Written response, February 24, 1998.
48. Conner, Written response, January 5, 1998.
49. Davison, "Grossly Underbid," 4.
50. USS *Stack* DD 406 Action Report, 2.
51. Allison, Written response, February 24, 1998.
52. Lanz, Written response, January 9, 1998.
53. Allison, Written response, February 24, 1998.
54. USS *Dunlap* DD 384 Action Report, 3.
55. USS *Dunlap* DD 384 Action Report, 3, 10.
56. USS *Dunlap* DD 384 Action Report, 3.
57. Allison, Written response, February 24, 1998.
58. Author's reconstructed events and dialogue as sourced through: Southard, Written response, December 1998, and follow-up by phone, December 4, 2006.
59. Author's reconstructed events and dialogue as sourced through: Southard, Written response, December 1998, and follow-up by phone, December 4, 2006.
60. Author's reconstructed events and dialogue as sourced through USS *Dunlap* DD 384 Action Report, 3, 10.
61. Author's reconstructed events and dialogue as sourced through USS *Dunlap* DD 384 Action Report, 3, 10.
62. Author's reconstructed events and dialogue as sourced through USS *Dunlap* DD 384 Action Report, 3, 10.
63. Author's reconstructed events and dialogue as sourced through USS *Dunlap* DD 384 Action Report, 3, 10.

64. Author's reconstructed events and dialogue as sourced through USS *Dunlap* DD 384 Action Report, 3, 10.

65. Author's reconstructed events and dialogue as sourced through USS *Dunlap* DD 384 Action Report, 3, 10.

66. Author's reconstructed events and dialogue as sourced through USS *Dunlap* DD 384 Action Report, 3, 10.

67. Author's reconstructed events and dialogue as sourced through USS *Dunlap* DD 384 Action Report, 3, 10.

68. Author's reconstruction of events and dialogue as sourced through: Haden, Written response, undated, approximately February 1998, and untitled/undated essay written a few days after the battle.

69. Author's reconstructed events and dialogue as sourced through USS *Dunlap* DD 384 Action Report, 3, 10.

70. Hara, *Japanese Destroyer Captain*, 187.

71. Hara, *Japanese Destroyer Captain*, 187.

72. Hara, *Japanese Destroyer Captain*, 187.

73. Morison, *History of the United States Naval Operations in World War II, Vol. VI*, 214–15.

74. Hara, *Japanese Destroyer Captain*, 187–88.

75. Hara, *Japanese Destroyer Captain*, 188.

76. Hara, *Japanese Destroyer Captain*, 188.

77. Pritchett, Written response, June 2, 1998.

Chapter Eight: Execute: The Moment of Truth

1. USS *Dunlap* DD 384 Action Report, 4, 10.
2. USS *Dunlap* DD 384 Action Report, 4, 10.
3. USS *Craven* DD 382 Action Report, 2.
4. Davison, "Grossly Underbid," 5.
5. USS *Dunlap* DD 384 Action Report, 4, 10.
6. USS *Dunlap* DD 384 Action Report, 4, 11.
7. Author's reconstructed event and dialogue as sourced through: Haden, Written response to author, undated, approximately February 1998, and untitled/undated essay written a few days after the battle.
8. USS *Dunlap* DD 384 Action Report, 4, 11.
9. Southard, Written response, December 1998.
10. Crenshaw, *South Pacific Destroyer*, 210.
11. Davison, "Grossly Underbid," 5.
12. Davison, "Grossly Underbid," 3.
13. USS *Dunlap* DD 384 Action Report, 5.
14. Haden, Untitled/undated essay written a few days after the battle; USS *Dunlap* DD 384 Action Report, 3, where it is noted that "visibility [was] approximately 3500 to 4000 yards. The sky was completely overcast and the ship encountered intermittent light rain squalls prior to and during the engagement."

15. Haden, Untitled/undated essay written a few days after the battle; and Haden, Written response, undated, approximately February 1998.
16. USS *Dunlap* DD 384 Action Report, 11.
17. Olsen, Written response, January 29, 1998.
18. Gaither, Written response, February 1998.
19. Haden, Untitled/undated essay written a few days after the battle.
20. Commander in Chief, U.S. Fleet, *Information Bulletin No. 11, Chapter 58, Battle Experience Naval Operations Solomon Islands Area 12 July–10 August 1943: Night 6-7 August 1943, Battle of Vella Gulf Between Task Group 31.2 and Japanese Light Forces,* Moosbrugger, 17.
21. Davison, "Grossly Underbid," 6.
22. USS *Dunlap* DD 384 Action Report, 16.
23. Commander in Chief, U.S. Fleet, *Information Bulletin No. 11, Chapter 58, Battle Experience Naval Operations Solomon Islands Area 12 July–10 August 1943: Night 6-7 August 1943, Battle of Vella Gulf Between Task Group 31.2 and Japanese Light Forces*, 8.
24. Hara, *Japanese Destroyer Captain*, 188.
25. Reconstructed event and dialogue as sourced through: Hara, *Japanese Destroyer Captain*, 188.
26. Reconstructed event and dialogue as sourced through: Morison, *History of the United States Naval Operations in World War II, Vol. VI*, 216.
27. Hara, *Japanese Destroyer Captain*, 188.
28. Davison, "Grossly Underbid," 6.
29. Wallick, Written response, February 12, 1998.
30. Peters, Written response, January 12, 1998.
31. Peters, Written response, January 12, 1998.
32. Haden, untitled/undated essay written a few days after the battle.
33. Lazarz, Written response, January 2, 1998.
34. Reconstructed events and dialogue as sourced through: Morison, *History of the United States Naval Operations in World War II, Vol. VI*, 218.
35. Reconstructed events and dialogue as sourced through: Morison, *History of the United States Naval Operations in World War II, Vol. VI*, 218.
36. Reconstructed event and dialogue as sourced through: Hara, *Japanese Destroyer Captain*, 188–90.
37. Reconstructed event and dialogue as sourced through: Hara, *Japanese Destroyer Captain*, 188–90.
38. Hara, *Japanese Destroyer Captain*, 188–90.
39. Reconstructed event and dialogue as sourced through: Hara, *Japanese Destroyer Captain*, 190.
40. Wallick, Written response, February 12, 1998.
41. USS *Craven* DD 382 Action Report, Statement of Patrick Gerald Lynch, FC2c, Enclosure "C," 2.
42. USS *Craven* DD 382 Action Report, Statement of Martin Woodrow Hullender, Y1c, Enclosure "C," 5.
43. Poitevin, Written response, January 2, 1998.

44. Barber, Written response, January 5, 1998.

45. Fultz, Written response, January 20, 1998.

46. Commander in Chief, U.S. Fleet, *Information Bulletin No. 11, Chapter 58, Battle Experience Naval Operations Solomon Islands Area 12 July–10 August 1943: Night 6-7 August 1943, Battle of Vella Gulf Between Task Group 31.2 and Japanese Light Forces*, 12.

47. Commander in Chief, U.S. Fleet, *Information Bulletin No. 11, Chapter 58, Battle Experience Naval Operations Solomon Islands Area 12 July–10 August 1943: Night 6-7 August 1943, Battle of Vella Gulf Between Task Group 31.2 and Japanese Light Forces*, 12.

48. Shear, Interview transcript as given to Paul Stillwell, *Reminiscences of Admiral Harold Edson Shear*, 75.

49. Reconstructed dialogue as sourced through: Hara, *Japanese Destroyer Captain*, 190.

50. Reconstructed dialogue as sourced through: Hara, *Japanese Destroyer Captain*, 190.

51. Reconstructed dialogue as sourced through: Hara, *Japanese Destroyer Captain*, 191.

52. Reconstruction of events and dialogue of the "one ship was escaping" report is sourced through: Iverson, *Some Observations on the Battle of Vella Gulf*, 2. However, it should be noted that no direct reference of this is given in any of the action reports, only an indirect reference of "at 2349 [11:49 P.M.] the lagging contact grew noticeably smaller . . . until at 2351 [11:51 P.M.] it disappeared . . ." is given by Iverson in *Information Bulletin No. 11, Chapter 58, Battle Experience Naval Operations Solomon Islands Area 12 July–10 August 1943: Night 6-7 August 1943, Battle of Vella Gulf Between Task Group 31.2 and Japanese Light Forces*, 22.

53. Commander in Chief, U.S. Fleet. *Information Bulletin No. 11, Chapter 58, Battle Experience Naval Operations Solomon Islands Area 12 July–10 August 1943: Night 6-7 August 1943, Battle of Vella Gulf Between Task Group 31.2* and Japanese Light Forces, 21. It should be noted here that this deficiency was concurrent on all six of the destroyers, but especially so on *Dunlap* having the PPI scope a deck below in the chart house (all others were located directly behind the bridge in the captain's emergency cabin) and that Moosbrugger stated that this correction could not be made "soon enough."

54. Commander in Chief, U.S. Fleet, *Information Bulletin No. 11, Chapter 58, Battle Experience Naval Operations Solomon Islands Area 12 July–10 August 1943: Night 6-7 August 1943, Battle of Vella Gulf Between Task Group 31.2* and Japanese Light Forces, 22. By 11:59 P.M. the reported "escaping" target had faded away, and by 12:00 midnight a third blip on the radar screen had disappeared. By this time, it was believed that only two enemy ships were remaining afloat. But, Moosbrugger had no hard confirmations, so he acted with the presumption that all four enemy combatants still remained—and it would prove wise of him to do so.

55. Calhoun, *Tin Can Sailor*, 122.

56. Calhoun, *Tin Can Sailor*, 123.

57. Gray, Written response, December 11, 1998. Contact was actually first made at 11:33 P.M. Gray's point was that the execution was going on time as planned.

58. Gray, Written response, December 11, 1998.

59. Lee, Written response, September 12, 2004.

60. Southard, Written response, December 1998.

Chapter Nine: Commence Fire: Finishing the Deed

1. Reconstructed dialogue as sourced through: USS *Lang* DD 399 Action Report, 3.
2. USS *Lang* DD 399 Action Report, 3.
3. USS *Stack* DD 406 Action Report, 3.
4. USS *Stack* DD 406 Action Report, 3.
5. Commander in Chief, U.S. Fleet, *Information Bulletin No. 11, Chapter 58, Battle Experience Naval Operations Solomon Islands Area 12 July–10 August 1943: Night 6-7 August 1943, Battle of Vella Gulf Between Task Group 31.2 and Japanese Light Forces*, 8; USS *Dunlap* DD 384 Action Report, 11.
6. Commander in Chief, U.S. Fleet, *Information Bulletin No. 11, Chapter 58, Battle Experience Naval Operations Solomon Islands Area 12 July–10 August 1943: Night 6-7 August 1943, Battle of Vella Gulf Between Task Group 31.2 and Japanese Light Forces*, 9.
7. Conner, Written response, January 5, 1998.
8. Conner, Written response, January 5, 1998.
9. Barber, Written response, January 5, 1998.
10. USS *Maury* DD 401 Action Report, 3.
11. USS *Dunlap* DD 384 Action Report, 6, 21; USS *Craven* DD 382 Action Report, 3.
12. Reconstructed events and dialogue by author as sourced through: USS *Dunlap* DD 384 Action Report, 6, 21; Commander in Chief, U.S. Fleet, *Information Bulletin No. 11, Chapter 58, Battle Experience Naval Operations Solomon Islands Area 12 July–10 August 1943: Night 6-7 August 1943, Battle of Vella Gulf Between Task Group 31.2 and Japanese Light Forces*, 22.
13. USS *Dunlap* DD 384 Action Report, 12.
14. Reconstructed events and dialogue by author as sourced through: USS *Craven* DD 382 Action Report, 3–5.
15. Reconstructed events and dialogue by author as sourced through: USS *Maury* DD 401 Action Report, 3; Crenshaw, *South Pacific Destroyer*, 214.
16. USS *Dunlap* DD 384 Action Report, 6.
17. USS *Dunlap* DD 384 Action Report, 6.
18. USS *Dunlap* DD 384 Action Report, 26.
19. Reconstructed events and dialogue by author as sourced through: Peters, Written response, January 12, 1998.
20. USS *Maury* DD 401 Action Report, 2–3.
21. Commander in Chief, U.S. Fleet, *Information Bulletin No. 11, Chapter 58, Battle Experience Naval Operations Solomon Islands Area 12 July–10 August 1943: Night 6-7 August 1943, Battle of Vella Gulf Between Task Group 31.2 and Japanese Light Forces*, 9.
22. USS *Maury* DD 401 Action Report, 3.
23. USS *Dunlap* DD 384 Action Report, 12.
24. Sherman, *The Battle of Vella Gulf*, U.S. Naval Institute Proceedings, 69.
25. Reconstructed events and dialogue by author as sourced through: USS *Dunlap* DD 384 Action Report, 6, 12.
26. Reconstructed dialogue by author as sourced through: Commander in Chief, U.S. Fleet, *Information Bulletin No. 11, Chapter 58, Battle Experience Naval Operations Solomon*

Islands Area 12 July–10 August 1943: Night 6-7 August 1943, Battle of Vella Gulf Between Task Group 31.2 and Japanese Light Forces, 11.

27. Reconstructed dialogue by author as sourced through: Commander in Chief, U.S. Fleet, *Information Bulletin No. 11, Chapter 58, Battle Experience Naval Operations Solomon Islands Area 12 July–10 August 1943: Night 6-7 August 1943, Battle of Vella Gulf Between Task Group 31.2 and Japanese Light Forces*, 11.

28. Reconstructed event and dialogue by author as sourced through: USS *Dunlap* DD 384 Action Report, 7, 12; Commander in Chief, U.S. Fleet, *Information Bulletin No. 11, Chapter 58, Battle Experience Naval Operations Solomon Islands Area 12 July–10 August 1943: Night 6-7 August 1943, Battle of Vella Gulf Between Task Group 31.2 and Japanese Light Forces*, 11.

29. Reconstructed event and dialogue by author as sourced through: USS *Dunlap* DD 384 Action Report, 7, 12; Commander in Chief, U.S. Fleet, *Information Bulletin No. 11, Chapter 58, Battle Experience Naval Operations Solomon Islands Area 12 July–10 August 1943: Night 6-7 August 1943, Battle of Vella Gulf Between Task Group 31.2 and Japanese Light Forces*, 11.

30. USS *Dunlap* DD 384 Action Report, 7.

31. Reconstructed dialogue by author as sourced through: Hara, *Japanese Destroyer Captain*, 191.

32. Hara, *Japanese Destroyer Captain*, 191.

33. Hara, *Japanese Destroyer Captain*, 190–92.

Chapter Ten: Scenes of Victory: God This Is Awful

1. USS *Dunlap* DD 384 Action Report, 13.

2. United Press, "Vela Gulf Victory Called One of War's Most Decisive Battles," September 16, 1943.

3. Commander in Chief, U.S. Fleet, *Information Bulletin No. 11, Battle Experience Naval Operations Solomon Islands Area 12 July–10 August 1943: Chapter 58, Night 6-7 August 1943, Battle of Vella Gulf Between Task Group 31.2 and Japanese Light Forces*, 13.

4. Sherman, *The Battle of Vella Gulf*, U.S. Naval Institute Proceedings, January 1945, 69.

5. Davison, "Grossly Underbid," 7.

6. Robinson, "Vella Gulf Victory Made Murder by Clean Surprise," International News Service, August 10, 1943.

7. Davison, "Grossly Underbid," 7.

8. USS *Maury* DD 401 Action Report, 4–5.

9. USS *Dunlap* DD 384 Action Report, 13.

10. Crenshaw, *South Pacific Destroyer*, 216.

11. U.S. Navy, Office of Naval Intelligence, *Combat Narratives, Solomon Islands Campaign*, 10; and Commander in Chief, U.S. Fleet, *Information Bulletin No. 11, Chapter 58, Battle Experience Naval Operations Solomon Islands Area 12 July–10 August 1943: Night 6-7 August 1943, Battle of Vella Gulf Between Task Group 31.2 and Japanese Light Forces*, 11.

12. U.S. Navy, Office of Naval Intelligence, *Combat Narratives, Solomon Islands Campaign*, 10; and Commander in Chief, U.S. Fleet, *Information Bulletin No. 11, Chapter 58,*

Battle Experience Naval Operations Solomon Islands Area 12 July–10 August 1943: Night 6-7 August 1943, Battle of Vella Gulf Between Task Group 31.2 and Japanese Light Forces, 11.

13. USS *Lang* DD 399 Action Report, 5; and Lee, Written response, September 12, 2004.

14. USS *Lang* DD 399 Action Report, 5; and U.S. Navy, Office of Naval Intelligence, *Combat Narratives, Solomon Islands Campaign*, 11 (including the notation: "The word was probably *Kowai*, a Japanese ejaculation of fear.")

15. USS *Lang* DD 399 Action Report, 5; and Robinson, "Vella Gulf Victory Made Murder by Clean Surprise," International News Service, August 10, 1943.

16. Calhoun, *Tin Can Sailor*, 125.

17. Lee, Written response, September 5, 2004.

18. USS *Lang* DD 399 Action Report, 5; and numerous *Lang* eyewitness accounts as given to the author, various dates.

19. Crenshaw, *South Pacific Destroyer*, 216.

20. Crenshaw, *South Pacific Destroyer*, 216.

21. General quarters remained in effect until 3:40 A.M., when Division 15 had safely "passed Visuvisu Point and the entrance to Kula Gulf . . . ," USS *Stack* DD 406 Action Report, 3.

22. Peters, Written response, January 12, 1998.

23. Olsen, Written response, January 29, 1998.

24. Barber, Written response, January 5, 1998.

25. Huber, Written response, January 12, 1998.

26. Allen, Personal diary for August 6, 1943 (author's personal collection).

27. Southard, Written response, December 1998.

28. Gray, Written response, December 11, 1998.

29. Crenshaw, *South Pacific Destroyer*, 218.

30. Crenshaw, *South Pacific Destroyer*, 218.

31. Crenshaw, *South Pacific Destroyer*, 218.

32. Crenshaw, *South Pacific Destroyer*, 218.

33. Crenshaw, *South Pacific Destroyer*, 218.

34. USS *Dunlap* DD 384 Action Report, 8, 13.

35. USS *Dunlap* DD 384 Action Report, 8, 13. The time is recorded as "0359" (3:59 A.M.).

36. Allison, Written response, February 24, 1998.

37. Yannotti, Written response, January 2, 1998.

38. On December 7, Wilfong was present at Pearl, as the commanding officer of the *Wasmuth* (DMS 15).

39. Davison, "Grossly Underbid," 7.

40. Hansen, Written response, January 1, 1998.

41. Shear, Interview transcript as given to Paul Stillwell, *Reminiscences of Admiral Harold Edson Shear*, 75.

42. Haden, Written response, undated, approximately February 1998.

43. Crenshaw, *South Pacific Destroyer*, 223.

44. Crenshaw, *South Pacific Destroyer*, 218.

45. USS *Dunlap* DD 384 Action Report, 8, 14.
46. USS *Dunlap* DD 384 Action Report, 8.
47. Morrison, *History of the United States Naval Operations in World War II, Vol. VI*, 221; U.S. Navy, Office of Naval Intelligence, *Combat Narratives, Solomon Islands Campaign*, 11.
48. Morrison, *History of the United States Naval Operations in World War II, Vol. VI*, 227.
49. Hara, *Japanese Destroyer Captain*, 192.
50. Davison, "Grossly Underbid," 7.
51. USS *Dunlap* DD 384 Action Report, 8.
52. Davison, "Grossly Underbid," 7.

Chapter Eleven: Well Done: Summation of Victory

1. Commander Task Force 31, U.S. Naval Communication Service, Wilkinson to Moosbrugger communiqué for August 7, 1943.
2. Harmon, U.S. Naval Communication Service, General Harmon to Moosbrugger communiqué for August 7, 1943.
3. Commander Motor Torpedo Boat Flotilla One, U.S. Naval Communication Service, Commander Calvert to Task Group 31.2 communiqué for August 7, 1943.
4. Commander South Pacific Forces, U.S. Naval Communication Service, Halsey to Moosbrugger communiqué for August 7, 1943.
5. Commander Task Group 31.2, U.S. Naval Communication Service, Moosbrugger to Task Group 31.2 communiqué for August 7, 1943.
6. Commander Southwest Pacific Forces, U.S. Naval Communication Service, MacArthur to Halsey communiqué for August 10, 1943 (Forward) to Task Group 31.2.
7. Hara, *Japanese Destroyer Captain*, 193.
8. Hara, *Japanese Destroyer Captain*, 192–93.
9. Hara, *Japanese Destroyer Captain*, 193.
10. Hara, *Japanese Destroyer Captain*, 193.
11. Hara, *Japanese Destroyer Captain*, 193–94.
12. Hara, *Japanese Destroyer Captain*, 194.
13. Hara, *Japanese Destroyer Captain*, 194.
14. Commander Destroyer Division Fifteen—USS *Lang* (399) Newspaper, Press Radio Newscast for Monday Morning August 9, 1943, Mackay Radio transcript, Associated Press.
15. Robinson, "Vella Gulf Victory Made Murder by Clean Surprise," International News Service, August 10, 1943.
16. McCarthy, "Warship Wants FDR Photo," United Press, September 1, 1943.
17. McCarthy, "Warship Wants FDR Photo," United Press, September 1, 1943.
18. McCarthy, "Warship Wants FDR Photo," United Press, September 1, 1943.
19. Robinson, "Vella Gulf Victory Made Murder by Clean Surprise," International News Service, August 10, 1943.
20. Author's reconstructed events and dialogue as sourced through: Southard, Written response, December 1998 and follow-up by phone December 4, 2006. This commentary regarding the controversy over the damaged photo of FDR is described as fully detailed by Capt. Pemberton Southard in an unrecorded phone conversation with the author

in December of 2004. In the 1998 interview, Captain Southard stated of Commodore Simpson and Pat Robinson that, "after the Pres. Roosevelt picture falling episode, I didn't trust either one of them." It is the understanding of the author that Captain Southard did not directly witness the event as it occurred on the bridge, but that he was later told of the incident by Captain Wilfong. Captain Southard went on to state that of Commodore Simpson and Captain Wilfong that "they didn't like each other, I felt, and the Commodore got into ship's business at times—much to the displeasure of Capt. Wilfong—He and I talked frequently about it."

21. Iverson, *Some Observations on the Battle of Vella Gulf*, 3.

22. Allen, Personal diary for August 9, 1943.

23. Commander in Chief, U.S. Fleet, *Information Bulletin No. 11, Chapter 59, Battle Experience Naval Operations Solomon Islands Area 12 July–10 August 1943: Vella Gulf Encounter, Night 9-10 August 1943 Between Task Group 31.2 and Japanese Barges.*

24. Allen, Personal diary for September 8, 1943.

25. Iverson, *Some Observations on the Battle of Vella Gulf*, 3.

26. Iverson, *Some Observations on the Battle of Vella Gulf*, 3.

27. Iverson, *Some Observations on the Battle of Vella Gulf*, 3–4.

28. Iverson, *Some Observations on the Battle of Vella Gulf*, 3–4.

29. Iverson, *Some Observations on the Battle of Vella Gulf*, 4.

30. Iverson, *Some Observations on the Battle of Vella Gulf*, 4.

31. Bureau of Naval Personnel Information Bulletin No. 326, "Frederick Moosbrugger—Citation."

32. Iverson, *Some Observations on the Battle of Vella Gulf*, 4.

33. United Press, "Vela Gulf Victory Called One of War's Most Decisive Battles," September 16, 1943.

34. Southard, Letter to author, July 29, 2004.

35. Navy Log Memories, ID # 130154, "Pemberton Southard."

36. Olsen, Written response, January 29, 1998.

37. Southard, Written response, December 1998.

CHAPTER TWELVE: FINAL NOTES: DEBATES, CONTROVERSIES, AND CONCLUSIONS

1. Arthur, Conversation with author in 2004. The Arthur family was close friends, and Kenny and I had numerous conversations regarding *Lang* history and about what he observed that night. He was always adamant regarding the "cruiser" belief.

2. Allen, Personal diary for August 6, 1943.

3. U.S. Navy, Office of Naval Intelligence, *Combat Narratives, Solomon Islands Campaign*, 11–12.

4. Commander in Chief, U.S. Fleet, *Information Bulletin No. 11, Chapter 58, Battle Experience Naval Operations Solomon Islands Area 12 July–10 August 1943: Night 6-7 August 1943, Battle of Vella Gulf Between Task Group 31.2 and Japanese Light Forces*, 13.

5. USS *Dunlap* DD 384 Action Report (underscore added by the author), 15.

6. USS *Craven* DD 382 Action Report, 4. This report included as part of the descriptions of the "cruiser" a "high catapult (with a '?') abaft mainmast."

7. Olsen, Written response, January 29, 1998.

8. Rowland and Boyd, *U. S. Navy Bureau of Ordnance in World War II*, 98; Regarding the depth issue with the Mark 15 torpedo, "In 1938, for example, a destroyer command engaging in battle practice off Coronado, Calif., found that half its torpedoes failed to function properly. When many surfaced in 90 feet of water with the exercise heads covered with mud, deep running was obvious . . . The incident failed to shake official faith in the procedures of the Naval Torpedo Station. For three more years the inadequacies of torpedoes were obscured by misplaced faith in faulty procedures and an inaccurate recording device."

9. Commander in Chief, U.S. Fleet. *Information Bulletin No. 11, Chapter 58, Battle Experience Naval Operations Solomon Islands Area 12 July–10 August 1943: Night 6-7 August 1943, Battle of Vella Gulf Between Task Group 31.2 and Japanese Light Forces*, 20.

10. Fisher, By phone, August 28, 1999.

11. Crenshaw, Letter to author, October 19, 1999.

12. Fisher, By phone, August 28, 1999.

13. USS *Maury* DD 401 Action Report, 7.

14. Olsen, Written response, January 29, 1998.

15. Crenshaw, Letter to author, October 19, 1999.

16. Hara, *Japanese Destroyer Captain*, 191–92.

17. Shear, Interview transcript as given to Paul Stillwell, *Reminiscences of Admiral Harold Edson Shear*, 74.

18. Shear, Interview transcript as given to Paul Stillwell, *Reminiscences of Admiral Harold Edson Shear*, 77.

19. Shear, Interview transcript as given to Paul Stillwell, *Reminiscences of Admiral Harold Edson Shear*, 77.

20. Commander in Chief, U.S. Fleet, *Information Bulletin No. 11, Chapter 58, Battle Experience Naval Operations Solomon Islands Area 12 July–10 August 1943: Night 6-7 August 1943, Battle of Vella Gulf Between Task Group 31.2 and Japanese Light Forces*, 26.

21. Commander in Chief, U.S. Fleet, *Information Bulletin No. 11, Chapter 58, Battle Experience Naval Operations Solomon Islands Area 12 July–10 August 1943: Night 6-7 August 1943, Battle of Vella Gulf Between Task Group 31.2 and Japanese Light Forces*, 32.

22. Ballantine, Written response, January 1998.

23. Ballantine, Letter to author, December 8, 2000.

24. Lee, Letter to author, September 5, 2004.

25. Gray, Letter to author, September 30, 2002.

26. Southard, Letter to author, June 2004.

27. A good example of this danger was exhibited at Pearl Harbor on December 7, 1941, when the destroyer *Monaghan* used a depth charge at shallow depth and at too slow of a speed against a midget submarine found inside the harbor. The explosion destroyed the submarine but also severely damaged *Monaghan*'s rudder, causing the destroyer to lose steering and to crash into a dock along the shore.

28. It is not known if Ballantine had read the Shear interview, as, unfortunately, the author admits to not having made this important inquiry. His responses to the author were certainly post of Shear's published comments to Stillwell. If so, this might explain

some triggering of Ballantine's belief that he too had recollection of such occurring. Both men made the comments some fifty years after the fact, and time does tend to blur memories. The author fully believes that both men were being forthright with their recollections and honest with what they thought had occurred. It was an exciting night, fast and furious with multiple events evolving in a very short period of time. The author greatly respects these two men, and he respects their comments. On this occasion, however, the evidence appears to affirm the opposite.

29. Potter, *Admiral Arleigh Burke*, 84–85.

30. Edward Moosbrugger, Letter to author, August 13, 1998.

31. Commander in Chief, U.S. Fleet, *Information Bulletin No. 11, Chapter 58, Battle Experience Naval Operations Solomon Islands Area 12 July–10 August 1943: Night 6-7 August 1943, Battle of Vella Gulf Between Task Group 31.2 and Japanese Light Forces*, 26–27.

32. Potter, *Admiral Arleigh Burke*, 85.

33. Southard, Follow-up by phone, December 4, 2006.

34. Davison, "Grossly Underbid," 7.

35. Gray, Letter to author, May 25, 2004.

36. Helen Fultz, Letter to author, May 22, 2004.

Bibliography

Books

Arey, Richard W., and Robert G. Tower. *The 1942 Lucky Bag: The Annual of the Regiment of Midshipmen, United States Naval Academy, Annapolis, MD.* Buffalo, NY: Baker, Jones, Hausauer, Inc., 1942.

Calhoun, C. Raymond. *Tin Can Sailor: Life Aboard the USS Sterett, 1939–1945.* Annapolis, MD: Naval Institute Press, 1993.

Crenshaw, Russell Sydnor, Jr. *South Pacific Destroyer: The Battle for the Solomons from Savo Island to Vella Gulf.* Annapolis, MD: Naval Institute Press, 1998.

Cohen, Stan. *East Wind Rain: A Pictorial History of the Pearl Harbor Attack.* Missoula, MT: Pictorial Histories Publishing Company, 1981.

Dull, Paul S. *A Battle History of the Imperial Japanese Navy (1941–1945).* Annapolis, MD: Naval Institute Press, 1978.

Hara, Tameichi. *Japanese Destroyer Captain.* New York: Ballantine Books, 1961.

Harms, Norman E. *Hard Lessons Vol. 1: U. S. Naval Campaigns Pacific Theater February 1942–1943.* Beaverton, OR: Scale Specialties, 1987.

Hoyt, Edwin P. *The Glory of the Solomons.* New York: Stein and Day, 1983.

Ienaga, Saburo. *The Pacific War 1931–1945.* New York: Pantheon Books, 1978.

King, Larry. *Love Stories of World War II.* New York: Crown Publishers, 2001.

Knight, Rex A. *Riding on Luck: The Saga of the USS Lang (DD-399).* Ashland, OR: Hellgate Press, 2001.

Koburger, Charles W., Jr. *Pacific Turning Point: The Solomons Campaign, 1942–1943.* Westport, CT: Praeger, 1995.

Lanier, William D., Jr., and Joseph P. Morray. *The 1940 Lucky Bag: The Annual of the Regiment of Midshipmen, United States Naval Academy, Annapolis, MD.* Buffalo, NY: Baker, Jones, Hausauer, Inc., 1940.

McGee, William L. *Amphibious Operations in the South Pacific in WWII, Volume II: The Solomons Campaigns, 1942–1943, From Guadalcanal to Bougainville, Pacific War Turning Point.* BMC Publications, 2002.

Morison, Samuel Eliot. *History of United States Naval Operations in World War II, Vol. III: The Rising Sun in the Pacific, 1931–April 1942.* Boston: Little, Brown, 1984.

———. *History of United States Naval Operations in World War II, Vol. IV: Coral Sea, Midway and Submarine Actions, May 1942–August 1942.* Boston: Little, Brown, 1984.

———. *History of United States Naval Operations in World War II, Vol. V: The Struggle for Guadalcanal, August 1942–February 1943.* Boston: Little, Brown, 1984.

———. *History of United States Naval Operations in World War II, Vol. VI: Breaking the Bismarcks Barrier, 22 July 1942–1 May 1944.* Boston: Little, Brown, 1984.

———. *History of United States Naval Operations in World War II, Vol. VII: Aleutians, Gilberts and Marshalls, June 1942–April 1944.* Boston: Little, Brown, 1984.

———. *The Two-Ocean War: A Short History of the United States Navy in the Second World War.* Boston: Little, Brown, 1963.

Moulton, H. D., and M. W. Hibschman. *The 1931 Lucky Bag. The Annual of the Regiment of Midshipmen, United States Naval Academy, Annapolis, MD.* Chicago: Rogers Printing Company, 1931.

Pihl, P. E., and W. D. Johnson Jr. *The Lucky Bag of 1921: The Annual of the Regiment of Midshipmen, United States Naval Academy, Annapolis, MD.* 1921.

Potter, E. B. *Admiral Arleigh Burke: A Biography.* New York: Random House, 1990.

Robinson, Pat. *The Fight for New Guinea: General Douglas MacArthur's First Offensive.* New York: Random House, 1943.

Roscoe, Theodore. *United States Destroyer Operations in World War II.* Annapolis, MD: U.S. Naval Institute, 1953.

Tanaka, Raizo. *The Japanese Navy in World War II.* An anthology of articles by former officers of the Imperial Japanese Navy and Air Defense Force originally published in the *U.S. Naval Institute Proceedings.* Annapolis, MD: U.S. Naval Institute, 1969.

Watts, Anthony J. *Japanese Warships of World War II.* Sheperton, UK: Ian Allen Ltd., 1966.

Withington, F. S. *The Lucky Bag of 1923: The Annual of the Regiment of Midshipmen, United States Naval Academy, Annapolis, MD.* 1923.

Official Reports / Government Documents

Chief of Naval Operations, Navy Department, History Division. *Dictionary of American Naval Fighting Ships, Volumes I–VIII.* U.S. Government Printing Office, 1959–1981.

Commander in Chief, U.S. Fleet. *Information Bulletin No. 11. Chapter 58, Battle Experience Naval Operations Solomon Islands Area 12 July–10 August 1943: Night 6-7 August 1943, Battle of Vella Gulf Between Task Group 31.2 and Japanese Light Forces.* College Park, MD: National Archives and Records Administration.

———. *Information Bulletin No. 11. Chapter 59, Battle Experience Naval Operations Solomon Islands Area 12 July–10 August 1943: Vella Gulf Encounter, Night 9-10 August 1943 Between Task Group 31.2 and Japanese Barges.* College Park, MD: National Archives and Records Administration.

Commander in Chief, Pacific Fleet. *Pacific Fleet Tactical Bulletin No. 4TB-42. Subject: Pacific Fleet Radar Doctrine.* Serial 03443, November 26, 1942.

Commander Destroyers, Pacific Fleet. *CIC Handbook for Destroyers Pacific Fleet.* Serial 0624, June 24, 1943.

———. *Destroyers, Pacific Fleet Radar Gunnery Notes.* Serial 0428, June 1943.

Commander Motor Torpedo Boat Flotilla One. U.S. Naval Communication Service. Commander Calvert to Task Group 31.2 communiqué for August 7, 1943

Commander South Pacific Forces. U.S. Naval Communication Service. Halsey to Moosbrugger communiqué for August 7, 1943.

Commander Southwest Pacific Forces. U.S. Naval Communication Service. MacArthur to Halsey communiqué for August 10, 1943 (Forward) to Task Group 31.2.

Commander Task Force 31. U.S. Naval Communication Service. Wilkinson to Moosbrugger communiqué for August 7, 1943.

Commander Task Group 31.2. U.S. Naval Communication Service. Moosbrugger to Task Group 31.2 communiqué for August 7, 1943.

Harmon. U.S. Naval Communication Service. General Harmon to Moosbrugger communiqué for August 7, 1943.

Joint Army-Navy Assessment Committee. *Japanese Naval and Merchant Shipping Losses During World War II By All Causes.* U.S. Government Printing Office, February 1947.

Navy Department. *The Bluejacket's Manual.* U.S. Naval Institute, 1944.

Rowland, Buford, and William B. Boyd. *U. S. Navy Bureau of Ordnance in World War II.* Department of the Navy, Bureau of Ordnance, undated.

U.S. Navy, Office of Naval Intelligence. *Combat Narratives. Solomon Islands Campaign: XI Kolombangara and Vella Lavella 6 August–7 October 1943.* Publications Branch, 1944.

USS *Craven* DD 382 Action Report. *Report of Vella Gulf, Night Action of August 6-7, 1943.* Serial 081, August 8, 1943. Office of Naval Records and Library.

USS *Dunlap* DD 384 Action Report. *Action Report of U.S.S. Dunlap (384), Battle of Vella Gulf 6-7 August 1943.* Serial 012, August 18, 1943. Office of Naval Records and Library.

USS *Lang* DD 399 Action Report. *Action Report of Surface Engagement in Vella Gulf, Night of 6-7 August 1943.* Serial 0141, August 15, 1943. Office of Naval Records and Library.

USS *Lang* DD 399 Log Report. *Log Book of the U.S.S. Lang (399) Rate, Commanded by Lieutenant Commander E. A. Seay, U.S. Navy, Destroyer Division Fifteen, Destroyer Squadron Eight, United States Atlantic Fleet, Commencing Monday December 1, 1941, at Sea, and ending Wednesday December 31, 1941, at Bermuda, B.W.I.* No Serial, January 22, 1942. Department of the Navy, Bureau of Navigation.

USS *Maury* DD 401 Action Report. *Report of Night Destroyer Attack Against Japanese Surface Ships in Vella Gulf, Night of August 6, 1943.* Serial 012, August 15, 1943. Office of Naval Records and Library.

USS *Stack* DD 406 Action Report. *Action Report for Night of 6-7 August 1943 (Surface Action in Vella Gulf).* Serial 008, August 14, 1943. Office of Naval Records and Library.

USS *Sterett* DD 407 Action Report. *Report of Action for Night of 6-7 August 1943 (Night Action in Vella Gulf).* No Serial, August 10, 1943. Office of Naval Records and Library.

NEWSPAPER, MAGAZINE, AND INTERNET ARTICLES

Arlington National Cemetery Website. "Theodore Starke Wilkinson, Jr. Vice Admiral, United States Navy." www.arlingtoncemetery.com/tswilkin.htm. Last visited March 17, 2001.

Bureau of Naval Personnel Information Bulletin No. 325 (April 1944). "Gelzer Loyall Sims—Citation." www.homeofheroes.com/valor/1_Citations/03_wwii-nc/nc_06wwii_navyS.html. Last visited January 15, 2008.

Bureau of Naval Personnel Information Bulletin No. 326 (May 1944). "Frank G. Gould—Citation." www.homeofheroes.com/valor/1_Citations/03_wwii-nc/nc_06wwii_navyG.html. Last visited January 15, 2008.

———. "Clifton Iverson—Citation." www.homeofheroes.com/valor/1_Citations/03_wwii-nc/nc_06wwii_navyI.html. Last visited January 15, 2008.

———. "Frederick Moosbrugger—Citation." www.homeofheroes.com/valor/1_Citations/03_wwii-nc/nc_06wwii_navyM.html. Last visited January 15, 2008.

———. "Roy Arthur Newton—Citation." www.homeofheroes.com/valor/1_Citations/03_wwii-nc/nc_06wwii_navyN.html. Last visited January 15, 2008.

———. "Rodger Whitten Simpson—Citation." www.homeofheroes.com/valor/1_Citations/03_wwii-nc/nc_06wwii_navyS.html. Last visited January 15, 2008.

———. "John Lester Wilfong—Citation." www.homeofheroes.com/valor/1_Citations/03_wwii-nc/nc_06wwii_navyV.html. Last visited January 15, 2008.

———. "Francis T. Williamson—Citation." www.homeofheroes.com/valor/1_Citations/03_wwii-nc/nc_06wwii_navyV.html. Last visited January 15, 2008.

Commander Destroyer Division Fifteen—USS *Lang* (399) Newspaper. Press Radio Newscast for Monday Morning August 9, 1943. Mackay Radio transcript. Associated Press.

Cordes, Jeff. "A Moonless Night in Vella Gulf: One Man's War—Joe Poitevin Remembers a Watershed Battle, 58 Years Ago." *Idaho Mountain Express*, week of July 4–10, 2001. www.mtexpress.com/2001/01-07-04/01-07-04craven.htm. Last visited June 10, 2003.

DeMarco, Mario. "Skippers in the Spotlight—Francis T. Williamson." *Navy Times*, October 20, 1962, 4.

East Carolina University, Special Collections Digital Exhibit, *Day of Infamy 1941–2001, Biographical Sketch of Russell S. Crenshaw, Jr. (USS Maury)*, Digital.lib.ecu.edu/special/pearlharbor/ph/CREN/hCREN.html.

Geocities. "Rear-Admiral Raizo Tanaka." www.geocities.com/dutcheastindies/tanaka.html. Last visited September 7, 2004.

Hailey, Foster. "Lure of the 'Tin Cans.'" *New York Times Magazine*, May 16, 1943.

Hamilton, Robert A. (copy of *New London Day* article—Admiral Harold Shear death notice—February 1999). www.ussvi.org/names/admshear.htm. Last visited June 10, 2004.

IJN, materials of (Naval Academy Class 46). "Kaju Sugiura." www.homepage2.nifty.com/nishidah/e/px46.htm. Last visited May 22, 2003.

IJN, materials of (Naval Academy Class 41). "Raizo Tanaka." www.homepage2.nifty.com/nishidah/e/px41.htm. Last visited May 22, 2003.

Knight, Rex A. "Clean Sweep By Destroyers." *World War II*, March 1990, 43.

Kyle, Roberta. "One Man's Navy Family." *Shipmate*, June 1988, 27.

McCarthy, Francis. "Warship Wants FDR Photo—First Was Damaged in Battle." United Press, September 1, 1943.

Muir, Dan. "Order of Battle—Battle of Vella Gulf—6-7 August 1943." www.warships1.com/W-Order_of_Battle/OOB_WWII_Pacific/OOB_WWII_Vella-Gulf.htm. Last visited March 17, 2001.

Navy Log Memories. ID # 130154. "Pemberton Southard." www.lonesailor.org/Navyvoice_display.php?ID=130154&page=1&pages=1&lastname=SOUTHARD.htm. Last visited December 26, 2002.

Nease, I. B. "Henry Donald Davison: USS Arizona Survivor Stories." www.ussarizona.org/survivors/davison/index.html. Last visited April 21, 2008.

Nevitt, Allyn D. "IJN Arashi: Tabular Record of Movement." www.64.124.221.191/arashi_t.htm. *Long Lancers*, 1998. Last visited September 1, 2002.

———. "IJN Hagikaze: Tabular Record of Movement." www.64.124.221.191/hagika_t.htm. *Long Lancers*, 1998. Last visited September 1, 2002.

———. "IJN Kawakaze: Tabular Record of Movement." www.64.124.221.191/kawaka_t.htm. *Long Lancers*, 1998. Last visited September 1, 2002.

O'Hara, Vincent P. "Battle of Vella Gulf—August 6-7, 1943." www.microworks.net/pacific/battles/vella_gulf.htm. Last visited April 7, 2004.

Robinson, Pat. "Vella Gulf Victory Made Murder by Clean Surprise." International News Service, August 10, 1943.

"Republican China," www.chaos.umd.edu/history/republican.html.

Sherman, V. A., Lieutenant, U.S. Naval Reserve. "The Battle of Vella Gulf." U.S. Naval Institute Proceedings, January 1945, 61.

"Solomons Bombardment & Reinforcement Missions." www.pacific.valka.cz/forces/ijn/solomons.htm. Last visited September 7, 2004.

United Press. "Vela Gulf Victory Called One of War's Most Decisive Battles; Full Story Is Told." September 16, 1943.

USS *Arleigh Burke* (DDG 51). "About the Destroyer's Name, About Admiral Arleigh Burke." www.navysite.de/dd/ddg51.htm. Last visited May 19, 2003.

USS *Forrest Sherman* (DD 931). "Capt. Russell S. Crenshaw—1955–1957." www.ussforrestsherman.org/cdr_crenshaw.htm. Last visited May 26, 2008.

USS *Moosbrugger* (DD 980). "About the Destroyer's Name, About Vice Admiral Frederick Moosbrugger." www.navysite.de/dd/dd980.htm. Last visited May 19, 2003.

USS *Richmond K. Turner* (CG-20). "Admiral Richmond Kelly Turner." www.navysite.de/cg/cg20.htm. Last visited June 10, 2003.

USS *Simpson* (FFG 56). "About the Ship's Name, About Rear Admiral Rodger Whitten Simpson." www.navysite.de/ffg/FFG56.HTM. Last visited December 30, 2002.

USS *Wasmuth* DMS 15 Action Report. "Report of Pearl Harbor Attack." Serial 280, December 12, 1941. Department of the Navy—Naval Historical Center. www.history.navy.mil/docs/wwii/pearl/ph120.htm. Last visited April 13, 2004.

Wikipedia. "Tameichi Hara." www.en.wikipedia.org/wiki/Tameichi_Hara. Last visited July 16, 2008.

———. "Kaju Sugiura." www.en.wikipedia.org/wiki/Kaju_Sugiura. Last visited July 22, 2008.

Williamson, Francis T., Rear Admiral, U.S. Navy. "Adm. Williamson's Sea Stories Too Varied for Our Artist." An excerpt of a letter from Admiral Williamson to the *Navy Times*. *Navy Times*, October 20, 1962, 4.

Yamashiro, Katsunori. "The True Story of Pres. John F. Kennedy's PT109 Collision." www.newcomermuseum.com/images/a1480.jpg. Last visited December 30, 2002.

Materials—Unpublished or Privately Published

Allen, Glenn E. [Store Keeper 2/c aboard USS *Dunlap*]. Personal diary for dates 10/21/42 through 8/21/44.

Davison, Henry D. [Lieutenant aboard USS *Craven*]. "Grossly Underbid." Undated.

Fleming, Denver [Shipfitter 1/c aboard USS *Lang*]. *The Mighty Lang*. USS *Lang* Printing, undated.

Haden, William P. [Torpedoman 2/c aboard USS *Craven*]. Untitled/undated essay written a few days after the battle.

Iverson, Clifton [Commander aboard USS *Dunlap*]. *Some Observations on the Battle of Vella Gulf*. Nine Star General Press, undated.

Muleahy, E. J. [Machinist's Mate 1/c aboard USS *Dunlap*]. Personal diary for dates 11/23/43 through 8/30/44.

Novak, Raymond P., Alex Telfer, and Charles W. Stirrup [Yeomen aboard USS *Lang*]. *USS Lang—Fifth Anniversary*. USS *Lang* Printing, March 30, 1944.

Putnam, Walt [Quartermaster aboard USS *Craven*]. *The Battle of Vella Gulf*. Printed for members of the USS *Craven* Reunion group. Nine Star General Press, 1991.

———. *The Ensign*. Printed for USS *Craven* Reunion, September 18–21, 1991.

Interviews—Personal, Written, and Phone

Allison, Richard Lee [Quartermaster 2/c aboard USS *Craven*]. Written response, February 24, 1998.

Arthur, Kenneth [Gunner's Mate 1/c aboard USS *Lang*]. Personal conversation, summer 2004.

Ballantine, John W. [Ensign aboard USS *Lang*]. Written responses, January 1998 and November 16, 2000.

Barber, Ralph Emmett [Pharmacist's Mate 1/c aboard USS *Dunlap*]. Written response, January 5, 1998.

Caylor, William L., Jr. [Machinist's Mate 2/c aboard USS *Craven*]. Written response, January 9, 1998.

Conner, Clyde Alston [Seaman 1/c aboard USS *Dunlap*]. Written response, January 5, 1998.

Fisher, James W. [Acting Chief Torpedoman aboard USS *Maury*]. By phone, August 28, 1999, and in person, August 8, 2008.

Fultz, Wilber O. [Coxswain aboard USS *Craven*]. Written response, January 20, 1998.

Gaither, Patrick J. [Fire Controlman 1/c aboard USS *Craven*]. Written response, February 1998.

Gilmore, Jack G. [Machinist's Mate 1/c aboard USS *Craven*]. Written response, January 2, 1998.

Gray, Dandridge M. [Lieutenant (jg) aboard USS *Lang*]. Written responses, December 11, 1998 and September 30, 2002; by phone, May 2004.

Haden, William P. [Torpedoman 2/c aboard USS *Craven*]. Written response, undated, approximately February 1998.

Hall, John A. [Machinist's Mate 1/c aboard USS *Craven*]. Written response, February 24, 1998.

Hansen, Gene V. [Carpenter's Mate 2/c aboard USS *Craven*]. Written response, January 1, 1998.

Huber, John William [Boatswain's Mate 2/c aboard USS *Dunlap*]. Written response, January 12, 1998.

Lanz, Carl W. [Gunner's Mate 2/c aboard USS *Craven*]. Written response, January 9, 1998.

Lazarz, William A. [Coxswain aboard USS *Craven*]. Written response, January 2, 1998.

Lee, Charles H. [Gunner's Mate 2/c aboard USS *Lang*]. Written responses, September 5 and 12, 2004.

Lucia, Anthony P. [Fireman 1/c aboard USS *Craven*]. Written response, January 2, 1998.

Moosbrugger, Dave [Son of Frederick Moosbrugger]. By phone, September 22, 2004.

Moosbrugger, Edward [Son of Frederick Moosbrugger]. By phone, September 29, 2004.

Olcott, John T. [Torpedoman 3/c aboard USS *Maury*]. Written response, August 22, 1999.

Oliver, James Davis, Jr. [Lieutenant (jg) aboard USS *Craven*]. Written response, January 7, 1998.

Olsen, Albert R. [Lieutenant aboard USS *Dunlap*]. Written response, January 29, 1998. Follow-up phone interview, September 29, 2004.

Peters, Loyd [Fire Controlman 3/c aboard USS *Dunlap*]. Written response, January 12, 1998.

Poitevin, J. Joe [Ensign aboard USS *Craven*]. Written response, January 2, 1998.

Pritchett, George [Radioman 1/c aboard USS *Craven*]. Written response, June 2, 1998.

Rivera, William [Fireman 1/c aboard USS *Dunlap*]. Written response, January 8, 1998.

Schaffer, Max Ernest [Fire Controlman 3/c aboard USS *Dunlap*]. Written response, December 23, 1997.

Shear, Harold Edson [Lieutenant (jg) aboard USS *Stack*]. Interview transcript as given to Paul Stillwell, *The Reminiscences of Admiral Harold Edson Shear, U. S. Navy (Retired)*, Annapolis, MD: U.S. Naval Institute Press, 1997.

Southard, Pemberton [Lieutenant aboard USS *Lang*]. Written response, December 1998; By phone, December 4, 2006.

Turner, Elaine [Niece to Frederick Moosbrugger and family historian]. By phone, April 2008.

Wallick, Robert [Torpedoman 2/c aboard USS *Dunlap*]. Written response, February 12, 1998.

Yannotti, Ferdinand S. [Machinist's Mate 2/c aboard USS *Craven*]. Written response, January 2, 1998.

Correspondence

Ballantine, John W. [Ensign aboard USS *Lang*]. Letter to author, December 8, 2000.
Barber, Ralph E. [Pharmacist's Mate 1/c aboard USS *Dunlap*]. Letters and emails to author, various dates.
Calhoun, C. Raymond [Author of *Tin Can Sailor*, USS *Sterett*]. Emails to author, various dates.
Crenshaw, Russell S., Jr. [Lieutenant aboard USS *Maury*]. Letters to author, various dates.
Fultz, Helen [Widow to Wilber Fultz, USS *Craven*]. Letter to author, May 22, 2004.
Gray, Dandridge M. [Lieutenant (jg) aboard USS *Lang*]. Letters to author, various dates.
Moosbrugger, Edward [Son of Frederick Moosbrugger]. Letter and emails to author, various dates.
Olsen, Albert R. [Lieutenant aboard USS *Dunlap*]. Letters to author, various dates.
Peters, Loyd [Fire Controlman 3/c aboard USS *Dunlap*]. Letters and emails to author, various dates.
Shear, Harold E. [Lieutenant (jg) aboard USS *Stack*]. Letter to author, January 3, 1998.
Southard, Pemberton [Lieutenant aboard USS *Lang*]. Letters to author, various dates.

www.ingramcontent.com/pod-product-compliance
Ingram Content Group UK Ltd.
Pitfield, Milton Keynes, MK11 3LW, UK
UKHW011915150926
8656IPUK00002B/6

9 780811 778480